East Asia Strategic Review

Major Powers and the Korean Peninsula: Politics, Policies and Perspectives

East Asia Strategic Review

Major Powers and the Korean Peninsula: Politics, Policies and Perspectives

Editor

Titli Basu

KNOWLEDGE WORLD

KW Publishers Pvt Ltd
New Delhi

INSTITUTE FOR DEFENCE STUDIES & ANALYSES
रक्षा अध्ययन एवं विश्लेषण संस्थान

Institute for Defence Studies and Analyses
No. 1, Development Enclave, Delhi Cantt.
New Delhi-110010
Phone: +91-11-26717983
Website: www.idsa.in

ISBN 978-93-89137-15-6 Hardback

Published in India by Kalpana Shukla

KW Publishers Pvt Ltd
4676/21, First Floor, Ansari Road
Daryaganj, New Delhi 110002
Phone: +91 11 23263498/43528107
Marketing: kw@kwpub.com
Editorial: production@kwpub.com
Website: www.kwpub.com

Printed and bound in India

Contents

Acknowledgements

The East Asia Centre at the Institute for Defence Studies and Analyses (IDSA) has been publishing annually a comprehensive compendium focussing on one of the major themes dominating the East Asian security architecture. As major powers engage North Korea, the denuclearisation of the Peninsula is unfolding as one of the most defining challenges in shaping regional security. As the future of the region continues to remain plagued by the developments in the Korean theatre, the theme of this volume, *Major Powers and the Korean Peninsula: Politics, Policies and Perspectives*, was decided with the objective of advancing understanding and analyses on critical issues shaping the future designs in the Peninsula.

IDSA's maiden volume on the Korean Peninsula would not have been possible without the erudite and dynamic leadership from Director General, Amb. Sujan R. Chinoy. I would like to express my deepest gratitude for the institutional support extended by IDSA leadership in facilitating this volume. This work has been enriched by the unfailing support and encouragement from my colleagues at the East Asia Centre. I would particularly like to thank Dr. Jagannath P. Panda, Coordinator of the East Asia Centre, for his guidance in the early stages of planning this volume. My colleague, Mr Vivek Kaushik has been greatly supportive in providing editorial assistance and administrative support for this publication.

I would like to thank all the authors for bringing in their wealth of expertise into this volume. I deeply appreciate them for investing time in participating and brainstorming during the workshop held in May 2018, and subsequently develop their analyses, as reflected in the chapters. This volume is intended to advance academic debates, discussions and scholarly deliberations on critical issues in the Korean Peninsula. However, neither IDSA nor the editor assumes any responsibility for the author's individual arguments and perspectives. Any factual incongruities in any of the chapters in the volume are the sole responsibility of the individual author.

Dr. Titli Basu

List of Contributors

Amb. **Vishnu Prakash** is a lawyer (a gold medallist) by training and a diplomat by profession. He retired as India's High Commissioner to Canada in November 2016 after over 35 years in the Indian Foreign Service. Prior to that he was Ambassador to South Korea, Official Spokesperson of the Ministry of External Affairs, and Consul General to Shanghai. He also served at various positions in Tokyo, New York, Moscow, Islamabad, Vladivostok, and Cairo. Ambassador Prakash spent a sabbatical with the Asia-Pacific Center for Security Studies in Hawaii in 1996. In 2013, he was conferred an Honorary Doctoral degree in Business Administration by Tongmyong University, Busan (South Korea). He got recognition as the 'Ambassador of the Year 2014' by the Asia Society, Korea Centre. Presently he is a foreign affairs analyst and columnist. His areas of interest include the Indo-Pacific region, especially North East Asia, the ASEAN region, and Pakistan, as also the US, Canada, and Israel. He has been writing for the *Hindustan Times*, *The Asian Age*, *The Korea Times*, *The Quint* and various think tanks, among others. He is widely published and regularly appears as an expert panelist on electronic media.

Dr. **Manpreet Sethi** is a Distinguished Fellow at the Centre for Air Power Studies, New Delhi where she heads a project on nuclear security. She is the recipient of the prestigious K. Subrahmanyam Award, an honour conferred for excellence in strategic and security studies. This recognises her contribution to the fields of nuclear energy, strategy, non-proliferation, disarmament, arms and export controls, and BMD over the last 20 years. She has published over

90 articles in several reputed journals, and has eight books to her credit. Her book, *Nuclear Strategy: India's March towards Credible Deterrence* (2009) is deemed essential reading for many courses. She lectures regularly at all premier establishments of the Indian Armed Forces, the Indian Police, and the Indian Foreign Service. She was a Member of the Prime Minister's Informal Group on Disarmament in 2012, and has been part of India's Track-II initiatives. She has been a Member of the Executive Board of the Indian Pugwash Society, and is a Consultant with the global Nuclear Abolition Forum and Board Member, Asia-Pacific Leadership Network.

Kapil Patil is Associate Fellow at the Vivekananda International Foundation (VIF), New Delhi. His research focuses on nuclear energy, WMD-proliferation, science, technology and national security-related issues. He submitted his doctoral thesis at the Jawaharlal Nehru University and is currently awaiting the Ph.D defence. Prior to joining the VIF, he worked as Senior Research Fellow with the Indian Pugwash Society, New Delhi for the BRNS-DAE research project. He is a co-author of the book, *India's Nuclear Energy Programme: Challenges, Prospects, and Public Concerns*, published in 2014. He is the recipient of the 2018 Emerging Leaders Fellowship conferred by the Korean Ministry of Unification, and also an alumnus of the Nuclear History Boot Camp (2011) jointly organised by the Woodrow Wilson International Center for Scholars, Washington DC and the University of Roma Tre. His research is featured in academic journals as well as in current affairs magazines such as *Global Energy Monitor*, *Nautilus*, *The Diplomat*, *Swaraj*, and the *CBW Magazine*.

Amb. **N. Parthasarathi** is a career diplomat, with more than three decades of service in the Indian Foreign Service. From 2005–2008, he served as Ambassador of India to South Korea. Amb. Parthasarathi joined the Indian Foreign Service in 1981 and has served as a diplomat in Pakistan, Belgium, the United Kingdom, and Syria as well as in many countries in Africa. He is a member of the India-Korea Strategic

Dialogue. He has published two books: *The Reluctant Assassin*, a fictional thriller published in Delhi in January 2005, and *The Legend of an Ayodhya Princess in Korea*, a fictional novel linking the ancient history of India and Korea. The latter was translated into the Korean language as *Bi Dan Hwang Hoo* (Silk Empress), and was published in Seoul in June 2007, and later, the National Book Trust of India published a children's book *Sriratna-Kim Suro* based on this novel. Following his retirement, he engages in mentoring start-ups and advising organisations and universities on many issues of business interest. He writes regularly on international politics in the print media, and participates in discussions on electronic media. Amb. Parthasarathi's hobbies include writing, spirituality, mentoring youth, golf, and bridge. After retirement from the Foreign Service, he served as the Secretary General of the Federation of Karnataka Chambers of Commerce and Industry (FKCCI) and currently he is the CEO of the Karnataka State Cricket Association (KSCA).

Major General **G.G. Dwivedi** retired as Assistant Chief Integrated Defence Staff in 2009, after a distinguished career in the Indian Army spanning over 38 years. A veteran of the Bangladesh War, he later commanded Battalion in Siachen, Brigade in the Kashmir Valley and Division in the Eastern Sector, amidst an intense counter-insurgency environment. A graduate of the National Defence Academy, he holds MBA, double M.Phil (in Strategic Studies) degrees from Madras University and Ph.D (in International Relations) from Jawaharlal Nehru University, New Delhi. Besides completing interpretership course in Chinese language from the School of Foreign Language (MOD, India), he also attended senior executive education programmes in 'Art & Practice of Leadership Development' and 'Senior Executives Programme in National and International Security' at the Harvard Kennedy School. General Dwivedi served as Defence Attaché in China, North Korea, and Mongolia from 1997–99. In China, he closely followed the 'Third Generation' leadership transition; facilitated high level military exchanges and astutely articulated India's position post Pokhran II. In North

Korea, he had opportunity of visiting North Korean People's Army (NKPA) units deployed astride the 'Military Demarcation Line', thus gaining first hand insight into politico-military significance of the DMZ. An alumnus of the National Defence College, he has been faculty at Indian Military Academy, Dehradun and at Defence Services Staff College Wellington. From 2013–17, General Dwivedi was Professor and Founder Chair of the Faculty of International Studies in Aligarh Muslim University, where he was instrumental in building the department. He is currently visiting faculty at premier institutions, including Foreign Services Institute, New Delhi, Punjab University, Chandigarh and North Cap University, Gurgaon. He has authored five books including the *War in Korea 1950–53*; published over 60 articles on geo-strategy, security, and leadership in leading professional journals, besides more than 70 short pieces in the national dailies. A member of leading think tanks, he is invited speaker at reputed 'Centres of Excellence' in India and abroad, frequently appears as panellist on the national television.

Major General **Mandip Singh** is a serving officer in the Indian Armed Forces. Currently he is the Dean at the prestigious Army War College in Mhow. Having completed his Master's in Defence Studies from the University of Madras, and his M.Phil from DAVV Indore, he was a Senior Fellow at IDSA from 2011 to 2013. During this time, he also headed the East Asia Centre as its Coordinator. A prolific writer on military issues, he is particularly focussed on China and its military, having contributed to various military journals and publications. He also lectures regularly at the Naval, Air, and Army War Colleges, and is a visiting faculty at paramilitary institutions of the BSF, the ITBP, and Punjab University. He has also participated in various Track-II dialogues with China and East Asian nations in India and abroad. He is presently pursuing his Ph.D from Punjab University.

Dr. **Namrata Goswami** is an author, strategic analyst, and consultant on counter-insurgency, counter-terrorism, alternate futures, and great power politics. After earning her Ph.D in International

Relations from Jawaharlal Nehru University, she served for nearly a decade in the Institute for Defence Studies and Analyses (IDSA), New Delhi, working on ethnic conflicts in India's Northeast as well as on the India-China border conflict. She is the author/editor of three books: *India's National Security and Counter-Insurgency*, *Imagining Asia in 2030: Trends, Scenarios and Alternatives*, and *Asia 2030: The Unfolding Future*. Her research and expertise has generated opportunities for collaborations abroad, and she accepted visiting fellowships at the Peace Research Institute, Oslo, Norway; the La Trobe University, Melbourne, Australia; and the University of Heidelberg, Germany. In 2012, she was selected to serve as a Jennings-Randolph Senior Fellow at the United States Institute of Peace (USIP), Washington DC where she studied India-China border issues, and was awarded a Fulbright-Nehru Senior Fellowship that same year. Shortly after establishing her own strategy and policy consultancy, she won the prestigious MINERVA grant awarded by the Office of the US Secretary of Defense (OSD) to study great power competition in the grey zone of outer space. She was also awarded a contract with Joint Special Operations University (JSOU), to work on a project on 'ISIS in South and Southeast Asia'. With expertise in international relations, ethnic conflicts, counter insurgency, war gaming, scenario building, and conflict resolution, she has been asked to consult for audiences as diverse as Wikistrat, USPACOM, USSOCOM, the Indian Military and the Indian Government, academia, and policy think tanks. She was the first representative from South Asia chosen to participate in the George C. Marshall European Centre for Security Studies NATO Partnership for Peace Consortium (PfPC) 'Emerging Security Challenges Working Group'. She also received the Executive Leadership Certificate sponsored by the Harvard Kennedy School of Government, National Defence University (NDU), and the Asia Pacific Center for Security Studies (APCSS). Currently, she is working on two book projects: one on 'Ethnic Narratives', to be published by Oxford University Press; and the other on 'Great Power Ambitions" to be published by Lexington Press, an imprint of Rowman and Littlefield.

Dr. **Jagannath P. Panda** is a Research Fellow and Centre Coordinator for East Asia at the Institute for Defence Studies and Analyses (IDSA), New Delhi, India. He is in charge of East Asia Centre's academic and administrative activities, including Track-II dialogues with the Chinese, Japanese, and Korean think-tanks/ institutes. He is the author of the recently published book *India-China Relations: Politics of Resources, Identity and Authority in a Multipolar World Order* (Routledge, 2017), and *China's Path to Power: Party, Military and the Politics of State Transition* (Pentagon Press, 2010). He has published many articles in peer-reviewed journals like *Rising Powers Quarterly*, *Journal of Asian Public Policy* (Routledge), *Journal of Asian and African Studies* (Sage), *Asian Perspective* (Lynne Reiner), *Journal of Contemporary China* (Routledge), *Georgetown Journal of Asian Affairs* (Georgetown), *Strategic Analysis* (Routledge), *China Report* (Sage), *Indian Foreign Affairs Journal* (MD Publications), *Portuguese Journal of International Affairs* (Euro Press), etc.

Dr. **Jojin V. John** is a Research Fellow at the Indian Council of World Affairs, New Delhi. Prior to this, he taught Political Science in Christ University, Bangalore, and held visiting research positions at National Chengchi University, Taipei; the Institute of Chinese Studies, Delhi; and at Seoul National University and Academy of Korean Studies, Korea. Dr. John obtained his Ph.D from the School of International Studies, Jawaharlal Nehru University. His research interests include International Relations in East Asia, Korean foreign policy, and India-East Asia relations. Dr. John coordinates the India-South Korea Annual Dialogue (Track-1.5).

Dr. **Manabhanjan Meher** is a Research Analyst at Europe and Eurasia Centre, Institute for Defence Studies and Analyses (IDSA). His research interests include society, politics, and ethnic conflicts in post-Soviet republics and Afghanistan. His research has mainly focused on foreign policy and security issues, including SCO, CSTO and EAEU. He has published articles on these topics in journals like *World Focus* and *Aakrosh*. He holds a Ph.D from Jawaharlal Nehru University, New Delhi.

Dr. **Titli Basu** is an Associate Fellow at the East Asia Centre, Institute for Defence Studies and Analyses (IDSA). Her research interests include strategic affairs in East Asia with focus on Japan and Korean Peninsula, and great power politics in the Indo-Pacific. She was a Visiting Fellow at the National Institute for Defense Studies (NIDS, Tokyo) in 2017. Earlier, she was with the Institute of Social Science, The University of Tokyo in 2010–11. She has published several research articles on these issues in *The Korean Journal of Defence Analysis*, *India Quarterly: A Journal of International Affairs*, *Tamkang Journal of International Affairs*, *The Asan Forum*, *Global Asia*, *The Diplomat*, *Asia-Pacific Bulletin*, *East Asia Forum*, *Asian Journal of Public Affairs*, and the *Indian Foreign Affairs Journal*. Dr. Basu has co-edited a book titled, *China-India-Japan in the Indo-Pacific: Ideas, Interests and Infrastructure* (Pentagon Press, 2018). She completed her doctoral thesis from Jawaharlal Nehru University in New Delhi. She was a recipient of the Japan Foundation fellowship in 2010. Previously, she interned with the Institute for Global Environmental Strategies, Japan.

Dr. **Prashant Kumar Singh** holds M.Phil and Ph.D degrees in Chinese Studies from Jawaharlal Nehru University, New Delhi, India. He is Associate Fellow in the East Asia Centre at the Institute for Defence Studies and Analyses (IDSA), New Delhi, India. He follows Chinese affairs, India and East Asia, the Indo-Pacific, and Indian Foreign Policy. He has been a recipient of many prestigious scholarships and fellowships, field-trips, and travel grants.

Dr. **M.S. Prathibha** is an Associate Fellow at the East Asia Centre in IDSA. Her research interests include China's Nuclear Policy, Strategic Force Modernisation, Chinese Views on War and Strategy,

Chinese Foreign Relations, and Chinese Civilisation and Philosophy. Currently, she is working on Missile Defence and China. She is a Member of the Editorial Board of *Strategic Analysis* (Routledge). She has published in journals such as *Strategic Analysis* (Routledge), *China Report* (Sage), and various international publications. She had received the Human Resource Development (India) and the China Government Scholarship, and completed her fellowship at the School of Political Science and International Studies, Beijing Normal University from 2009–2011. She had also conducted field trips to China in 2015 and 2016. Dr Prathibha had completed her Ph.D at the Chinese Studies Division of the East Asia Centre in the School of International Studies, Jawaharlal Nehru University. She completed her Master's in International Studies from Stella Maris College, Chennai and won the Best Dissertation Award. She obtained her Bachelor's degree in Mathematics at Ethiraj College for Women, Chennai.

Dr. **Anushree Chakraborty** is currently Assistant Professor at Vidyasagar College for Women, University of Calcutta. She has co-edited a book titled *Look East to Act East Policy: Tracking the Challenges and Opportunities in the Indo-Pacific* with Prof. Manmohini Kaul. She completed her doctorate from the Centre for South, Central, Southeast, and South West Pacific Studies, School of International Studies, Jawaharlal Nehru University. She was an ICSSR Post-Doctoral Fellow from 2013 to 2014.

Dr. **G. Balachandran** is a Consultant at IDSA. He has a Ph.D in Economics and Computer Science from the University of Wisconsin. His specialisation includes issues related to economics and technology.

Jyotishman Bhagawati is a Junior Research Fellow at Jamia Millia Islamia. He completed his post-graduation in International Relations from South Asian University. He is also a graduate in Political Science from the University of Delhi. His broad research interests include

China's strategic culture, maritime security in the Indo-Pacific region and the role of disruptive technologies in future warfare. After completing his post-graduation, he joined the New Delhi based National Maritime Foundation as a Research Associate. He has also worked with the Institute for Defence Studies and Analyses (IDSA) and the Institute of Chinese Studies (ICS). He is a recipient of the Huayu Enrichment Scholarship, given by the Ministry of Education of Taiwan. He has also written widely on strategic affairs for various think-tanks and journals.

1. Introduction: Mapping the Korean Conundrum

Titli Basu

The Korean Peninsula has remained a contested theatre for the major powers. Brutal wars have been fought involving imperial Japan, Czarist Russia, the Union of the Soviet Socialist Republics (USSR), Qing China, the People's Republic of China, and the United States (US) which left the Peninsula conquered, colonised, and divided, starting with Chosun (Yi) Korea from 1392–1910 to colonial Korea from 1910–45 to divided Korea since 1945.[1] Subsequently, the Korean War from 1950–53 defined the character of the Cold War in Northeast Asia. The strategic choices in the Korean theatre have been influenced by the competing geopolitical interests of regional stakeholders. In the post-Cold War era, the Peninsula remained a key variable in shaping the Northeast Asian security architecture since the Democratic People's Republic of Korea or North Korea continued to employ the strategic use of nuclear brinksmanship.

The public policy debate on whether to adapt a confrontational strategy or engage North Korea is decades old. The academic literature in the post-Cold War era indicates that while there is a school of thought which argues that the threat assessment vis-à-vis North Korea is overestimated and it recommends a more open approach, there are counter-arguments which are more sceptical. However, in both cases, irrespective of the regime's intentions and goals, the 'commanding rationale' and 'default policy' recommendation supports an engagement strategy.[2] The Korean Peninsula constitutes the strategic pivot of Northeast Asian security. Three of the five permanent members of the United Nations Security

Council (UNSC) are stakeholders in Korean denuclearisation, who are also the original nuclear weapons states under the Nuclear Non-Proliferation Treaty (NPT) regime. Northeast Asia was one theatre in Cold War politics without nonaligned states,[3] and a few Cold War structures continue to serve the goal of furthering the US-led regional order to this day.

This book aims to situate some of the important issues in the Korean Peninsula within the competing geopolitical interests of the major powers. For a nuanced understanding of the Korean conundrum, it is imperative to grasp the politics, policies, and perspectives that major powers hold, and analyse their approaches towards the key issues in the Peninsula. The objective is to evaluate the developing policy debates among the major powers, and assess how they have pursued their interests in the Peninsula. The de-escalation of the North Korean threat will be considerably shaped by the way the major powers manage their unsettled power rivalries, conflicting policy agendas, and develop a shared vision for the Peninsula's future.

Denuclearisation, Armistice Agreement and Peace Declaration

As major powers engage North Korea, the denuclearisation of the Peninsula is unfolding as one of the most defining challenges in shaping Northeast Asian security. Several key questions complicate this strategic puzzle, including the question of what defines the contours of denuclearisation in the Korean Peninsula. More importantly, the other question that arises is what is the best model for pursuing denuclearisation in the Korean Peninsula? Unlike Iran, the North Korean nuclear weapons programme is relatively more advanced. Contesting models of denuclearisation are proposed by the major stakeholders, with China's dual-track approach, North Korea's corresponding measures approach, and the US's maximum pressure approach. For the US and its allies, denuclearisation conventionally implies the dismantling of North Korea's nuclear weapons, its ballistic missile programme, and its chemical and biological weapons under international monitoring in a complete, verifiable, and irreversible manner. Meanwhile, China advocates a dual-track—pursuing parallel negotiations concerning denuclearisation of the Korean Peninsula as well as the establishment of a peace mechanism replacing the Armistice Agreement.[4] For North Korea, it entails the removal of the US nuclear umbrella and extended deterrence from the Korean theatre, the removal of US troops, and the wearing down of the US 'hostile' policies towards the regime.

The complex discourse on denuclearisation has become further convoluted following the push for a possible peace declaration ending the War, and replacing the Armistice Agreement. Given the fluidity in regional geopolitics, this, in turn, has unleashed a larger discussion on the prospects of an eventual peace treaty that may very well reorient the existing Cold War structures in the Peninsula, raising pertinent questions about the future of United Nations Command (UNC), established by UNSC Resolution 84 in 1950; US Forces Korea (USFK), established in 1957 as part of the South Korea–US Mutual Defense Treaty; and the relevance of the US alliance with South Korea. Sequencing the two issues, that is denuclearisation and peace treaty, is debated. The US favours steering peace talks only after headway on denuclearisation; but China advocates parallel negotiations over denuclearisation and the peace treaty. However, any failure to link a peace treaty with considerable advancement in North Korean denuclearisation would establish a dangerous imbalance between the two Koreas, impacting regional security and stability.[5] If the UNC—whose key task includes monitoring the Armistice—is disbanded, it would necessitate a new UN Security Council resolution, contingent on the Chinese and Russian veto, in case forces are to be reinstated in a Korean crisis. Also, if the UNC is disbanded, the UNC (Rear) in Japan would also be dissolved within 90 days consistent with the Agreement Regarding the Status of the UN Forces in Japan (UN SOFA).[6]

Literature reflects the usage of several terms, including peace treaty, peace agreement, peace declaration, peace regime, and peace mechanism to define the process and end-state of a permanent peace on the Peninsula. While some argue that a peace regime must pave the way for a peace agreement, the progressives have called for pursuing a peace declaration as the preliminary step.[7] In his negotiations with the Trump administration, Chairman Kim Jong-un has prioritised creating a 'peace regime on the Korean Peninsula', extracting 'security guarantees',[8] and the easing of economic sanctions. However, the end of the Armistice Agreement and designing a peace regime is fiercely debated among major powers. Whose national security interests are furthered by such a peace treaty? How will a peace declaration, which will pave the way for a peace treaty, impact the regional security architecture? What should be the sequencing? And, who are the parties that should be involved in crafting this peace regime? Peace declaration in the longer term will have geopolitical implications since, strategically and structurally, the existence of the USFK is perceived as a 'dagger to China's throat'.[9]

The North Korean threat is often used to justify the presence of the USFK as also the deployment of Terminal High Altitude Area Defense (THAAD) missile battery in South Korea which threatens China's regional strategy. North Korea's long-term objective behind the end of the Korean War and building a peace regime is ensuring the withdrawal of US forces from the Peninsula and attenuating the alliance, having an impact on the strategic posture across East Asia. These echo Chinese objectives of waning American influence in East Asia. As a party to the Armistice, China would exert influence in furthering its interests during any negotiations related to a peace treaty. Meanwhile, there is a school of thought which argues that North Korea is manoeuvring the peace treaty issue as a ploy to trap the US into an extended discussion, thereby buying it time to further advance their nuclear weapons programme.[10]

Traditionally, North Korea has preferred negotiating directly with the US bypassing South Korea;[11] but any peace treaty negotiations would have a colossal impact for South Korean security which has led the US (including the Bill Clinton and George W. Bush administrations) insist that South Korea be part of any formal negotiations. South Korea is not a signatory to the Armistice Agreement. Deliberations over a permanent peace regime in the 1990s and the 2000s involved the key stakeholders in the Korean conflict. President Moon Jae-in has underscored that 'the resolution of the North Korean nuclear issue and establishment of permanent peace' is a key component of his 'peace and prosperity' approach to North Korea.[12] The April 2018 'Panmunjom Declaration for Peace, Prosperity and Unification of the Korean Peninsula' underscored that 'establishing a firm peace regime on the Korean peninsula is a historic mission that must not be delayed any further'.[13]

However, denuclearisation and peace declaration are not the only variables shaping the Korean strategic calculus. Academic and policy debates have intensified over the stability of the North Korean regime, the effectiveness of economic sanctions as viable policy tools in influencing the behaviour of North Korea, the competing strategic interests of the great powers in the Peninsula, the dilution of non-proliferation regime and global norms, among others.

Security Guarantee, Regime Stability, and the Politics of Sanctions

As the strategic discourse in the US shifted from 'strategic patience' to the 'maximum pressure' campaign with 'all options on the table'—and some hardliners, for instance, the National Security Advisor John Bolton advocating the 'Libya model'—the primary objectives of Chairman Kim Jong-un are to ensure regime stability and ease economic sanctions. The 2018 US Nuclear Posture Review argues that any North Korean nuclear attack against the US or its allies is 'unacceptable and will result in the end of that regime'.[14] For North Korea, regime stability has remained one of the primary objectives of the Supreme Leader (*Suryong*) and dynastic ruling of the Kim family. At the Singapore Summit, President Trump 'committed to provide security guarantees to the DPRK'[15] in return for Kim Jong-un's pledge to complete denuclearisation. North Korea has pursued the nuclear and ballistic missile programmes as tools serving regime stability and national security. The 'axis of evil' formulation by President Bush furthered North Korea's nuclear defiance.

Even though the academic and policy debate on the legitimacy of the North Korean regime is contested and status of a nuclear state questioned, Kim Jong-un amended the Constitution in 2013 to pronounce North Korea as a 'nuclear state'. The regime argues that it needs to wield the nuclear threat as deterrence against US pre-emption. This, in turn, makes the goal of denuclearisation a monumental challenge for regional stakeholders. In its latest assessment in January 2019, US intelligence—including the FBI Director Christopher Wray, CIA Director Gina Haspel, and Director of National Intelligence Dan Coats—argued to the Senate Intelligence Committee that North Korea is unlikely to dismantle its nuclear capabilities since nuclear weapons are perceived critical to regime survival.[16] The US has pursued the politics of democracy promotion in authoritarian states and, in some instances, effected regime changes. But regime change may not be the objective of President Trump as the risks, costs, and consequences of initiating a regime change are colossal. Even though much of the discourse on forced regime change centres on the colossal economic costs of reunification and a possible refugee crisis for bordering states, the geopolitical implications for the US may not necessarily be favourable.[17]

The debate over political survival and the impending collapse of the authoritarian regime can be traced back to the death of the North Korean leader, Kim Il-sung. Despite the resilience of this opaque regime surviving the worst economic period in the late 1990s, there is a school of thought among a few western scholars[18] and American intelligence which have argued for the potential instability of Kim Jong-un's regime. However, quite on the contrary, he has consolidated power on the domestic front through various political organs, including the Worker's Party of Korea (WPK), and maintains a hybrid authoritarian regime that seeks its sustainability through party apparatuses.[19] He pursued ideological legitimacy by instituting *Kimilsungism-Kimjongilism* as the official ideology of the Party which synergizes the *Juche* revolutionary idea of Kim Il-sung and the Military First Politics of Kim Jong-il.[20]

There are arguments that Chairman Kim was forced to turn to the negotiating table since President Trump created pressure through primary and secondary sanctions with the objective of deterring third parties from offering goods or financial services which contribute to the North Korean economy. The effective utilisation of secondary sanctions—in addition to the primary sanctions strategy—has affected Chinese and Russian firms, entities, and individuals. For instance, the imposition of secondary sanctions against Dandong Bank by the US Treasury Department for violating Section 311 of the US Patriot Act by way of laundering money for Dandong Hongxiang Industrial Development (DHID), which ran a money laundering scheme for the North Korean government. The Bank of Korea estimated that North Korea's GDP contracted by 3.5 per cent in 2017,[21] with severe waning in the mining sector prompted by harsher UN sanctions. One of the reasons why economic sanctions worked well in 2017 and the first quarter of 2018 is because China was forced to implement them stringently, and the US created disincentives for evading UN sanctions on coal or other exports, and on petroleum imports.

The sequencing of denuclearisation and the easing of sanctions constitute a major faultline as the US-North Korea negotiations intensified between the Singapore and the Hanoi Summits.[22] Given the challenges associated with the use of force, the international community has employed sanctions since 2006 in order to manage the behaviour of North Korea. However, great power politics in shaping the UNSC sanctions debate, and the difficulties involved in the efficient implementation and quantification of the impact of sanctions have complicated the discourse over the years. Pyongyang has nurtured a series of sophisticated evasion tactics, such as the direct swapping of goods; ship-to-ship transfer of petroleum and related products; smuggling; and the illegal transfers of arms; forging ship registry papers; a network of fraudulent companies and joint ventures; and the misuse of diplomatic cover as underscored in the UN Panel Report (S/2018/171).

Additionally, North Korea has misused several gaps in the international financial system to transfer and receive funds illegally, and maintain a few offshore bank accounts to transfer funds internationally. Also, the joint ventures with overseas companies are one of the primary means of evading sanctions. The primary challenge for the effective implementation of sanctions stems from the absence of requisite capacity among the states.

As President Trump has categorically refused to ease any sanctions until the goal of denuclearisation is realised, China and Russia have coordinated their position, and urged the UNSC to ease sanctions on North Korea as a means of rewarding initial steps towards disarmament. Furthermore, a China-Russia-North Korea joint communiqué in October 2018 articulated that attaining the goal of denuclearisation of the Korean Peninsula should be done step-by-step, synchronised and complemented by reciprocal steps from the involved states. It is not in Chinese or Russian national interest to push North Korea towards instability owing to the effective implementation of sanctions. Severe sanctions could destabilise the regime and, in an extreme situation, lead to a regime collapse which may pave the way for a pro-US reunified Korea, considerably altering the power balance in Northeast Asia.

North Korea and Proliferation

Even though the overriding national security objective of the US with North Korea is to remove its capability to threaten continental US with nuclear weapons, the North Korean experience has intensified a larger global debate on the effectiveness of the non-proliferation regime. North Korea signed the Non-Proliferation Treaty (NPT) in 1985. As the international community commemorates the 50th anniversary of the NPT, founded on mutually reinforcing pillars of non-proliferation, disarmament, and peaceful uses of nuclear energy, North Korea diluted the essence of the treaty considerably as it withdrew from the treaty with no adverse costs for non-compliance. Despite the fact that the NPT has secured nuclear restraint from numerous states, there are concerns that the North Korean example would be undermining global norms, and encourage wilful proliferation if there are no consequences. In tracing the trajectory of proliferation to North Korea, the role of three major contributors to its nuclear and missile programmes—the USSR/Russia, Pakistan, and China—and the risk of onward proliferation from North Korea to others, constitutes a critical challenge. The mechanisms for managing North Korea, including through the NPT, Agreed Framework, the Six-Party Talks, and UNSC sanctions have failed to influence North Korea to abandon its nuclear ambitions.

North Korea's role in the proliferation network, its implications for international security, and the risk of nuclear proliferation to non-state actors who might be interested in carrying out acts of nuclear terrorism poses a colossal threat to the regional security situation. North Korea has a record of circumventing sanctions to engage in the trade of dual-use materials related to nuclear and ballistic missile activities, in addition to selling conventional arms and military equipment. Pyongyang has supplied missiles and missile technology to several countries, including Egypt, Iran, Libya, Pakistan, Syria, and Yemen. It has shipped containers of uranium hexafluoride to A.Q. Khan in Pakistan, which was then shipped to Libya. Moreover, there are strong indications of transfer of prohibited ballistic missiles as well as conventional arms-related and dual-use goods to Syria. There is also evidence of Myanmar getting ballistic missile systems in addition to a range of conventional weapons, including multiple rocket launchers and surface-to-air missiles from North Korea. The August 2018 International Atomic Energy Agency (IAEA) report suggested that the 'continuation and further development of the DPRK's nuclear programme and related statements by the DPRK are a cause for grave concern'.[23]

Competing Interests and Major Powers

The US-China strategic competition is playing out in the Korean theatre. The end state on the Korean Peninsula and how it is realised will influence the regional balance of power. The US and China have differing priorities. The US's top priority is to realise denuclearisation. The US lays emphasis on eliminating the threat posed by Pyongyang's nuclear weapons and missile programme, reassuring the regional allies of US commitment and deny China the prospect of using the North Korean issue to advance its larger strategic ambitions. While China supports the goal of denuclearisation but does not consider Pyongyang's nuclear and missile programme as a direct threat. Beijing's primary interest is to maintain a stable external environment by way of upholding regime stability, and averting any possibility of war on the Korean Peninsula. China's economic development—which is crucial for its ambition of becoming a great power and the legitimacy of the Communist Party—is contingent on a stable external environment. The Korean Peninsula is an important variable in shaping this stable external environment. With the exception of North Korea, China is surrounded by traditional US allies, including Japan and South Korea, hosting US forward deployment in the Asia-Pacific. Thus, China is keen on ensuring a stable regime in Pyongyang, which is relatively more inclined towards Beijing. As China taps into the period of strategic opportunity for development, it wants North Korea to focus more on economic development as well as integration with the regional economy of China's northeast which, in turn, will give China a greater foothold in North Korea, or a reunified Korea. China has stakes in shaping the outcome of US-North Korea negotiations as Beijing's interests are served in averting a military confrontation and regime collapse. Moreover, the North Korean question will also test China's great power ambitions in terms of securing the interests of its sole treaty ally with whom it fought the Korean War.[24]

While South Korea under President Moon Jae-in preferred to sit in the 'driver's seat' to achieve the denuclearisation of the Korean Peninsula, and invested profoundly in North-South reconciliation, China continues to enjoy considerable leverage and perform a critical role in the Peninsula. Following the Singapore Summit, developments in the Korean Peninsula largely resonated China's 'suspension for suspension' proposal. China's key security objective is regional stability, and preserving the strategic balance in Northeast Asia. As Kim Jong-un launched his charm offensive with a diplomatic whirlpool, the pace of China-North Korea reset in 2018 suggests Kim Jong-un's cognisance that he is better placed negotiating with the US if China is in his corner. Prior to 2018, relations were tense to the point that Xi Jinping and Kim Jong-un had never held a summit. It also reiterates North Korea's strategic significance to China, and stresses China's resolve not to be sidelined in negotiations that could conclusively affect Chinese interests. While China's role in the Peninsula has remained a challenge for the US and Trump has blamed China for North Korea's lack of progress towards denuclearisation, excluding China, is not an option; in fact, it has pushed China to refresh its relations that had dipped to a low point after Kim Jong-un assumed power.

In the meantime, North Korea has played into the US-China strategic competition as it seeks to revive China-North Korea political and economic relations while engaging with the US directly for negotiating denuclearisation and sanctions. In the future, it is unclear whether the North will resort to the strategy of playing one country off against the other to maximise its gains.[25] North Korea requires Chinese support to expand its leverage while negotiating with the US, and China as a stakeholder would play its part to make certain that its interests are represented.

Unlike previous negotiations, the current phase of dialogue between the Trump administration and Chairman Kim Jong-un is taking place in a greatly altered circumstances. The North Korea of 2018/2019 is a much more confident actor than before, with tested nuclear and intercontinental ballistic missile capability which Pyongyang believes has given it a stronger negotiating edge.[26] Contrary to the narrative of North Korea as an irrational actor, it has emerged as a shrewd and a skilled strategic player, especially under Chairman Kim Jong-un. North Korea's belligerence is influenced by its coercive bargaining rationale whose hope is to leverage the crises more to its advantage. The policy debate has gained traction following Kim Jong-un's marked departure from the relentless testing of nuclear and ballistic missiles through 2017 to an effective charm offensive beginning 2018, which has enabled Pyongyang to position itself relatively favourably within the great power politics.

2018 has witnessed shifts in the strategic balance in the Korean Peninsula. Chairman Kim arrived on the international stage as a crafty statesman in his dealing with President Trump at the Singapore Summit. He has garnered considerable concessions for North Korea, including no mention of a complete, verifiable, and irreversible denuclearisation (CVID) in the Joint Statement; no definite timeline for achieving denuclearisation; safeguarding regime stability; the unilateral suspension of the US-South Korea war games; besides an invitation to the White House. Additionally, South Korean President Moon Jae-in's cautious optimism—balanced with a pragmatic approach—has paved the way for meaningful inter-Korea cooperation that has translated into economic gains for Pyongyang with inter-Korea infrastructure projects, and strategic gains with the historic military agreement. Furthermore, he has consolidated support from China and Russia, which gives Pyongyang's national interest greater latitude in debates on phased denuclearisation as well as UNSC sanctions.

North Korea engages in maximising its gains by taking advantage of the differences among major regional powers. For instance, North Korea has engaged in trilateral talks with China and Russia while furthering its top priority of easing sanctions. The trilateral talks have called for 'reciprocity, and parallel, synchronous and gradual steps', and have argued that denuclearisation in the Korean Peninsula should follow the Russian-Chinese roadmap, which contradicts the Trump administration's approach that sanctions must continue to remain in place until denuclearisation has been achieved and verified. China and Russia are mindful of upholding regime stability in North Korea in the context of tight economic sanctions. Regime collapse would have adverse effects on both China and Russia as they share borders with North Korea. Moreover, in the case of a reunification leading to a pro-US Korea would significantly shift the regional balance of power. Besides regional geopolitics, China and Russia are guided by their respective national interests. Russia pursues North Korea as a key variable in realising its regional economic project and development of the Far East. China's relation with the North, on the other hand, is shaped by the 1961 Sino-North Korean Treaty of Friendship, Cooperation, and Mutual Assistance which is up for renewal in 2021. China's approach to North Korea is determined by its ideological underpinnings, and the need to economically stimulate China's northeast. The US-China-Russia equation in managing North Korea in the backdrop of a US-China trade war and US-Russia escalating tensions (including economic sanctions and the erosion of the INF Treaty) defines the complexity of the problem. Policy decisions should weigh North Korea in the context of Sino-US and Russia-US relations, and US policy choices should not have unintended geopolitical outcome of consolidating China-Russia strategic relations.[27] China and Russia will oppose measures that expand American influence in Northeast Asia. For making progress on denuclearisation and averting military contingency, the US would need constructive engagement with both China and Russia.

Meanwhile, China is also acting from a stronger strategic position as it has consolidated its economic and military strengths. As the strategic competition intensifies with the US, China has not shied away from employing a coercive economic approach, with US allies in pursuit of its national interests. For instance, the economic retaliation by the Chinese over the THAAD issue targeted South Korea despite the fact that it was fundamentally a case of competing power projections between the US and China.[28] Beijing believes that THAAD would disturb the regional strategic balance and nuclear deterrence capabilities of China and Russia since the monitoring scope of the X-Band radar goes far beyond the defence needs of the Korean Peninsula.[29] In this regard, China has converging strategic interests with Russia, and thus both have coordinated their positions in opposing the extension of US-led regional missile defence as part of a broader American strategy to manage China.

China has argued that the American deployment of global missile defence systems will hinder the nuclear disarmament process; initiate regional arms race; and increase military confrontation. It believes that the THAAD system will not accomplish the denuclearisation of the Peninsula. Its deployment will 'severely undermine the strategic security interests of regional countries including China and disrupt regional strategic balance, to which China is firmly opposed, and China will take necessary measures to defend national security interests and regional strategic balance'.[30] There is a school of thought which argues that North Korea is the 'winner' since the THAAD provides it the justification for development of nuclear weapons and missiles, and drives a wedge between China and South Korea by making use of the THAAD deployment.[31] Moreover, the THAAD strengthens strategic cooperation between China and Russia and countermeasures may include actions intended to overcome the US missile defence architecture, possibly comprising further complex missile defence exercises; the development of new missile variants and technologies; coordinated missile deployments; and increased data and information sharing between the two countries.[32]

As President Trump pursues the goal of denuclearisation in the Korean Peninsula, one of his key assets will be the US regional allies. The Asia Reassurance Initiative Act encompasses North Korea in its scope and authorises spending for pursuing US interests. But, how President Trump's America First policy—which is reshaping the US hub-and-spokes San Francisco system of alliances—will shape the structure of regional security in Northeast Asia remains to be seen. At a time when the US-South Korea alliance commemorated its 65th anniversary, the absence of discussion with allies before unilaterally suspending the US-South Korea war games—calling them 'very expensive', 'very provocative' and 'inappropriate',[33] demonstrates not just President Trump's unconventional understanding but also gives into one of the key North Korean demands. President Trump's effort to 'keep its partners in Seoul and Tokyo in the loop' leaves much to be desired in terms of alliance management. This may present North Korea 'potential openings to create fissures' and decouple the US alliance framework.[34] One key concern for America's regional allies is whether President Trump is moving away from the 'ironclad' security commitment in support of his 'America First' policy. The decisive role performed by South Korean President Moon Jae-in in de-escalating tensions by charting the course of dialogue and enabling the process of engagement not only with regard to inter-Korea relations but also with US-North Korea relations cannot be undervalued. In pursuit of his 'America First' policy, Trump appears to be disregarding the nuances of alliance management, and prioritising a transactional approach in terms of burden sharing. Some of Trump's actions may have diluted confidence in the decades-old alliance framework that served as the fulcrum of regional stability.

Beyond this, the North Korean nuclear programme has emerged as a key variable, testing the resilience of Japan's post-war security orientation. Considerable advancement in North Korea's nuclear and ballistic missile programme has raised fierce policy debates in Japan on how to evolve a better alliance management mechanism, and balance the US's extended deterrence commitment versus the intensification of alliance de-coupling concerns. As North Korean missiles flew over Hokkaido, Japan took a policy decision to 'drastically'[35] develop ballistic missile defence capabilities, and advance the political debate on acquiring strike capabilities (*teki kichi kōgeki*). Since Prime Minister Abe came to power in December 2012, Japan has unmistakably marked a departure in its post-war security orientation. His resolve to buttress Japan's deterrent capabilities has raised concerns in the region that still suffers from complex historical baggage. As Japan adapts to the fast altering regional security environment; incrementally expands the scope of Article 9 and creates more latitude for SDF operations; bolsters the missile defence systems; and reinforces deterrence capabilities; it has prompted a regional response.

Inter-Korea Dialogue

Alongside US-North Korea negotiations on denuclearisation, inter-Korean dialogue gained traction in 2018 owing to President Moon Jae-in's pragmatic approach. In addition to the three inter-Korea summits, President Moon has served as an important channel between the US and North Korea. South Korean policy discourse has focused on three objectives for inter-Korean relations, including denuclearisation and instituting permanent peace; advancing sustainable inter-Korean relations; and the realisation of a new economic community in the Peninsula. With the Panmunjom and Pyongyang Declarations in 2018, both Koreas have decided to pursue military confidence building measures, cooperative economic initiatives, and interpersonal exchanges.

> Developments in inter-Korean relations are not the by-effects of progress in the relationship between the North and the United States. Rather, advancement in inter-Korean relations is the driving force behind denuclearisation of the Korean Peninsula.
>
> —President Moon Jae-in on Korea's
> 73rd Liberation Day, August 15, 2018

However, the pace of North Korean denuclearisation juxtaposed with the speedy developments in inter-Korean relations which have unfolded a host of economic, cultural, and security initiatives with the North is critically analysed in the US. Managing the delicate balancing act between two unpredictable leaders, consolidating the alliance under the Trump Presidency, and reconciliation with North Korea under Chairman Kim Jong-un is a colossal challenge for President Moon. Decelerating the speed of rapprochement as a response to US reservations may be tough to sell to Chairman Kim Jong-un. Moreover, America's resolve on the strict implementation of sanctions might lead to a stalemate in inter-Korean economic cooperation, thus waning Pyongyang's desire for dialogue. Even if South Korea eases the unilateral sanctions imposed on Pyongyang subsequent to the sinking of the *Cheonan*, the existing international sanctions regime impedes any meaningful economic engagement with the North, including in the Kaesong Industrial Zone. Similar to the inter-Korean railways project, progress on both Kaesong and Kumgang is restricted by the scope of UNSC sanctions that stop bulk cash transfers to the North. As Chairman Kim Jong-un is focusing on the easing of sanctions and developing the North Korean economy, productive relations with the South is an important factor.

Meanwhile, there is a school of thought arguing that Chairman Kim Jong-un is playing on Seoul's expectation of meaningful progress on denuclearisation while leveraging his ability to influence the leadership in Seoul. President Trump now has the task of restricting the North from manipulating the peace process without giving the impression that the US is a hindrance to peace.[36] While the unconventional approach of the Trump Presidency has put the decades old alliance on test, whether it is scaling down joint military exercises or renegotiating the military cost-sharing agreement, neither the alliance nor the forward deployment are on the negotiating table as President Moon seizes the historic opportunity to infuse momentum in inter-Korea relations.

From Singapore to Hanoi to the DMZ

Following the Singapore Summit, complex negotiations among the interlocutors culminated in the lack of agreement at the Hanoi Summit regarding what is entailed in denuclearisation and corresponding measures as President Trump urged North Korea to part ways with its entire nuclear weapons programme before any possible easing of sanctions. Sanctions relief is perceived as subsidising the development of weapons of mass destruction in North Korea. The US wanted the dismantlement of the plutonium and uranium enrichment facilities that extend beyond the scope of Yongbyon—for instance, the facility at Kangson.[37] Meanwhile, North Korea has demanded partial relief of sanctions in return for the permanent dismantlement of all nuclear material production facilities in Yongbyon. This is likely to remove the source of plutonium production, slow the rate of highly enriched uranium accumulation, and end one of North Korea's few potential sources of tritium.

Beyond the optics presented at the Singapore Summit and the latest meeting at the DMZ, if both leaders are genuinely interested in an agreement then Hanoi presented a reality check.

President Trump will likely continue with the present position that Yongbyon alone is not enough for effective sanctions relief. Following the Hanoi Summit, whether North Korea reverts back to serious provocation—for example, the rebuilding of Tongchang-ri and Sanum-dong—remains to be seen. The 2019 US Missile Defense Review stressed that North Korea continues to pose an extraordinary threat 'since the intentions of potential adversaries can change directions unexpectedly and more rapidly than we can develop and field defensive capabilities'.[38] Going forward, it needs to be comprehended that while complete, irreversible and verifiable denuclearisation is the desired goal, North Korea has invested heavily in building its nuclear weapons programme and any denuclearisation attempts—especially according to the timeframe outlined by the Trump administration—is highly unlikely. Owing to the infrastructure of North Korea's nuclear programme that needs to be dismantled, denuclearisation would be a long, phased process, and *quid pro quo* may have to be provided along the course.[39] A good starting point could be arriving at a common understanding and outlining a roadmap for denuclearisation. What follows from the Trump-Kim meeting at the DMZ in late June 2019 and the subsequent launching of several short-range ballistic missiles by North Korea in the following weeks and whether it can lead to advancing constructive dialogue on denuclearisation depends on the political will and intentions of the leaders.

A vast array of policy means have been employed over decades. All have aimed at de-escalating tensions in the Peninsula, including bilateral talks; multilateral talks with the Six-Party framework; diplomacy and pressure; and the use of carrots and stick approach. America's 'strategic patience' approach, China's 'three no's' (encompassing no war, no instability, no nukes), besides the Agreed Framework failed to realise the policy objectives in the Korean Peninsula. Making tangible progress in managing the North Korean threat will involve periodic setbacks; it demands an enduring diplomatic engagement coordinated among all regional stakeholders, holding the ability to influence the outcomes.

This volume is an endeavour to bring together leading Indian experts including former Indian ambassadors to South Korea, senior members from the defence community and members from the strategic community to analyse the developments in the Peninsula, especially in 2017 and 2018.

Notes

1. Samuel S. Kim, *The Two Koreas and the Great Powers,* Cambridge University Press, New York, 2006.
2. For more, see, Victor D. Cha and David C. Kang, *Nuclear North Korea: A Debate on Engagement Strategies,* Cambridge University Press, New York, 2003.
3. Samuel S. Kim, note 1.
4. 'Foreign Minister Wang Yi Meets the Press,' March 8, 2017, Ministry of Foreign Affairs of the People's Republic of China at http://www.fmprc.gov.cn/mfa_eng/zxxx_662805/t1444204.shtml, accessed on December 10, 2018.
5. Bruce Klingner 'Challenges to Transforming the Korean Armistice into a Peace Treaty', *The Journal of East Asian Affairs*, 25(1), Spring/Summer, 2011, pp. 59–84.
6. Yasuaki Chijiwa, 'The "Termination" of the Korean War, the "Dissolution" of the United Nations Forces and their Influence on Japan', NIDS Commentary No. 80, July 11, 2018.
7. Bruce Klingner, note 5.
8. 'Joint Statement of President Donald J. Trump of the United States of America and Chairman Kim Jong Un of the Democratic People's Republic of Korea at the Singapore Summit', The White House, June 12, 2018 at https://www.whitehouse.gov/briefings-statements/joint-statement-president-donald-j-trump-united-states-america-chairman-kim-jong-un-democratic-peoples-republic-korea-singapore-summit, accessed on December 10, 2018.
9. Seong-hyon Lee, 'The Shift of Security Environment in Northeast Asia: The US–China Conflict and its Implications for Korea', *Journal for Peace and Nuclear Disarmament*, 1(2), 2018, pp. 352–362.
10. Jung H. Pak, 'Kim Jong-un Has a Maximum Pressure and Engagement Strategy of His Own,' Brookings Brief, April 19, 2018.
11. Emma Chanlett-Avery, Susan V. Lawrence, Mark E. Manyin, Mary Beth D. Nikitin, 'A Peace Treaty with North Korea?' Congressional Research Service, April 19, 2018 at https://fas.org/sgp/crs/row/R45169.pdf, accessed on December 10, 2018.

12. 'Moon Jae-In's Policy on the Korean Peninsula', Ministry of Unification, December 2017 at https://www.unikorea.go.kr/eng_unikorea/policylssues/koreanpeninsula/goals/, accessed on December 10, 2018.
13. 'Panmunjom Declaration for Peace, Prosperity and Unification of the Korean Peninsula', Ministry of Foreign Affairs Republic of Korea, April 27, 2018 at http://www.mofa.go.kr/eng/brd/m_5478/view.do?seq=319130&srchFr=&srchTo=&srchWord=&srchTp=&multi_itm_seq=0&itm_seq_1=0&itm_seq_2=0&company_cd=&company_nm=&page=1&titleNm, accessed on December 10, 2018.
14. 'Nuclear Posture Review 2018', Office of the Secretary of Defense, February 2018 at https://media.defense.gov/2018/feb/02/2001872886/-1/-1/1/2018-nuclear-posture-review-final-report.pdf, accessed on December 10, 2018.
15. The White House, note 8.
16. 'US Intel Heads List North Korea, Not Border, as Threat to US', The Associated Press, January 29, 2019 at https://www.nytimes.com/aponline/2019/01/29/us/politics/ap-us-global-threats.html, accessed on February 10, 2019.
17. Richard Sokolsky and Aaron David Miller, 'Regime Change in North Korea: Be Careful What You Wish For', 38 North, August 2, 2017 at https://www.38north.org/2017/08/rsokolskyamiller080217/, accessed on December 10, 2018.
18. Bruce W. Bennett, 'Preparing for the Possibility of a North Korean Collapse', RAND Corporation, 2013; Snyder S and Draudt D., 'First mover responses to North Korean instability: the intervention-legitimacy paradox', *International Journal of Korean Unification Studies,* 24, 2015, pp. 99–126.
19. B.S. Koo, J.Y. Choi, and J. Kim, 'Analyzing Kim Jong-un's survival strategy from the comparative authoritarian perspective', *Pacific Focus,* XXXI, 2016, pp. 211–231.
20. Hanhee Lee, 'Analyzing the Political Survival Prospects of Kim Jong-un's North Korean Regime through the Framework of Selectorate Theory', *Japanese Journal of Political Science*, 19 (3), 2018, pp. 474–488.
21. 'Gross Domestic Product Estimates for North Korea in 2017', Bank of Korea, July 20, 2018 at https://www.bok.or.kr/eng/bbs/E0000634/view.do?nttId=10046123&menuNo=400069&pageIndex=10, accessed on December 10, 2018.
22. 'Remarks by President Trump in Press Conference, Hanoi, Vietnam', The White House, February 28, 2019 at https://www.whitehouse.gov/briefings-statements/remarks-president-trump-press-conference-hanoi-vietnam/, accessed on March 10, 2019.

23. 'Application of Safeguards in the Democratic People's Republic of Korea', IAEA Board of Governors General Conference, GOV/2018/34-GC(62)/12, August 20, 2018.
24. Ferial Saeed, 'What Will North Korea Negotiations Mean For The US-China Balance Of Power?' War On The Rocks, July 26, 2018 at https://warontherocks.com/2018/07/what-will-north-korea-negotiations-mean-for-the-u-s-china-balance-of-power/, accessed on December 10, 2018.
25. Fei Su, 'China's Potential Role as Security Guarantor for North Korea', 38 North, October 24, 2018 at https://www.38north.org/2018/10/fsu102418/, accessed on December 10, 2018.
26. Jinwook Choi, 'How to stop North Korea's nuclear ambition: failed diplomacy and future options', *Journal of Contemporary East Asia Studies*, 7:1, 2018, pp. 1–15.
27. Mercy A. Kuo, 'China, Russia, and US Sanctions on North Korea: Insight from Sharyl Cross', *The Diplomat*, November 13, 2018 at https://thediplomat.com/2018/11/china-russia-and-us-sanctions-on-north-korea/, accessed on December 10, 2018.
28. Seong-hyon Lee, 'The Shift of Security Environment in Northeast Asia: The US–China Conflict and its Implications for Korea', *Journal for Peace and Nuclear Disarmament*, 1:2, 2018, pp. 352–362.
29. 'Wang Yi Talks about US's Plan to Deploy THAAD Missile Defence System in ROK', Ministry of Foreign Affairs of the People's Republic of China, February 2, 2016 at https://www.fmprc.gov.cn/mfa_eng/zxxx_662805/t1340525.shtml, accessed on December 10, 2018.
30. 'Statement by Ambassador WANG Qun, Director-General of the Arms Control Department of the Ministry of Foreign Affairs of China, at the General Debate of the First Committee of the 71st Session of the UNGA', Ministry of Foreign Affairs of the People's Republic of China, October 10, 2016 at https://www.fmprc.gov.cn/mfa_eng/wjdt_665385/zyjh_665391/t1405391.shtml, accessed on December 10, 2018.
31. Fan Gaoyue, 'ROK: The Biggest Loser of THAAD,' China-US Focus, August 9, 2016 at http://www.chinausfocus.com/foreignpolicy/rok-the-biggest-loser-of-thaad, accessed on December 10, 2018.
32. Ethan Meick, 'China-Russia Military-to-Military Relations: Moving toward a Higher Level of Cooperation,' U.S.-China Economic and Security Review Commission, March 20, 2017, pp. 11–12 at https://www.uscc.gov/sites/default/files/Research/China-Russia%20MilMil%20Relations%20Moving%20Toward%20Higher%20Level%20of%20Cooperation.pdf, accessed on December 10, 2018.
33. 'Press Conference by President Trump', The White House, June 12, 2018 at https://www.whitehouse.gov/briefings-statements/press-conference-president-trump/, accessed on December 10, 2018.

34. Victor Cha and Katrin Fraser Katz, 'A Better North Korea Strategy: How to Coerce Pyongyang Without Starting a War', *Foreign Affairs*, June 1, 2018.
35. 'Defense of Japan 2018 (Digest)', Ministry of Defense, August 2018 at http://www.mod.go.jp/e/publ/w_paper/pdf/2018/DOJ2018_Digest_0827.pdf, accessed on September 20, 2018.
36. David Maxwell and Mathew Ha, 'At the Latest Inter-Korean Summit, Kim Jong-un Created a Diplomatic Minefield for the United States', War on the Rocks, October 31, 2018 at https://warontherocks.com/2018/10/at-the-latest-inter-korean-summit-kim-jong-un-created-a-diplomatic-minefield-for-the-united-states/, accessed on December 10, 2018.
37. Ankit Panda and Vipin Narang, 'The Hanoi Summit Was Doomed From the Start', *Foreign Affairs Snapshot*, March 5, 2019 at https://www.foreignaffairs.com/articles/north-korea/2019-03-05/hanoi-summit-was-doomed-start, accessed on March 19, 2019.
38. 'Missile Defence Review', Department of Defence, 2019 at https://assets.documentcloud.org/documents/5687662/2019-MISSILE-DEFENSE-REVIEW.pdf, accessed on March 10, 2019.
39. Taeyong Cho, 'The Hanoi Summit: A Blessing in Disguise but What Now? A View from Seoul', 38 North, March 20, 2019 at https://www.38north.org/2019/03/tcho032019/, accessed on March 30, 2019.

PART I
Politics and Policies in the Korean Peninsula

2. Is it Spring Time in the Korean Peninsula?

Vishnu Prakash

The only constant in the Korean Peninsula is change. 'If you don't like the weather in New England now, just wait a few minutes,' said Mark Twain once. This is as applicable to the political and security climate in the Korean Peninsula, which morphs with astounding speed, living up to its billing as a theatre of the unexpected. And, the unexpected did happen yet again, in Singapore and Hanoi, when President Trump and Chairman Kim Jong-un held their historic summits. Ever since the Armistice in 1953, the Korean Peninsula has been and remains one of the volatile flashpoints on the planet. Big power politics, divergent political ideology, perceived existential crisis by North Korea, and missed opportunities have made it so. In the last two decades, North Korea added WMD to this combustible cocktail. Efforts were made by the protagonists, time and again, to find a modus vivendi. Periodically, green shoots of hope and peace sprouted through the frost, only to wither as quickly. Will it be any different this time around, is the big question?

The author was privileged to fly the Indian flag in Seoul for over three years till early March 2015. South Korea is one of the most fascinating countries in the world and, arguably, the greatest success story of the 20th century. It rose from the ashes of the three-year devastating inter-Korean war, to become an OECD member-nation in 1996. No country has managed this feat before or after. The democratic transition in 1987 reflects the resilience of the nation. There is everything going for South Korea save two critical items of unfinished business: the normalisation of inter-Korean ties, and eventual reunification. Both sides believe—and rightly so—that Korean Peninsula was torn asunder by the big powers in pursuit of their own interests. Sustained efforts have been made, over the preceding decades, by the South Koreans to ease tensions with North Korea, and at least foster a modicum of economic and people-to-people engagement. Instead, Pyongyang has generally chosen to play hardball, and extract a price from Seoul for the smallest of 'concessions'.

It also openly engaged in hostilities—especially in the 1960s to 1980s—when its assailants infiltrated into South Korea to carry out political assassinations. In 1968, North Korea commandoes were intercepted just 100 metres from the Presidential Palace (Blue House) in Seoul, thwarting their mission to kill President Park Chung-hee. In 1983, an attempt was made on President Chun Doo-hwan's life in Rangoon (Yangon), during which 21 South Koreans (including ministers) perished. The sinking of the South Korea navy frigate Cheonan and the shelling of the Yeonpyeong Island in 2010, which resulted in casualties, are still fresh in public memory. Yet, the yearning for reunification, especially among South Korean politicians and a sizable percentage of its populace remains unquenched. They have learnt to take North Korean bellicosity and provocations in their stride. In early 2013, when Pyongyang threatened to douse Seoul in a 'Sea of Fire', people didn't skip a beat, and the stock market remained rock steady. The youngsters, who have little sense of history and have only witnessed prosperity, are obviously not enamoured. Overall support for reunification has fallen considerably in South Korea over the last 70 years. Given that the per-capita income of South Koreans is 20 times that of their northern compatriots, Seoul shudders at the challenges and cost of reunification which is variously estimated up to US$ 5 trillion.

That is the broad background against which the dramatic developments since the advent of President Trump on the scene needs to be viewed. Consider this, as 2017 drew to a close, the sides were all jaw-jaw, hurling invectives at each other and threatening mutual destruction. President Trump had been warned by his predecessor that North Korea was likely to be his biggest foreign policy challenge.[1] In the ensuing months, President Trump blew hot and cold, alternately warning of a 'major, major conflict', or calling Kim Jong-un 'little rocket man', and stating, 'if it would be appropriate for me to meet with [Kim Jong-un], I would absolutely, I would be honoured to do it.'[2] Chairman Kim reciprocated the 'compliments' by dubbing Trump a 'dotard'. He nonchalantly doubled down on efforts to upgrade his WMD arsenal. The Trump administration and the United Nations Security Council (UNSC) imposed a series of debilitating sanctions, proscribing most of North Korea exports and imposing severe restrictions on the import of oil and petroleum. In September 2017, North Korea conducted its sixth and most powerful nuclear-test. In November 2017, North Korea successfully tested Hwasong-15 ICBM which, on a standard trajectory, could traverse a distance of 13,000 km, bringing the US mainland within its range for the first time. However, experts believe that North Korea has yet to master the ICBM and missile re-entry technologies, as well as suitably miniaturise a nuclear warhead for being mounted on the missile delivery system. It is noteworthy that, under Kim Jong-un's rule since December 2011, North Korea has conducted 86 missile tests—20 in 2017 alone—compared to a mere 16 during his father's 17-year regime.

US intelligence agencies and experts have consistently underestimated North Korea's determination and capabilities. The Trump administration was assured early on that 'there was still ample time—upward of four years—to slow or stop the development of its missile capable of hitting a US city with a nuclear warhead ...' In an interview, Lieutenant General H.R. McMaster, President Trump's former National Security Adviser, acknowledged that Kim's race to the finish line 'has been quicker and the timeline is a lot more compressed than most people believed.'[3] It is noteworthy here that North Korea has the ability to fire some 20,000 conventional rockets, artillery pieces, and heavy mortars within minutes of the beginning of hostilities, causing serious fatalities and devastation in

Seoul, which is merely 56 km from the DMZ (Demilitarized Zone). Thus, as the year drew to a close, the doomsday clock was ticking furiously and the possibility of a conflict was steadily sharpening.

The January 2018 Dialogue Offer by Kim Jong-un

And then, out of the blue, on January 1, 2018, Chairman Kim stated that he was 'open to a dialogue' with South Korea, and also offered to participate in the PyeongChang Winter Olympics, taking everyone by complete surprise. He termed North Korea as a 'peace-loving and responsible nuclear power'.[4] Things moved at breath-taking pace thereafter. Within days, officials of both sides met. An agreement was reached for their sports teams to march together under the unification flag at the opening ceremony. They also decided to field a unified women's ice hockey team. South Korea athletes flew down to North Korea for joint training. A hotline was restored between the two nations.

As if that was not dramatic enough, Chairman Kim despatched his sister, Kim Yo-jong, as his special envoy, along with North Korea's nominal head of state, Kim Yong-nam, to the Olympics. She became the first member of the Kim clan to set foot on southern soil. She handed over a personal letter from Kim Jong-un to President Moon Jae-in stating his willingness to improve inter-Korean relations. She also conveyed her brother's invitation to him to 'visit Pyongyang at his earliest convenience'[5] for a meeting. Kim Jong-un could not have staged a bigger propaganda coup against South Korea.

The Moon Jae-in Factor and the Dramatic U-turn by Kim Jong-un

No South Korean leader can afford to turn down a summit invite, least of all Moon Jae-in, the son of North Korean immigrants who has been a steadfast votary of dialogue and détente with the North. He had visited North Korea in 2004, along with his mother under the government-sponsored family reunion programme, to see her younger sister. On the eve of assuming office in May 2017, he had reiterated, 'under the right conditions, I will also go to Pyongyang.

For peace on the Korean Peninsula, I will do everything that I can do.' In July 2017 in Berlin, President Moon had outlined a comprehensive peace plan with the North. It sought neither North Korean collapse or regime change, nor an artificially expedited unification, but a denuclearised Korean Peninsula that guaranteed the North Korean system. He proposed initial steps that included the resumption of the reunion of separated families, an invitation to the North to participate in the PyeongChang Winter Olympics, the suspension of all hostile activities along the DMZ, and the holding of talks on inter-Korean cooperation. The US was taken aback, and its displeasure was duly conveyed to Seoul in strong terms. But, President Moon persisted, and even renewed his call for inter-Korean military talks on a later occasion.

Hitherto, only two inter-Korean summits had taken place. Both were held with Kim Jong-il (father of Kim Jong-un). The first, in 2000, was the result of President Kim Dae-jung's 'Sunshine Policy' of constructive engagement with North Korea. He was even awarded a Nobel Prize for his outreach. However, the sheen wore off once it became known that South Korea had bribed the North with a clandestine payment of US$ 500 million for agreeing to the meeting. The second summit was held in 2007, when Moon Jae-in's mentor, Roh Moo-hyun, was the President. Neither of the summits eventually produced the desired results, except for the establishment of South Korea financed Kaesong Industrial Complex in North Korea. Coming back to Kim Jong-un's invite, President Moon promptly sent a five-member delegation—led by National Security Advisor Chung Eui-yong to Pyongyang on March 5. The latter has been engaged with the North Korean file for over 20 years. They held a three-hour dinner meeting with the reclusive North Korean leader.

Affecting a complete turnaround Kim Jong-un expressed 'understanding' for the forthcoming US-South Korea annual joint military exercise. The visitors were assured that for the time being, there would be no further provocations by North Korea. And what's more, Kim Jong-un agreed to talks without any preconditions with the US and even dangled the carrot of denuclearisation if his regime's security was guaranteed. Next, the South Korean National Security Advisor flew to Washington in March 2018 to convey Kim Jong-un's willingness to meet President Trump. The latter agreed on the spot to unconditionally meet Kim Jong-un towards end of May, or early June. North Korea had been seeking this big prize for decades. Addressing the media at the White House and knowing which buttons to press, Chung observed 'I explained to President Trump that his leadership and his maximum-pressure policy, together with international solidarity, brought us to this juncture.'

Back-channels between the US and North Korea

It now transpires that Washington and Pyongyang were in direct contact for some time and holding confidential talks, at Beijing, New York and even in Pyongyang, notwithstanding the absence of any diplomatic or consular ties. 'We're not in a dark situation, a blackout, we have a couple, three channels open to Pyongyang,'[6] the then Secretary Tillerson had said as much in Beijing in September 2017, when asked if China was acting as a go-between for communication with North Korea. He added that the US had its 'own channels—we can talk to them, we do talk to them.'[7] This earned the hapless Tillerson a public reprimand from President Trump, even though he confirmed the same during the visit of Prime Minister Abe. It was disclosed that Mike Pompeo had a top-secret and positive meeting with Chairman Kim in Pyongyang.[8]

Chairman Kim Jong-un Mends Fences with China

In parallel, Chairman Kim managed to renew ties with China. He and President Xi Jinping have met five times since their first summit in Beijing in March 2018. For weeks it had appeared that Seoul was calling the shots in fostering a thaw in the Korean Peninsula. Her diplomats were clocking up thousands of air-miles in briefing key world leaders, including Presidents Putin and Xi Jinping, as well as Prime Minister Abe. Japan was uncomfortable, but could do little except to advise caution and keep in touch with Washington. Prime Minister Abe travelled to the US to meet President Trump in April 2018. China, North Korea's sole even if estranged benefactor, refused to be sidelined, and decided to get into the act. Beijing was determined to reclaim and maintain its centrality in Korean Peninsula.

An invitation for an unofficial meeting was extended by President Xi to Chairman Kim, which was grabbed with alacrity. Both sides stood to gain. China attempted to reinforce its leverage with North Korea, and signal that a solution to the Korean Peninsula imbroglio could only be found with its blessings. It effectively sought a spot at the negotiating table. Setting his reservations aside, President Xi Jinping accorded all state-honours to Kim, who had left North Korea for the first time since coming to power in 2011. The mollycoddling worked—not that Kim Jong-un needed any. Friendless and isolated, the invite had come to him as a Godsend. It improved his bargaining position forthwith, knowing that China, which was loath to see an increased US role in Korean Peninsula, was being supportive. President Xi and Kim held four follow-up meetings in Dalian on May 7–8, in Beijing on June 19–20, 2018 and January 8–9, 2019 as also in Pyongyang on June 20 –21, 2019. Kim stated in Beijing during his first visit:

> The issue of denuclearisation of the Korean Peninsula can be resolved, if South Korea and the United States respond to our efforts with goodwill, create an atmosphere of peace and stability while taking progressive and synchronous measures for the realisation of peace.[9]

He expectedly introduced caveats which were difficult for President Trump to accept. The latter was (and is) demanding an upfront commitment from North Korea to completely, verifiably, and irreversibly denuclearise (CVID), before easing sanctions. The stage was thus set for bruising and gruelling negotiations. Consequently, though hope was in the air, there was also a sense of déjà vu, given the numerous false starts towards normalisation in the Korean Peninsula. All the same, it is instructive to examine the reasons for Kim Jong-un's dramatic turnaround.

Why North Korea needed to Shift Gears

North Korea had virtually become an international pariah. At the urging of the US a number of nations, including Kuwait, Mexico, Malaysia, Peru, Philippines, Spain, and Thailand, had begun downsizing relations with Pyongyang. Several rounds of ever-tightening UN and American sanctions had begun to bite. North Korea's export avenues and revenues had begun to dry up. Even its trade with China had declined by about one-third in 2017, and more perceptibly in 2018. Similarly, India had halted all exports, except for food products and pharmaceuticals. Pyongyang was facing a serious foreign exchange crunch. The international opinion was coalescing against Chairman Kim's adventurism and threats. What was more, the US, Japan, and South Korea had begun singing from the same music sheet. North Korea's sole benefactor China was getting increasingly frustrated with it. Under relentless pressure from President Trump, Beijing was left with no choice but to endorse UN sanctions, while scouting for loopholes and creative ways to circumvent them on the ground. President Trump's sabre-rattling was sowing confusion in Pyongyang. It appeared that Kim Jong-un had finally found his match. But the decisive factor was that, for the first time, North Korea had managed to acquire the requisite ballistic missile and nuclear capability, to deter a possible American military strike.

Hence, there was an urgent need to deflect pressure, buy time, pitch for easing sanctions, and humanitarian assistance. Somehow a wedge had to be driven between South Korea and the US. South Korea had to be weaned away, with an offer of dialogue and summit. Pyongyang also needed to swiftly make-up with China and Russia—the two veto wielding members of the UNSC—and participants in the Six-Party Talks (SPT). These talks, hosted in Beijing, had meandered for six years before being called off in 2009. Thus, with consummate speed, Chairman Kim shifted gears and fell-back on the time-tested ploy of extending the olive branch of denuclearisation.

The Inter-Korea Summits

President Moon and Chairman Kim had a productive meeting on April 27, 2018. Kim Jong-un was conscious that the big prize of a direct engagement with President Trump was contingent on a positive outcome of the inter-Korean summit. He walked across the DMZ, becoming the first North Korean leader to enter the South's territory. They shook hands warmly and later in the day, embraced each other. Kim jong-un looked relaxed, and even participated in an unprecedented live media event, jointly with President Moon.

The 2018 'Panmunjom Declaration for Peace, Prosperity and Unification of the Korean Peninsula' was issued, stating 'that there will be no more war on the Korean Peninsula and thus a new era of peace has begun'.[10] They agreed to 'transform the demilitarized zone into a peace zone'. They further agreed to 'carry out disarmament in a phased manner, as military tension is alleviated and substantial progress is made in military confidence-building'. This clause did not sit well with the US which wanted to frontload disarmament commitments on North Korea's part before easing sanctions. The Koreas 'confirmed the common goal of realising, through complete denuclearisation, a nuclear-free Korean Peninsula'. This would be the toughest to implement for reasons mentioned below.

The sides declared their intention to convert the Armistice into a peace treaty in the course of the year, in consultation with US and also China. US officials have, similarly, been talking of such a possibility. The two Koreas cannot do so independently, since the UN, China, and North Korea were parties to the Armistice Agreement, and not South Korea. In addition, the North and the South agreed to regular military-to-military contacts, and step-up family reunions.

Their second brief summit took place at short notice, in May, to sort out the impasse posed by the divergent positions of Pyongyang and Washington on the denuclearisation issue. President Moon Jae-in visited Pyongyang from September 18 to 20, 2018 for the third inter-Korea summit which resulted in the significant 'Pyongyang Declaration'. North Korea pledged to 'permanently dismantle' the ICBM engine test and launch site at Tongchang-ri, in the presence of inspectors, as also the critical Yongbyon nuclear facility, if the US took 'corresponding steps'. Trump termed the developments as 'very exciting'. He ordered preparations for the second summit with Kim.

The Denuclearisation Challenge

As late as in March 2018, the North's official newspaper *Rodong Sinmun* had thundered, 'Hoping that the North Korea would abandon its nuclear programs is as foolish an act as trying to wish seas to get dried up'.[11] The Constitution enshrines North Korea as a nuclear weapons state. This is no idle speak. North Korea believes that it faces an existential crisis. Its conventional warfare superiority has been eroded. Pyongyang views its own WMD as key to regime survival, and insurance against pre-emptive military strikes. The Kim clan has staked everything in its WMD programme, sacrificing economic development, coping with widespread starvation deaths in the 1990s, and facing international opprobrium. It has tapped all avenues, legitimate and illicit, in that pursuit.

North Korean embassies have served as conduits for sourcing technology, material, and critical components for its WMD programme. In the initial years, Pyongyang got missile technology from the USSR. On the other hand, it is well known that Pakistan got nuclear weapons technology and components from China, which also proxy tested its nuclear device in Lop Nor in 1990.[12] Former Pakistani Prime Minister, Benazir Bhutto, on a state visit to North Korea in 1993, smuggled in critical data on uranium enrichment—a route to making a nuclear weapon—to help facilitate a missile deal with Pyongyang.[13] She carried back ballistic missile blueprints from North Korea.

As noted above, the US demanded that North Korea commits to CVID upfront. But, on the other hand, Seoul wanted to remain under the US security umbrella, and retain US troops on its soil. Nuclear weapons had already been pulled out of South Korea in 1991, as a prelude to the two Koreas' joint declaration on the denuclearisation of Korean Peninsula. However, that was poor comfort to Kim Jong-un as the US maritime, land-based and airborne nuclear and missile assets could be used against North Korea any time. Nevertheless, the US piled tremendous pressure on North Korea to concede to its demand.

Security Guarantees

Kim Jong-un had also sought security guarantees to enable North Korea to denuclearise, and therein lay the rub. Kim trusts no one and nothing, other than his WMD arsenal and own instincts, honed by three generations during their over 70-year-long uninterrupted reign. Notwithstanding western propaganda, the North Korean leadership is well informed and follows global strategic affairs closely. Pyongyang has drawn the requisite lessons from the fate of Saddam Hussain and Gaddafi, who had given up their WMD programmes at American behest. President Trump's decision to pull out of the Iran deal (JCPOA) reinforced Kim's conviction about American unpredictability and transactional disposition.

North Korea's sense of vulnerability was further heightened by the elevation of hawks like John Bolton and Mike Pompeo in President Trump's inner circle, who stood for regime change. The annual US-South Korea joint military exercises, including overflights of long distance B-2 stealth bombers, also rattled North Korea no end. The fact remains that Pyongyang sees them as a rehearsal for an armed strike. North Korea questions American and South Korean motives for holding such exercises. Thus, no security guarantee short of retaining some amount of WMD is good enough for Kim Jong-un. The President of Israel, the late Shimon Peres, had quoted Thomas Hobbes as writing in *The Leviathan*, the 'reputation of power is power'. His theory, observed Peres, '... was its corollary: The reputation of nuclear is deterrence. And deterrence, I believed, was the first step on the path toward peace.'[14] To astute observers of global strategic affairs, that message seems to have been fully imbibed by the North Korean leadership.

As such, Kim Jong-un dug-in even when President Trump threatened to, and actually called-off, the proposed summit in May. After all, the Kim clan had perfected the art of brinkmanship while instinctively knowing when to pull back. Kim Jong-un further had the advantage of being in total control, and not being encumbered by public/media scrutiny. He rightly assessed that President Trump was as keen on the summit and, indeed, it was the latter who blinked. The US conceded that denuclearisation was a 'process' which needed time. In less than 48 hours, President Trump announced that the summit was back on track. It turned out that Kim was a better poker player, even with odds heavily stacked against him.

First Kim-Trump Summit

The US and North Korea have rarely held direct political talks, leave alone at the summit level. By that token, the first ever US-North Korea summit in Singapore on June 12, held without elaborate groundwork, was highly unusual in the annals of global diplomacy. Normally, a series of preparatory talks are held at various levels, to pave the way for a meeting of the principals. The Kim clan had been craving for this big prize for decades, and it is astounding that it fell into their lap so easily. President Trump is known to be impulsive, with little understanding of history or patience for protracted diplomacy. He prides himself as a deal-maker. Embroiled in numerous controversies, personal and professional, he urgently needed a big success story. Perhaps he sensed an opportunity for crafting history, and went all out while also threatening to walk away if talks did not proceed as per his expectations. On a self-congratulatory note, he remarked: 'I know when someone wants to deal and I know when they don't'.[15]

The two leaders, one half the age of the other, met as equals. President Trump was at his charming best. They had a one-on-one meeting, followed by delegation level talks, and a working lunch. At the conclusion, they signed a short joint statement, in which 'President Trump committed to provide security guarantees to North Korea, and Chairman Kim Jong-un reaffirmed his firm and unwavering commitment to complete denuclearisation of the Korean

Peninsula'.[16] It is noteworthy that Kim agreed to denuclearisation of Korean Peninsula, not just North Korea. There was no reference to CVID or any timelines. It was mentioned, though, that the sanctions would be lifted once denuclearisation happen.

However, President Trump was not done yet. At his press conference the same day, he announced that the US-South Korea joint military exercises would be suspended.

> We will be stopping the war games, which will save us a tremendous amount of money, unless and until we see the future negotiation is not going along like it should. Plus, I think it's very provocative. ... And South Korea contributes, but not 100 percent, which is certainly a subject that we have to talk to them about also.[17]

He could also not stop gushing about his interlocutor. Speaking to Fox News the same evening, this is what he had to say about Kim: 'He's got a very good personality, he's funny, and he's very, very smart ... He's a great negotiator, and he's a very strategic kind of a guy.' And, on the very next day in Washington, Trump declared that 'There is no longer a nuclear threat' from Pyongyang. At the outset, President Moon's salutary role needs to be commended in felicitating the US-North Korea dialogue and engagement. Suave, erudite, and self-effacing, he truly played the honest broker by keeping the sides suitably informed, and periodically nudging them in the right direction.

On the other hand, at first glance it appeared that President Trump had been outwitted. Many critics accused him of giving away the store. No doubt, since January 1, Kim had come across as nimble footed and crafty beyond his years. He took control of the narrative, managed to crack the anti-North Korea front, relegated Japan to the side-lines, and created day-light between South Korea and the US. He appeared to know that 'the US had a long tradition of positing a maximalist posture in public while adopting a practical approach in practice'.[18] All the same, Trump displayed realism. The US side crafted a practical, flexible and balanced deal, which was not too onerous for North Korea. When asked, 'how long it would take to denuclearise the Korean Peninsula', President Trump replied, 'I don't know—I think we will do it as fast as it can be done scientifically, as fast as it can be done mechanically'.

Second Kim-Trump Summit

Preparations for the second meeting began in right earnest with senior interlocutors on both sides shuttling back and forth. For some inexplicable reason, the US reverted to its maximalist demand on denuclearisation, instead of seeking a middle-ground. North Korea insisted on a reciprocal step-by-step arrangement, to build mutual trust and confidence. It also sought progressive easing of sanctions and conclusion of a peace accord. Speaking at the UNGA in September 2018, North Korean Foreign Minister Ri Yong-ho did not mince words:

> The U.S. insists on the 'denuclearization-first' and increases the level of pressure by sanctions to achieve their purpose in a coercive manner, and even objecting to the 'declaration of the end of war'—Without any trust in the U.S. there will be no confidence in our national security and under such circumstances there is no way we will unilaterally disarm ourselves first.[19]

Both sides continued to stare down each other while ensuring that talks were not interrupted. Trump did say publicly that he was in no rush for speed but did not want any further tests. There were reports that the negotiators had hammered out a broad understanding, barring some critical elements which only the principals could decide. Thus, there was a sense of anticipation as the two leaders headed for Hanoi for their second engagement in February 2019.

News of talks breaking down on February 28, therefore, came as a surprise. Mutual recriminations followed. The US alleged that North Korea wanted complete withdrawal of sanctions, in exchange for dismantling the vital Yongbyon nuclear complex, which was unacceptable. North Korea countered that it had only sought partial relief on sanctions, but the US reverted to its 'all or nothing' demand on denuclearisation. Fortunately, Trump and Kim continued to express mutual admiration.

Does India have a Role in Korean Peninsula?

Traditionally, India has had cordial relations with Korea. As per legend, Princess Suriratna of Ayodhya, travelled three months by sea to Korea in 48 AD, to marry King Kim Suro and become Queen Hur Hwang-ok. There are beautiful memorials dedicated to the royal couple in Gimhae. In Ayodhya too, there is a memorial of sorts. India was also supportive of the Korean struggle against Japanese colonial rule in the early 20th century. Independent India, notwithstanding its limited resources, positioned a medical mission at the theatre during the Korean War. Its work was much-appreciated. A Neutral Nations Repatriation Commission (NNRC) was established after the War, under India's chairmanship, to decide the fate of over 20,000 prisoners of war (POW) from both sides, which again did a commendable job. On humanitarian considerations, India took-in over 80 POWs who wanted to settle in neutral countries.[19] As such, India is respected in both Koreas as a benign rising power. India also stands to strategically gain from, and supports Korean reunification.

In this context, some Indian scholars have been advocating that India should play a role to help resolve the Korean tangle. However, during the author's tenure in South Korea, not one Korean interlocutor broached the subject, in spite of India's strategic partnership and rapidly expanding ties in recent years. On the other hand, India's relations with North Korea have remained tepid since the mid-1990s, when its clandestine WMD collaboration with Pakistan came to light, that directly impinged on India's security. India did provide some humanitarian assistance to Pyongyang under the UN aegis, and maintained limited trade relations—which too were severely curtailed due to UN sanctions. Minister of State, V.K. Singh, did pay a visit to Pyongyang on May 15–16, 2018; but it was essentially a flag showing exercise.

India happens to be geographically distant from the Korean theatre, with rather limited stakes. Only four nations around Korean Peninsula—the US, China, Russia, and Japan, to varying degrees—can play a meaningful role. Even so, the latter two have limited clout. The reality is that the US and China are the only two powers that can make a difference in the Korean Peninsula, using both carrot and stick. India has neither as it lacks the necessary leverage with the Koreas. India will do well to stay out.

The Road Ahead

Truth be told, North Korea is a de-facto nuclear power, and no nuclear weapons state has ever disarmed in history except for South Africa. So long as the Kim clan is in the saddle, North Korea is unlikely to completely give up or rollback its WMD programme. Surgical strikes to take out its WMD assets are practically no longer feasible as they are widely dispersed and secured. Conflict is not an option as the human and economic costs will be too high. North Korea can be adventurist, but it is not suicidal. It will not launch an unprovoked frontal attack on South Korea, Japan, or the US, as it knows the consequences.

Occasionally, the US does display some flexibility on the pace and scope of denuclearisation. On his way to Pyongyang on July 5, 2018, Secretary Pompeo had tweeted: 'looking forward to continuing our work toward the final, fully verified denuclearisation (FFVD) of DPRK as agreed to by Chairman Kim'. Washington may continue to play hardball, but does (or should) realise by now that Pyongyang at best, will settle for a roll-back/freeze on its advanced nuclear and ICBM programme, under IAEA safeguards, to address American security concerns. In other words, a Progressive, Limited and Conditional Denuclearisation (PLCD).

In return, North Korea will expect a continued freeze on joint military exercises, the reduction of the US troops in South Korea, a peace accord, immediate rollback of sanctions, normalisation of ties and liberal developmental assistance. China, Russia, and South Korea can more or less live with such an outcome. Japan—over whose territory, North Korean missiles have flown—may feel short-changed; but may be able to do little. The big question is whether President Trump still has the requisite political capital and will to clinch the deal? The big fear is that both sides may overplay their hand, squandering a rare opportunity. Post-Hanoi, the road ahead has become bumpier. Still there is a sliver of hope for a positive resolution of the Korean conundrum.

Notes

1. Ian Bremmer, 'As North Korea grows more aggressive, Trump will have to figure out ways to handle it', *The Hindustan Times*, May 24, 2017 at https://www.hindustantimes.com/columns/as-north-korea-grows-more-aggressive-trump-will-have-to-figure-out-ways-to-handle-it/story-WAOtCEtolOy4AK1usa9r5M.html, accessed on September 12, 2018.
2. 'Transcript: President Donald Trump's Interview With Bloomberg News', Bloomberg News, May 2, 2017 at https://www.bloomberg.com/news/articles/2017-05-01/president-donald-trump-interviewed-by-bloomberg-news-transcript, accessed on September 2, 2018.
3. 'U.S. intelligence failed to foresee North Korea's nuclear strides', *The New York Times*, January 6, 2018 at https://dailygazette.com/article/2018/01/06/u-s-intelligence-failed-to-foresee-north-korea-s-nuclear-strides, accessed on September 2, 2018.
4. 'North Korea's Kim Jong-Un Says 'Open to Dialogue' With South Korea, Will Only Use Nukes If Threatened', Reuters, January 1, 2018 at https://www.ndtv.com/world-news/north-koreas-kim-jong-un-says-open-to-dialogue-with-south-korea-will-only-use-nukes-if-threatened-1794411, accessed on September 2, 2018.
5. Kim Rahn, 'Kim Yo-jong's historic 3-day stay here', *The Korea Times*, February 11, 2018 at http://www.koreatimes.co.kr/www/nation/2018/02/103_244001.html, accessed on September 2, 2018.
6. Emily Rauhala, 'Tillerson: U.S. is in direct contact with North Korea, is 'probing' talks', *The Washington Post,* September 30, 2017 at https://www.washingtonpost.com/world/tillerson-us-is-in-direct-contact-with-north-korea/2017/09/30/eecb3ed2-a5c3-11e7-8c37-e1d99ad6aa22_story.html?noredirect=on&utm_term=.88fbc864a0d4, accessed on June 12, 2018.
7. 'Rex Tillerson: US in contact with North Korea', Al Jazeera, September 30, 2017 at https://www.aljazeera.com/news/2017/09/rex-tillerson-china-korea-talks-170930035204341.html, accessed on September 2, 2018.
8. Shane Harris, Carol D. Leonnig, Greg Jaffe and David Nakamura, 'CIA Chief Made Top-Secret Visit To North Korea's Kim Jong Un Weeks Ago', *The Washington Post,* April 18, 2018.

9. Uri Friedman, 'What Does 'Denuclearization' Mean to Kim Jong Un? A close reading of what the Korean leader reportedly told Xi Jinping in Beijing', *The Atlantic*, March 28, 2018 at https://www.theatlantic.com/international/archive/2018/03/kim-jong-un-china-xi-jinping-train-nuclear-trump-summit/556679/, accessed on September 16, 2018.
10. 'Panmunjom Declaration for Peace, Prosperity and Unification of the Korean Peninsula', Ministry of Foreign Affairs Republic of Korea, April 27, 2018 at http://www.mofa.go.kr/eng/brd/m_5475/view.do?seq=319649, accessed on May 4, 2018.
11. Christine Kim, 'South Koreans meet North Korean leader Kim for talks about talks', Reuters, March 5, 2018 at https://www.reuters.com/article/us-northkorea-missiles-southkorea/south-korean-team-heads-to-north-in-bid-to-bring-u-s-north-to-nuclear-talks-idUSKBN1GH030, accessed on May 4, 2018.
12. Chidanand Rajghatta, 'China tested nukes for Pakistan, gave design', *The Times of India*, September 5, 2008 at http://toi.in/Ff3EXa/a19fi, accessed on May 4, 2018.
13. Glenn Kessler, 'Bhutto Dealt Nuclear Secrets to N. Korea, Book Says', *The Washington Post*, June 1, 2008 at http://www.washingtonpost.com/wp-dyn/content/story/2008/06/01/ST2008060100007.html, accessed on May 4, 2018.
14. Shimon Peres, *No Room for Small Dreams: Courage, Imagination, and the Making of Modern Israel*, Custom House, 2017.
15. 'Trump-Kim summit: Donald Trump vows to "end war games" in "new history" with North Korea', *The Telegraph*, June 13, 2018 at https://www.telegraph.co.uk/news/2018/06/11/donald-trump-kim-jong-un-summit-live-latest-news-updates-us/, accessed on September 14, 2018.
16. 'Trump Kim summit: Full text of the signed statement', BBC, June 12, 2018 at https://www.bbc.com/news/world-asia-44453330, accessed on September 14, 2018.
17. 'Press Conference by President Trump', The White House Press Briefings, June 12, 2018 at https://www.whitehouse.gov/briefings-statements/press-conference-president-trump/, accessed on September 14, 2018.
18. Brahma Chellaney, at a seminar in New Delhi on April 17, 2018.
19. 'If North Korea says no way will disarm unilaterally without trust', Reuters, September 29, 2018 at https://www.reuters.com/article/us-un-assembly-northkorea-idUSKCN1M90JF, accessed on January 20, 2019.
20. Jairam Ramesh, 'India's role in ending the Korean war', *The Hindu*, May 3, 2018 at https://www.thehindu.com/opinion/op-ed/indias-role-in-ending-the-korean-war/article23750989.ece, accessed on September 14, 2018.

3. Proliferation and the Korean Peninsula: The Making of North Korea's 'Mature' Nuclear Enterprise

Manpreet Sethi

Till such time as President Trump and Chairman Kim Jong-un actually came face to face on June 12, 2018 in Singapore, the attention of the international community on the nuclear stand-off between the US and the Democratic People's Republic of Korea (DPRK)[1] had been largely focused on the dangers of nuclear war in the Korean Peninsula. American unwillingness to accept a deterrent relationship with the country, and Chairman Kim Jong-un's consistent march towards more sophisticated nuclear and missile capabilities, had dominated the security discourse. Much analyses and writings have deliberated upon how the US should respond to the changed strategic calculus with North Korea. Should the US pursue diplomatic engagement? Or, should it use its military might to forcibly denuclearise North Korea? Can it do so? At what cost to the Peninsula and the US mainland? Meanwhile, non-proliferation hardliners have been worried about what the North Korean example would mean for the NPT and the wider non-proliferation regime in the long run. Would it end up undermining global norms that stigmatise nuclear weapons development? Would it cause a setback to non-proliferation?

These are valid concerns. And, still remain so, despite the summit meetings in Singapore and Hanoi. It is still unclear as to what tangible results will Trump's Korea policy yield. But, in the meanwhile, it is equally important to understand how North Korea got here. How has it managed to develop strategic programmes that have consistently improved in size, sophistication, and capability? Pyongyang has conducted six nuclear tests since 2006; numerous missile tests ranging from those of intermediate range ballistic missiles (IRBMs) to inter-continental ballistic missiles (ICBMs); these have been conducted from all kinds of platforms—from ground facilities (Musudan and Nodong),[2] from submarines (Pukkuksong–1),[3] and from mobile transporter-erector-launchers (Hwasong–6);[4] it has claimed the conduct of a hydrogen bomb test in January 2016;[5]miniaturisation capability in March 2016;[6] and the testing of a 'multi-functional thermonuclear weapon' in September 2017.[7] It has showcased the ability of its nuclear warhead to withstand shock, vibration, and temperature changes associated with ballistic missile flight and re-entry. All these capabilities involve fairly advanced technologies and special materials that are not available for the asking in the commercial market, and certainly not to a country that has been under such heavy sanctions as North Korea has been. But, the frequency of missile tests, 20 in 2017 alone, indicates the continued availability of the necessary financial and material resources. Indeed, as the 2013 UN panel tasked to monitor sanctions implementation stated that, despite sanctions, it had found instances of 'import of fine-grain graphite, classified documents, and machine tools for missile technology development'.[8]

From where has this help been forthcoming? Which countries have been involved in proliferation to North Korea that has brought it to this threshold of capability today? How deep is the proliferation network? And what implications does this have for international security? It is imperative that the nature of the network and the manner in which proliferation has taken place be well understood. Such an understanding may not be able to roll back what has already happened in North Korea; but it could minimise the chances of a repeat performance. In order to lessen the negative consequences for the future of non-proliferation, offenders need to be identified, and seen to be brought to justice as a deterrent for such future activity.

This is even more essential since the risk of nuclear proliferation to non-state actors who might be interested in carrying out acts of nuclear terrorism is of a high order in contemporary times. States that may be tempted to wilfully proliferate, for whatever reasons, must be conscious of possible consequences for themselves.

In tracing the story of proliferation to North Korea, this chapter examines the role of three major contributors to its nuclear and missile programmes: USSR/Russia, Pakistan, and China. It also explores the possibility of further onward proliferation from North Korea to others. It concludes with the impact of such developments on international security, and why it is necessary to get to the bottom of the proliferation activity.

With a Little Help from Friends: Contributors to the North Korean Strategic Capability

North Korea was the industrial hub of the Korean Peninsula at the time of its partition. This was largely the result of industrial development that the Japanese colonial administration brought to the resource-rich part of the Koreas in the 1920s. In 1945, 65 per cent of the Korean heavy industry was in the North. However, most of this was destroyed during the Korean War. Its recovery was subsequently enabled by North Korea's abundant natural resources and labour force, ably sustained by generous Soviet and Chinese support. Also, the ability of the country to bounce back can be credited to the existence of a certain level of domestic industrial capability and expertise.

The base so provided also came in useful for the build-up of nuclear and missile programmes. Of course, North Korea has gained from the external infusion of technology, special materials, and designs. But, the fact that it could effectively absorb the imported technologies and even undertake the reverse engineering of products it acquired was possible because of the availability of indigenous expertise.[9] This was enabled, as also further honed, by the high emphasis on self-reliance or the idea of *Juche* by the Kim dynasty. Kim Jong-Il, for instance, had stated, decades ago, that,

> scientists and technicians should work to overcome by their own efforts the problems which require an urgent solution for the development of the national economy of our country, and to introduce the scientific and technical successes of developed countries in accordance with its specific reality.[10]

Indeed, North Korea's indigenous capability became the backbone for its strategic programmes and enabled the absorption of outside help. But, of course, domestic capability was ably supported and enhanced by external help, whether received openly or clandestinely.

From the USSR: The First Helping Hand

The beginning of the North Korean nuclear programme, ostensibly for peaceful purposes, can be traced back to Soviet assistance as far back as the mid-1950s. About the same time, as the Atoms for Peace initiative was announced by the then US President Eisenhower for America's friends and allies, a parallel endeavour to promote technological development in countries of its own bloc was also initiated by the USSR. North Korea became a beneficiary of this initiative. Kim Il-sung quickly grabbed the opportunity to sign an agreement for the development of the peaceful use of nuclear energy with the Soviet Union in 1956. As a part of this, North Korea signed the founding charter of the Joint Institute for Nuclear Research (JINR), co-founded by eleven Socialist countries in the Kalinin region of the USSR, to further scientific progress. The JINR charter established that the, 'results achieved in scientific research carried out in the Institute shall be used exclusively for peaceful purposes for the benefit of human mankind'. Going along with this mandate, and perhaps, satisfied for the moment to, at least, have its hand in the nuclear cookie jar, North Korea funded 0.05 per cent of the JINR budget and, in return, received access to nuclear equipment and training from physicists that the Soviet Union gathered at Dubna. It also established its own Atomic Energy Research Institute in 1955.[11]

However, there is enough circumstantial evidence to show that the military dimension of the nuclear capability was not lost on Kim Il-sung. In fact, the end of the Korean War can, perhaps, be taken as the beginning of the nuclear ambitions of the leader. Having lost 12–15 per cent of his population to American aerial attacks on cities, and living under the fear of a possible nuclear strike, it is not surprising that he had grasped the value of having nuclear weapons of his own.[12]As stated by one analyst, 'The war against the US, more than any other single factor, gave North Koreans a collective sense of anxiety and fear of outside threats that would continue long after the war's end.'[13] Subsequently, when the US deployed tactical nuclear weapons in South Korea in 1958, it is likely that it gave a further impetus to North Korean nuclear weapons ambitions. This illustrates that North Korea's desire for nuclear weapons was primarily security-driven, and they have not let the history of the atrocities that were mounted on them die down.

Without publicly voicing any such intentions though, North Korea carried on slowly developing its nuclear programme, with significant Soviet assistance. In 1959, it entered into another agreement where Moscow agreed to build a research reactor (IRT-2000) to produce radioisotopes and a nuclear research centre at Yongbyon. This laid the foundation of what eventually became a big nuclear complex at this place. The USSR also offered training at the Dubna complex, and North Korea's Academy of Sciences sent several promising scientists to be trained there for its own nuclear programme. Between 1956 and 1961, North Korea made use of this cooperation to facilitate the development of related curriculum in its science and technology universities. In 1962, two atomic energy research centres were established, at Pakchon and Yongbyon.[14]As a result of these efforts, the first 2 MWth nuclear reactors in North Korea went operational in 1965. By 1974, the engineers of North Korea were able to indigenously upgrade the IRT-2000 reactor to 4 MWth and, in the late 1980s, to even 8 MWth.[15]Meanwhile, in 1973, North Korea also signed an agreement with Poland on technical and scientific cooperation that included the provision for three North Korean technical experts to be trained in Poland in nuclear technology. The fact that both Poland and North Korea were part of JINR must have made this cooperation easier.

A major expansion phase of North Korea's nuclear programme came next, in the 1980s. North Korea began a programme to build three graphite-moderated natural uranium-fuelled Magnox-type reactors independently, using information from open sources as well as its own experience. The first and the smallest of these, a 5 MWe reactor, was completed in 1985. This reactor has served as the core of North Korea's nuclear programme from the late 1980s to about 2000, also used to produce weapons-grade plutonium for its nuclear tests. In 1984, the construction of a 50 MWe reactor of the same type was also started, followed subsequently by one 200 MWe reactor. However, neither of these was ever completed. Nevertheless, during the decade of the 1980s, North Korean nuclear activities had expanded to include uranium milling facilities, a fuel rod fabrication complex, a 5 MWe nuclear reactor, and R&D institutions. Pyongyang was also acquiring plutonium reprocessing technology from USSR.

Not surprisingly, North Korea's growing nuclear activity caught US attention, and it put pressure on the USSR to force its ally to accede to the NPT and accept international safeguards through the International Atomic Energy Agency (IAEA). North Korea joined the treaty in 1985, though it did not sign the safeguards agreement with IAEA until 1992. That happened only after the US withdrawal of its nuclear weapons from South Korea, the 1991 Joint Declaration on Denuclearisation of the Korean Peninsula, and South Korea's promise to suspend its joint military exercises with the US. Meanwhile, in return for its signature, Pyongyang did extract from the USSR an agreement for economic, scientific, and technological cooperation, including the provision of new Light Water Reactors (LWRs).[16] The LWRs never materialised though. Rather, the North Korea-USSR relationship came in for a turbulent phase with the collapse of the Soviet Union in 1989. Nevertheless, the breakdown of the USSR also presented the opportunity to North Korea to grab some Soviet scientists and engineers who suddenly found themselves jobless. Sixty such scientists were arrested at Moscow airport in 1992 on their way to Pyongyang. But, many unknown incidents of transfer may have occurred.[17] Such a conclusion is partly corroborated by the fact that some of the North Korean missiles being tested in recent times seem to closely resemble old Soviet designs.

North Korea began its missile endeavour by importing full missile systems, particularly Scud missiles, from Egypt in the 1970s. It managed to reverse-engineer them within a decade. The availability of Soviet expertise in the 1990s may have been useful in expediting North Korean efforts at developing the Nodong, a scaled-up Scud design, and in experimenting with longer-range missiles, such as the Taepodong which, anyway, were based on engines of the shorter-range systems.[18] A NIAS study of the missiles from the available pictures indicates a close similarity between the Hwasong engines and the RD 250 and RD-50 models, manufactured at Russia's Energomachoconcern and Ukraine's KB Yuzhnoye.[19] It has also been alleged that smuggling networks in China and Pakistan helped in facilitating the transfer of these high performance liquid propellant engines from Russia/Ukraine in the period 2014–2017. These gave a big boost to North Korea's missile programme, helping it transit from short and medium range missiles to the intermediate range Hwasong 12 and the ICBM Hwasong 14.[20]

To get back to the North Korean nuclear programme, in the 1990s, Pyongyang planned a third phase of nuclear infrastructure expansion, wanting to complete the larger capacity reactors that it had begun constructing in the previous decade. However, not much was achieved on this front owing to the collapse of its biggest ally, the death of Kim Il-sung, a debilitating famine, and an ensuing economic crisis. The country also came in for pressure to open its nuclear facilities to IAEA inspections. With the Soviet Union no longer available to shield it from a hard-line US position, and having seen the US attack on Iraq in pursuit of suspected WMD, North Korea conceded. As inspections began in 1992, discrepancies were pointed out. In July 1992, the IAEA alleged that North Korea had attempted reprocessing three times, and not just once as it had claimed.[21] Cornered, North Korea chose to use a new tactic. Kim Jong-Il threatened to walk out of the NPT. From the North Korean perspective, this blackmail worked perfectly, since it led to the Agreed Framework in 1994. North Korea bargained the political utility of its nuclear programme, and agreed to halt the plutonium production programme in return for 500,000 tons of heavy oil and two 1000 MWe each LWRs.

However, its nuclear weapons ambition had not gone away, and new proliferation mechanisms and instruments were soon found. Domestic work on nuclear research and development continued relatively unabated since its strategic programmes had, by then, 'sufficient numbers of personnel from indigenous educational programmes'.[22]

It cannot be said with any certainty whether the USSR ever intended to make North Korea a nuclear weapons possessor. But, there is no doubt that extensive Soviet assistance, starting from the 1950s, laid the foundation for its strategic programmes. Many a times, private Russian industry was found guilty of proliferation. For instance, in 1997, British customs intercepted a shipment of maraging steel on a British Airways flight from Moscow to Islamabad. An economic counsellor at the North Korean embassy at Islamabad was behind facilitating the deal with the All-Russian Institute of Light Alloys in Moscow on behalf of Pakistan.[23] Other Russian companies were also used to source mass spectrometers, lasers, and carbon fibre.[24] North Korea's own ability to learn fast, and take the technology further, including up-rating reactors, building new ones, and enhancing missile range capabilities, must be given due credit.

From Pakistan: Missile for Uranium Enrichment Swap and More

However, important contributions were made by two other states too. Ever since the revelations of the A.Q. Khan network broke in 2003, many articles and books based on investigative and archival research have clearly established that Pakistan shared its nuclear technology with Iran, Libya, and North Korea. By the time the network was discovered, it had most likely been running for fifteen years—at least since 1987. In fact, A.Q. Khan's overtures to Pyongyang go back to the early 1980s in the context of providing joint missile help to Iran which was then engaged in a conflict with Iraq. Reportedly, Pakistani and North Korean engineers, technicians, and contractors worked together on the Iranian missile programme.[25] Subsequently, there are reports of Pakistan giving North Korea a US stinger missile in 1990, and itself seeking its help for Scud missile technology in 1991.[26]

Early relations came on a more sure footing in 1992, with the visit of the North Korean Foreign Minister Kim Yong-nam to Pakistan (besides Syria and Iran). In May 1993, A.Q. Khan, in his capacity as Khan Research Laboratories (KRL) director, was invited to witness a test firing of the Nodong missile. Having seen its capability, and espying in it the potential of being used for nuclear weapons delivery, A.Q. Khan engineered and used a visit of then Prime Minister Benazir Bhutto to Pyongyang in December 1993 to seal the deal for the purchase of these missiles. Thereafter, Khan made several trips to Pyongyang, and high-level North Korean delegations regularly visited Islamabad. One such visit was led by the Vice Chairman of the DPRK National Defence Commission, who also bore the responsibility for North Korea's nuclear procurement programme. He was allowed into the KRL and its enrichment halls in November 1995. The Vice Chairman also visited Pakistan's missile production facility and the missile test site. 'During this visit North Korea signed a further agreement to provide Pakistan with fuel tanks, rocket engines, and between 12–25 complete Nodong missiles.... In return, Khan agreed to host North Korean missile experts in a joint training programme.'[27]

By 1997, this cooperation had turned into a barter exercise because Pakistan did not have the financial resources to pay for the missiles it had contracted for. So, it offered the transfer of uranium enrichment technology, the expanse and capability of which had already been showcased to North Korea in 1995. For Pyongyang, this turned out to be the perfect deal since the 1994 Agreed Framework had put a stop to its access to plutonium. Still harbouring ambitions for a nuclear weapons programme (if not for establishing deterrence then to once again use the capability to drive a hard bargain as had been done in the past with the Agreed Framework), Pakistan came in handy as a conduit for uranium enrichment technology.

Not all of what was passed on to Pyongyang as part of the arrangement with Pakistan is still known because the then President Musharraf blocked any international interrogation of A.Q. Khan. But, enough details have emerged from various sources. In 2003, A.Q. Khan himself admitted in a signed statement that he had supplied 'old and discarded centrifuge and enrichment machines, together with sets of drawings, sketches, technical data, and depleted hexafluoride gas to North Korea.[28] Former Pakistan President, Pervez Musharraf, has written in his memoirs that A.Q. Khan provided North Korea with 'a flow meter, some special oils for centrifuges, and coaching on centrifuge technology, including visits to top-secret centrifuge plants.'[29] Pakistan admits that this cooperation continued until 2002, using chartered or Pakistan Air Force aircraft. Besides hardware and designs, Pakistan also furnished North Korea with what Gaurav Kampani calls 'integrated shopping solutions in a fragmented market.'[30] This included lists of manufacturers, clandestine procurement, and smuggling techniques, names of middlemen and companies based across Southeast Asia, the Middle East, Africa, and Europe. Khan travelled to North Korea a dozen times during 1997–99, and is believed to have provided technical briefings to North Korean scientists. Besides, North Korean scientists received training at KRL too.[31] In fact, President Musharraf has himself admitted that, while he was in office, he had received a 'report suggesting that some North Korean nuclear experts, under the guise of missile engineers, had arrived at KRL, and were being given secret briefings on centrifuges, including some visits to the plant.'[32] Interestingly, it has also been reported that,

> not only were North Koreans present at the Pakistani tests but that Pakistanis may have actually tested a North Korean device for them in addition to their own. This may have been the sixth and final test, which took place at a different location and had a different signature, including traces of plutonium when the other bombs were thought to be only uranium.[33]

Though there is no conclusive evidence on this, an analysis by the US Los Alamos Nuclear Laboratory has pointed out that 'as North Korea and not Pakistan was working on this kind of technology at the time, the conclusion drawn by the US was that the test had been conducted by Pakistan on behalf of its nuclear partner.'[34] Also intriguing is the fact that, in June 1998, a week after Pakistan conducted its nuclear tests, a North Korean woman, wife of the North Korean Economic Counsellor in the embassy in Islamabad, who was also a representative of the North Korean company that provided Nodong missiles to Pakistan in 1994, was shot dead outside the KRL guest house. According to the CIA, this happened because she was preparing to pass information about the Pakistan-North Korea nuclear deal to the West. Though this remains officially uncorroborated, there are reports that, in the Pakistan Air Force aircraft that flew out her body to Pyongyang, was also A.Q. Khan, along with 'five crates of luggage, two of them large, which no one was allowed to check ... suspected to carry P-1 and P-2 centrifuges, drawings, technical data, and uranium hexafluoride.'[35]

As part of its cooperation with Pyongyang, Pakistan is also believed to have helped them 'conduct a series of cold tests using supercomputers', and giving Pyongyang advice on how to 'fly under the radar', hiding nuclear research from American satellites and global intelligence agencies.'[36] Pakistan has even used a C-130 transport plane provided by Washington to help fight the war on terror, to fly nuclear equipment to Pyongyang, and fly back with missile parts. On April 3, 2003, German intelligence intercepted a cargo vessel in the Suez Canal carrying aluminium tubing of the specifications required for manufacturing outer casings for P-2 centrifuges headed for North Korea.[37] Therefore, as Gordon Corera notes, the relationship was 'far deeper than a simple one-off barter of missiles for centrifuge'.[38]

The association has continued in recent times too, and is now suspected in the cooperation on MIRVed capabilities. Pakistan tested the *Ababeel* in 2017. It is a missile that claims to have MIRVed capability. A similar warhead design was seen atop the Hwasong-12, also tested by DPRK in the same year, and claimed as being capable of carrying multiple warheads.[39] The origin of both is believed to be in China, though it is unclear whether the warhead designs, or the warhead itself, was passed on to Rawalpindi, and through there to Pyongyang, or the other way around.

In any case, these routes are not of recent origin. After all, it was in January 1994 that Pakistan, China, and North Korea signed a 'formal technical assistance pact'.[40] Much transpired under this arrangement. Transactions more pertinent to recent times include transfers to North Korea of special nickel alloys Inconel and Monel, which are corrosion resistant and used for uranium enrichment, and chemical weapons production by Galaxy Corporation Pvt. Ltd., a company affiliated to the Pakistan Atomic Energy Commission.[41] Vacuum induction melting furnaces that can be used in forging uranium and plutonium metal into hemispheres for fissile pits, are also believed to have been passed on from Pakistan to Pyongyang. And these, in turn, are supposed to have come from Suntech Technologies, a Beijing based company.[42] Indian intelligence sources have claimed that a cargo by ship was delivered from Suntech Technologies to Pakistan; this has been corroborated through open source research based on information received from Pakistani shipping records.[43] Records of shipments from Suntech to Galaxy Corporation Pvt. Ltd. between January-April 2016 included 'dual-use goods with potential utility in the nuclear fuel cycle and WMD-related applications.'[44]

In its longstanding nuclear and missile relationship with North Korea, Pakistan has not only undertaken proliferation, but also wilfully undermined international agreements and sanctions imposed on a country that the rest of the world was trying to stall from moving towards nuclear weapons.

From China: The Relationship between Lips and Teeth

In the years immediately after the end of the Korean War, North Korea enjoyed the advantage of being wooed by both the USSR and China as they tried to establish the primacy of their version of communism. Pyongyang gained economic and military assistance from both. With China it even entered into a Sino-North Korean Mutual Aid and Cooperation Friendship Treaty in 1961. There under, China committed to provide immediate military and other assistance to its ally against any outside attack.[45] In fact, in 1963, in the context of the Cuban missile crisis, Kim Il-sung expressed disappointment with the Soviet Union for showing 'weakness by backing down.'[46] When China tested its nuclear weapons in 1964, it must have gladdened his heart. Surprisingly, not much literature is available on direct Chinese help to the North Korean nuclear programme. But the absence of a direct footprint does not rule out the presence of cooperation in a more indirect manner through the use of other nations. As mentioned earlier, China, Pakistan and North Korea signed a nuclear cooperation agreement in 1994.

China has provided tacit support to North Korean positions on non-proliferation, besides the facilitation of illicit links with Pakistan. Much of this has been already stated in the section on Pakistan's proliferation to North Korea. Other evidence is available in, for instance, the case of Taepodong 1, a solid-fuelled missile that resembles the Pakistani missile Hatf, which itself is modelled on the Chinese M-11. As compiled by one author,

> A total of 5233 Chinese companies have traded, including in dual use technology, with North Korea, between 2013 and 2016 ... Chinese company Dandong Dongyuan Industrial Co. Ltd., which exported US$ 28.5 million worth of material to North Korea during 2013–2016, including a shipment of US$ 790,000 worth of 'radio navigational aid apparatus in June 2016.[47]

When the UN raised questions regarding China's sale of certain products and technologies, the latter answered with absurd responses. For instance, Chinese supplies of six TELs to North Korea were explained to the UN by providing an end user certificate declaring their transfer for 'purpose of transporting timber'.[48] However, the use of TELs for providing mobility to missiles is well known, especially since the manufacturer of these TELs was China's Hubei Sanjiang Space Wanshan Special Vehicle Company, a subsidiary of the China Aerospace Science and Industry Corporation that makes Shenzhou rockets and missiles. Besides transport trucks for missiles, China has also provided 'the biconic warhead design of the Hwasong-14, and other missile components.'[49] This warhead design is believed to be the same as used by Pakistan. Rick Fisher, of the International Assessment and Strategy Centre, has speculated that 'it is possible that Chinese technology was originally given to North Korea which fashioned the new warhead that was tested by Pakistan as *Ababeel*.'[50]

It is not very difficult to understand China's reasons for nuclear and missile proliferation to North Korea. China considers it a 'welcome dynamic' that North Korea should be a 'weak but persistent and reckless annoyance to US policy in East Asia, sapping much diplomatic energy and absorbing a significant portion of its power-projection capability in the region.'[51] But the nuisance value that China hopes would be outwards only, came back to bite when the threat perceptions of Seoul and Tokyo elicited militaristic responses like the deployment of missile defences or started debating the development of own nuclear weapons. Indeed, as put by some scholars,

> while a nuclear North Korea pursuing nuclear weapons short of a strategic nuclear deterrent may have been a net positive for China, a North Korean strategic nuclear deterrent and a regime willing to act at odds with Beijing risks the worst outcomes that Chinese leaders are working hard to avoid.[52]

Indeed, the number of writings that question the conventional wisdom of China's hesitation at pushing North Korea to denuclearise, or being unduly worried about instability on the Peninsula, or even the requirement of a buffer state between China and South Korea, are steadily increasing. As suggested by one analyst, 'China's increasing confidence about its capabilities and regional influence' is changing its strategic calculations on DPRK.[53] Enjoying the advantage of geography, force posture, manpower, and access to early warning indicators, China no longer feels hostage to the need to succumb to North Korean machinations.

Indeed, China's contribution to the North Korean nuclear and missile programme has been less than straightforward, quite like its overall relationship with the country. The signature of Chinese origin products can be found in North Korea; but Beijing has managed, in a rather clever manner, to do so through private companies or other third countries. Besides material help, even more significant has been the indirect help in terms of the tacit backing for North Korea's efforts in capability build-up as a means of increasing the complexity for US security interests in the region. Therefore, despite sanctions, China has continued to provide energy, food, and other requirements to the Kim regime. It is only quite recently that China may be re-assessing its interests, but as far as North Korean proliferation is concerned, the die has already been cast.

Other Inadvertent Proliferators

Several reports released by the UN Panel of Experts on North Korean Sanctions have highlighted North Korea's continued use of illicit procurement techniques to acquire dual use items for its nuclear and missile programmes. The ingenuity of the country to exploit export control loopholes by procuring material that falls just below the radar of national control lists has enabled a continuance of its efforts towards building more sophisticated capabilities despite the elaborate sanctions net that has been cast by the United Nations. In this process, sometimes quite unlikely candidates seem to have inadvertently helped North Korea. For instance, when South Korea recovered some of the wreckage of the Unha-3 rocket used to test a long range missile in December 2012, British, Chinese, Russian, South Korean, Swiss, and American manufactured components were found.[54] Most of these components were off-the-shelf items requiring no licensing for exports. Using such sub-control threshold goods has allowed North Korea to use diverse sources, and escape the scrutiny of national authorities.

Two conclusions are evident from the above. One, that the people behind the North Korean strategic programme do have a very good understanding of what they need, and how to procure and use such items. Secondly, it reveals the large scale use of deception by North Korea to procure items through front companies, thereby evading end-user verifications. Investigations have established that North Korea uses 'circuitous procurement routes and deceptive practices'[55] to obtain necessary parts from unwitting private players. The implications of this for further proliferation should not be underestimated.

From North Korea to Others: Outward Proliferation Possibilities

The manner in which North Korea has received its nuclear technology through clandestine trade and procurement techniques, the use of middlemen and shell companies, falsified end user certificates, and the diversion of industrial goods and technologies using circuitous routes has obviously taught it the tricks of doing the same for others. Indeed, the further outward proliferation from Pyongyang to other state and non-state actors is a grave concern. Going a step further, the US Department of Defense Report to the Congress has expressed additional concern over the possibility of North Korea being 'more willing to sell fissile material or complete nuclear weapons (as opposed to only nuclear technology or equipment) as the size of its arsenal grows.'[56]

It may be recalled that, from 2002 onwards, there have been indications that North Korea could emerge as a nuclear supplier of equipment and material. As mentioned by Gordon Corera in his book, 'North Korean front companies also received a number of payments routed through the Khan network. This would make no sense if they were simply a customer of the network.'[57] Obviously, they were acting as suppliers to some others too. The case of North Korean technical help to build a Yongbyon type nuclear reactor in Syria, Al-Kibar, in the early to mid-2000s is well known. In 2010, the US was worried about the expanding military relationship between DPRK and Myanmar, which was suspected to encompass 'sale of small arms, missile components and technology possibly related to nuclear weapons.'[58] Pyongyang is also known to have sold missile parts and/or technology to countries like Egypt, Iran, Libya, Myanmar, Syria, Yemen, and UAE. 'Sales of missiles and telemetric information from missile tests have been a key source of hard currency for the Kim regime.'[59] The risks of the further transfer of nuclear material or weapons to terrorist organisations cannot be ruled out.

For such possibilities to be minimised, it is important that North Korea be brought into the non-proliferation regime, especially through the application of safeguards on its nuclear programme. For this to happen, some sort of engagement with the country is important. That would not only bring down the risk of inadvertent or accidental nuclear war, but also rein in the programme from the proliferation point of view. It is wishful thinking to seek the denuclearisation of North Korea as the first step in the negotiation strategy. It may be recalled that North Korea has categorically stated that its nuclear programme is 'not a bargaining chip to be exchanged for something else', and that it will continue to 'qualitatively and quantitatively' expand its nuclear forces 'until denuclearisation of the world is realised'.[60] In its own Constitution, it has declared itself a full-fledged nuclear weapons state. Given the circumstances, it would serve the international community well to open negotiations with the country, and seek ways of bringing the programme under some kind of safeguards to enhance nuclear security. One small step seems to have been taken in this direction with the engagements between President Trump and Kim Jong-un, and the follow-ups between the government officials thereafter. However, the links are still pretty tenuous, with little confirmed information available in the public domain on the progress being made. However, there is no alternative other than getting North Korea to accept IAEA safeguards as one viable way of minimising the risks of onward proliferation.

Conclusion

The history of attempts at resolving the knotty North Korean nuclear issue shows that these have focused on somehow 'freezing' its nuclear programme with the ultimate objective of full denuclearisation. Seemingly forgotten in all these efforts is the manner in which North Korea got there in the first place. It has used extensive proliferation networks to achieve this feat and, what is even more worrisome, is the fact that these could still be active. In fact, their next customers may even be terrorist organisations which would not only be non-deterrable in the classical sense, but also not open to negotiations on terms that nations may find acceptable. Therefore, while it is imperative to deal with the problem of North Korea, it is equally important that attempts be made to get a full disclosure on all networks that have been operating. This can only be possible from the actors who have been involved in the enterprise. Pakistan, and its well-known citizen A.Q. Khan, would be the key to this, and it is time for the international community to demand some hard answers on the extent of proliferation that was undertaken.

In fact, this would also help towards the resolution of the North Korean nuclear issue since one of the difficulties in negotiating with North Korea has been the lack of knowledge on the extent of its capability. As Corera points out, no one is sure 'how far North Korea has actually been able to turn the nuclear material they have into a weapon ... whether Khan has provided weapons design information that would short circuit'[61] a long process. There is little information on where and how big the North Korea enrichment facilities are, and how long they have been operational, or how much HEU could have been accumulated. The lack of this information makes the negotiators blind as they go into a deal and the chances of cheating, as has happened in the past, cannot be dismissed. Getting answers on the proliferation activities could lead to a more constructive solution. It would also foster a sense of closure to the activities, and the knowledge of the modus operandi would alert nations to future such endeavours.

Nuclear security is indeed the need of the times, and the North Korean nuclear and missile programme could be both the problem, as also a part of the solution. Good thinking is needed to turn the crisis into an opportunity for the sake of larger international security.

Notes

1. Though this is the official name of the country, the paper uses North Korea.
2. Ralph Savelsberg and James Kiessling, 'North Korea's Musudan Missile: A Performance Assessment', 38 North, December 20, 2016 at https://www.38north.org/2016/12/musudan122016/, accessed on October 6, 2018.
3. 'KN – 11 At a Glance', CSIS at https://missilethreat.csis.org/missile/kn-11/, accessed on October 6, 2018.
4. 'Hwasong – 6 At a Glance', CSIS at https://missilethreat.csis.org/missile/hwasong-6/, accessed on October 6, 2018.
5. Elise Hu, 'North Korea Claims Hydrogen Bomb Test', NPR at https://www.npr.org/sections/thetwo-way/2017/09/03/523913820/north-korea-possibly-conducts-sixth-nuclear-test-south-korea-says, accessed on October 6, 2018.
6. Justin McCurry, 'North Korea may have Capability for Miniaturised Warhead, Says Japan', *The Guardian*, August 7, 2017 at https://www.theguardian.com/world/2017/aug/08/north-korea-nuclear-miniaturised-warhead-advanced-considerably-japan, accessed on October 6, 2018.
7. 'North Korea has Missile Ready Nuclear Weapon', BBC News, September 3, 2017 at https://www.bbc.com/news/world-asia-41138834, accessed on October 6, 2018.
8. Daniel M. Gerstein, 'How Did North Korea Get its Nuclear Capabilities So Far So Fast?', RAND Blog, August 14, 2017 at https://www.rand.org/blog/2017/08/how-did-north-korea-get-its-nucelar-capabilities-so.html, accessed on October 6, 2018.
9. In contrast, Libya for instance, could not make use of the centrifuges and other technologies that the A.Q. Khan network made available to it owing to the lack of any indigenous industrial expertise.

10. Kim Jong Il, 'Selected Works', Vol. 10, pp. 195–196, as cited in Stephen Blancke, *Examining Allegations that Pakistan Diverted Chinese-origin Goods to the DPRK*, Proliferation Case Study Series, Project Alpha, August 2, 2016.
11. Olli Heinonen, 'North Korea's Nuclear Enrichment: capabilities and Consequences', Belfer Center, June 22, 2011 at https://www.belfercenter.org, accessed on October 6, 2018.
12. Blaine Harden, 'The US War Crime North Korea Won't Forget', *The Washington Post*, March 24, 2015.
13. Charles Armstrong, 'The Destruction and Reconstruction of North Korea, 1950–1960', *The Asia-Pacific Journal*, 8(51):2, December 20, 2010.
14. Joseph S Bermudez, Jr., 'North Korea's Development of a Nuclear Weapons Strategy', North Korea's Nuclear Future Series, US Korea Institute at SAIS, 2015, p. 8.
15. The up-rated reactor required 80 per cent highly enriched uranium which Russia provided until 1990. As the fuel expended, it has been less clear as to how, and whether at all, the reactor has been kept operational.
16. Fu Ying, 'The Korean Nuclear Issue: Past, Present and Future—A Chinese Perspective', Strategy Paper 3, Washington DC: John L. Thornton China Centre at Brookings, May 2017.
17. Daniel Brown, 'Russian Scientists in the 90s may have Given North Korea its Newest Missile Designs', Business Insider, January 2, 2018 at http://www.businessinsider.com, accessed on October 6, 2018.
18. 'Why did sanctions against North Korea's missile program fail?', The Conversation, July 8, 2017 at http://theconversation.com/why-did-sanctions-against-north-koreas-missile-program-fail-80666, accessed on October 6, 2018.
19. Arun Vishwanathan, S. Chandrashekhar, L.V. Krishnan, and Lalita Sundaresan, 'North Korea's 2016 Nuclear Tests: An Analysis', January 10, 2016, International Strategic and Security Studies Programme, NIAS.
20. Michael Elleman, 'The Secret to North Korea's ICBM Success', IISS, August 14, 2017 at http://www.iiss.org/en/iiss%20voices/blogsections/iiss-voices-2017-adeb/august-2b48/north-korea-icbm-success-3abb, accessed on October 6, 2018.
21. 'Fact Sheet on DPRK Nuclear Safeguards', IAEA at https://www.iaea.org/newscenter/focus/dprk/fact-sheet-on-dprk-nuclear-safeguards, accessed on October 7, 2018.
22. Bermudez, note 14, p. 11.
23. Adrian Levy and Catherine Scott-Clark, *Deception: Pakistan, the United States and the Global Nuclear Weapons Conspiracy,* Penguin Books, London, 2007, p. 279.

24. Ibid., pp. 279–280.
25. Indrani Bagchi, 'Pak-Pyongyang Links Date to 1970s', *Times of India*, October 10, 2006.
26. Adrian Levy and Catherine Scott-Clark, note 23, p. 245.
27. Ibid., p. 250.
28. As cited by Christopher Clary, 'Dr Khan's Nuclear WalMart', *Disarmament Diplomacy*, Issue no. 176, March/April 2004.
29. Pervez Musharraf, *In the Line of Fire: A Memoir,* Simon & Schuster Ltd. London, 2006, p. 294.
30. Gaurav Kampani, 'Proliferation Unbound: Nuclear Tales from Pakistan', CNS Research Story, Centre for Non-proliferation Studies, February 23, 2004.
31. David Sanger, 'In North Korea and Pakistan: Deep Roots of Nuclear Barter', *New York Times*, November 22, 2002.
32. P. Musharraf, note 29, pp. 286–287.
33. David E. Sanger and William J. Broad, 'Did North Koreans Fuel Pak Bomb?', *International Herald Tribune*, February 28, 2004.
34. Hassan Abbas, *Pakistan's Nuclear Bomb: A Story of Defiance, Deterrence and Deviance,* Penguin Random House, London, 2018.
35. Paul Watson and Mubashir Zaidi, 'Death of North Korean Woman Offers Clues to Pakistani Nuclear Deals', *Los Angeles Times*, March 1, 2004.
36. Adrian Levy and Catherine Scott-Clark, note 23, p. 336.
37. Ibid., p. 347.
38. Gordon Corera, *Shopping for Bombs: Nuclear Proliferation, Global Insecurity and the Rise and Fall of the AQ Khan Network,* Foundation Books, New Delhi, 2006, p. 93.
39. Prabha Rao, 'How North Korea was Armed', IDSA Issue Brief, October 30, 2017.
40. Adrian Levy and Catherine Scott-Clark, note 23, p. 249.
41. Prabha Rao, note 39.
42. 'Pakistan Continuing to Sell Nuclear Materials to North Korea, Reveal US Sources', ANI Exclusive, June 22, 2016. As cited by Stephan Blancke, note 10, p. 10.
43. Ibid., pp. 12–13.
44. Ibid., p. 13.
45. The treaty has been extended a couple of times, and has validity until 2021.
46. Adrian Levy and Catherine Scott-Clark, note 23, p. 246.
47. Prabha Rao, note 41.
48. Anders Corr, 'Chinese Involvement in North Korea's Nuclear Missile Program: From Trucks to Warheads', *Forbes*, July 5, 2017 at https://www.

forbes.com/sites/anderscorr/2017/07/05/chinese-involvement-in-north-koreas-nuclear-missile-program, accessed on October 7, 2018.

49. Ibid.
50. Ibid.
51. Michael D. Cohen and Sung Chull Kim, 'Introduction: A New Challenge, A New Debate', in Sung Chull Kim and Michael D Cohen (eds), *North Korea and Nuclear Weapons: Entering the New Era of Deterrence*, Georgetown University Press,Washington DC, 2017, p. 7.
52. Ibid., p. 8.
53. Oriana Skylar Mastro, 'Why China Won't Rescue North Korea', *Foreign Affairs*, January/February 2018.
54. 'UN Sanctions Panel North Korea Report Shows UK Companies Contributed to Missile Programme', Project Alpha, April 27, 2014 at https://projectalpha.eu/un-sanctions-panel-north-korea-report-shows-uk-companies-contributed-to-missile-programme/#more-1901, accessed on October 7, 2018.
55. 'North Korean Rocket Reportedly Used Foreign-Made Components', Project Alpha, February 11, 2016 at https://www.projectalpha.eu/north-korean-rocket-reportedly-used-foreign-made-components/, accessed on October 7, 2018.
56. Dennis C Blair, 'Annual Threat Assessment of the Intelligence Community for the Senate Select Committee on Intelligence: Testimony before the Committee', February 12, 2009.
57. Gordon Corera, note 38, p. 243.
58. John Pomfret, 'US Increasingly Wary as Burma Deepens Military Relationship with North Korea', *Washington Post*, March 4, 2010.
59. Emma Chanlett-Avery *et al.*, 'North Korea: US Relationship, Nuclear Diplomacy, and Internal Situation', CRS Report, January 15, 2016.
60. Laurence Norman, 'North Korea Says Nuclear Program Isn't Bargaining Chip', *Wall Street Journal*, September 27, 2014.
61. Gordon Corera, note 38, p. 101.

4. Sanctions as an Instrument of Non-proliferation Policy: The North Korean Experience

Kapil Patil

Since time immemorial up to the present day, states have long used economic and military sanctions to force a change in the behaviour of a target state, group, or individual.[1] The sanctions are most commonly used in cases where the country or regime is violating human rights, aiding and abetting terrorism, or posing a grave danger to international peace and security. The efficacy of sanctions as an instrument of statecraft, however, remains a subject of much contestation. This is particularly the case with certain regimes or groups which not only defy the collective international will but also remain undeterred by most stringent sanctions. The Hermit Kingdom of North Korea is one such archetype, which has been reeling under sanctions for the past 12 years but has shown little signs of halting or reversing its nuclear and missile programmes. The international community has long regarded North Korea's proliferation activities as a serious threat to global peace and stability. Since its first nuclear test in 2006, the United Nations (UN) has extensively used sanctions to curb North Korea's nuclear and ballistic missile programmes, and gradually widened the scope of denials to coerce Pyongyang. From arms embargoes to denying access to sensitive materials, technologies, asset freezes, and travel bans, etc., the sanctions against Pyongyang have become much more sophisticated and institutionalised to affect a change in its proliferation behaviour. In 2016–2017 alone, the UN Security Council (UNSC) has adopted as many as six new resolutions which have imposed the strongest-ever sanctions on North Korea than it has ever imposed on any country.[2]

The new sanctions have specifically targeted Pyongyang's clandestine trade activities which constitute a primary source of revenue for the regime that enabled it to sustain nuclear and missile activities.[3] Additionally, the Trump administration's new sanctions decree has sought to target Chinese companies that are commercially engaged with North Korea in violation of the UN resolutions.[4] Despite such a widened scope of sanctions, the North Korean regime has not only remained defiant but, to the contrary, significantly improved its ability to form new procurement channels to service its WMD programmes. Amidst the inability of sanctions to restrain Chairman Kim Jong-un's unbridled nuclear ambitions, the successful summit meeting between President Trump and Chairman Kim Jong-un held in June 2018 had generated renewed hopes for a diplomatic solution to North Korea's nuclear programme.[5] In the immediate aftermath of the summit, the flurry of reports highlighting North Korea's continuing expansion of nuclear facilities have, nevertheless, raised further doubts about Kim's regime willingness to scrupulously honour the commitment it undertook to 'work towards [the] complete denuclearisation of the Korean peninsula'.[6]

North Korea's persistent evasion of embargoes has, thus, called into question the utility of sanctions, and raises several other pertinent questions. First, what role can sanctions play in halting North Korea's nuclear and missile programmes? Second, what are the peculiar factors that enable North Korea to withstand the most stringent sanctions? And third, what generic policy lessons does it offer for revisiting the use of sanctions to deal with North Korea's Kim Jong-un regime? Assessing the impact of sanctions in the North Korean case presents several difficulties due to the opaque nature of its society and the wide variety of embargoes imposed on the country. Further, the lack of access to any credible data from North Korea compels one to limit the assessment of information provided in the reports of the UN Panel of Experts, which is responsible for monitoring the implementation of various UNSC resolutions.

This chapter, thus, seeks to provide a qualitative assessment of the impact of sanctions and the extent to which they have served the desired policy objectives. It mainly argues that the primary objective of sanctions—that is, to prevent and roll back Pyongyang's proliferation activities—has become mostly obsolete owing to North Korea's persistently defiant behaviour. Notwithstanding the pressure of the most crippling sanctions, the regime is determined to maintain its nuclear and missile development activities. Sanctions as an autonomous instrument of non-proliferation have, therefore, a very limited scope to force a change in North Korea's longstanding nuclear policies. Sanctions can, nonetheless, play a complementary role in negotiating a long-term 'political deal' with the Kim Jong-un regime which can not only restructure the post-war regional security order but also bring Pyongyang into a benign security relationship with Japan and South Korea.

In this context, the chapter is organised as follows. The following section will present an overview of the literature on sanctions as a tool of non-proliferation policy, and offer conceptual as well as policy-relevant insights. The third section will map the evolution of sanctions on North Korea, while the fourth section will subsequently provide an assessment of sanctions and challenges associated with their implementation. The fifth section will analyse various opportunities and challenges for using sanctions as a strategic tool to bargain for peace and stability in the Korean Peninsula, and lastly, the concluding section will summarise the findings of the study.

Non-proliferation Sanctions

In the international system, states often use sanctions to exercise influence on the policies of others.[7] Governments employ them both, unilaterally or multilaterally, to punish a range of activities, including the violation of human rights, waging a war, or endangering international peace and security. Given the difficulties involved in dealing with recalcitrant regimes as well as the challenges associated with the use of force, states often find sanctions a viable policy tool between war and diplomacy.[8] The use of sanctions in affecting the behaviour of states, however, remains a subject of much debate. This is further complicated by the challenges involved in assessing the impact of sanctions due to wide-ranging measures as well as the difficulties associated with capturing their impacts quantitatively. Notwithstanding such challenges, there has been a steady growth in the literature on sanctions and their impact on state behaviour. For instance, the pioneering studies on sanctions by Baldwin and Hufbauer et al., offer diverging perspectives on the utility of sanctions as a tool of foreign policy and statecraft.[9]

Hufbauer, Schott, and Elliot provide a qualitative assessment of 103 cases of sanctions since World War I and find only 40 cases (34 per cent) to have been successful in achieving their desired objectives.[10] Their study mainly underlines the fact that sanctions tend to work rather quickly or not at all, and have a better chance to succeed when the target country's economy is in trouble. Additionally, they also caution against campaigns designed to squeeze the target in a sustained manner over a period of time, as seen in the case of Iraq, Pakistan, and North Korea. On other the hand, Baldwin notes that, in the 'nuclear age', sanctions as an instrument of economic statecraft have a greater value in demonstrating political resolve to deter the target without resorting to military means. Taking this research further, a study by Lopez and Cortright identifies various conditions under which sanctions can be effective.[11] They note that sanctions can make an impact on the target country by imposing more than two per cent economic cost to its gross national product (GNP), and also by ensuring swift, strict, and complete coordination among the trading partners of the targeted country to limit sanctions evasion. In their follow-up study, Hufbauer, Schott, Elliot, and Oegg modify their views and suggest that '... even if sanctions did not contribute to inducing policy change in the target state, it does not mean that it was a mistake to impose them'.[12]

Specifically, in the context of non-proliferation, Miller argues that sanctions have served as an important policy tool for states, and especially the US, in preventing proliferation though its effects have remained largely hidden due to 'selection effects'. The rationale for Miller's contention is that:

> rational leaders assess the risk of sanctions before initiating a nuclear weapons programme, which produces a selection effect whereby states highly vulnerable to sanctions are deterred from starting nuclear programmes in the first place, so long as the threat is credible.[13]

Thus, Miller attributes fewer instances of proliferation to the successful use of sanctions as opposed to large instances of proliferation predicted by the nuclear domino theories.[14] Similarly, several sanctions optimists—namely Martin, Kunis and others—point out cases where sanctions or the threat of sanctions, imposing heavy economic costs have been effective in curbing proliferation in countries such as Taiwan, Brazil, Argentina, South Africa, Libya, and Iran.[15] Also, in the case of India and Pakistan, where the threat of sanctions failed to prevent the nuclearisation of these countries, Morrow and Carriere argued for maintaining embargoes as a relevant policy threat against vertical proliferation.[16] The pessimists like Lopez and Cortright, on the other hand, cite unsuccessful cases to show that not only sanctions not serve any major purpose in achieving their political objectives but may also end up causing more harm than any good.[17] Given such diverging assessments over the efficacy of sanctions, their utility as a generic or non-proliferation policy tool remains a subject of debate.

Some of the notable studies on proliferation dynamics, including Solingen, Marinov, Escriba-Folch and Wright, Stein, and Haggard and Noland have provided useful insights in cases of 'nuclear proliferation' as well as 'nuclear reversal' and singled out factors that are critical for making impacts through sanctions.[18] Stein, for instance, suggests that 'since the results of sanctions depend critically on the relationship between state and society within the sanctioner and the sanctioned, [the] regime type is a critical factor in assessing the prospects for, and the outcomes of, economic sanctions'.[19] Similarly, Marinov finds that 'economic pressure works in at least one respect—it destabilises the leaders it targets'.[20] He contends that if pressure is effective in destabilising the leaders it targets, then the leaders are most likely to compromise and change the course of action. Therefore, sanctions may be more effective in securing policy change than was thought previously. Marinov's findings, nevertheless, curiously escape the North Korean case where the leadership has invented newer ways of escaping pressure, and to successfully channel hardships to the ordinary populace.[21] In this respect, Escriba-Folch and Wright conducted an important study that examined the impact of sanctions on regime types, such as personalists, military, and single-party state regimes. Based on their investigation of regimes from 1967 to 1997, they contend that:

> the effect of sanctions is mediated by the type of authoritarian regime against which sanctions are imposed. Because personalist regimes and monarchies are more sensitive to the loss of external sources of revenue ... these regimes are more likely to be destabilised by sanctions than leaders in other types of regimes.[22]

In contrast, they note that 'when dominant single-party and military regimes are subject to sanctions, they increase their tax revenues and reallocate their expenditures to increase their levels of co-optation'.[23]

The study, therefore, concludes that military and single-party regimes are less likely to be destabilised by the pressure of sanctions; and 'if sanctions are to be effective in destabilizing dictators, they should strike at revenue sources the dictator needs to stay in power'.[24] Finally, the most recent research by Haggard and Noland suggests that the strategies of 'sanctions and engagement' employed by the international community towards North Korea are premised on highly flawed economic logic.[25] Derived from the analysis of Chairman Kim Jong-un's policies, they contend that sanctions only increase the sufferings of ordinary Koreans whereas the Kim Jong-un regime manages to insulate its core party elite from the adversities of sanctions. Based on a data released by Chinese and South Korean firms doing business with North Korea, they point to persistent coordination difficulties in imposing costs on the North Korea regime and express doubts about the utility of even increased sanctions.

The existing research on sanctions and non-proliferation dynamics, therefore, offers several important insights which are relevant to the North Korean case. Firstly, sanctions are most likely to be effective when the target country's economy is in trouble.[26] Two, it reinforces Hufbauer et al.'s assessment that 'the effect of economic sanctions on despotic systems tends to be relatively small and, in general, the effect of economic sanctions is weaker on states that are hostile and despotic'. Finally, addressing coordination issues in multilateral sanctions can effectively improve the impact of sanctions, especially in the case of determined proliferators.

The Evolution of Sanctions on North Korea

The extant research on North Korea presents a largely pessimistic picture about the efficacy of sanctions in altering Pyongyang's proliferation behaviour. This is mainly due to the regime type as well as the various difficulties involved in the enforcement of sanctions. At present, North Korea is subjected to some of the most stringent sanctions that the UN has ever imposed on any country. Besides the UN sanctions, a number of other countries, including the US, the European Union, South Korea, and Japan, have also unilaterally imposed sanctions on North Korea for posing a grave threat to peace and security in the region. For close to two decades, North Korea has been engaged in the development of nuclear weapons and long-range missile systems. To prevent its nuclear programme from crossing the threshold, a group of countries including China, the US, North and South Korea, Japan, and Russia launched negotiations with North Korea under the framework of Six-Party Talks in 2003.[27] Though the Six-Party Talks produced breakthroughs at least on two different occasions, they failed mainly because of Pyongyang's non-compliance and unscrupulous behaviour, and ended abruptly in April 2009.[28]

Since its first nuclear test in 2006, the ambit of sanctions on North Korea has widened considerably through the adoption of various resolutions by the UNSC (see, Table 1). These resolutions urge Pyongyang to dismantle its nuclear weapons programme in a 'complete, verifiable, and irreversible manner'. North Korea, however, continued to blatantly disregard the UNSC resolutions and has dramatically increased the pace of nuclear and missile testing. In 2017, North Korea carried out its sixth largest nuclear test in which it claimed to have tested a thermonuclear device, and also flight-tested an intercontinental ballistic missile capable of striking the US mainland.[29] The unprecedented levels of threat led the international community to adopt four new resolutions in a year's time through which it bolstered the existing sanctions alongside introducing new measures, including a ban on export of petroleum and crude oil to North Korea.[30]

Table 1: UNSC Resolutions on North Korea

UNSC Resolution	Trigger	Scope of Sanctions
S/RES/1718 (2006)	1st Nuclear Test, October 2006	Imposes arms embargo, assets freeze, ban on imports and exports to prohibit the DPRK's Nuclear programme, a travel ban on persons involved in the DPRK's nuclear programme.
S/RES/1874 (2009)	2nd Nuclear Test, May 2009	Expands arms' exports and imports, prevent the provision of financial services or the transfer of financial resources that could contribute to prohibited programmes/activities.
S/RES/2087 (2012)	Ballistic Missile Test, December 2012	To seize and destroy material suspected of being connected to the DPRK's weapons development or research.
S/RES/2094 (2013)	3rd Nuclear Test, February 2013	Imposes targeted financial sanctions; expands the prohibited items list concerning WMDs, and the provision of a non-exhaustive list of prohibited luxury goods.

UNSC Resolution	Trigger	Scope of Sanctions
S/RES/2270 (2016)	4th Nuclear Test, March 2016	Expands the arms embargo and non-proliferation measures, a ban on operating DPRK vessels or using DPRK flags; assets freeze on Government of the DPRK and its Workers' Party entities.
S/RES/2321 (2016)	5th Nuclear Test, November 2016	Placing an annual cap on the amount/value of coal exports by the DPRK; ban sale, supply, and transfer of copper, nickel, silver, and zinc by the DPRK.
S/RES/2356 (2017)	SLBM Test, August 2016	Designates additional 14 individuals and 4 entities.
S/RES/2371 (2017)	DPRK's violation & flagrant disregard of previous UNSC resolutions.	Introduces a full ban on coal, iron and iron ore, and adds lead and lead ore to the banned commodities, subject to sectoral sanctions. Prohibits the export by the DPRK of seafood.
S/RES/2375 (2017)	6th Nuclear Test, September 2016	Introduces a full ban on the supply, sale or transfer of all condensates and natural gas liquids to the DPRK; the limit for all refined petroleum products, restrictions of crude oil to the DPRK in any period of 12 months.
S/RES/2397 (2017)	ICBM Test (Hwasong-15), November 29	Introduces a limit of 4 million barrels or 525,000 tons in the aggregate amount per a twelve-month period as of December 22, 2017.

Source: Compiled by the author.

Thus, the wide-ranging UNSC sanctions on North Korea include stringent arms embargoes; the denial of sensitive dual-use technologies for its nuclear and missile programmes; the supply of industrial machinery, goods, and heavy vehicles; freezing assets of key personnel engaged in WMD programme; banning the import of coal, minerals, and seafood; resections on North Korean workers in foreign countries; limits on natural oil, gas, and petroleum products; as well as curtailing fishing rights, etc. In addition to such embargoes, the US has also unilaterally imposed a range of sanctions on North Korea targeting its individuals, financial institutions, and businesses. In 2008, President George W. Bush passed an Executive Order (E.O.) 13466 which designated North Korea as a threat to US national security.[31] The E.O. further served as the basis for the Obama administration to pass another E.O. 13570 in 2011, which expanded and toughened existing sanctions against North Korea.[32] The US Congress also passed the Iran, North Korea, and Syria Non-proliferation Act (INKSA) in 2011, primarily aimed at targeting individuals and entities that scrupulously evade the sanctions to trade with these three rogue states. For instance, the US has recently fined some non-North Korean entities, like China's ZTE, for violating US export controls with regard to North Korea and Iran.[33] Most recently, the Trump administration has also enacted new measures that seek to ban foreign entities doing business with North Korea, and from entering the US financial system.

Similarly, countries like South Korea, Japan, and EU have placed a host of supplementary sanctions on North Korea.[34] South Korea's approach, however, has been a mixed one. While some of South Korean leaders have adopted a conciliatory stance toward Pyongyang and called for increased bilateral exchanges along with the expansion of aid as a path to peaceful coexistence, other leaders have mostly toed the Western line. South Korea imposed the most stringent sanctions on May 24, 2010, after the attack on its naval warship *Cheonan* by North Korea. The main provisions of the sanctions include the banning of all South Korean visits to North Korea, apart from the Kaesong Industrial Complex; forbidding all North Korean ships from entering South Korean waters; halting inter-Korean trade and the prohibition of new investments in North Korea.[35] Further, in 2016, Seoul imposed new sanctions suspending all the commercial activities with Pyongyang at the Kaesong industrial complex. Japan, too, has prohibited all commercial and diplomatic exchanges with North

Korea since its 2006 nuclear tests. Although Japan partially lifted some sanctions in 2014 in return for Pyongyang's promise to investigate the disappearance of Japanese nationals in North Korea in the 1970s and 1980s, the understanding soon ended, and Tokyo renewed embargoes in response to North Korea's nuclear tests in 2016 and 2017. The new sanctions not only banned the entry of North Korean workers into Japan but also curbed the transfer of remittances from Japan.[36]

The European Union has aligned its own restrictive measures with the latest UN sanctions on Pyongyang which were adopted in response to the North Korea's non-proliferation activities. The supplemental restrictions of the EU prohibit the admission and residency of persons who have facilitated North Korea's weapons programme, ban the participation of North Koreans from specialised training in the EU, the suspension of any kind of commercial exchanges and investments, and a cap on remittances to North Korea.[37] Despite such a wide variety of sanctions, the hardliners in the Trump administration as well individual experts have called for imposing more sanctions on Pyongyang to punish the regime.[38] However, the sceptics, on the other hand, urge for a review of the existing measures as well as for assessing and improving their implementation.[39]

Impact of Sanctions on North Korea

In line with the above approach, this section assesses the impact of new sanctions on North Korea, and its implications for existing policies and practices. Assessing the efficacy of sanctions in North Korea's case presents several difficulties, and calls for exercising much caution. Though the international community has time and again responded to North Korea's nuclear and ballistic missile provocations by imposing newer types of sanctions, they have nonetheless proven inadequate to restrain Pyongyang from conducting nuclear weapons and missile tests. The North Korean case, thus, begs the most pressing question: what practical purpose can sanctions serve as a policy tool in North Korea's case?

In recent years, several assessments have shown that Pyongyang is violating the most stringent embargoes in myriad ways. A most noteworthy analysis, in this respect, is provided in the latest report of the UN Panel of Experts released on March 5, 2018.[40] The UN Experts Panel was set up pursuant to resolution 1874 (2009) passed by the UNSC and is mainly responsible for monitoring various mandated embargoes, which include restrictions on arms transfers, assets freeze, and so on. The latest Panel Report (S/2018/171), which is drawn as per the mandate of resolution 2345 (2017), highlights widespread violations as well as sophisticated evasion tactics adopted by the Kim regime.[41] Besides, several media reports and scholarly analyses, over the years, extensively reveal how brazenly Pyongyang evades sanctions and carries out illicit trading activities which ensure a steady stream of finances and necessary supplies to the country.

The panel report details various areas as well as the diversified business linkages that Pyongyang has established around the world through sophisticated evasion tactics. Among others, it reports a number of evasion tactics, such as direct swapping of goods, ship-to-ship transfer of petroleum and related products, smuggling and illegal arms transfers, forging ship registry papers, a network of fraudulent companies and joint ventures, the misuse of diplomatic cover, etc. First, in the area of petroleum sanctions, it shows how Pyongyang relies mostly on illicit ship-to-ship transfers through a number of international brokers, ship vendors, and also the reputed international oil suppliers and trading firms.[42] The local fishing companies based out of Taiwan and Hong Kong were reportedly found involved in arranging the ship-to-ship transfer of petroleum in the East China and the Yellow Seas.[43] Such transfers take place mostly at night, and the North Korean vessels involved in such transfers frequently redesign and restructure their physical attributes, including hulls, cranes, flags, as well as the permanent registration number (called IMO) to hide their identities.[44] Additionally, the panel report notes that the high-intensity sanctions have created enormous incentives for middlemen who illegally procure petroleum for North Korea while exporting its natural gas to far away locations.[45] The report, therefore, makes specific recommendations to prevent the evasion of petroleum sanctions and to improve their enforcement by member states.

Second, North Korea manages to export almost all prohibited goods, despite the most comprehensive exports ban. Illegal exports constitute a major revenue source for the regime and, between January and September 2017; Pyongyang reportedly generated nearly US$ 200 million through such exports.[46] Third, amongst the various commodities banned from exports, coal amounts to be the highest transferred item through measures like trans-shipment, forged documentation, signal manipulation by ships, etc. to hide the identity of its original supplier. The UNSC Resolution 2371, passed in August 2017, has completely banned North Korea's coal exports; Pyongyang, nevertheless, continues to sell large quantities of coal through trans-shipments via Russian ports.[47] The trans-shipments mostly take place through international vessels which load coal from North Korea and carry it to Russian ports, where the coal is then unloaded and picked up by other vessels, which eventually ship it to the destination countries.[48] Through such tactics, coal exports generate significant revenues for the Kim Jong-un's regime.

Fourth, the report extensively details North Korea's ongoing military cooperation with countries such as the Syrian Arab Republic, Myanmar, and a number of countries in Africa.[49] For long, North Korea has been supplying large quantities of conventional arms and military hardware to these countries clandestinely. The sale of small arms and military hardware constitutes yet another important source of cash for the regime, with customers spanning the world. The modus operandi for such transfers involves hiding arms consignments inside the bulk shipments of legitimate goods (such as sugar or loose iron ore, etc.), whereas the deals for such transfers are carried out by North Korean trade representatives posted in various diplomatic missions around the world.[50] In doing so, the North Korean officials blatantly abuse their diplomatic immunity under the Vienna Convention on Diplomatic Relations.

Fifth, in recent years, North Korea has exploited several gaps in the global financial system to transfer as well as receive funds unlawfully.[51] The weak implementation of financial sanctions enables North Korea to maintain several offshore bank accounts to transfer funds globally. Also, the joint ventures with overseas companies are one of the primary means of evading sanctions and generating cash for Pyongyang.[52] Through these companies, North Korean firms conceal their identities at multiple levels and manage to easily escape cursory scrutiny required by banking embargoes. Uncovering such forged identities poses serious difficulties for the authorities, especially in those countries that lack rigorous monitoring mechanisms. Further, they also exploit the common Korean identity by posing as South Korean natives and carry out transactions by producing essential licenses and registry papers in the ethnic Korean language.

An independent study has shown that 'financial sanctions have had the unintended net effect of actually strengthening the North Korean procurement networks'.[53] Based on 21 in-depth interviews with former officials of North Korean firms, their study found that stringent sanctions have forced Pyongyang to form closer business partnerships with private Chinese companies through persons called 'hwagyo' middlemen.[54] These hwagyo middlemen, who possess Chinese citizenship, can easily trade with international companies and evade sanctions to benefit the North Korean regime. The study has revealed the existence of such strong business linkages between many Chinese firms and North Korean STCs, which enables Pyongyang to source a range of materials and circumvent sanctions. In sum, the UN panel report points to the several loopholes in the global trading, shipping, and financial systems which North Korea exploits without fear, and deceives the enforcement authorities from the full implementation of sanctions.[55]

In view of such persistent evasions, the report concludes by noting that the 'expansion of sanctions is yet to be matched by the requisite political will, international coordination, prioritisation, and resource allocation necessary to drive effective implementation', and calls for improved coordination and information sharing among the member states. Although several countries in recent years have improved the implementation of sanctions, and are keen on improving it further, the foremost challenge emanates from the lack of requisite capacity among the states. This is further compounded by the lack of information sharing on serial offenders, poor awareness, and the additional monitoring burden which leads to disregarding the UNSC mandate. The existence of such challenges makes it difficult to improve coordination among states despite several efforts from UN agencies.

The role of Chinese and Russian agencies, in this respect, also remains a suspect. In recent years, several instances of breaches have been reported from Chinese and Russian locations, and their inability to curb such activities has led to intense criticism. Although China has responded positively to international appeals by closing off ports to North Korean ships and cracked down on several publicly known Chinese-North Korean joint ventures, its actions are widely deemed to be inadequate. Several independent studies, including by Haggard and Noland (2017), have also pointed to China's reluctance in taking steps against individuals and entities involved in assisting North Korea to evade sanctions.[56] Consequently, North Korea continues to exploit loopholes in the system, and carry on with illicit activities with impunity. Unless such discrepancies are actively removed, the sanctions will have little scope for imposing serious costs on Pyongyang and serve as an effective tool in advancing policy objectives.

Rethinking Sanctions

The assessment of sanctions from various official and unofficial sources suggests that their impact on North Korea's political elite has, so far, remained quite insignificant. Although several analysts have called for imposing 'smart' sanctions against Chairman Kim and his core party elite, there is considerable evidence pointing to difficulties involved in enforcing such sanctions effectively. Although the implementation of the existing sanctions must be tightened as much as possible as per the recommendations of the UN panel report, in all likelihood, it appears unlikely that sanctions alone could force Pyongyang to accept any limits on its nuclear programme, and force it to renounce nuclear weapons that it has built assiduously over the years. Sanctions are, therefore, only creating a chimera of toughness on the part of the US and its allies, while their original objective—which is to freeze and rollback Pyongyang's nuclear programme—has become largely obsolete.

Given the widespread challenges associated with the use of toughest sanctions against North Korea, a fierce debate has been raging among US policymakers on whether sanctions alone can force Pyongyang to give up its nuclear programme; whether more sanctions can be imposed on the defiant regime; and whether China can be cajoled to do more in enforcing sanctions on Pyongyang.[57] As a result, the international community, including the US and its allies, are forced to reconsider the objectives of the sanctions policy and re-deploy other policy tools—such as diplomacy—rather than becoming a dead end in itself.

North Korea's successful acquisition of formidable deterrent capabilities through high-yield nuclear warheads and long-range delivery systems has most clearly eliminated the possibility of any American military strike on North Korea. The changed strategic reality has led several influential scholars, including Stanford University's Scott Sagan and MIT based Vipin Narang, to advocate a change in US policies by the simultaneous pursuit of deterrence and diplomacy with North Korea.[58] There is growing realisation within the US too about the complementary role that sanctions play in the deterrence strategy which relies primarily on effective military capabilities. Sagan, however, recommends the deterrence strategy somewhat reluctantly, given the challenges involved in deterring the authoritarian regime in Pyongyang, and also due to President Trump's dangerous escalatory rhetoric which makes such strategy far riskier than ever experienced in the past.[59]

Similarly, Vipin Narang also advocates a deterrence strategy; but cautions that an 'effective deterrence policy depends on clarity, consistency, coherence, and communications'. Reckoning with the new strategic realities on the Korean Peninsula, the US, and its allies formulated a deterrence strategy that aims to dissuade Pyongyang from embarking upon any mindless misadventure. The Trump administration's latest Nuclear Posture Review (NPR) underlines this approach quite unambiguously by noting that 'any North Korean nuclear attack against the United States or its allies and partners is unacceptable and will result in the end of that regime'.[60] It further warns Pyongyang by noting that 'there is no scenario in which the Kim regime could employ nuclear weapons and survive.' To ensure the credibility of this threat, the NPR has pledged to maintain and deploy a range of strategic assets—such as missile defence and other prompt response capabilities—that can effectively respond to North Korea's military overtures.

Amidst the raging debate over the future of sanctions and military strategy, the opening-up of diplomatic opportunity to hold talks with North Korea has drastically changed the scenario on the Korean Peninsula and generated immense hopes for establishing peace in the region. The Trump administration, and especially his former secretary Tillerson, have been reportedly looking for diplomatic avenues to hold talks with North Korea. The most important overture in this direction, however, came from Chairman Kim who, after announcing the successful completion of his country's nuclear programme, adopted a markedly different approach in seeking rapprochement with the international community. In his New Year address, Chairman Kim agreed to send a North Korean delegation for the Winter Olympics in South Korea and, on its side-lines, held talks with his South Korean counterparts. Through successful inter-Korean dialogue, Chairman Kim dramatically stepped up his game by extending a direct invitation to President Trump for a summit meeting through the visiting South Korean officials. In an equally dramatic gesture, President Trump accepted Chairman Kim's invitation on the spot, which culminated in the historic Singapore Summit between the two leaders on June 12, 2018.

Future of Sanctions Post Kim-Trump Meetings

The summit meeting between Chairman Kim and President Trump has been widely hailed by countries around the world for making a definite progress towards creating peace and stability in the region. Through the summit meeting, President Trump has secured a tangible gain by securing a freeze on nuclear and missile tests, and also by committing North Korea to dismantle its nuclear tests sites.[61] More importantly, as part of the summit declaration, North Korea has agreed to 'work towards complete denuclearisation of the Korean peninsula'. This commitment of denuclearisation, however, is markedly different from Washington's long-stated goal of seeking 'complete, verifiable and irreversible dismantlement (CVID) of North Korea's nuclear arsenal'.[62] Although the freeze has clearly minimised the risks of an accidental breakout of conflict, many in the Trump administration realise that, for future progress, the Singapore Summit is just the beginning of a long, tortuous set of negotiations with North Korea, and that only one such summit meeting would not be enough for Chairman Kim to give up the nuclear programme that his country has built assiduously over the years. This is evident from the flurry of reports about North Korea's continuing expansion of nuclear facilities within a few weeks after the Singapore Summit.

Consequently, the Trump administration seems to have adopted a hardline approach towards denuclearisation and has desisted from granting any immediate relief to North Korea on sanctions. This is clear from the statement issued by White House which made it clear that the US will not revoke sanctions at any stage, and will maintain the policy of 'maximum pressure' through sanctions on North Korea.[63] US officials believe that such a hard-line approach will enable the US to seek credible assurances from North Korea during future negotiations. Although it is difficult to predict how long the two sides will remain engaged in the diplomatic process, the summit meeting has clearly opened up a window for creating peace and stability on the Korean Peninsula.[64]

Clearly, much will depend on how much flexibility both the sides are willing to show in future summits. Having secured short-term gains, the US and its allies can also leverage sanctions to seek a larger diplomatic breakthrough in the form of a 'deal' that will not only resolve the longstanding conflict on the Peninsula but would also pave the way for North Korea's denuclearisation. For long, the Korean Peninsula has remained divided due to extra-territorial interventions, and the ideological split precipitated by the breakout of the Cold War. Although the Cold War has long been over, and the ideological barriers have been fully shattered, the conflict on the Korean Peninsula remains alive as a legacy of the Cold War and continuing extra-regional interests in the region. Resolving such a security conundrum requires forging a 'political deal', or some kind of 'Peace Treaty' that North Korea has always demanded from Washington and Seoul. The Trump administration's North Korea Policy must take these realities into account, and work towards achieving a diplomatic breakthrough with Pyongyang.

The US and its allies should make use of ongoing diplomatic engagement to seek a 'political deal' which will not only alter fundamental security dynamics in the region by bringing North Korea into a benign alliance with South Korea and Japan but also paving its way towards denuclearisation in the long-run. Sensing the risk of such imminent breakthrough, however, China already seized the initiative by hosting Kim Jong-un in Beijing, and firming up their Cold War-era alliance. Despite such developments, the US and South Korea could still pursue diplomatic efforts toward denuclearisation by taking appropriate policy steps. In this regard, President Trump's policy of 'maintaining sanctions till North Korea denuclearises fully' can be made more flexible so that it does not negate the possibility of using sanctions to bargain for both short and long terms diplomatic gains. The US could adopt such an approach by showing the requisite flexibility towards North Korea during the actual process of negotiations. By deftly using the summit opportunity, President Trump has not only hard-bargained peace with Kim Jong-un but also successfully turned the tables on China. In the future too, sanctions can well be America's 'Trump Card' that will help to bring lasting peace to the Korean Peninsula.

Conclusion

This chapter mainly contends that sanctions as an instrument against North Korea's non-proliferation policy has reached its limits, and is unlikely to force Pyongyang to give up its nuclear and missile programmes. This is mainly due to the regime's ability to weather the most stringent sanctions, and channelling hardships caused by embargoes to the ordinary Korean people. As the US and its allies seek to recalibrate policies towards North Korea by adopting both deterrence and diplomacy, they can still leverage sanctions to secure certain short term as well as long-term strategic gains. For this purpose, Washington will have to invest considerably in building diplomatic leverage over North Korea. Also, the success of diplomacy critically depends on how the US and its allies can bring North Korea into a closer political security alliance with Japan and South Korea. Fostering such a strategic transformation should clearly be the way forward for US diplomacy which will not only alter the security dynamics in America's favour but also facilitate North Korea's denuclearisation in the long-run.

Notes

1. In modern times, international sanctions are mostly evoked in accordance with Article 41 of the UN Charter in cases where the country or regime is found violating human rights, waging war, or endangering international peace and security (see, Article 41, Charter of the United Nations, 1945). Since the dawn of the atomic age, sanctions have been widely used to prevent the proliferation of nuclear weapons as also to deter potential proliferators from doing so.
2. 'Documents on North Korea', Security Council Reports, United Nations 2018 at http://www.securitycouncilreport.org/un-documents/dprk-north-korea/, accessed on March 12, 2018.
3. K. Calamur, 'What's New About the Latest UN Sanctions Against North Korea?', *The Atlantic*, August 7, 2017 at https://www.theatlantic.com/international/archive/2017/08/north-korea-sanctions/536082/, accessed on March 18, 2018.
4. T. Mitchell and X. Liu, 'China's trade with North Korea targeted by Trump', *Financial Times*, April 23, 2017 at https://www.ft.com/content/14e6fe4c-27e0-11e7-9ec8-168383da43b7, accessed on March 26, 2018.

5. T. Dalton and A. Levite, 'When Trump Meets Kim Jong Un', *Foreign Affairs*, March 26, 2018, at https://www.foreignaffairs.com/articles/north-korea/2018-03-26/when-trump-meets-kim-jong-un, accessed on March 30, 2018.
6. B. Haas and J. McCurry, 'Optimism and Confusion in Seoul over Trump-Kim Summit', *The Guardian*, June 12, 2018 at https://www.theguardian.com/world/2018/jun/12/north-korea-sanctions-may-be-lifted-after-summit-says-china, accessed on August 25, 2018; and, N. Smith, 'North Korea expands weapons facilities despite US pressure to disarm', *The Telegraph*, July 2, 2018 at https://www.telegraph.co.uk/news/2018/07/02/north-korea-expands-weapons-facilities-despite-us-pressure-disarm/, accessed on August 25, 2018.
7. U. Friedman, 'Smart Sanctions: A Short History', *Foreign Policy*, April 23, 2012 at http://foreignpolicy.com/2012/04/23/smart-sanctions-a-short-history/, accessed on March 25, 2018.
8. I. Eland, 'Economic sanctions as tools of foreign policy', in D. Cortright, (ed.), *Economic Sanctions: Panacea or Peace-building in A Post-cold War World?*, Routledge, New York, 2018, pp. 29–42.
9. D.A. Baldwin, *Economic Statecraft*, Princeton University Press, Massachusetts, 1985; and G.C. Hufbauer, J.J. Schott, and K. Ann Elliott, *Economic Sanctions Reconsidered: History and Current Policy,* Vol. 1, Institute for International Economics, Washington, 1985.
10. Ibid.
11. G.A. Lopez, and D. Cortright, 'The Sanctions Era: An Alternative to Military Intervention'. *Fletcher Forum of World Affairs*, 19, 1995, p. 65.
12. G.C. Hufbauer, J.J. Schott, K.A. Elliott, and B. Oegg, *Economic Sanctions Reconsidered*, Third edition, Peterson Institute for International Economics, Washington, 1990.
13. N.L. Miller, 'The Secret Success of Non-proliferation Sanctions', *International Organization*, 68(4), 2014, pp. 913–944.
14. Ibid.
15. L.L. Martin, 'Credibility, costs, and institutions: Cooperation on economic sanctions', *World Politics,* 45(3), 1993, pp. 406–432; and S.J. Kunis, 'Non-proliferation Sanctions: Taking the "Profit Out Of Proliferation?"', thesis submitted to Centre For International Security & Cooperation, Freeman Spogli Institute for International Studies, Stanford University, 2015.
16. D. Morrow, and M. Carriere, 'The economic impacts of the 1998 sanctions on India and Pakistan', *The Non-proliferation Review*, 6(4), 1999, pp. 1–16.
17. See, G.A. Lopez, and D. Cortright, note 11.
18. E. Solingen, (ed.), *Sanctions, Statecraft, and Nuclear Proliferation,* Cambridge University Press, Cambridge, 2012; N. Marinov, 'Do economic sanctions destabilize country leaders?' *American Journal of Political Science*,

49(3), 2005, pp. 564–576; A. Escribà-Folch and J. Wright, 'Dealing with tyranny: International sanctions and the survival of authoritarian rulers', *International Studies Quarterly*, 54(2), 2010, pp. 335–359; S. Haggard, and M. Noland, *Hard Target: Sanctions, Inducements, and the Case of North Korea*, Stanford University Press, Palo Alto, 2017.

19. A. Stein, 'Sanctions, inducements, and market power', in E. Solingen, (ed.), *Sanctions, Statecraft, and Nuclear Proliferation,* Cambridge University Press, Cambridge, 2012.
20. See N. Marinov, note 18.
21. Ibid.
22. A. Escribà-Folch, and J. Wright, 'Dealing with tyranny: International sanctions and the survival of authoritarian rulers', *International Studies Quarterly*, 54(2), 2010, pp. 335–359.
23. Ibid.
24. Ibid.
25. See, S. Haggard and M. Noland, note 18.
26. See, G.A. Lopez, and D. Cortright, note 11.
27. K. Davenport, 'The Six-Party Talks at a Glance: Fact Sheets', Arms Control Association, July 2017 at https://www.armscontrol.org/factsheets/6partytalks, accessed on March 22, 2018.
28. After several rounds of negotiations, the Six-Party Talks led to an agreement in 2005 in which North Korea agreed to renounce the pursuit of nuclear weapons. The agreement, however, failed within few months of its negotiations, and led to North Korea's first nuclear test in October 2006. Under the pressure from Six-Party members and especially China, North Korea returned to the six-party talks, and agreed to a denuclearisation plan in February 2007. The denuclearisation plan called for freezing North Korea's nuclear programme in return for the release of aid and assets. Although Pyongyang agreed to the denuclearisation plan, and began dismantling its nuclear complex at Yongbyon in agreed phases, it still tested the Taepo Dong-2 three-stage rocket, calling it a part of its civilian space programme. The UN Security Council responded to the test by imposing a new set of sanctions, upon which North Korea Pyongyang declared, on April 14, 2009, that it would no longer participate in the Six-Party Talks. Subsequently, in May 2009, Pyongyang conducted the second nuclear test which effectively ended the Six-Party Talks.
29. Associated Press, 'A Look at This Year's North Korean Nuclear and Missile Tests', *Time*, November 29, 2017 at http://time.com/5040375/north-korea-nuclear-missile-tests-2017/, accessed on March 14, 2018.
30. 'Fact Sheet: UN Security Council Resolution 2397 on North Korea', United States Mission to the United Nations, State Department, December 22, 2017 at https://usun.state.gov/remarks/8238, accessed on March 20, 2018.

31. Executive Order 13466 of June 26, 2008: 'Continuing Certain Restrictions with Respect to North Korea and North Korean Nationals' at https://www.treasury.gov/resource-center/sanctions/Documents/nkeo.pdf, accessed on March 20, 2018.
32. Executive Order 13570: 'Prohibiting Certain Transactions with Respect to North Korea' at https://obamawhitehouse.archives.gov/the-press-office/2011/04/18/executive-order-13570-prohibiting-certain-transactions-respect-north-kor, accessed on March 20, 2018.
33. See also, Iran, North Korea, and Syria Non-proliferation Act Sanctions (INKSNA) at https://www.state.gov/t/isn/inksna/, accessed on December 23, 2018.
34. E. Albert, 'What to Know about the Sanctions on North Korea: Backgrounder', Council on Foreign Relations, January 3, 2018 at https://www.cfr.org/backgrounder/what-know-about-sanctions-north-korea, accessed on March 12, 2018.
35. 'Moon Chung-in alludes to adjusting May 24 sanctions on North Korea', *The Hankyoreh*, May 25, 2017 at http://english.hani.co.kr/arti/english_edition/e_northkorea/796240.html, accessed on April 24, 2018.
36. Mina Pollmann, 'Japan Unveils Unilateral Sanctions on North Korea', *The Diplomat*, February 12, 2016 at https://thediplomat.com/2016/02/japan-unveils-unilateral-sanctions-on-north-korea/, accessed on April 11, 2018.
37. E. Albert, note 34.
38. J. Stanton, Sung-Yoon Lee and B. Klingner, 'Getting Tough on North Korea: How to Hit Pyongyang Where It Hurts', *Foreign Affairs*, May/June 2017 at https://www.foreignaffairs.com/articles/north-korea/2017-04-17/getting-tough-north-korea, accessed on March 29, 2018.
39. S. Eckert, 'United Nations Sanctions on DPRK: Implementation Evasion, and Opportunities to Strengthen.' Watson Institute for International and Public Affairs, Providence, June 15, 2015.
40. 'Report of the Panel of Experts established pursuant to resolution 1874', UNSC Report, United Nations Security Council, S/2018/171, March 5, 2018 at http://www.un.org/ga/search/view_doc.asp?symbol=S/2018/171, accessed on October 27, 2018.
41. Ibid.
42. Saul Faulconbridge, and Nikolskaya, 'Russian tankers fuelled North Korea via transfers at sea—sources', Reuters, December 30, 2017 at https://in.reuters.com/article/northkorea-missiles-russia-oil-exclusive/exclusive-russian-tankers-fuelled-north-korea-via-transfers-at-sea-sources-idINKBN1EN1PP, accessed on March 23, 2018.
43. R. Jennings, 'Taiwan investigators say ship transferred oil to North Korea in defiance of sanctions', *Los Angeles Times*, January 4, 2018 at http://www.latimes.com/world/asia/la-fg-taiwan-north-korea-oil-20180104-story.html, accessed on March 26, 2018.

44. 'North Korea Flouts UN Sanctions on Oil, Coal', *The Maritime Executive*, August 8, 2018, at https://www.maritime-executive.com/article/north-korea-flouts-un-sanctions-on-oil-coal; and C. Sang-Hun, 'South Korea Seizes Ship Suspected of Sending Oil to North Korea', *New York Times*, December 29, 2017 at https://www.nytimes.com/2017/12/29/world/asia/south-korea-ship-seized.html, accessed on March 20, 2018.
45. 'North Korea flouts UN sanctions earning millions, say experts', *The Telegraph*, February 3, 2018 at https://www.telegraph.co.uk/news/2018/02/03/north-korea-flouts-un-sanctions-earning-millions-say-un-experts/, accessed on March 14, 2018.
46. 'North Korea earned $200 million from banned exports: UN', Deutsche Welle, February 3, 2018 at http://www.dw.com/en/north-korea-earned-200-million-from-banned-exports-un/a-42437240, accessed on March 19, 2018.
47. T. F. Chan, 'North Korea reportedly "laundered" coal through Russia in an apparent breach of sanctions', Business Insider, March 5, 2018 at https://www.businessinsider.in/North-Korea-reportedly-laundered-coal-through-Russia-in-an-apparent-breach-of-sanctions/articleshow/63165315.cms, accessed on March 19, 2018.
48. J. Warrick, 'High seas shell game: How a North Korean shipping ruse makes a mockery of sanctions', *The Washington Post*, March 3, 2018 at https://www.washingtonpost.com/world/national-security/high-seas-shell-game-how-a-north-korean-shipping-ruse-makes-a-mockery-of-sanctions/2018/03/03/3380e1ec-1cb8-11e8-b2d9-08e748f892c0_story.html?utm_term=.e7eb90dd9020, accessed on March 29, 2018.
49. M. Nichols, 'North Korea earned $200 million from banned exports, sends arms to Syria, Myanmar: U.N. report', Reuters, February 3, 2018 at https://in.reuters.com/article/northkorea-missiles-un-exclusive/exclusive-north-korea-earned-200-million-from-banned-exports-sends-arms-to-syria-myanmar-u-n-report-idINKBN1FM2UH, accessed on March 27, 2018.
50. See J. Warrick, note 48.
51. Sigal, 'How North Korea Evades Financial Sanctions', *Foreign Affairs*, May 3, 2013 at https://www.38north.org/2013/05/lsigal050313/, accessed on October 14, 2018.
52. David Thompson, 'Risky Business: A system-level analysis of the North Korean Proliferation Financing System', *C4ADS*, 2011 at https://c4ads.org/risky-business/, accessed on March 25, 2018.
53. The North Korean STCs, he noted, are tightly connected to the Korean People's Army (KPA), the Worker's Party of Korea (WPK), and the Cabinet. Over the years, their linkages have evolved; and they have also adapted their business methods in the face of increasing sanctions and international isolation. Additionally, the North Korean STCs are known to have

formed a highly intricate 'self-financed networked model of procurement' from which the Kim regime and WPK are able to glean the majority of profits through bribes and mandatory taxes in the form of 'revolutionary funds.' See, J. Park, and J. Walsh, 'Stopping North Korea, Inc.: Sanctions Effectiveness and Unintended Consequences', Massachusetts Institute of Technology, August 2016 at https://www.belfercenter.org/sites/default/files/legacy/files/Stopping%20North%20Korea%20Inc%20Park%20and%20Walsh%20.pdf, accessed on March 19, 2018.

54. 'Hwagyo' middlemen are the ethnic Han Chinese, but possess dual Chinese and North Korean citizenship, which allows them to travel freely across the border.
55. N. Bhatiya, 'The Missing Piece in the World's North Korea Strategy', *The Diplomat*, January 30, 2018 at https://thediplomat.com/2018/01/the-missing-piece-in-the-worlds-north-korea-strategy/, accessed on March 15, 2018.
56. See, S. Haggard and M. Noland, note 18.
57. K. Hewitt, 'Rethinking North Korean Sanctions: Lessons and Strategies for Long-Term Planning', 38 North, January 16, 2018 at https://www.38north.org/2018/01/khewitt011618/, accessed on March 25, 2018; and C. Russell, 'China buys record North Korean coal as sanctions ignored: Russell', Reuters, September 26, 2016 at https://www.reuters.com/article/us-column-russell-coal-china/china-buys-record-north-korean-coal-as-sanctions-ignored-russell-idUSKCN11W0CO, accessed on April 1, 2018.
58. S. Sagan, *et al.*, 'Why Nuclear Deterrence can Work on North Korea', The Centre for International Security and Cooperation, the Freeman Spogli Institute for International Studies, November 14, 2017 at https://cisac.fsi.stanford.edu/news/why-nuclear-deterrence-can-work-north-korea; and Vipin Narang, 'Why nuclear deterrence can work on North Korea', Centre for International Security and Cooperation, Stanford University, November 14, 2017 at https://cisac.fsi.stanford.edu/news/why-nuclear-deterrence-can-work-north-korea, accessed on April 7, 2018.
59. S.D. Sagan, 'The Korean Missile Crisis: Why Deterrence Is Still the Best Option', *Foreign Affairs*, November/December 2017 at https://www.foreignaffairs.com/articles/north-korea/2017-09-10/korean-missile-crisis, accessed on April 2, 2018.
60. DoD, 'Nuclear Posture Review', Office *Of The Secretary Of Defense,* February 2018 at https://media.defense.gov/2018/feb/02/2001872886/-1/-1/1/2018-nuclear-posture-review-final-report.pdf, accessed on April 11, 2018.
61. Kapil Patil, 'Forging a "Korean Nuclear Deal": The Beginning of a Long Road', Vivekananda International Foundation, March 23, 2018 at http://www.vifindia.org/article/hindi/2018/march/23/forging-a-korean-nuclear-deal-the-beginning-of-a-long-road, accessed on April 11, 2018.

62. A. Panda, '3 Takeaways From Kim Jong-un's 2018 New Year's Address', *The Diplomat*, January 1, 2018 at https://thediplomat.com/2018/01/3-takeaways-from-kim-jong-uns-2018-new-years-address/; and A. Panda and V. Narang, 'The Trump-Kim Summit and North Korean Denuclearization: The Good, the Bad, and the Ugly', War on the Rocks, March 14, 2018 at https://warontherocks.com/2018/03/the-trump-kim-summit-and-north-korean-denuclearization-the-good-the-bad-and-the-ugly/, accessed on March 29, 2018.
63. Besheer, 'US Maintains "Maximum Pressure" on North Korea Ahead of Possible Summit', Voice of America, March 12, 2018 at https://www.voanews.com/a/us-maximum-pressure-north-korea-possible-summit/4296047.html, accessed on April 5, 2018; also see, 'Trump's 'maximum pressure' on North Korea is working. Now what?' *The Washington Post*, March 6, 2018 at https://www.washingtonpost.com/opinions/global-opinions/trumps-maximum-pressure-on-north-korea-is-working-now-what/2018/03/06/917d3c36-217d-11e8-badd-7c9f29a55815_story.html?utm_term=.69803cf74c04, accessed on March 28, 2018.
64. A. Fifield, D. Nakamura, and Seung Min Kim, 'Trump accepts invitation to meet with North Korean leader Kim Jong Un', *The Washington Post*, March 8, 2018, at https://www.washingtonpost.com/world/asia_pacific/north-korean-leader-kim-jong-un-has-invited-president-trump-to-a-meeting/2018/03/08/021cb070-2322-11e8-badd-7c9f29a55815_story.html?utm_term=.349618772706, accessed on April 1, 2018.

5. North Korean Economy: Failure of UNSC Sanctions

N. Parthasarathi

North Korea remains an enigma to the outside world as not much is known about its economy or its trade with other countries. As the Mid-Term Report (September 5, 2017) of a Panel of Experts established pursuant to Resolution 1874 (2009) of the UN Security Council, states, 'the most comprehensive and targeted sanctions regime in United Nations history' has been imposed on North Korea.[1] These sanctions should have further isolated the country. However, observers who watch North Korea agree that the country has not only managed to defy the US-led comprehensive UN sanctions but the North Korean economy has continued to grow in the past decades.

How has North Korea managed to absorb the shocks and make its economy resilient? Before comprehending the mindset of North Korea's leaders in defying the UN sanctions, it is necessary to understand and appreciate the reasons and the depth of the country's hostility towards the US. As Kim Il-sung, the 'Great Leader' and founder of North Korea has explained, 'the most important thing for his country was to prepare for war and educate his people to hate US imperialism'.[2] The hatred is rooted in the reality of the destruction and suffering of the North Korean people at the hands of US forces during the Korean War. During the war, the US Air Force bombed across North Korea. The US Air Force General Curtis LeMay, Head of the Strategic Air Command during the War, boasted in an interview he gave in 1984, saying, 'So we went over there and fought the war and eventually burned down every town in North Korea anyway ... over a period of three years or so, we killed off—what—twenty percent of the population'.[3] American aircraft dropped more bombs on North Korea than they did in the entire Pacific Theatre of World War II—635,000 tons vs. 503,000 tons out of these around 32,000 tons were Napalm bombs, flammable liquid weapons that burst just above ground level and stick to human flesh inflicting excruciating pain.[4] Dean Rusk, who later became the US Secretary of State, claimed that the US bombed 'everything that moved in North Korea, every brick standing on top of the other'.[5] US bombers also destroyed hydro-electric and irrigation dams, destroying entire crops.

Many decades later, North Korean leaders have kept these tragic memories fresh in the minds of their people. North Koreans are repeatedly told that fighting against such heavy odds, it was the brilliance of Kim Il-sung that saved North Korea, and ensured the defeat of a great imperialist power that was the US. It is to be remembered that the Korean War ended with an Armistice (not a peace treaty), and hence North Korea is technically still at war with the US. Joint military exercises between the US and South Korea reinforced North Korean's belief that the US could attack them any day. President Trump's rhetoric that he will 'totally destroy North Korea' sounded like a serious threat to North Korea.[6] In fact, hostility towards the US and developing the ability to fight the US are among the major justifications for the Kim family to continue ruling in North Korea.

The North Koreans have endured sanctions for decades, and that is why *Juche* or self-reliance has become the prime objective of their existence. Their leaders have also understood that they cannot compete in a conventional arms race with South Korea or the US because of the size of their economies. They have learnt lessons from the US led war on Iraq, Afghanistan, and Libya—that for the survival of their regime and to safeguard their country's security, they need to have nuclear weapons and inter-continental ballistic missile programmes. Accordingly, they have invested more and more resources on the development of these weapon systems, irrespective of the suffering it causes to the normal lives of their people.

The regime believed in severely restricting communication with the outside world and is adept at transferring the pain of UN sanctions to its people. Available resources are reserved for a small number of the political elite, the top brass of their defence forces, and the nuclear weapon and missile programmes. People are urged to endure the suffering caused by imperialist US that wants to test them, and make them give up their freedom. North Korean leader Kim Jong-un can be belligerent but he is also intelligent and practical.

North Korean Economic Path—The Past

In 1945, about 65 per cent of Korean heavy industry was located in Northern Korea because of the availability of raw material resources and other inputs. Owing to the brutal bombings by the US forces, North Korean industry was destroyed beyond recognition during the Korean War. After the war, under the authoritarian and charismatic leadership of Kim Il-sung, North Korea mobilised its people to exploit the available resources for economic development. In 1956, Kim Il-sung declared *Juche* or self-reliance to be the guiding principle of their economy. The three fundamental principles of *Juche* included political independence cooperating with other socialist countries and countries that were members of the non-aligned movement; economic self-sustenance focussing on national economy based on heavy industries and technological prowess; and self-reliance in defence.

With the help of substantial amounts of economic aid from the Soviet Union and the People's Republic of China, North Korea's centrally planned, self-reliant development strategy was able to accord high priority to developing heavy industry, with parallel development in agriculture and light industry. Almost half of the state investment went into the industrial sector during the 1954–1976 period.[7] Many other communist countries have believed in a similar strategy. It may be noted that North Korean growth rates in most industrial sectors remained higher than that of South Korea till 1965 the country made great strides in education for children, establishing universities, energy and industrial production. The living standards of people kept rising into the 1970s.

In the 1970s, North Korean leadership decided on a couple of major policies to make their country stronger and self-reliant. One of the primary objectives of such policies was to reduce its dependence on aid from the Soviet Union and China by borrowing foreign funds and investing in the local mining industry. It borrowed large funds and imported diverse equipment for mineral extraction and processing. It also imported petro-chemical, steel, cement, and paper making plants from abroad, including from Japan and Denmark. North Korea believed that it can pay off the debt through the increased sales of its minerals in international markets. The second decision was to invest large amounts of borrowed funds in military industries to avoid dependence on foreign arms suppliers, and also to promote exports in the defence sector.

Unfortunately, as a result of the 1973 oil-crisis, international prices of many raw materials, including those produced by North Korea, fell. North Korea crumbled under debt, and it defaulted on most of its foreign debt. As the country suffered, the leaders learnt a lesson not to depend on outside funds but to become self-sufficient in their own way, thus reinforcing their *Juche* strategy. Even if North Korea wanted, it was extremely difficult to borrow funds from outside. As North Korea struggled with its old-world steel and mines economy, other countries (such as South Korea) were moving ahead with electronics and computer technologies. South Korea also depended on large external borrowings, but their higher economic growth was able to service the country's debt.

Further disaster awaited North Korea. With the collapse of the Soviet Union, North Korea lost its principal source of external support in terms of aid and trade. Added to that, the oil price shock due to the war in Iraq by an US-led coalition, deprived North Korea's ability to buy required oil as demands were made that they be paid in hard currency. This, in turn, affected fertiliser and electricity production which had a greater impact on agriculture.

Chronic trade deficit, mounting foreign debt, and vanishing foreign aid crippled the North Korean economy. Even during those difficult times, it is generally believed that the country still allocated around 20 per cent of its budget for defence. In addition, from 1994 to 1998, North Korea suffered severe famine, including record floods in 1995. More than a million people are said to have perished due to starvation and disease. The North Korean economy is estimated to have shrunk between 25 per cent and 50 per cent during that decade.[8] The outside world still remembers the horrifying images of floods and starvation of that era, and still perceives that North Korea's economy is stuck in those times 'due to the inhuman dictatorial regime that only knows how to repress its people and divert funds for the benefit of a selected elite and for the development of missile and nuclear programmes'. As North Korea continues to remain isolated and information and reliable data is hard to find, the above perception has been reinforced over the last decade and a half.

Mitsuhiro Mimura, Senior Research Fellow at Japan's Economic Research Institute for Northeast Asia, has a different view of North Korea. Having visited North Korea several times during the last two decades, Mimura describes North Korea as the 'poorest advanced economy in the world'. He says that the country, though it has a comparatively low GDP, has built a sophisticated production environment. He explains that,

> the country has a comprehensive production structure including both labour-intensive and capital-intensive industries. They are able not only to produce capital goods to run their society, like railroad locomotives and carriages, cargo vessels, turbines and generators for power plants, numerically controlled lathes, but they also make most of the things needed for military use, from small arms to ballistic missiles and nuclear weapons, trucks, jeeps, destroyers, and diesel engines.

Mimura further explains as to how the entrepreneurial spirit at the level of individuals including housewives has been accepted through 'socialist cooperation', and such monetisation of economic activity has been adding to the resilience of the North Korean economy. He adds that 'in North Korea, even for the leadership, reality prevails over ideology. The North Koreans are practical people, adept at survival, adapting to reality—and that includes the leaders'.[9] Mimura is not alone in believing that North Korea has achieved considerable economic progress in recent years. In an article titled, 'Best guesses, How to measure North Korea's economy, *The Economist* says that,

> [the] North Korean economy has made great strides since the country's famine in the 1990s. The government has tacitly allowed the market economy to grow ... Although the rest of the country is still indisputably poor, visitors to Pyongyang, at least, cannot help but note the rise of shops and taxis ...The size of the country's apparently bourgeoning service sector is a complete mystery.[10]

In his article, 'Underground Markets in North Korea', Hyung Min-Joo is more categorical when he says,

> The outside world is well aware of the 'totalitarian' side of North Korea. Much less well known, however, is the 'capitalistic' aspect of the country in which an illicit 'bottom-up marketisation' has enveloped the everyday lives of people for the last 15 years or so.[11]

David Volodzko explains the phenomenon further, by saying,

> At the same time, economic reforms made in 2011 have begun to take hold allowing factory managers to set salaries, find their own suppliers, and hire and fire employees. Farming collectives have been replaced by a family-based management system, which has led to far greater harvests. The government has even come to tolerate private enterprise on a limited basis. The results are striking. Street vendors, once rare, are now a common sight in Pyongyang. Some neighbourhoods have new

luxury high-rises, modern supermarkets, fashionable shops, and streets busy with Mercedes-Benzes and BMWs. Although the government denies having abandoned the old socialist system, the evidence is undeniable: by some estimates, the private sector now accounts for up to half of GDP.[12]

Ruediger Frank, Professor and Head of the Department of East Asian Studies at the University of Vienna, a renowned expert on North Korea, has compiled the official annual growth rates of the North Korean state budget based on details published by *Rodong Sinmun* and Korean Central News Agency. He is of the opinion that,

> considering the dominant state ownership in the North Korean economy, these numbers are at least correlated, if not equivalent to, what we would call GDP growth'. He says that the budget reports 'imply that that North Korean state has for many years run a surplus to which revenue from 'local' sources-including-markets-have contributed.[13]

Figure 1: Annual Growth Rate of North Korean Budget (in percentage, 2006-2016)

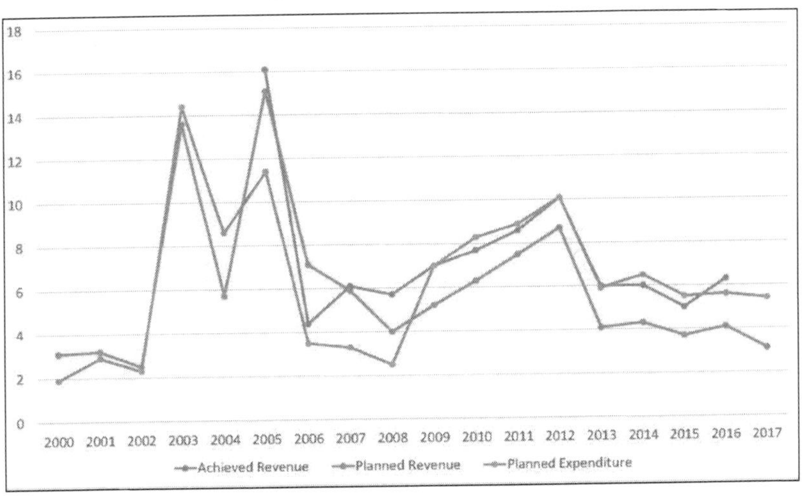

Source: *Rodong Sinmun* and KCNA, compiled by Rudiger Frank.

Referring to the speech of the North Korean leader at the Parliamentary session in April 2017, Ruediger Frank is of the opinion that, the state considering the production of consumer goods, indicates the moderately growing wealth at least among a part of the population. The promise to increase the production of higher quality agricultural products is indicative that the economy though poor is not in crisis anymore.[14]

In its report on North Korea, the Bank of South Korea (BoK) estimated that, in 2015, North Korea produced 2.01 million tons of rice compared to 4.32 million tons produced by South Korea.[15] It is also to be noted that North Korea has a population of around 25 million compared to around 51 million in South Korea. Thus, North Korea, with half the population of South Korea, has been able to produce around half the quantity of rice produced by South Korea. This is clear evidence that North Korea is no more in a crisis situation for its staple food. Although the general perception is that North Korea is isolated, economy is struggling, the people are starving or malnourished and any further sanctions would make the economy collapse, and the desperate people will revolt leading to a change in regime, this is not really true. Those experts who have been visiting North Korea regularly believe that the economy is not facing any crisis situation.

The Size of the North Korean Economy

Before any assessment can be made to validate the North Korean economy, how seriously it has been affected by UN sanctions, whether it has managed to grow despite them, it is essential to know the size of the North Korean economy, its constituents, its previous record of growth, and factors that impact its economy. Unfortunately, there are no published statistics on North Korea that are reliable. North Korea stopped publishing economic performance statistics from 1965 onwards, and its last state budget containing budget figures was in the financial year 2001. Since then, it releases annual budgets only with percentage changes in different sectors. As North Korea does not release its own data, much of the data on the country comes from observers such as the Bank of South Korea (BoK), the Ministry of Unification of South Korea, the Korea Trade-Investment Promotion Agency (KOTRA), and the CIA Fact book. Such data are not comprehensive and are, at best, educated guesstimates. In the absence of reliable data, there is no option but to explore whatever data that is available.

The BoK[16] estimates that the North Korean economy grew at an average rate of 1.2 per cent between 2012 and 2016. BoK also estimates North Korea's GDP at 31.996 trillion won, approximately US$ 28.1 billion and after 31.161 trillion won approximately US$ 27.37 billion for 2016. BoK data also indicates that the North Korean economy had shrunk by 1.1 per cent during 2015, and its GDP stood at 31.161 trillion won.[17] According to the CIA Fact Book,[18] the GDP of North Korea was estimated at US$ 28 billion (2013), a rise of 1.1 per cent over the year 2012. If it is assumed that the country's economy grew by 1 per cent in 2014, the estimated GDP for 2014 would be US$ 28.28 billion. Then, the economy contracted by 1.1 per cent in 2015—that is, the GDP would work out to US$ 27.97 billion. Then again, the economy grew by 3.9 per cent for the year 2016. Hence, the estimated GDP works out to US$ 29.06 billion for 2016. This estimate varies by around US$ 1 billion compared to the estimate of GDP provided by the BoK.[19]

Figure 2: North Korean GDP

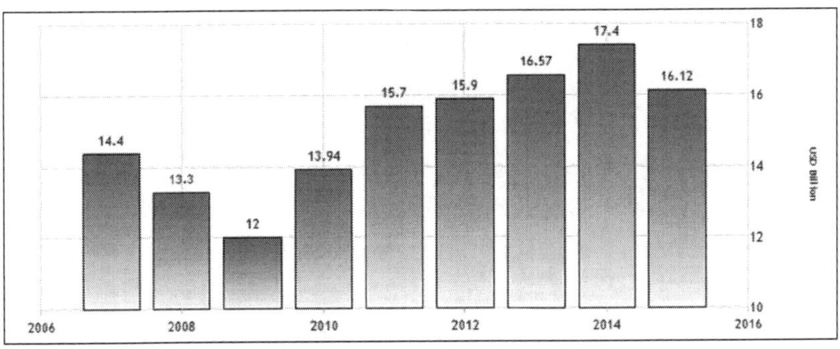

Source: Trading Economics website.

The above estimates of North Korean GDP demonstrate the serious challenges in finding reasonable economic data on North Korea.

In the words of Marcus Noland, an acknowledged scholar on North Korea and the Executive Vice President and Director of Studies at Peterson Institute for International Economics, 'it is possible that North Korea's economy may not be as bad as many outside countries wish to believe. It is possible that the observers have not factored in various economic reforms that are providing resilience to the economy'. Noland rightly points out that 'nowhere else is the gap between what we know and what we think we know so wide'. He is of the opinion that, 'North Korean statistics are fragmentary, subject to gross error and even intentional deception'.[20] Even the available data, however approximate and unreliable, become more complex due to various factors.

North Korea is not new to sanctions. In response, partially to such sanctions, North Korea followed the *Juche* strategy of self-reliance and has managed, over decades, to build a manufacturing base to meet its requirements, particularly in the defence sector. It has managed to overcome the disastrous effects on its economy in the 1990s, and has brought back its economy to follow an ascending curve.

UN Sanctions on North Korea

With continued defiance of the international community and regardless of the warnings of 'grave consequences', North Korea conducted a nuclear test in 2006, which led the UNSC unanimously adopt Resolution 1718 under Chapter VII of the UN Charter (but barring military enforcement under Charter's Article 41). The Resolution demanded North Korea to cease nuclear testing, and return immediately to multilateral talks. The Resolution imposed an embargo on large scale arms, assets freeze and travel ban on persons related to North Korea's nuclear programme, and a ban on a range of imports and exports, including luxury goods. The Resolution also established a Security Council Sanctions Committee.[21] Subsequently in 2009, North Korea successfully tested another nuclear device with up to 8 kiloton yield that proved its technological capabilities. This led UNSC to unanimously adopt Resolution 1874 tightening sanctions to block funds for nuclear, missile, and proliferation activities. It widened the ban on arms imports-exports. The Resolution called upon member states to prevent the provision of financial services or the transfer of financial resources that could contribute to North Korea's nuclear, missile, or WMD related activities. It required member states to 'inspect cargo vessels, if states have "reasonable grounds" to believe, [it] contain[s] prohibited items'. It also established a seven-member Panel of Experts to assist the Sanctions Committee.[22] These nuclear test and several missile tests that were conducted were viewed as an attempt by the ailing Leader Kim Jong-il to prove North Korean capabilities before his death.[23] No new nuclear tests took place in 2010 and 2011. Kim Jong-Il passed away on December 28, 2011, and his second son, Kim Jong-un was declared the Supreme Leader of the hermit kingdom.

Without losing time, the Chairman Kim Jong-un focussed on missile and nuclear programmes and in April 2012, attempted the launch of a satellite aboard an Unha-3 rocket that ended in failure. Undeterred, he persisted, and in December 2012, successfully launched a satellite into orbit aboard a three stage rocket. After the satellite launch, the UNSC unanimously adopted Resolution 2087 in 2013, that clarified a state's right to seize and destroy cargo suspected of heading to, or from, North Korea for the purposes of military research and development.[24] Soon after, in February 2013, North Korea claimed that it had tested a miniaturised and lighter nuclear device with higher yield. International observers pointed out that it could be a uranium device, and miniaturisation could mean that North Korea could soon produce a weapon that would fit on a long range missile that could target the US.

In response, the UNSC unanimously adopted Resolution 2094 in March 2013 that took significant steps in imposing sanctions on money transfers aiming to isolate North Korea from the international financial system.[25] In response, North Korea threatened South Korea not to cooperate on UN sanctions. It also threatened the US which deployed the THAAD system in Guam. The 2013 UN sanctions would, no doubt, have had an adverse impact on North Korea's economy, but they could not halt the momentum of its missile and nuclear programmes. On the contrary, it would appear that they strengthened the resolve of North Korea in speeding up such weapons programmes to achieve adequate means to reach miniaturised nuclear weapons to mainland US.

In 2013, North Korea conducted further missile tests and its third nuclear test which led to the imposition of UNSC resolution 2094. In January 2016, after threatening to attack South Korea and the US, North Korea announced that it had successfully tested a hydrogen bomb. A couple of months later, in March, North Korea announced that it had succeeded in miniaturising a nuclear weapon to fit on its missiles. North Korea genuinely believes that once it has the proven capability to launch nuclear weapons, the threat of a destructive attack by the US—as on Iraq, Libya, etc.—could be prevented. In 2016, North Korea declared that it had successfully conducted its fourth and fifth nuclear test which led the UNSC to adopt resolution 2270 and 2321. The yields were much higher than the bomb US had dropped on Hiroshima. Undeterred, North Korea stepped up its missile launches in 2017 including Pukguksong-2, Hwasong-12, tested a new rocket engine that can be fitted to an ICBM, Hwasong-14 ICBM, in addition to the sixth nuclear test. After President Trump put North Korea back on the list of 'State Sponsors of Terrorism', North Korea successfully tested its Hwasong-15 in November 2017, a newly developed sophisticated ICBM that could deliver nuclear warheads anywhere in the United States. Despite growing sanctions, in 2017 alone, North Korea has conducted several missile launches and a major nuclear test. Since January 2017,

> UN and other countries' sanctions as well as promises of action from China have failed to rein in its nuclear programme. Less remarked upon, but perhaps more surprising, is that sanctions have also not had much effect on the North Korean economy.[26]

Where does North Korea find the Money?

Back in 2012, mainstream western media reported that the South Korean government estimated that Pyongyang spent around US$ 1.3 billion on its rocket programme in 2012.

> The two rockets launched this year (2012)—this week's mission and a failed attempt in April—cost US$ 600 million, while the launch site itself is estimated at US$ 400 million. Other related facilities add another US$ 300 million, according to an official from South Korea's Ministry of reunification.[27]

If these are reasonable estimates, then North Korea would have spent more than a couple of billion dollars in 2017 alone as it has launched missiles and conducted a major nuclear test. Hence, the estimates appear to be exaggerated, without an understanding of the real cost of production in North Korea. Unfortunately, realistic estimates of the costs involved in the North Korean missile and nuclear programmes as well as the expenditure on tests conducted are not available. Nevertheless, if not billions of dollars, North Korea must be spending hundreds of million dollars on these tests alone. Despite sanctions, how does North Korea sustain its economy, and allocate more funds for its nuclear and missile programmes? As has been pointed out in *The Economist*,

> In part this is because not all UN sanctions are meant to cripple the economy. Many are more narrowly targeted. Asset freezes and travel bans target individuals close to the regime; prohibiting the sale of military supplies is meant to hobble the army. But even those that are broad-based have not always been effective.[28]

More importantly, China and Russia have not allowed the US to have its way in getting through tough UNSC Resolutions that could really cripple the North Korean economy until recently. Moreover, since 1994 when the Clinton administration signed a Framework Agreement with North Korea, the US focus on North Korea has not been consistent, leading to many crisis situations, perceptions of progress, and stalemates. Even after the 2006 UN Resolution, while the focus has been mainly to deprive North Korea of funds, technology, and components to paralyse its WMD programmes, no serious efforts have been made towards the strict implementation of the UN Resolutions.

> The UN has only recently attempted to block North Korea's access to hard currency by capping the amount of coal the state can export, potentially depriving it of more than a quarter of its total export revenue. China, the buyer of 99 per cent of North Korea's reported coal sales, went further in February 2017, saying it would suspend all imports. Yet North Korean vessels have continued to dock at China's coal ports. And the North can earn foreign currency in other ways: using foreign agents as a front, the regime sells drugs, weapons and counterfeit goods. Mr Kim's government also earns more than $1 billion a year by forcibly sending labourers abroad.[29]

Whenever North Korean foreign trade is discussed, it is largely focused on its trade with China as it is assumed that China accounts for around 80 to 90 per cent of North Korean foreign trade. This may not be correct. For example, 'inter-Korean trade holds a unique place in South Korean trade data: South Korean government agencies do not consider inter-Korean trade as trade between two sovereign nations, and thus compile this trade data separately from South Korea's international trade data, and refer to 'inbound' and 'outbound' transactions with North Korea rather than imports and exports'.[30]

As may be seen from the table below, inter-Korean trade peaked at US$ 2.714 billion in 2015. Although most of these are imports and exports into and from the Kaesong Industrial Complex from South Korea, and the only benefit to North Korea was the salaries of over US$ 100 million paid to around 54,000 workers, these are not reflected in North Korean trade figures. In addition, South Korea has also provided humanitarian assistance of around US$ 3.05 billion to North Korea since 1995. These are obviously not reflected in any trade figures; but such assistance would have helped mitigate the impact of sanctions.

Figure 3: Inter-Korean Trade Volume by Year (Unit: US$ millions)

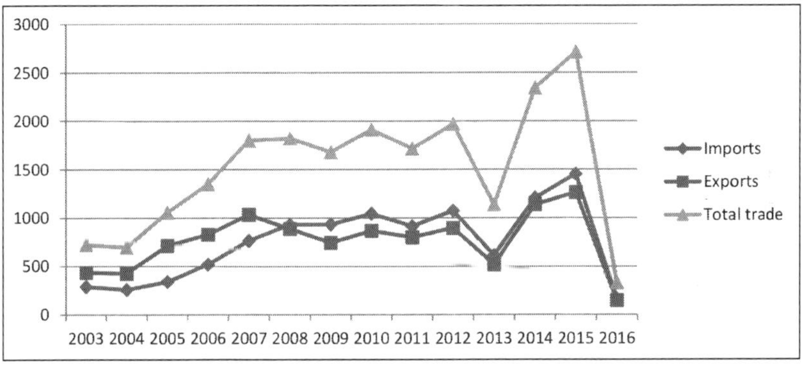

*The total for each year may differ from the actual total due to rounding errors.
Source: Trade data from Ministry of Unification; Graph prepared by the author.

As Marcus Noland explains,

> Because of budget cuts, or a desire to downplay North Korea's Middle East connections, KOTRA also ignores trade with many Middle Eastern countries like Algeria and Saudi Arabia, both of which report trade with North Korea to the UN statistical agencies. As a result, KOTRA greatly exaggerates the prominence of the trade partners that it does record, with important geopolitical implications.[31]

In July 2004, the Pakistani newspaper *Dawn* reported that, 'Pakistan's former Prime Minister Benazir Bhutto confirmed that Pakistan bought long-range missile technology from North Korea following a visit she made to Pyongyang in 1993'.[32] Pakistan allegedly continues its collaboration and trade with North Korea, particularly regarding weapons, including missiles. Similarly, Iran and North Korea supposedly have a long history of military cooperation and technology exchanges, and North Korea's missiles and nuclear trade with Iran could be important. As Samual Ramani points out in his article in *The Diplomat*, 'the collapse of the Soviet Union abruptly ended North Korea's access to subsidised oil in 1991. It forced North Korea to look to Iran, one of the few oil-rich countries with which it had diplomatic relations, as a potential energy source. Iran restructured North Korea's debt in 1987 and strengthened its energy linkages with the DPRK, in exchange for North Korean assistance in its missile technology and nuclear programmes.'[33]

In addition, trade with many countries in the Middle East, including Syria, Yemen and Libya as well as trade with countries in Africa could have contributed significantly to North Korean exports. It is interesting to note that, way back in 2000, during the fifth round of US-North Korean missile talks in Kuala Lumpur, North Korea is said to have repeated its demand for compensation, stated as US$ 1 billion per year, in return for halting missile exports. Even at that time, North Korea had a sizable weapons export capability. It could have only grown in recent years, with its improved and proven capabilities in these sectors.

Zeeshan Aleem refers to a recent report from the Institute for Science and International Security, a nonpartisan Washington based think tank focused on nuclear non-proliferation, and says that,

> A whopping 49 countries have violated UN Security Council sanctions imposed on North Korea between March 2014 and September 2017 ... Various countries have failed to observe different kinds of UN sanctions ... A number of them have participated in banned financial transactions and other business activities with North Korea, a group which includes Brazil, China, Egypt, Germany, India, Iran, Russia, Singapore, Sri Lanka, the United Arab Emirates, and others ... Some countries import goods and minerals from North Korea that they're not supposed to, a group that includes China, Egypt, France, Germany, India,

> Indonesia, Iran, Ireland, Mexico, Philippines, and Vietnam, and others ... Another group—which includes Brazil, China, Egypt, Greece, and Japan—has helped North Korea with the tricky business of shipping materials in and out of its country illicitly ... And the fourth major group highlighted is countries that have military ties with North Korea—participating in arms trading or military training. These tended to be poorer countries, including Angola, Cuba, the Democratic Republic of the Congo, Eritrea, Mozambique, Tanzania, Myanmar, and Syria.[34]

Hence, it would be reasonable to assume that North Korea continues to have diverse trading relationships with many countries, and a lot of trade remains unreported. Moreover, there is no doubt that the majority of North Korea's trade remains accounted for by China, and it is not in China's interests to seriously cripple the North Korean economy.

Figure 4: North Korea-China Trade, 2004–2014

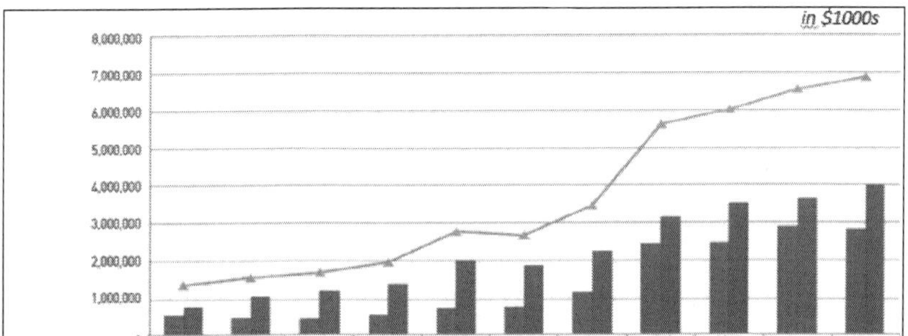

		2004	2005	2006	2007	2008	2009	2010	2011	2012	2013	2014
Exports	수출	585,703	499,157	467,718	581,521	754,046	793,048	1,187,861	2,464,188	2,484,699	2,913,624	2,841,476
Imports	수입	799,503	1,081,184	1,231,886	1,392,453	2,033,233	1,887,686	2,277,816	3,165,181	3,527,843	3,632,909	4,022,515
Total	수출입계	1,385,206	1,580,341	1,699,604	1,973,974	2,787,279	2,680,734	3,465,677	5,629,369	6,012,542	6,546,533	6,863,991

자료원: GTA

Source: 'North Korea Economy Watch', Archive for the 'Korea Trade-Investment Promotion Agency (KOTRA)' Category [35]

China's carrying out of sanctions is watched as an important pointer of Beijing's level of support on denuclearisation. Yun Sun, Co-Director of the East Asia Program and Director of the China Program at the Stimson Center, argues that, according to Chinese official statistics on trade,

> UN sanctions on North Korean exports do not appear to have been eased. According to the Chinese Customs, Sino-DPRK trade in the first half of 2018 was 7 billion RMB, down 59 per cent from the same period in 2017, including a decrease in Chinese exports to North Korea of 43 per cent, or 6.38 billion RMB; and a decrease in imports from North Korea of 88.7 per cent, or 690 million RMB. The same set of data also suggests that Chinese imports from North Korea have been in decline for 10 consecutive months since 2017.[36]

The Midterm Report of the Panel of Experts, established pursuant to UNSC Resolution 2345, 2017, was circulated by the Security Council in September 2017. In its summary, the Report categorically stated that,

> the Democratic People's Republic of Korea has made significant technological advances in its weapons of mass destruction capability in defiance of the most comprehensive and targeted sanctions regime in United Nations history ... The country also continues to flout the arms embargo and robust financial and sectoral sanctions, showing that as the sanctions regime expands, so does the scope of evasion ... The Democratic People's Republic of Korea continues to violate the financial sanctions by stationing agents abroad to execute financial transactions on behalf of national entities. Financial institutions in numerous member states wittingly and unwittingly have provided correspondent banking services to front companies and individuals of the Democratic People's Republic of Korea engaged in prohibited activities ... Involvement of diplomatic personnel of the Democratic People's Republic of Korea in commercial activities and the leasing of embassy property generate substantial revenue and are aided by multiple deceptive financial practices ... The Democratic People's Republic of Korea continued to violate sectoral sanctions through the export of almost all of the commodities prohibited in the resolutions, generating at least $ 270 million in revenue during the reporting period. Following China's

> suspension of coal imports from the country in February 2017, the Democratic People's Republic of Korea has been rerouting coal to other member states including Malaysia and Vietnam, and has shipped coal through third countries ... The Democratic People's Republic of Korea, led by its Maritime Administration Bureau, continued to hone its evasion tactics as member states took action to reduce the number of the country's vessels under foreign flags. This has also led to an increase of Democratic People's Republic of Korea-flagged vessels, many of which are formally owned or operated by foreign companies in violation of the resolutions.[37]

It is evident that the UNSC sanctions, starting from 2006 till date, have failed to achieve intended objectives. 'Lax enforcement of the sanctions regime coupled with the country's evolving evasion techniques are undermining the goals of the resolutions that the Democratic People's Republic of Korea abandon all weapons of mass destruction and cease all related programmes and activities'.[38] The North Korean economy has continued to grow, subject to the normal impact of drop in international prices of certain commodities involved, and global economic trends. In fact, the UNSC sanctions on North Korea's appear to be counter-productive as the speed of developments related to missile and nuclear programmes have gained greater momentum during this period.

Sanctions rarely succeed in forcing a sovereign country to abandon the pursuit of its objectives that are not acceptable to some members of the international community. The US and its allies still believe that UNSC sanctions are the main option to deal with North Korea, despite the fact that the country has defied earlier sanctions, and its missile and nuclear programmes have only gathered greater momentum. For sanctions to have a chance to succeed, it is essential that all the permanent members of the Security Council should share the main objectives of imposing such sanctions. They should have the commitment, urgency, and sincerity in implementing the UNSC resolutions and more. Implementing the sanctions should be in the interests of each of these member countries.

In the case of North Korea, the US has maintained sanctions for decades without being able to restrain North Korea from pursuing its objectives of achieving nuclear and missile capabilities to reach the American mainland. For decades, North Korea had the potential to achieve these, but the US had assumed that either persuasion or threat of massive force could stop, or indefinitely delay, North Korean goals. However now, it has become a national security priority for the US as Kim Jong-un has demonstrated the capabilities of targeting continental US.

President Trump believes that China has the ability to strictly enforce all UN resolutions and also cut off trade completely with North Korea, thus forcing it to abandon its nuclear ambitions. But, for China, North Korean missiles and nuclear weapons are not top priority. The Chinese are more worried about instability in North Korea, and the resultant possibility of the collapse of the North Korean regime. This could lead to millions of refugees entering China, the installation in Pyongyang of a puppet regime supportive of the US, leading to the real possibility of the US military at its borders. As North Korea has nuclear weapons, the possibility of these falling into the wrong hands, or even an accidental nuclear incident, could cause catastrophic problems for the region, including parts of China bordering North Korea. Hence, it is unrealistic to assume that China will do anything that could grievously hurt the North Korean economy, or bring so much pressure on Kim Jong-un that it could destabilise the country. That is the reason why China has ensured the watering down of the sanctions each time the US has proposed stronger measures against North Korea. Why would China help the US on North Korea if it resulted in serious consequences to itself? China would go to a certain extent to abide by UN sanctions; however, despite US pressure, it would not go beyond the tipping point that could destabilise the regime. China needs to protect North Korea to protect its own interests.

In 2017, President Donald Trump announced a new Presidential Executive Order empowering the US Department of the Treasury to impose additional sanctions on individuals and entities that do business with North Korea. The US believes that its sanctions campaign on the Iranian nuclear programme through secondary sanctions have forced Iran to agree to give up its nuclear programme. The US Treasury Department has imposed sanctions on a Chinese bank for allegedly laundering money for North Korea. However, North Korea cannot be compared to Iran. China has a greater stake in maintaining stability and economic viability in North Korea. The imposition of secondary sanctions on a large scale on Chinese entities are likely to trigger retaliatory measures that would not be in the interest of the US. More importantly, even if one assumes hypothetically that China agrees to use all its influence and threat to force North Korea to give up its nuclear programme, it is unlikely that North Korea would accede to China's wishes. North Korea has learnt from what happened in Iraq, Libya, and other countries. It is evident that more than a decade of UN sanctions, along with sanctions imposed by the US, Japan, and South Korea, has failed to achieve the intended objectives in the case of North Korea. Further sanctions, however comprehensive, strong, and specific are unlikely to force North Korea to give up its nuclear capabilities.

As Mimura points out,

> North Koreans tell me their country is safe because they have nuclear weapons. They point to Libya, Iraq and Ukraine as countries that had nuclear programmes, gave them up, and were then attacked by either the US or Russia. They say the DPRK made the right decision to stick with developing nukes. And now they have them. And now that their country is demonstrating the means to deliver those weapons wherever they want, including Washington, they believe the DPRK will be safe from American attack ... Since I started studying North Korea, in the 1980s, and made my first visit there in 1996, my conclusion is [that] the US has played an important role in helping the Kim family stay in power. When the outside world threatens the North, it makes the DPRK stronger. The people rally and come together to find a way to confront the threat—including the threat of sanctions.[39]

Nuclear weapons are considered vital not only for the survival of North Korea but more importantly for the survival of Kim Jong-un's regime. People are willing to suffer and rally behind the regime as long as they believe their leaders retain these weapons to protect the sovereignty of their country. This is where lies the challenge for the US. The US needs to understand this mindset. For long, the US wanted North Korea to renounce nuclear weapons as a precondition for talks. Chinese president Xi Jinping and Russian President Putin have made a 'freeze for freeze' proposal wherein a dialogue could begin with North Korea if it agrees to freeze its nuclear programme and if the US agrees to freeze its annual joint military exercises with South Korea. However, this has not been acceptable to the US. As US Secretary of State, Rex Tillerson, has insisted, mere 'freezing North Korea's nuclear program is unacceptable because Pyongyang's capabilities have already progressed too much and must be rolled back'.[40]

The US considers North Korea as a national security threat. Apart from its nuclear and missile capabilities, North Korea's cyber-attack capabilities are believed to be far superior to those of South Korea. 'In September 2016, North Korean intelligence services stole a huge batch of classified US and South Korean military plans—including a plan to assassinate North Korea's dictator Kim Jong-un and other top government officials'.[41] Apart from this, the hacking of banks, WannaCry ransom-ware, etc., have been attributed to North Korean sources. North Korea may even have the ability to disrupt the economy and security systems in South Korea, and even in the US, with cyber stealth capabilities and deniability.

While the situation remains grave, this is not the first time the US has faced such a situation with North Korea. For decades, the US has tried to end North Korea's nuclear and missile development programmes by imposing wide-ranging sanctions, through negotiations, by providing aid, by enlisting the support of China and Russia, and even by threatening to attack its nuclear and missile facilities. In June 1994, it is believed that the US had finalised its plans to attack the nuclear reactor at Yongbyon to prevent North

Korea fulfil its threat of going nuclear. Any such attack would have resulted in North Korean retaliation on South Korea, and a war in the Peninsula resulting in huge loss of life and destruction. The crisis was averted with the help of an 'Agreed Framework' signed wherein North Korea agreed to freeze and, in due course, dismantle its nuclear programme; and, the US agreed to provide fuel oil, light water reactors, and the normalisation of relations. But, the lack of trust between the two, and the differing strategic importance of North Korea to China, Russia, and the US have allowed North Korea to relentlessly pursue its WMD programmes.

The option of imposing comprehensive and targeted sanctions has not fully worked. If the sanctions are to be effective, then the sanctions regime monitoring system should become stronger, and all member countries should be willing to implement the sanctions in the right spirit. However, North Korea has diverse relationship with many countries that have their own interests and do not necessarily share the objectives of the US. In fact, Russia, China, and even perhaps South Korea, may not be interested in actually implementing sanctions that could lead to the collapse of the North Korean economy. That may not be in their best interests. It may not be difficult for President Trump to perceive that China is not doing what he thinks it should do on the strict implementation of sanctions. But, the US also realises that China is the only country that could possibly influence North Korea. The situation is, to some extent, comparable to Afghanistan where the US knows that Pakistan—which claims to fight alongside—has actually given a safe haven to terrorists. However, the US has no option but to depend on Pakistan as that is the only country that can be effective in Afghanistan if it genuinely wants to. Similarly, the US has no other option than to depend on China despite its ambiguous behaviour.

As 2017 drew to a close, the US and its allies continued to face a crisis situation on North Korea. The strongest military power in the world was unable to dictate its terms to North Korea. Despite the chest thumping rhetoric of 'Fire and Fury', the US understood that any military option could lead to millions of deaths, and hence, it started slowly stepping back. Stopping the rhetoric was also essential to avoid any untoward incident because of misunderstanding on either side. Despite some of the hardliners calling for strong action, then US Secretary of State, Rex Tillerson, wisely stated that the US was ready for talks with North Korea without any preconditions.

By this time, North Korea had demonstrated its capabilities in developing miniaturised nuclear weapons and ICBMs that could reach US territory. It could take a break from further testing. More importantly, while earlier UN sanctions could not achieve their objectives, the latest round of sanctions, if enforced strictly, could deprive North Korea of large funds by not allowing the export of its coal and textiles. Perhaps, considering all these factors, North Korea's leader Kim Jong-un, in his New Year's speech for 2018, signalled the possibility of sending athletes to the 2018 Winter Olympics in Pyeongchang in South Korea. South Korea seized the opportunity, and inter-Korean meetings were held swiftly. North and South Korean athletes marched together at the Olympics opening ceremony in February 2018. This not only eased tensions but enhanced the stature of Kim Jong-un and the possibility of a meaningful dialogue to resolve the crisis. Inter-Korean meetings continued, and three inter-Korean summits soon became a reality in 2018 when Kim Jong-un and Moon Jae-in met. Both leaders pledged to (i) work towards the denuclearisation of the Korean Peninsula; (ii) convert the Korean Armistice Agreement into a full peace treaty; and (iii) end hostile activities between the two nations. The first inter-Korea summit paved the way for the historic summit between Kim Jong-un and President Donald Trump in June.

In June 12, 2018, the US President Donald Trump and Chairman Kim Jong-un of North Korea created history by holding a summit meeting in Singapore. Since the creation of North Korea, no sitting President of the US had met the North Korean counterpart. After the summit, President Trump tweeted that there was no longer a nuclear threat from North Korea, and that his meeting with Kim Jong-un was an interesting and very positive experience. Critics accused President Trump of giving away major concessions to the

North Korean leader without getting anything in return. They claimed that: (i) the very fact of the US President holding a summit with a repressive dictator was itself a great victory for Kim Jong-un, and it gave legitimacy to the North Korean regime; (ii) by claiming that there is no longer a nuclear threat from North Korea, President Trump implicitly acknowledged that North Korea was a nuclear power; (iii) President Trump made a huge concession of suspending joint military exercises with South Korea; (iv) President Trump agreed to provide security guarantees to North Korea, and ignored serious human rights violations by Kim Jong-un's regime; and (v) President Trump did not extract any pledge from Kim Jong-un about the unilateral dismantling of the nuclear programme, and Kim Jong-un merely reaffirmed his commitment for the denuclearisation of the Korean Peninsula. This would be a long drawn process given the complex nature of the issues as witnessed in the Hanoi Summit. Much will depend on confidence building measures and various other concessions from the US. In fact, all the criticism heaped against President Trump appears valid. Only a few months ago, Trump had called Kim Jong-un the crazy 'little rocket man', and had threatened to launch 'fire and fury' to destroy North Korea completely. A war due to misreading of the situation or provocation was a real possibility.

Why did President Trump make a u-turn, and issued a vague joint statement without specific commitments from Kim Jong-un? Did he commit a grave mistake, and sacrifice US interests? The answer is no. He had the courage to do something really practical under the current circumstances. He knew that the comprehensive and targeted UN sanctions have not been very effective in weakening Kim Jong-un's regime or halt North Korea's nuclear programme. He seems to have understood that there is no military solution possible. Even when North Korea was not a nuclear power, any military option could have resulted in the loss of millions of lives, including thousands of American soldiers stationed in South Korea. Now that North Korea has demonstrated its ability to reach even US territory, the option of military force is no more feasible. Thus, by agreeing to engage

Kim Jong-un in talks, President Trump seems to have eliminated the possibility of an accidental war due to misunderstanding or provocation. Being a businessman, President Trump has talked of the natural resources and cheap labour available in North Korea and feels that outside investment can create profitable business ventures. If this can happen, then the people of North Korea will slowly get exposed to the outside world. The more the North Korean economy gets integrated into the world economy, the prospect of North Korea behaving in any irrational manner gets reduced, and President Trump's decision to engage North Korea would prove to be right. President Clinton had tried it in 1994 when he entered into a Framework Agreement with North Korea but due to criticism within his own country and lack of mutual trust, the agreement was abandoned. It is hoped that this time President Trump and his successors will continue the engagement.

Notes

1. S/2017/742 - 'Midterm report of the Panel of Experts established pursuant to resolution 1874', United Nations Security Council, September 5 2017 at http://undocs.org/S/2017/742, accessed on October 2, 2018.
2. Christopher Woody, 'US-North Korea tensions are ramping up, but the horrors of the Korean War are alive and well', Business Insider Australia, August 2, 2017 at https://www.businessinsider.in/US-North-Korea-tensions-are-ramping-up-but-the-horrors-of-the-Korean-War-are-alive-and-well/articleshow/59871255.cms, accessed on October 2, 2018.
3. An Interview with Generals Curtis E. LeMay, Leon W. Johnson, David A. Burchinal, and Jack J. Catton, *Strategic Air Warfare*, Office of Air Force History United States Air Force, Washington DC., 1988 at https://media.defense.gov/2010/Sep/29/2001329790/-1/-1/0/AFD-100929-052.pdf, accessed on October 2, 2018.
4. Charles K. Armstrong, 'The Destruction and Reconstruction of North Korea, 1950–1960', *The Asia-Pacific Journal: Japan Focus* at http://apjjf.org/-Charles-K.-Armstrong/3460/article.html, accessed on October 2, 2018.
5. Max Fisher, 'Americans have forgotten what we did to North Korea', Vox, August 3, 2015 at https://www.vox.com/2015/8/3/9089913/north-korea-us-war-crime, accessed on October 2, 2018.
6. US President Donald Trump's Address at the 72nd United Nations General Assembly at UN headquarters in New York, USA, YouTube, September

19, 2017 at https://www.youtube.com/watch?v=iUPcEYik2Oc, accessed on October 2, 2018.

7. Andrea Matles Savada (ed.), *North Korea: A Country Study*, GPO for the Library of Congress, Washington DC, 1993 at http://countrystudies.us/north-korea/48.htm, accessed on October 2, 2018.
8. 'The Economy of North Korea', Wikipedia at https://en.wikipedia.org/wiki/Economy_of_North_Korea#Crisis_and_famine, accessed on October 2, 2018.
9. Jeff Baron, 'What if Sanctions Brought North Korea to the Brink? Well, in 1941', 38 North, September 7, 2017 at http://www.38north.org/2017/09/jbaron090717/, accessed on October 2, 2018.
10. 'Best guesses: How to measure North Korea's economy, finance and economics', *The Economist*, February 9, 2017 at https://www.economist.com/finance-and-economics/2017/02/09/how-to-measure-north-koreas-economy, accessed on October 2, 2018.
11. Hyung-Min Joo, 'Underground Markets in North Korea', September 4, 2009, APSA 2009 Toronto Meeting Paper at https://ssrn.com/abstract=1452129, accessed on October 2, 2018.
12. David Volodzko, 'North Korea's Secret Weapon? Economic Growth: Rising living standards will limit the effect of sanctions', Bloomberg, September 15, 2017 at https://www.bloomberg.com/view/articles/2017-09-14/north-korea-s-secret-weapon-economic-growth, accessed on October 2, 2018.
13. Frank Ruediger, 'Economic Sanctions and the Nuclear Issue: Lessons From North Korean Trade', 38 North, September 18, 2017 at https://www.38north.org/2017/09/rfrank091817/, accessed on October 2, 2018.
14. Ibid.
15. 'N. Korea's per capita income unchanged at $1,179 last year: 2016/12/15', Yonhap News Agency at http://english.yonhapnews.co.kr/northkorea/2016/12/15/45/0401000000AEN20161215006500320F.html, accessed on October 2, 2018.
16. BOK cautions that, the statistics are based on estimates using methodologies applied to gauge South Korea's own economy. Thus, it is not desirable to directly compare this data with that of other foreign nations.
17. Archive for the 'Bank of Korea' Category at http://www.nkeconwatch.com/category/organizaitons/bank-of-korea/, accessed on October 2, 2018.
18. On PPP GDP data, the CIA Fact Book cautions that the data shown are derived from purchasing power parity (PPP) GDP estimates for North Korea that were made by Angus Maddison in a study conducted for the OECD; his figure for 1999 was extrapolated to 2015 using estimated real growth rates for North Korea's GDP and an inflation factor based on the US GDP deflator; the results were rounded to the nearest $ 10 billion.

19. CIA, 'The World Factbook' at https://www.cia.gov/library/publications/the-world-factbook/geos/kn.html, accessed on October 2, 2018.
20. Marcus Noland, 'The Black Hole of North Korea', *Foreign Policy*, March 7, 2012 at http://foreignpolicy.com/2012/03/07/the-black-hole-of-north-korea/, accessed on October 2, 2018.
21. Security Council Condemns Nuclear Test by Democratic People's Republic of Korea, unanimously adopting resolution 1718', 2006, UN Security Council Press release SC/8853, October 14, 2006 at https://www.un.org/press/en/2006/sc8853.doc.htm, accessed on October 2, 2018.
22. Security Council, Acting Unanimously, Condemns in Strongest Terms Democratic People's Republic of Korea Nuclear Test, Toughens Sanctions, UN Security Council Press release SC/9679, June 12, 2009 at https://www.un.org/press/en/2009/sc9679.doc.htm, accessed on October 2, 2018.
23. 'North Korea nuclear tests: What did they achieve?' BBC News, September 3, 2017 at http://www.bbc.com/news/world-asia-17823706, accessed on October 2, 2018.
24. 'Security Council Condemns Use of Ballistic Missile Technology in Launch by Democratic People's Republic of Korea', in Resolution 2087, Security Council, SC/10891, January 22, 2013 at https://www.un.org/press/en/2013/sc10891.doc.htm, accessed on October 2, 2018.
25. 'Security Council Strengthens Sanctions on Democratic People's Republic of Korea', in Response to 12 February Nuclear Test, Security Council, SC/10934-7 March 2013 at https://www.un.org/press/en/2013/sc10934.doc.htm, accessed on October 2, 2018.
26. 'Why the North Korean economy is growing: Despite sanctions, Kim Jong-un's regime continues to do business', *The Economist*, June 27, 2017 at https://www.economist.com/the-economist-explains/2017/06/27/why-the-north-korean-economy-is-growing, accessed on October 2, 2018.
27. Inocencio Ramy, 'North Korea's rocket launches cost $1.3 billion', CNN, December 12, 2012 at https://edition.cnn.com/2012/12/12/business/north-korea-rocket-cost/index.html, accessed on October 2, 2018.
28. *The Economist*, note 26.
29. Ibid.
30. 'North Korea in the World', The National Committee of North Korea, East West Centre at https://www.northkoreaintheworld.org/inter-korean/inter-korean-trade, accessed on October 2, 2018.
31. Marcus Noland, 'The Black Hole of North Korea: What economists can't tell you about the most isolated country on Earth', *Foreign Policy*, March 7, 2012 at https://foreignpolicy.com/2012/03/07/the-black-hole-of-north-korea/, accessed on October 2, 2018.

32. 'Missile technology bought from N. Korea: Benazir', *Dawn*, July 19, 2004 at https://www.dawn.com/news/364962, accessed on October 2, 2018.
33. Samuel Ramani, 'The Iran-North Korea Connection', *The Diplomat*, April 20, 2016 at https://thediplomat.com/2016/04/the-iran-north-korea-connection/, accessed on October 2, 2018.
34. 'Here's why North Korea's economy is able to survive sanction after sanction', Vox, December 7, 2017 at https://www.vox.com/world/2017/12/7/16745692/north-korea-sanctions-nuclear-economy, accessed on October 2, 2018.
35. 'North Korea Economy Watch, Archive for the 'Korea Trade-Investment Promotion Agency (KOTRA)' Category, 38 North at http://www.nkeconwatch.com/category/organizaitons/korea-trade-investment-promotion-agency-kotra/, accessed on October 2, 2018.
36. Yun Sun, 'The State of Play in Sino-DPRK Relations', 38 North, September 5, 2018 at https://www.38north.org/2018/09/ysun090518/, accessed on October 2, 2018.
37. 'UN midterm report on UNSC Resolution 2345', United Nations Security Council, September 5, 2017 at http://www.un.org/ga/search/view_doc.asp?symbol=S/2018/171, accessed on October 2, 2018.
38. Ibid.
39. Jeff Baron, note 9.
40. Rex Tillerson, 'Freezing N. Korea's nuclear program unacceptable', Yonhap News Agency, July 7, 2017.
41. Kelsey Atherton, 'How North Korean hackers stole 235 gigabytes of classified US and South Korean military plans: North Korea's impressive cyber capabilities', Vox, October 13, 2017 at https://www.vox.com/world/2017/10/13/16465882/north-korea-cyber-attack-capability-us-military, accessed on October 2, 2018.

6. Demilitarized Zone: Legacy of Status Quo

G.G. Dwivedi

The Korean Peninsula, given its geographic location has been the scene of great power rivalry as various stake holders have vied for influence in Northeast Asia. Since late nineteenth century, the Peninsula has been the focal point of confrontation and competition among—China, Japan, Russia and the US. No other region in the world assumed such symbolic importance to these countries as the Korean Peninsula. Prevailing political complexities and strategic expediencies are the fallout of numerous historic events. In earlier times, Korean Peninsula was known as Chosun—the land of morning calm. The Peninsula became a prize for China, Japan and Russia as any one of the trio could pose threat to each other by virtue of its domination. In 1910, Japan annexed Korea and made it integral part till 1945.[1]

At the 1943 Cairo Conference, President Roosevelt and Chiang kai-shek promised unity and independence of Korea. Later, at the Potsdam Conference, promise was reaffirmed as Russia had also adhered to the declaration. During the World War II, in the Pacific Theatre, there was a need for a demarcation line between US and USSR. The line approved was 38th Parallel. At the end of War, the Soviet forces moved into North Korea and received surrender of Japanese forces, stopping on reaching the arbitrary alignment—38th Parallel. Americans on the other hand landed at Inchon on September 8, 1945 and received Japanese surrender the next day. The boundary was respected by both sides. With the creation of Democratic People's Republic of Korea (North Korea) and Republic of Korea (South Korea) in 1948, the 38th Parallel became the de facto border.

Both Korea were heavily dependent upon their respective sponsor states. Consequently, ideological differences soon erupted and sanctity of the boundary was eventually lost. Fanatic communism and liberal democracy were two incompatibles for the national reconciliation and Korean unification. The 38th Parallel soon turned into an iron curtain. The division had no geographical or economical basis as North Korea was industrialised and South Korea was primarily agrarian. The tension began to build up across the Peninsula, giving rise to the fear of another global confrontation.

There was wide spread discontentment in the US on the promulgation of Truman administration 'containment policy'; which did not seek to destroy Communism but merely check its expansion. Defence of Europe being on the higher priority vis-à-vis Far East Asia coupled with the drive to cut the military expenditure resulted in the pulling out of American forces from Korean Peninsula. Strategic weakness of US policy in the region alongside political and economic chaos in South Korea was fully exploited by the North Korean leadership. South Korean leader Rhee's rhetorical statements of overrunning Kim Il-sung's North Korea in a fortnight were provocations enough for Pyongyang to plan for war. North Korea launched blitzkrieg offensive in June 1950, achieving absolute surprise. Collapse of Rhee's Republic of Korean Army (ROKA) in the face of speedy manoeuvre by North Korean People's Army (NKPA) completely upset the American calculations. It was only on the US intervention that combined UN Forces under General MacArthur were able to stall the NKPA around Pusan—a port at the southern tip of the Peninsula, by end July 1950.

General MacArthur was able to turn the tide by executing a strategic master stroke—the amphibious landing at Inchon in September 1950. Barely a month later, towards end October, the UN Forces were closing on to Yalu River as part of MacArthur's 'Home by Christmas Offensive'. Fearing aggression against the mainland by the US led UN Forces in conjunction with Chiang Kai-shek's Army prompted Mao Zedong to jump into the fray and thwart American design. The Chinese Communist Forces (CCF) Under Marshal Peng Dai Hui launched preemptive offensive in October 1950, inflicting crushing defeat on the UN Forces, driving them back to the 38th Parallel by the beginning of January 1951.

The crucial battles of Wonju and Chipyong-ni in February 1951 proved to be a turning point; the UN Forces delivering a devastating blow to the CCF. Having suffered losses with better part of fourteen divisions destroyed, Marshal Peng realised that opportunity to achieve a quick and decisive victory over next few months had slipped away. When he explained to Mao that Korean War could not be won any time soon, the latter gave clear instructions for conducting the war to resist US aggression and assist Korea; 'win a quick victory if you can—if you can't, win a slow one'.[2] Mao was prepared for long war evident from his communication to Stalin sometime around early June 1951; 'the position on the frontline in June—our forces will be comparatively weaker, in July will be stronger than June and in August even stronger-ready to make a stronger blow to the enemy'.[3]

By the mid-1951, feelers of Armistice were in the air. However, South Korean President Rhee was vehemently opposed to any peace overtures. Around mid-July, the Communists launched a major offensive against South Korean ROK II Corps in the area of Kumsong, to give 'bloody nose' to Rhee. During the Kumsong battle, the South Korean forces suffered over ten thousand casualties and dealt serious blow to Rhee's prestige.

To inflict maximum punishment on the Communist armies and pressurise its leadership to the negotiation table, the UN Forces launched air bombing campaign from April to June 1951. The strategic bombing proved to be effective in interdicting the North Korean rail and road networks, which imposed devastating constraint on the Chinese logistics. With front virtually static and under constant air attacks, the Chinese were forced to go underground. Thus tunnels, trenches and bunkers became the backbone of Communist ability to sustain operations. By the end of War, Chinese had built 1250 km of tunnels; virtually underground cities. While the air campaign did halt Chinese advance and contributed to the stalemate, it did not lead to the collapse of Communist will and pressurise China into settlement.[4]

The chapter provides insight into the establishment Demilitarized Zone (DMZ), its structural layout, role during and after the Cold War, efficacy as 'zone of peace' and quest of strategic equilibrium, concluding with brief prognosis.

Demilitarized Zone (DMZ)

Prelude to Armistice: MacArthur's bold plan to end the prevailing impasse by laying a radioactive belt around the narrow neck of Korean Peninsula was rejected by the Truman administration. With neither side making any tangible gains, on international intervention belligerents opted to negotiate for a favourable Armistice Agreement based on the 'status quo' partition of Korea. The public opinion in the US was strongly in favour of 'stalemated peace' than 'stalemated war'. The accepted mutually agreed principle by both sides was that the demarcation line should generally follow the battle line.

Initial meeting for the Armistice talks was held in July 1951 at Kaesong—the ancient capital city during Koryo Dynasty. As the town had large presence of North Korean and the Chinese soldiers, the venue was shifted to Panmunjom. Following marathon talks, the Armistice Agreement was signed on July 27, 1953. It was the first major 'hot war' in the Cold War era which resolved nothing, culminating in a stalemate. Ironically, the opposing forces stood facing each other, around the same positions they held three years back.

Operational Imperatives: As a sequel to the Armistice Agreement, DMZ was created, whereby each side agreed to pull back by two km from the frontline, creating a buffer zone of four km wide and 250 km long. The Military Demarcation Line (MDL) which runs through the centre of the DMZ indicates where the front was when agreement was signed. The DMZ intersects but does not follow the 38th Parallel—the de facto border before the war. The MDL broadly divides the Korean Peninsula in two halves. The North Limit Line (NLL), maritime demarcation line between the two Koreas in the Yellow Sea remains disputed.

In the absence of formal peace agreement, the two sides while in a theoretical stalemate, technically still remain at war. Given the hostile environment, both sides maintain large number of troops to guard against potential aggression, making it one of the most fortified defense lines in the world. Even the coast line and the islands on both sides of NLL are also heavily militarised. While the quantum of force levels and the weapon systems allowed to be deployed as per the Armistice Agreement have been specified, the adversaries maintain an offensive posture. The defences are based on series of positions held by company/platoon size subunits. Both sides patrol the areas and are expected to maintain the sanctity of the MDL. Post the Korean War, due to the parity of forces; the opponents have remained largely constrained, obviating a major confrontation. Hence, even six and half decades on, the DMZ continues to define the legacy of 'status quo' and 'state of equilibrium', defying any quest for rebalancing.

At Panmunjom, located near the western coast in the DMZ, Joint Security Area (JSA) has been designated. It is the only connection between the opposing sides astride the MDL. Interestingly, the MDL runs through conference room, across the central table where North Koreans and United Nations Command (primarily Americans and South Koreans) meet face to face. Here the soldiers from the two sides stand guard, at a hand shake distance.[5] JSA is the location where all the meetings since 1953 have been held. It has large number of building including the North Korean Phanmun Hall and South Korean Freedom House.

The North Korean side of the DMZ acts as a defence line against any invasion by South Korea. It also serves the functions akin to the erstwhile Berlin Wall to check any defection. Behind the wire fence which runs along the MDL are buried strips of mines. As the Defence Attaché, one had the opportunity of visiting the forward posts of NKPA. The troops remain in 'hair trigger' readiness.[6] The Pyongyang-Panmunjom road-150 km in length, is an eight lanes highway with designated stretches designed to act as air strips for the jet fighters during hostilities. The highway cuts through more than dozen tunnels, which offer excellent hides for both combat assets and logistics installations.[7] Almost 60 per cent of the North Korean artillery is deployed with in few kilometres of the DMZ to act as deterrent against the South Korean invasion.[8] It also ensures shorter lines of communications and minimum vulnerability to the enemy's air. In case of hostilities breaking out, it is estimated that North Korea has the capability to fire around half a million shells in the first hour, thus causing heavy damage to the South Korean population centres in the vicinity of the DMZ. For undertaking a major offensive, North Korea is known to have two corridors—Chorwon and Minsan, both in the middle section of the DMZ. On the West, Onjin Peninsula offers viable defensive line.[9]

Towards South of the DML, there is a concrete wall which stretches over 240 km from east to west, 5-8 m high and 3-7 m wide. It is reinforced with the wire entanglement and weapon emplacements, acts as a launch pad for any Northward offensive. The US and South Korea deny the existence of wall, while acknowledging the anti-tank obstacle along certain sections of the DMZ. The front line is manned by the South Korean troops. For the operational security, there is additional buffer zone delineated as 'Civilian Control Line' (CCL) which runs at a distance 5-20 km from the Southern Limit Line of the DMZ. The 'Civil Control Zone' which acts as additional buffer zone is an essential operational necessity for the military to regulate entry of civilians in the area. It was first activated in February 1954. The whole estuary of Han river is deemed to be a 'neutral zone', off limits to civilian vessels and treated like rest of the DMZ. Only the military personnel are allowed within the DMZ. Ara Canal which was completed in 2012 connects Seoul to the Yellow Sea. It is capable of handling only the small boats.

Both Koreas maintain peace villages on their respective sides of the DMZ, in the visual range; Daeseong-dong in the South and

Kijong-dong in the North. These are administered under the terms of DMZ. As symbols of one-upmanship, the two sides resorted to 'flagpole war'. In 1980, South Korea erected a 98.4 m high flag pole in Daeseong-dong to fly its flag. North Korea responded by building 160 m high pole in Kijong-dong-fourth tallest in the world. From 1953 onwards the two sides indulged in the propaganda war through loudspeakers, mounted on various buildings. In 2004, both agreed to end the broadcast only to resume again in 2016. In 2014, the defectors from North Korea even used balloons as a propaganda tool, wherein they scattered anti-Pyongyang leaflets, DVDs and US dollar bills. After the April 27, 2018 historic Panmunjom Summit, both sides have dismantled the propaganda blaring loudspeakers; for decades these were the instruments to wage 'war of words', across the DMZ. Over the years, due to its natural isolation and inaccessibility, the DMZ has emerged as one of the most well preserved park in the temperate region.

Cold War and After: During the Cold War, DMZ was perceived to be the most dangerous flash point as 2 million troops could be involved in case of hostilities breaking out. Towards the early phase of Cold War, envisaged role of DMZ was to act as an instrument for political and economic containment of Communism rather than just a military defence line. Subsequently, by the mid-1970s, the role of DMZ got redefined, as the key concern was regional stability in the wake of tectonic geopolitical changes that were triggered due to the cascading effect of Sino-American rapprochement, Sino-Soviet split and increasing Sino-Vietnamese tension.

The Korean War continued to be waged as series of local actions along the DMZ, although the nature of conduct had changed drastically. There were sporadic incidences of incursion and violence astride the DMZ. On January 21, 1968, North Korea sent 31 commandos across the DMZ to assassinate South Korean President Park at his official residence the 'Blue House'. Two days later, after the failed assassination attempt, North Korean captured USS Pueblo along with crew, off its coast, while the ship was in the international waters. It was a grave provocation for

America which could have led full scale fighting on the Korean Peninsula.[10]

During the period 1953-99 due to the sporadic clashes, the figure of casualties suffered by the opposing sides stood over 500 South Korean, 50 American and 250 North Korean soldiers. Last major incidence was in 1997 when 14 North Korean soldiers crossed the DML, resulting in heavy gunfire exchange.[11] While almost one thousand people flee from North to South every year, few venture to escape across the heavily manned MDL. Over the past three years, four North Korean soldiers defected across the DMZ. The last defection was reported in November 2017 when a North Korean soldier identified as 24-year-old Oh Chong Song made a daring dash across the DMZ under the cover of heavy fog to South Korea, through the JSA in Panmunjom. He was shot several times by the North Korean border guards and received five bullet injuries.[12] It was reported as a glaring violation of the 1953—Armistice Agreement and even drew strong reaction from the human rights organisation.

North Korea had dug tunnels under the DMZ to be used for sneaking special force into South during the first stage of operations. To counter this menace, 'Tunnel Neutralisation Teams' (TNTs) composed of small complement of US soldiers attached to South Korean army engineers were created. The major role of the TNT was to provide intelligence to South Korean army engineers. Wherever tunnel location was assessed, water-well rigs were used to dig holes to approach the site. Such search operations were undertaken whenever there were reports of underground compressors or drilling sounds. In this process some 3400 holes had been dug along the 250 km long DMZ. Over a period, three such tunnels had been located. One of these has become major tourist attraction.

In the post-Cold War period, situation on the Peninsula has been marked by recurring crisis. President Bill Clinton termed DMZ as the scariest place on the earth. Throughout President Obama's tenure, North Korean nuclear programme was a consistent cause of concern. Successful launches of intermediate range ballistic missiles (IRBMs) and inter-continental ballistic missiles (ICBMs) coupled with nuclear tests enabled North Korea to gain a de facto status of a nuclear weapons power, which threatened to disturb the delicate strategic balance. Gideon Rachman in his book 'Easternization-Asia's Rise and America's Decline' has quoted Even Medeiros who steered Asia Policy during Obama Administration as saying; 'North Korea is a land of bad options'.[13] Washington's policies of 'sanctions and subsidies' gave an impression of half-hearted approach in shaping the regional security architecture.

Efficacy-'Zone of Peace': Chairman Kim Jong-un stepping across the MDL for a historic handshake with President Moon Jae-in on April 27, 2018, the first among the top most leaders from North marked a watershed moment in the destiny of the Korean Peninsula. It set the clock re-ticking at Panmunjom which stood still since 1953—with signing of the Armistice Agreement. It was well calculated strategic move by Pyongyang with multiple objectives; to weaken the US-South Korean alliance and to provide relief to North Korea's battered economy.

Kim commenced the 'path breaking summit meeting' with sweeping promise by stating; 'I came here to put an end to the history of confrontation'. The two leaders pledged to end the Korean War. The Panmunjom Declaration envisages cession of hostile acts against each other and complete denuclearisation i.e. nuclear free Korean Peninsula. Announcing the beginning of 'new age of peace' both leaders agreed to transform the fortified border into peace zone, besides transforming 'Northern Limit Line' (NLL) in the West Sea into 'maritime peace zone'.[14]

As a sequel to the Panmunjom Declaration, an 'Agreement on the Implementation' was reached in September 2018 between the two Koreas; specific to the Military domain, primarily to ease military tension on the Korean Peninsula. Some of the salient facets are summarised below:

- South and North Korea agreed to completely ease all hostile acts against each other in every domain. This included actions to refrain infiltration, cease various military exercises along the MDL, including the live fire drills. To avoid an accidental military clash, five-step procedure has been evolved and implemented from November 2018.

- To transform the DMZ into 'Zone of Peace', the two sides agreed to completely withdraw all Guard Posts (GPs) within one km from each other; the action is in progress. The two sides also agreed to demilitarise the 'Joint Security Area'. A pilot project of 'Inter-Korean Joint Operation' to recover remains, within the DMZ has also been agreed to.
- As part of the process to devise various confidence building measures, the two sides agreed to continue consultations regarding installation of direct communication lines between respective military officials, review composition of the military committees and have a mechanism in place to regularly monitor implementation of the Agreement.

Another etymological development which followed on the heels of Panmunjom meeting was the Singapore Summit between President Trump and Chairman Kim in June 2018. Here again, the two leaders committed to build lasting peace regime on the Peninsula through complete denuclearisation. President Trump went on to announce suspending the US-South Korea war games-even terming these provocative and reduction in the 28,500 American soldiers currently deployed in South Korea.[15]

Given the above developments, current profile of the DMZ is set for a makeover. Meaningful future dialogue will certainly result in reduction of tension across the MDL. However, the process is likely to be a long drawn one given the prevailing complexities. It will entail adopting the confidence building measures route which will encompass opening channels of communications both at the strategic and operational levels. For this, effective institutional mechanism will need to be put in place. All this will require massive political effort coupled with astute diplomacy.

Strategic Equilibrium

As a sequel to the recent developments, prevailing geopolitical realignments in Northeast Asia are in for a reset, thus disrupting the prevailing equilibrium. All the four key players in the region namely China, Japan, Russia and the US have vested interests and genuine security concerns. South Korea being the frontline state, Japan's geographic proximity and China which shares border with North Korea, are directly affected with the developments in the Peninsula. All three have high stakes in an event of sudden political upheaval in North Korea. For the US, as a Pacific power, retaining influence in the Korean Peninsula is vital for safeguarding its strategic interests.

Every stakeholder has different connotation of denuclearisation and unification, seeking to alter the status of DMZ to its advantage. China does not favour unified Korea as it will mean US military presence right on its border. China is also skeptical about South Korea getting too deeply entrenched in the US-led security framework. On the other hand, China is seen by the West as having considerable leverage to manipulate North Korea to serve its ends. Given the zero-sum mind set, President Putin believes that constructive engagement with Pyongyang provides Russia leverage to play effective role in brokering peace in the region.

Japan is wary about the prospects of a unified Korea as it will create another power centre in the Far East. Besides, Japan and South Korea, despite being democracies and US allies carry a past historic baggage. American allies in the East Asian region remain skeptical about its commitment to address their security concerns and are recrafting their military strategies. Given the divergent national interests and prevailing geopolitical labyrinth, it becomes extremely difficult for nations in the region to cooperate for a viable solution.

Post-Korean War, Northeast Asian security architecture presents a classic case of balance of power dynamics, where parity of military potential between the adversaries created a state of equilibrium. Any entente between the stakeholders will imply significant shift in the prevailing geostrategic equations, which will have direct bearing on the status of DMZ.

Conclusion

Despite the Armistice Agreement and two Koreas still being technically at war, DMZ's sanctity has remained inviolable; incidences of transgression and incursion notwithstanding. It has defined the state of status quo and consistently withstood the quest for strategic rebalancing. Over the years, the role of DMZ got redefined, from containment of Communism to the fulcrum of stability. Since assuming power, Kim Jong-un adopted a bold aggressive approach, continuation of his father's policy on an accelerated mode in a bid to seek security of his regime. He adopted a strategy of *byungjin* pursuing military and economic developments simultaneously. During his 2018—new year's address, Chairman Kim made unexpected reconciliatory overtures. This set the tone for hyper paced political developments paving way for three inter-Korea summits and the two historic Trump-Kim summits.

For the time being, status quo serves the interest of all the parties as every stakeholder shuns war. At no cost Chinese would want the North Korean regime to collapse or a unified Korea as an US ally. Ideally, over a period of time, Chinese leadership would like gradual disengagement of US from the Korean Peninsula and East Asia. Despite the thaw and positive developments, considering the number of imponderables, the road to peace is not given. The DMZ defines the state of status quo and stands as a symbol of strategic equilibrium in the region. A prerequisite to obviate any catastrophic situation is to curb repeat of the past failed policies. Managing environment through diplomacy stands out as the best option; while substantial progress towards resolution of the issue even in the distant future remains a remote possibility.

Notes

1. David Rees, *Korea the Limited War*, Nataraj Publishers, Dehra Dun, 1978.
2. Peng Dai Hui, *Memoirs of Chinese Marshal*, Foreign Languages Press, 1984.
3. Mao-Stalin, CWHIP Bulletin 'Cold War in Asia'-No 6/7, Winter 1995, June 13, 1951.

4. Sheila Miyoshi Jager, *Brothers at War: The Unending Conflict in Korea,* WW Norton & Company, 2013.
5. Personal visits to DMZ as Military Attaché in North Korea (1997-99).
6. Ibid.
7. Ibid.
8. Bradley K Martin, *Under Loving Care of Father Leader*, Thomas Dunne Books, 2004.
9. Ibid.
10. 'Seizure of USS Pueblo', *New York Times,* January 28, 1968.
11. Bloger Daniel, *Scenes from Unfinished War: Low Intensity in Korea 1966-69*, Diane Publishing Co., Paperback Publishing House, 1991.
12. Clapper James, 'Kim Jing-un is God of North Korea', The Daily Beast, June 1, 2018 at https://www.thedailybeast.com/james-clapper-kim-jong-un-is-a-god-in-north-korea, accessed on October 4, 2018.
13. Gideon Rachman, *Easternization: Asia's Rise and America's Decline, From Obama to Trump and Beyond*, Other Press, 2017.
14. 'Panmunjom Declaration for Peace, Prosperity and Unification of the Korean Peninsula', Reuters, April 27, 2018 at https://reuters.com/article/uk-northkorea-southkorea-summit-statemen/panjunjom-declaration-for-peace-prosperity-and-unification-of-the-korea-peninsual, accessed on July 15, 2018.
15. 'Trump-Kim Summit Agreement', CNBC, June 12, 2018 at https://www.cnbc.com/2018/06/12/full-text-of-the-trump-kim-summit-agreement.html, accessed on July 17, 2018.

PART II
Major Powers and the Korean Peninsula

7. The US Grand Strategy and Preference in Korean Peninsula

Namrata Goswami

On June 12, 2018, US President Donald Trump and North Korean Chairman Kim Jong-un held a summit in Singapore. It was the first time that a sitting US President has met with a North Korean leader.[1] This was followed by a second summit between Trump and Kim in Hanoi, Vietnam in February 2019.[2] On June 30, Trump made history by becoming the first sitting US President to cross over to the North Korean side of the Demilitarized Zone (DMZ) where he shook hands with Kim Jong-un.[3] US-North Korea relations have been fraught with hostilities, which include the Korean War, the withdrawal of North Korea from the Nuclear Non-Proliferation Treaty (NPT), and North Korea's testing of Intercontinental Ballistic Missiles (ICBMs), with capability to reach the US homeland. After cancelling the summit due to stated hostilities from North Korea end May, President Trump agreed to hold the summit again after Kim Jong-un sent him a personal letter offering assurances that he would dismantle the missiles that threatened the US homeland.[4] In a Joint Statement released after talks, both sides agreed to establish a peaceful US-North Korea relationship, especially geared towards establishing a stable regime in the Korean Peninsula.[5]

Critically, from the US perspective, North Korea committed to work towards the denuclearisation of the Korean Peninsula, and the repatriation of Prisoners of War (POW) from the War, a topic of great emotional resonance within American society.[6] Just prior to the summit, Pyongyang dismantled its nuclear test site in the mountainous north eastern region of Punggye-ri. It was an action that could be perceived as signalling to President Trump of Kim Jong-un's commitment to denuclearisation.[7] In his press conference after the June 12, summit, President Trump, in a gesture of peace, pledged to halt military exercises with South Korea,[8] which were being viewed by North Korea as a 'threat of invasion' into its homeland.[9] Soon after he landed in the US, President Trump tweeted, 'Just landed—a long trip, but everybody can now feel much safer than the day I took office. There is no longer a Nuclear Threat from North Korea.'[10]

The June 12 summit has started a long-term process of building US-North Korea relations to be guided by the Panmunjom Declaration of April 2018. The Declaration specifies that both countries (North and South Korea) resolve to address the military tensions in the Korean Peninsula, bring an end to the 'unnatural armistice', carry out disarmament in a phased manner, and conduct trilateral as well as quadrilateral meetings involving the two Koreas, and the US and China to establish peace.[11] Both Koreas re-affirmed their commitment to a non-aggression agreement that removes the 'use of force' option from the region. The Kim-Trump summit statement referred to the Panmunjom Declaration, and North Korea reaffirmed its commitment 'to work toward complete denuclearization of the Korean Peninsula'.[12] Kim Jong-un showed willingness to close the Yongbyon nuclear facility, believed to have manufactured the materials used for its nuclear tests.[13] After a lull in the negotiation process for a few months since the summit, especially over the lack of progress in North Korea shutting down its nuclear production capacity, the US Secretary of State Mike Pompeo issued a statement in September 2018 where he stated that,

> This morning, I invited my counterpart Foreign Minister Ri Yong Ho to meet in New York City next week where we are both already scheduled to be in attendance at the United Nations General Assembly meeting. Likewise, we have invited North Korean representatives to meet our Special Representative for North Korea, Stephen Biegun, in Vienna, Austria at the earliest opportunity. This will make the beginning of negotiations to transform U.S.-

> DPRK relations through the process of rapid denuclearization of North Korea, to be completed by January 2021, as committed by Chairman Kim, and to construct a lasting and stable peace regime on the Korean Peninsula.[14]

Pompeo was headed back to North Korea on October 6 to meet with Kim Jong-un and other top officials to iron out differences and move the process forward.[15] Subsequently, the Hanoi Summit in February 2019 witnessed the two leaders coming together the second time. However, the complexities surrounding the denuclearisation and sequencing lead to the lack of agreement on both side. The Korean Peninsula has witnessed some quick and positive developments these past few months, after a year of escalatory missile tests by North Korea and some strong rhetorical signalling from President Trump, who threatened to destroy North Korea. Given the context in which the summit took place, it is useful to carry out a recap of the dynamics immediately preceding the summit. This essay explores the US grand strategic factors at play. It argues that, despite the demonstrated North Korean missile technologies and war rhetoric between Trump and Kim, the two summits indicated to the world that both leaders are willing to give peace a shot, for obviously strategic reasons.

For President Trump, it would establish his 'legacy in foreign policy'—as the US President who successfully ended the Korean War and denuclearised North Korea. This is something no other President before him has succeeded in doing. A summit level meeting indicates that the US takes very seriously North Korea's nuclear and ballistic missile capabilities. For Kim Jong-un, it would mean the lifting of sanctions, an investment in his long-term political survival, and South-North unification. For China, this scenario would mean not having to commit itself militarily to North Korea, especially in a context where the end results could put it at a disadvantage. A changed Korean Peninsula without a North Korean 'buffer' vis-à-vis the US is not in China's interest.

A Recap

The lead up to the summit was difficult and escalatory. It almost seemed like both leaders first engaged in war-mongering and then decided to hold a summit to address their 'war mongering' rhetoric. In his September 21, 2017 speech to the United Nations General Assembly (UNGA), President Trump threatened to totally destroy North Korea.[16] In an October 2017 visit to the Demilitarized Zone (DMZ) that separates North and South Korea, then US Defense Secretary James Mattis asserted that, 'North Korean provocations continue to threaten regional and world peace and despite unanimous condemnation by the United Nations Security Council, they still proceed'.[17] Consequently, President Trump's assertive stance towards North Korea escalated tensions in the Korean Peninsula, registering a call for a more nuanced approach from the South Korean President, Moon Jae-in, who is in favour of negotiations with the North. President Trump chided Moon, twitting, 'South Korea is finding, as I have told them, that their talk of appeasement with North Korea will not work, they only understand one thing!'[18] As talks were underway between South and North Korea, President Trump tweeted,

> with all of the failed 'experts' weighing in, does anybody really believe that talks and dialogue would be going on between North and South Korea right now if I wasn't firm, strong and willing to commit our total 'might' against the North. Fools, but talks are a good thing![19]

Mattis called for shoring up South Korea's defence mechanism vis-à-vis the North, with Vice President Mike Pence declaring the DMZ the 'historic frontier of freedom' during his visit there in April 2017.[20] Pence stated,

> I'm here to express the resolve of the people of the United States and the president of the United States to achieve that objective through peaceable means, through negotiations, but all options

> are on the table as we continue to stand shoulder-to-shoulder with the people of South Korea.[21]

Such deliberate visible posturing which included the military option brought about a strong response from North Korea. On November 28, 2017, North Korea test fired its strongest ICBM yet—the *Hwasong* 15—with boosted capabilities to reach anywhere in the continental US. In his New Year address, Kim Jong-un warned that, 'the US should know that the button for nuclear weapons is on my table ... The entire area of the US mainland is within our nuclear strike range'.[22] North Korea test-fired several missiles in the year 2017—now perceived as one of rapid progress of the country's missile technology. On August 28, 2017, it fired a ballistic missile over Japan's Hokkaido Islands that landed in the sea. The timing of the missile launch was significant as the US and Japan had completed a joint military drill in Hokkaido, which was viewed by the North as preparations for an invasion. North Korea's ambassador to the UN, Han Tae-song, stated that the missile test was a response to the US-Japan-South Korea military drills aimed at the North.[23] This view was reiterated by China, a major player in the Korean Peninsula, with the Foreign Ministry spokeswoman, Hua Chunying, asserting that the US and Japan's military drills have put pressure on North Korea to defend itself.[24] This missile, the *Hwasong* 12 fired by North Korea over Japan constitutes the strategic messaging of resolve by Kim Jong-un, to counter President Trump's assertion that he was buckling under US pressure. This was followed by a September 2017 missile test over the Hokkaido island, that flew 3,700 km, and reached an altitude of 770 km before landing in the Pacific. This test was intended not only at Japan but also at the US territory of Guam.

The US grand strategy vis-à-vis the Korean Peninsula is to maximise the security of its allies and its bases with a show of power. It accomplishes this with its tight knit security alliances with South Korea and Japan, and by a massive presence of its military in bases in both countries as well as its naval presence in the Pacific. The US aims to denuclearise North Korea in its efforts to maximise the security of the Korean Peninsula. However, Kim Jong-un's views US efforts as being aimed at regime change, resulting in his ouster. Consequently, he views his development of ballistic missiles as a deterrent and is unlikely to give it up, given the fate that befell dictators like Mohammad Gadhafi in Libya who agreed to dismantle its nuclear programme in 2003. The counterfactual is that had Gadhafi held on to his nukes, NATO would have 'thought twice' before bombing Libya in 2011.[25]

Just prior to the Trump-Kim summit, differences had cropped up, including remarks made by both the US National Security Advisor (NSA) John Bolton, and Vice President Mike Pence, that if North Korea does not give in to US demands of verified denuclearisation, then the country may suffer the same fate that befell Libya.[26] In response, North Korean Vice Foreign Minister, Choe Son-hui, threatened to abandon the summit, calling Pence's remarks as

> unbridled and impudent remarks that North Korea might end like Libya, military option for North Korea never came off the table ... as a person involved in the US affairs, I cannot suppress my surprise at such ignorant and stupid remarks gushing out from the mouth of the US vice president.[27]

The 'hard core', or so-called 'maximum pressure', bargaining strategy adopted by the US before the scheduled summit (that if North Korea did not make a deal, it might end up like Libya) backfired and, at the same time, demonstrated that the US could not keep matters quiet till the summit, which is usually how summits of such importance work. The contradictory stands of Trump, Bolton, and Pence created enough confusion about what the intent of the summit really was. Within the Trump administration, while Secretary of State Mike Pompeo is in favour of negotiating with Kim Jong-un, NSA John Bolton wrote two pieces before becoming NSA that made a legal case for pre-emptive strikes against North Korea. In his piece for *The Wall Street Journal*, Bolton argued that the threat from North Korea is imminent and, given the gaps in U.S.

intelligence about North Korea, we should not wait until the very last minute. That would risk striking after the North has deliverable nuclear weapons, a much more dangerous situation.[28]

Bolton quotes Pompeo, then CIA Director, who specified in January 2018, that the North was months away from being able to deliver a nuclear warhead on the US.[29] On April 29, Bolton advertised the 2003–2004 Libyan model for North Korea, stating that it will include a verified denuclearisation. Bolton specified that the US was also looking at what North Korea had committed to in order to give up nuclear weapons in 1992.[30] A lawyer by training, Bolton is well equipped to make a legal case as well as point out the limits of international law in dealing with a case such as this. Pompeo, on the other hand, is more careful when it comes to striking North Korea, and may not like to disrupt the peace in Northeast Asia. He has been at the forefront on negotiations with North Korea, including making two secret trips (early April as CIA Director, and May 2018 as US Secretary of State) to the North to meet Kim. North Korea pushed back on the Libya model with anger, prompting President Trump to contradict Bolton, saying that any deal with North Korea would include a promise of keeping Kim Jong-un in power, 'would be 'something where he'd be there, he'd be in his country, he'd be running his country, his country would be very rich.'[31]

However, President Trump's aggressive posturing against North Korea escalated Kim Jong-un's fears. For instance, in August 2017, President Trump stated that,

> North Korea best not make any more threats to the United States. They will be met with fire and fury like the world has never seen ... he has been very threatening beyond a normal state. They will be met with fire, fury and frankly power the likes of which this world has never seen before ...[32]

This immediately raised concerns of a US nuclear strike on the North. It is plausible that Kim Jong-un test fired his ICBMs as a 'deterrent signalling' against such an outcome. The war of words between President Trump and Kim Jong-un has been nasty as well, with the former calling the latter 'little rocket man', and Kim Jong-un calling President Trump, a 'dotard'.[33]

In light of all this, the US grand strategy towards the Korean Peninsula is hinged on the following three parameters: first, the denuclearisation of the Korean Peninsula; second, limit China's strategic influence over the North; and finally, maintain US primacy. This essay highlights these three parameters in light of recent developments as stated in the opening paragraphs, and ends by suggesting the contours of US strategy towards North Korea.[34]

The US Grand Strategy Towards the Korean Peninsula

The US grand strategy since the end of World War II has been to maintain US primacy by maximising its relative power. As a part of the configuration of the international system, the US has maintained 'off-shore' bases, especially in Japan and South Korea, to provide for hard core security, backed by military deployment. This can be traced back to the Korean War when North Korean tanks crossed the 38th parallel. This led to a 37 months long War whose objective was the 'withdrawal of the invading forces to positions north of the 38th parallel'. President Truman authorised the deployment of American troops in defence of South Korea vindicated by the 1950 United Nations declaration. The 1953 settlement between the North and American forces was a truce, and was never finalised into a peace treaty. The US lost 8,162 military personnel while achieving the limited war objective of securing the 38th parallel. However, the objectives were broadened by the UN from simply fighting off the North Koreans from the 38th parallel to the reunification of Korea. It was then that China entered, and reiterated its prior warnings that if American troops planned to advance to the Yalu river [their border with North Korea], they would join forces with the North.[35] This prolonged War resulted in a heavy loss of lives on all sides; finally there was a truce which showcased to the world the military capacity of Mao's People's Liberation Army (PLA). The end of the

Korean War led to two structural changes in the Korean Peninsula: the re-deployment of US military forces back to the Korean Peninsula after they left in 1949; and the US-South Korea relationship was cemented emotionally post 1950, given that 36,516 Americans had died defending South Korea from the North.

There are about 28,500 American troops present in South Korea.[36] The US maintains the Theatre High Altitude Air Defence (THAAD); the Patriot Air Missile defence system, especially the PAC-2; the MN3A1 Reconnaissance Vehicle especially as a protection against chemical agents in South Korea.[37] Consequently, the South Korean military coordinates closely with the United Nations Command led by US General Vincent Brooks, who also heads the US forces there. While it is assumed that, during wartime, the US will assume control of all South Korean forces, the South Korean President has to agree to that effect. Wartime Operational Control (OPCON) remains in force till 2020, despite insistence from current South Korean President Moon that it should end.[38]

As can be seen from the facts on the ground, the US grand strategy for the Korean Peninsula is deeply intertwined with South Korea remaining in a close-knit alliance. Both states share combined forces command, game out joint scenarios, and coordinate war plans. President Trump appears to have complicated the alliance by his statements about wanting South Korea to pay US$ 1 billion for the THAAD,[39] as well as renegotiate what he has termed an unfavourable trade deal. This has complicated the situation given an earlier commitment that the US will pay for the THAAD deployment while the South Koreans would offer land and infrastructure. This kind of posturing by President Trump, interpreted as a bargaining tactic by former US National Security Advisor, H.R. McMaster is, however, unhealthy as it creates fissures in the alliance, especially at a time when the North has demonstrated its capacity to launch missiles that can target the US. Nevertheless, in an interview to Reuters on April 27, 2017, President Trump stated that while a major US-North Korea conflict is plausible, he prefers a diplomatic peaceful path to resolution. He has identified North Korea as the biggest global challenge for his administration and recognises the role of Chinese President Xi Jinping in trying to reign in North Korea.[40]

The main challenge for the US and the Trump administration is to maintain 'strategic influence' given perceptions in the Korean Peninsula that President Trump's aggressive rhetoric against Kim Jong-un, and the deployment of THAAD has only bolstered North Korea missile development as a deterrent against any invasion.[41] The US-South Korea five day 'Vigilant Ace' military exercises started on December 4, 2017 was followed by a threat of nuclear war from North Korea. The 'Vigilant Ace' exercise included 12, 000 military personnel, 6 F22s, 18 F35s, and the B-1B bomber. The exercise included precision strikes and enemy infiltration, and focused on interoperability between US and South Korean military forces.[42] China, the lead major power in the region, viewed the deployment of the THAAD and the exercises as provocative and raking up regional tensions with its spokesman, Geng Shuang stating, 'We hope relevant parties can maintain restraint and not do anything to add tensions on the Korean peninsula'.[43] Significantly, Trump, in his post-Singapore summit press conference, declared that he was going to stop all war-games or military exercises between the US and South Korea, terming them 'inappropriate, expensive and provocative'.[44]

As stated earlier, there are three clear parameters to the US grand strategic design that it aims to achieve by utilising its diplomatic and economic clout, backed by a massive display of military power. First, denuclearisation of the Korean Peninsula. Second, limit China' strategic influence over the North, and finally, maintain US primacy.

The Parameters of US's Grand Strategy in the Korean Peninsula

The Denuclearisation of the Korean Peninsula

For the longest time, the US has desired North Korea to give up its nukes. This is despite the fact that North Korea has walked away from every agreement meant to achieve that purpose, and focused on enhancing its missile technology that could deliver its nuclear war-heads. In 1985, North Korea acceded to the NPT, but conditioned its International Atomic Energy Agency (IAEA) safeguards requirement to the withdrawal of the 100 US nuclear weapons from South Korea. In 1991, President George H.W. Bush declared a unilateral withdrawal of all land-based and naval nuclear weapons abroad. This was followed by the 1991 declaration by South Korea on the 'Denuclearization of the Korean Peninsula' by which South Korea promised not to develop or produce, possess, store, or use nuclear weapons. In 1992, South and North Korea signed the 'Joint Declaration of the Denuclearisation of the Korean Peninsula', committing both countries to 'not test, manufacture, produce, receive, possess, store, deploy or use nuclear weapons'.[45]

In 1992, North Korea signed an IAEA safeguards agreement, and submitted its declaration of nuclear material sites to the IAEA. On inspection, the IAEA discovered discrepancies in the amount of plutonium processed by North Korea, asked for clarifications, and requested for the 'special inspection' of two nuclear sites that possessed nuclear wastes. In response, North Korea announced its intention to withdraw from the NPT citing the Article X rationale of extreme national security. This was followed by largely failed consultations with the US and, in the wake of reports that North Korea had developed its first nuclear weapon, it withdrew from the NPT. US amplified diplomatic efforts to freeze North Korea's nuclear weapons, to include the 1994 Agreed Framework by which Pyongyang committed to freezing its plutonium weapons programme in exchange of aid. The US agreed to ease economic sanctions in exchange for a dialogue on missile proliferation. However, North Korea rejected US suggestions that it should adhere to the Missile Technology Control Regime (MTCR), asserting that the US should pay for revenues lost by North Korea for giving up on the proliferation and sale of ballistic missile components and technology.[46] In response, the US imposed sanctions. On August 31, 1998, North Korea launched the three-stage *Taepodong* 1 rocket, with a range of 1,500 and 2,000 km. As bilateral talks continued between the US and North Korea, the latter rejected US demands for the termination of its missile programme in exchange of relief from

US economic sanctions. While North Korea agreed to a moratorium on its testing of long range missiles while talks were underway with the US, it was discovered that the North Korean firm, Changgwang Sinyong Corporation, was proliferating missile technology probably to Iran. This led to increased US sanctions.[47]

In 2000, as the new millennium broke, South and North Korea signed an agreement on reunification. This was followed by a bilateral meeting between North Korea and the US in Kuala Lumpur, in which the North demanded US$ 1 billion a year as compensation from the US for giving up its missiles. The US rejected that offer and, in 2001, imposed sanctions on Changgwang Sinyong Corporation for proliferation to Iran. The tone and tenor of the George W. Bush administration was viewed by North Korea as hostile, and it declared its dual commitment to both dialogue and war. In his January 2002 'State of the Union' address, President Bush declared North Korea as an 'axis of evil', and North Korea responded strongly against the US posture of nuclear weapons use against it. In 2002, North Korea demanded IAEA inspectors leave its territory, and resumed operations on its nuclear facilities. In January 2003, North Korea withdrew from the NPT, and restarted its nuclear reactor that was frozen under the 1994 Agreed Framework.

With the failure of US-North Korea bilateral meetings, China entered the scene. In April 2003, in a trilateral meeting between the US, China, and North Korea, for the first time, North Korea informed the US that it possessed nuclear weapons. This was followed by the Six-Party Talks in August 2003 aimed at the US, Japan, and South Korea working to dismantle North Korea's nuclear programme. In the meantime, North Korea continued to proliferate its nuclear weapons technology, giving it to Iran, Pakistan, and Libya. This was followed by several years of dialogue in the Six-Party framework, which resulted in the September 2005 Joint Statement by which North Korea committed 'to abandoning all nuclear weapons and existing nuclear programme and returning, at an early date, to the Treaty on the Non-Proliferation of Nuclear Weapons and to IAEA safeguards.'[48] This commitment was not followed in letter and spirit, with North Korea continuing to process fuel rods, resulting in US sanctions against North Korean firms. In July 2006, North Korea tested seven ballistic missiles, and included the failed test of the *Taepodong* 2, its longest-range missile, which was viewed by the US as a provocative act. The United Nations Security Council (UNSC) adopted Resolution 1695 condemning North Korea's missile tests.

In 2007, the Six-Party Talks ended with an agreed 'action-plan' to halt North Korea's Yongbyon nuclear facility, and reward North Korea with an initial 50,000 tons of heavy fuel followed by an additional 950,000 tons in exchange for a complete declaration of its nuclear programme. The US also agreed to begin the process of removing North Korea from the list of 'state sponsors of terrorism'. In the sixth round of the Six-Party Talks, the North Korean delegation insisted that the US unfreeze US$ 25 million in frozen North Korean funds held in Banco Delta Asia or it would leave the talks. This was followed by the US agreeing to unfreeze the funds.[49] In a reciprocal response, North Korea shut down its Yongbyon nuclear facility, which was confirmed by IAEA inspectors. After several rounds of talks in 2008, the US tabled a draft verification protocol describing procedures to verify North Korea's nuclear programme, including uranium enrichment. North Korea made its nuclear dismantlement contingent on it being removed from the US list of 'state sponsor[s] of terrorism'. In December 2008, the Six-Party Talks ended in a stalemate due to the failure to arrive at a verification agreement. In April 2009, North Korea launched the three-stage Unha-rocket, and followed up by withdrawing from the Six-Party Talks. In 2010, North Korea informed Chinese news agency *Xinhua*, that it was ready to talk again on its nuclear programme. However, relations between the North and South deteriorated after the sinking of South Korean ship *Cheonan*—most likely by a North Korean torpedo, which the North denied. In November 2010, North Korea revealed to a team of visiting US-North Korean specialists that it had constructed a 2,000 uranium enrichment facility, and admitted for the first time that it can produce UF6.[50] This resulted in US suspicion that the North had more such facilities.

Into this scenario entered China in 2011, proposing a three-step revitalisation of multilateral talks. They began with the North-South talks, followed by North Korea-US talks, followed by the Six-Party talks. In February 2012, after a meeting in Beijing between North Korea and the US, both sides issued a statement by which North Korea agreed to suspend operations at its Yongbyon uranium enrichment plant, invite IAEA inspectors to monitor the suspension, and implement moratoriums on nuclear and long-range missile tests. In response, the US agreed to provide the North with 240,000 metric tons of food aid. However, in violation of that understanding, in April 2012, North Korea displayed six KN-8 ICBMs in its 100 years birthday celebration of its founder, Kim Il-sung. This was followed up by Leon Panetta, the then US Defence Secretary, claiming that China was helping North Korea's missile development.[51] On December 12, 2012, North Korea successfully launched the Unha-3. In August 2013, satellite images revealed that North Korea had restarted its heavy Yongbyon nuclear reactor.[52] This was followed by a March 2014 declaration by China that war cannot be permitted in the Korean Peninsula; North Korea responded by the testing of two medium range *Nodong* missiles into the Sea of Japan. In April 2015, the ICBM, K-N8 became operational, and North Korea launched a ballistic missile from a submarine. This was followed, a year later, by the test of the *Musudan*, an inter mediate range ballistic missile. On August 24, 2016, North Korea successfully tested the SLBM, KN-11. On September 6, 2016, the North conducted a nuclear test, the fifth of its kind.

In February 2017, the North tested the *Pukguksong*-2, a new type of ballistic missile. Several missile tests subsequently followed, including the May 2014 successful testing of the *Hwasong*-12 missile, with a range of 4,800 km. In July 2017, an ICBM test by North Korea indicated that it was capable of firing over a range of 10,400 km, thereby putting Los Angeles, Denver, and Chicago within range. Then, in September 2017, North Korea conducted its sixth nuclear test, with a seismic magnitude of 5.8. And, as stated earlier, in November 2017, North Korea tested its latest ICBM.

This chronology of US efforts to denuclearise North Korea is critical to document, as it reveals a dismal failure to meet that objective. The pattern that emerges is that US attempts to put pressure on North Korea by sanctions and calling it an 'axis of evil' only heightened North Korea's need for security, and its viewing of its missiles and nukes as 'survival weapons'. President Trump's aggressive posturing with 'threats to destroy North Korea', and the visible military exercises and deployment of the US navy near North Korean waters only emboldened Kim Jong-un to view his 'cache of weapons' and the visible demonstration of their capacity as a deterrent vis-à-vis any future US aggression. While President Trump asserts that unpredictability towards North Korea was a deal-maker, the North's response indicates that it has been a 'deal-breaker' as far as the failure of America's coercive strategy to motivate North Korea towards denuclearisation. Instead, the North has heavily upgraded its missile and nuclear technology, with 2017 registering the highest number of such tests. Clearly, the flurry of missile activity was aimed at one thing: the strategic signalling of North Korea's capability purely to act as dissuasion against US aggression.

Limit China's Strategic Influence over the North

China's strategic influence on North Korea is pegged on two parameters: its role in maintaining the Kim Jong-un regime, and its growing role in the negotiation with North Korea, including the Six-Party Talks. On November 1, 1950, China took the US by surprise when it entered the war on behalf of North Korea. Fresh and buoyant from their victories in Incheon and the successful defence of Pusan, the US army and the Marine Corps along with South Korean forces, marched deep inside North Korea towards the Chinese border. The objective was to reunify Korea and effectively bringing about a change in the North Korean regime. To their operational surprise, they were met by massive PLA resistance, seemingly coming out of nowhere, and a successful Chinese counter-offensive that led to a massive loss of lives on all sides, and pushed the US and South Korean advance back to the South Korean side of the 38th parallel (now DMZ). Some regard it as a stunning victory for China and a massive defeat for General Douglas MacArthur. Incidentally, General MacArthur had prior warning via 'Indian diplomatic channels' that China would not tolerate any presence of the US led UN troops near their borders. However, General MacArthur made little of Chinese capability, and US military observers with knowledge of the Chinese infantry during World War II believed that they were poorly equipped and trained, and stood little chance against the allied forces. They were proved wrong.[53]

Since then, China's influence on North Korea has loomed large. China is North Korea's largest trading partner (US$ 6.86 billion in 2014), and has historically worked to limit international sanctions against North Korea. The relationship appeared strained in the light of North Korea's nuclear test in October 2006 and China supported sanctions against the North via UNSC Resolution 1718. China, has, however worked to limit the effect of the economic sanctions imposed on North Korea as well as made sure to criticise international efforts that disparaged the North Korean regime's human rights violations. Chinese banks—the Agricultural Bank of China, the China Construction Bank, and the Bank of China—offer financial aid to North Korean businesses. China also runs a high-speed railway between the city of Dandong and Shenyang, and maintains special economic zones in North Korea, like the Sinujia and Rason zones.[54] After the Six-Party Talks collapsed, China remains the sole provider of economic aid. All this is geared towards maintaining North Korea as the 'buffer state' between China and US troop presence in South Korea. China strongly protested the deployment of the THAAD to South Korea, asserting that it is provocative to regional peace and stability. It also views Kim Jong-un's regime as beneficial to Chinese interests, no matter the costs of his antics. President Xi categorically stated that 'The U.S. deployment of an advanced anti-missile system in South Korea gravely harms the strategic security interests of China, Russia and other countries in the region.'[55] Being North Korea's largest trading partner is the leverage China utilised to pressurise the South over US missile shield deployment by imposing a year-long economic blockade of the South.[56] This negative pressure to not buy South Korean goods in China cost the South US$ 7.5 billion, reducing its GDP by 0.5 per cent.[57]

The pressure was removed when the South agreed not to accept any more THAAD missiles, and gave a commitment not to join a regional missile defence system in cooperation with the US and Japan. South Korea's current President, Moon Jae-in, is favourable towards diplomacy with North Korea and has cautioned the US against a military strike on North Korea given the massive US military build-up in the region.[58] Increasingly, Chinese diplomats and security analysts assert that the country that threatens to destabilise a prosperous Northeast Asian region is not China but the US with its war mongering rhetoric and the irresponsible statements uttered by its current President thereby exacerbating insecurity in the region.[59] The Chinese Ambassador to the US stated that,

> Honestly, I think the United States should be doing ... much more than now, so that there's real effective international cooperation on this issue ...They should refrain from issuing more threats. They should do more to find effective ways to resume dialogue and negotiation.[60]

Given the atmosphere of growing US military deployment in South Korea, China realised the practical necessity of maintaining the North Korean barrier. There is also a historical dimension to the China-North Korea relationship. On the one hand, the US aims to limit China's influence in the Korean Peninsula, reunify Korea and, simultaneously, remove a hostile regime that threatens the US. It aims to operationalise this by building upon its allies (Japan, South Korea, Philippines) in the region, and emphasise a deeper strategic partnership with countries like India and Vietnam. With an aim to limit China's influence and reach, the US, India, Australia, and Japan held their first 'quadrilateral meeting' in Manila in November 2017, as an effort to maintaining US primacy in the region, including the Korean Peninsula.[61] Recently, the US renamed its largest military command, Pacific Command (PACOM) as the Indo-Pacific Command (INDOPACOM)—a nod at India, and a shot at China.[62]

On the other hand, in response to the US and South Korea's five-day 'Vigilant Ace' military exercise in December 2017, the PLA Air Force (PLAAF) and PLA Navy (PLAN) conducted air and seaborne exercises on December 7, 2017 to demonstrate their combat readiness with more than 40 warships from PLAN taking part in the East China Sea.[63] The exercises tested the Navy's advanced HHQ-10 anti-missile system. On December 4, coinciding with the US-South Korea joint exercises,[64] the PLAAF conducted exercises near the Korean Peninsula, and included fighter jets, reconnaissance aircraft, and surface to air missiles. Li Jie, a military expert based in Beijing, believes that, 'the timing of this high-profile announcement by the PLA is also a warning to Washington and Seoul not to provoke Pyongyang any further'.[65] It showcases China's strategy with regard to its ally, North Korea, and its willingness to deter war in order to maintain North Korea as the 'buffer' between South Korea and US troops stationed there.[66] While the US aspires to reunify Korea, as well as limit China's influence, China aims to maintain the status quo.

Maintain US Primacy

US's grand strategy is to maintain US primacy based on a favourable and sustainable great power balance of power, investing in building the capacity of its 'allies' and punishing rogue actors like North Korea. The existence of the nuclear capable North Korean regime is viewed as a direct threat to the US and the international order that it has crafted which helps maintain its primacy. The rise of China with a different political regime is viewed as a threat to that primacy as well. China's help in sustaining the nuclear armed North Korean regime is not lost on the US which also views China's acquisition of enormous economic and military power as a threat to its own leverage in the Asia-Pacific. As a consequence, the primary goal of the US is to ensure that no rival state accumulates so much power that it is capable of threatening the US and its allies. China's assertive behaviour in the South China Sea and the East China Sea is viewed as a demonstration of its increased power potential. The US senator from Arkansas, Tom Cotton (viewed as rather influential within the Trump administration), has accused China of lying about North Korea for 25 years, asserting that China benefits from a nuclear North Korea. Cotton has stated, 'That's why they've been playing both sides of the street, saying one thing to Western officials in public but doing nothing to stop North Korea from getting nuclear weapons or now to get them to denuclearise.'[67]

China's role in the present North Korean crisis vis-à-vis the US is significant, given that diplomatic channels to North Korea have historically run through Beijing. The Trump administration has increased pressure on North Korea. On November 20, 2017, President Trump declared North Korea 'a state sponsor of terrorism'.[68] The US sanctioned North Korean entities to put economic pressure. As stated by the US Treasury Secretary, Steven T. Mnuchin, 'As North Korea continues to threaten international peace and security, we are steadfast in our determination to maximize economic pressure to isolate it from outside sources of trade and revenue ...'[69]

Significantly, the US imposed sanctions on Chinese and Russian companies conducting business with North Korea, and included the Chinese companies Dandong Rich Earth Trading Company, accused by the US of buying vanadium ore from Korea Kumsan Trading Corporation; the Mingzheng International Trading Limited, suspected to be a 'front company' for North Korea's Foreign Trade bank; and companies that were already included in the UNSC sanctions list of August 2017 under UNSC Resolution 2371. The UN sanctions prohibited UN members from buying coal and iron ore from North Korea, a move to restrict the North's export earnings, thereby squeezing its economy. While announcing the sanctions to include oil imports, the US Department of Treasury stated that, 'North Korea generates a significant share of the money it uses to fuel its nuclear and ballistic missile programme by mining natural resources and selling those resources abroad'.[70] Included in the US unilateral sanctions were Russian oil companies that traded with North Korea as well.[71] US Treasury Secretary, Steven Mnuchin, stated that the US 'will continue to increase pressure on North Korea by targeting those who support the advancement of nuclear and ballistic missile programme and isolating them from the American financial system.'[72]

However, China believes that such economic pressure tactics have not worked in the past, and will not work today. Instead, the US would have to ensure that they are not looking for regime change in North Korea. For China, North Korea's quest for nuclear weapons is based on a clear threat perception they perceive from the US—more so after the fall of its close ally, the Soviet Union. The US, on the other hand, views North Korea's nukes as propelled by aggressive objectives, particularly its goal to reunify the Korean Peninsula and push the US out of South Korea. The US has suffered from North Korea not meeting its bilateral obligations, including the 1994 Agreed Framework and the food-for-aid programme, and remains wary of negotiating with a country that is not viewed as reliable. China, on the other hand, perceives North Korea as a reliable partner, and argues that its need for enriching uranium, and developing its nukes is a deterrent it built to respond to the mixed signals coming out of the US. The latter demanding an end to its nuclear programme while, at the same-time, naming North Korea a state sponsor of terrorism has fed into its fears of regime change.[73]

The US grand strategy and preference for the Korean Peninsula are determined by these three factors: the US grand preference—spanning several administrations including the Trump administration—is to ensure that North Korea gives up its nuclear weapons. Unlike the US-USSR Cold War and Mutually Assured destruction (MAD) logic, where rationality and trust was inbuilt into the system, the US does not trust North Korea, despite Trump now stating that he trusts Kim Jong-un. Significantly, given the criticality of 'homeland defence', the Republicans, since the time of the Regan administration have aimed to establish a space-based missile shield, which would have the potential to avert North Korean missiles.[74] Regan's 1983 Strategic Defense Initiative (SDI) was aimed at building a space-based defence system that would knock out incoming Soviet ICBMs. While the SDI was ended in 1993, President Bill Clinton signed the National Missile Defense Act in 1999, committing to develop a missile defence system. President Trump has expressed a similar desire to 'develop a state-of-the-art missile defence system to protect against missile-based attacks from states like Iran and North Korea.'[75] The deployment of the radar based THAAD in South Korea is a continuation of that desire. While not being as distressed by the North Korean nuclear and missile tests, China is alarmed by the deployment of the US THAAD in Asia as it has the capability to avert Chinese missiles as well, if there is a conflict. This only means that the US is able to expand its power beyond the Korean Peninsula, to other regions of Asia. A US space based missile defence system would not only avert North Korean missiles but will have the potential to avert Chinese missiles in case a conflict ensues with countries like India or Japan. The growing US-India strategic partnership only heightens such Chinese concerns.

Some argue that President Trump's escalatory rhetoric against North Korea as well as secondary sanctions against Chinese and Russian companies have played a part in Kim Jong-un agreeing to meet President Trump, though surely that cannot be the sole cause. It was Kim Jong-un's demonstration of advanced nuclear and missile capabilities, especially in 2017, and President Trump's willingness to start a process without having water-tight concessions from Kim Jong-un on North Korea's path to disarmament that resulted in a summit. According to Tong Tong Zhao, a North Korea analyst and fellow at the Carnegie-Tsinghua Center for Global Policy, 'I think Kim Jong-un is now [in] a different position after the Hwasong-15 (long-range missile) testing. At a minimum, North Korea has achieved a rudimentary strategic deterrent and can afford to not continue testing....'[76] This allows North Korea bargaining leverage vis-à-vis the US.

What does the US gain from the Singapore Summit?

The US is starting to take leadership of the North Korean issue, delegated to other countries in the lead; namely, China. President Trump can showcase to his 'voter-base' that he is in control; that he is expecting Kim Jong-un to meet his obligations and, in due course, if those obligations of denuclearisation are met, sanctions could be removed. Cleverly, President Trump has made it clear that it will take time to denuclearise even as he will at the same time incrementally establish diplomatic relations. He portrayed the 'war-games' or military exercises with South Korea as expensive, even while flying US bombers from Guam, covering about six and a half hours. He argued that it was inappropriate to be conducting war games so close to the North Korean border, especially in the context that he and Kim Jong-un are now seeking to establish a peaceful regime in the Korean Peninsula. This was an interesting reference by Trump to context changing as well as highlighting the changing dynamic from war-mongering to seeking peace. The US gains by demonstrating that it is still the primary mover in Asia, given the amount of attention the summit generated in this region. It offered President Trump enormous bragging rights, and he can now repeatedly mention his 'deal-making' powers as well as his willingness to take risks to his voter-base. No doubt he has an eye on 2020.

What does North Korea gain from the Summit?

North Korea gains a lot from the summit, perhaps much more than the US. For one, Kim Jong-un gets to meet the leader of the world's strongest nation, a great honour for him resulting in his reputation gain and positive propaganda back home. Second, North Korea has created enormous bargaining power via-à-vis China, especially in the context of its neighbourhood. China had played into North Korean fears of US military presence as threatening to North Korea to continue creating the 'buffer' as well as treat Kim Jong-un as a junior partner. That dynamic might have changed now. Third, North Korea cleverly utilised its escalatory ballistic missile tests, explaining their existence as provoked by the US military presence in South

Korea as well as the joint US-South Korean military exercises. That rationale appears to have convinced President Trump for now who has halted those exercises.

The Risks

Realising the goals laid out at the joint statement issued following the Singapore summit presents an enormous challenge. Sequencing the goals of denuclearisation and easing of sanctions led to the breakdown of talks at Hanoi. For the US, the risks are that North Korea will commit to denuclearisation on paper, while continuing to keep its nuclear option alive and ready. This situation had arisen before, only for the US to discover—after commitments to do otherwise—that North Korea had continued with plutonium enrichment. The second risk is to be unable to have a 'verifiable and irreversible' denuclearisation process, one that is internationally vetted. The third risk is for President Trump to commit to halting joint military exercises only to find out that North Korea has not done much, barring token promises on paper, to appease him.

For North Korea, getting too cosy with the US will alienate one of its biggest guarantors, China. Hence, Kim Jong-un will have to walk a tight rope between keeping China close, while at the same time, developing a credible relationship with the US. The second risk is that given President Trump has invested so much in this summit, any walking back towards more nukes create risks of war. This seems unlikely, given the involvement of South Korea, specifically its President's personal commitment to the process. Finally, though it may appear that President Trump and Kim Jong-un are on an equal footing, this cannot be further from the truth. The power difference between them is enormous, and the US military machine is a threat North Korea cannot take lightly. Significantly, US engagement with North Korea reveals more of a tactical manoeuvre rather than any long term strategic move, and those tactics could be working. For now, it all seems a bit surreal for Kim Jong-un, and he indicated as much soon after he met President Trump by saying, 'it sure feels like a science fiction movie'.[77]

Notes

1. Veronica Rocha, *et al.*, 'President Trump Meets Kim Jon- Un', CNN, June 12, 2018 at https://www.cnn.com/politics/live-news/trump-kim-jong-un-meeting-summit/, accessed on June 12, 2018.
2. Everett Rosenfeld, 'Trump and Kim Meet Face-to-Face in Vietnam as Second Summit Kicks Off', CNBC, February 27, 2019 at https://www.cnbc.com/2019/02/27/trump-and-kim-meet-face-to-face-in-vietnam-as-second-summit-kicks-off.html, accessed on August 2, 2019.
3. David Jackson, 'Donald Trump Meets Kim Jong Un in DMZ, Steps onto North Korean Soil', *USA Today*, June 29, 2019 at https://www.usatoday.com/story/news/politics/2019/06/29/donald-trump-looks-brief-handshake-meeting-kim-jong-un/1608092001/, accessed on August 2, 2019.
4. 'Pushing the Envelope? Kim Jong-Un's Massive Letter to Trump', CBS, June 2, 2018 at https://www.cbsnews.com/news/pushing-the-envelope-why-kim-jong-uns-letter-to-trump-was-so-massive/, accessed on June 12, 2018.
5. 'Trump and Kim's Joint Statement,' Reuters, June 12, 2018 at https://www.reuters.com/article/us-northkorea-usa-agreement-text/trump-and-kims-joint-statement-idUSKBN1J80IU, accessed on June 12, 2018.
6. Ibid.
7. Kim Jaewon, 'North Korea "dismantles" nuclear test site', Nikkei Asian Review, May 24, 2018 at https://asia.nikkei.com/Spotlight/North-Korea-crisis-2/North-Korea-dismantles-nuclear-test-site, accessed on June 12, 2018.
8. 'President Trump's Full Press Conference on Summit with Kim Jong', CNBC, June 12, 2018 at https://www.cnbc.com/video/2018/06/12/president-trumps-full-press-conference-on-summit-with-kim-jong-un.html, accessed on June 13, 2018.
9. 'Trump Says US will End Joint Military Exercises with South Korea', *Time*, June 12, 2018 at http://time.com/5309515/trump-kim-summit-south-korea-end-military-exercises/, accessed on June 12, 2018.
10. @realdonaldtrump at https://twitter.com/realDonaldTrump/status/1006837823469735936, accessed on June 13, 2018.
11. 'Panmunjom Declaration of Peace', *Los Angeles Times*, April 27, 2018 at http://documents.latimes.com/panmunjom-declaration-peace/, accessed on June 13, 2018.
12. Ibid.
13. 'US "Ready to Start Negotiations" with North Korea', BBC, September 20, 2018 at https://www.bbc.com/news/world-asia-45581281, accessed on October 6, 2018.
14. Amanda Macias and Mark Calia, 'Pompeo Says North Korea Nuclear Talks to be Completed by January 2021', CNBC, September 19, 2018

at https://www.cnbc.com/2018/09/19/pompeo-says-north-korea-nuclear-talks-must-be-done-by-january-2021.html, accessed on October 6, 2018.

15. Conor Finnegen, 'Mike Pompeo Heads to North Korea with Low Expectations but High Pressure', ABC News, October 6, 2018 at https://abcnews.go.com/International/mike-pompeo-heads-north-korea-low-expectations-high/story?id=58310367, accessed on October 6, 2018.
16. Ali Vitali, 'Trump Threatens to "Totally Destroy" North Korea in First U.N. Speech', NBC News, September 21, 2017 at https://www.nbcnews.com/news/us-news/trump-un-north-korean-leader-suicide-mission-n802596, accessed on December 5, 2017.
17. Phil Stewart, 'Mattis Talks Diplomacy on North Korea Ahead of Trump's Asia Tour', Reuters, October 26, 2017 at https://www.reuters.com/article/us-northkorea-missiles/mattis-talks-diplomacy-on-north-korea-ahead-of-trumps-asia-tour-idUSKBN1CW04W, accessed on January 4, 2018.
18. @realDonaldTrump, Twitter, September 3, 2017 at https://twitter.com/realdonaldtrump/status/904309527381716992?lang=en, accessed on December 5, 2017.
19. @realDonaldTrump, Twitter, January 4, 2018 at https://twitter.com/realDonaldTrump/status/948879774277128197?ref_src=twsrc%5Egoogle%7Ctwcamp%5Eserp%7Ctwgr%5Etweet, accessed on January 4, 2018.
20. Cherlyn Pellerin, 'Pence Thanks US, South Korea Troops at "Historic Frontier of Freedom"', US Department of Defense, April 17, 2017 at https://www.defense.gov/News/Article/Article/1153606/pence-thanks-us-south-korean-troops-at-historic-frontier-of-freedom/, accessed on December 5, 2017.
21. Ibid.
22. 'Kim Jong-Un Warns "button for nuclear weapons is on my table"', CBS, January 1, 2018 at https://www.cbsnews.com/news/kim-jong-un-north-korea-completed-nuclear-forces/, accessed on January 4, 2018.
23. 'North Korea Fires Missile over Japan in "Unprecedented Threat"', BBC, August 29, 2017 at http://www.bbc.com/news/world-asia-41078187, accessed on December 5, 2017.
24. Charlotte Gao, 'China Refuses to Condemn North Korea's New Missile Launch', *The Diplomat*, August 30, 2017 at https://thediplomat.com/2017/08/china-refuses-to-condemn-north-koreas-new-missile-launch/, accessed on January 4, 2018.
25. Reza Sanati, 'A Troubling Lesson from Libya: Don't Give up Nukes', *The Christian Science Monitor*, August 30, 2011 at https://www.csmonitor.com/Commentary/Opinion/2011/0830/A-troubling-lesson-from-Libya-Don-t-give-up-nukes, accessed on December 5, 2017.

26. David Chol, 'Mike Pence Issues Warning to Kim Jong-un if the North Korean Leader "doesn't make a deal" with Trump', Business Insider, May 21, 2018 at http://www.businessinsider.com/mike-pence-north-korea-libya-model-kim-jong-un-summit-2018-5, accessed on May 24, 2018.
27. David Chol, 'North Korea Claps Back at Mike Pence's "Ignorant and Stupid" Remarks Leaving Summit with the U.S. Hanging in a Thread', Business Insider, May 24, 2018 at http://www.businessinsider.com/north-korea-mike-pence-us-summit-threatened-2018-5, accessed on May 24, 2018.
28. John Bolton, 'The Legal Case for Striking North Korea First', *The Wall Street Journal*, February 28, 2018 at https://www.wsj.com/articles/the-legal-case-for-striking-north-korea-first-1519862374, accessed on May 23, 2018.
29. Ibid.
30. Tim Harris, 'John Bolton: North Korea will follow "Libya 2004" Model of Verified Nuclear Denuclearization', Real Clear Politics, April 29, 2018 at https://www.realclearpolitics.com/video/2018/04/29/john_bolton_north_korea_will_go_by_libya_2004_model_of_denuclearization.html, accessed on May 23, 2018.
31. Patrick Goodenough, 'Trump: We're Not Looking at the "Libya Model" for North Korea, But a Deal That Would See Kim Jong un 'Running his Country', CNS, May 17, 2018 at https://www.cnsnews.com/news/article/patrick-goodenough/trump-were-not-looking-libya-model-north-korea-deal-would-see-kim, accessed on May 24, 2018.
32. Jim Sciuttu, *et al.*, 'Trump Promises North Korea "fire and fury" over Nuke Threat', CNN, August 9, 2017 at http://www.cnn.com/2017/08/08/politics/north-korea-missile-ready-nuclear-weapons/index.html, accessed on December 5, 2017.
33. Mahita Gajanan, 'Kim Jong Un Called President Trump a "dotard": What does that mean?', *Time*, September 21, 2017 at http://time.com/4952750/kim-jong-un-donald-trump-dotard-north-korea/, accessed on December 5, 2017.
34. For those interested in a North Korean perspective, please see, Namrata Goswami, 'North Korea's Grand Strategy', *Live Encounters Magazine*, June 7, 2018 at https://liveencounters.net/2018-le-mag/06-june-2018/dr-namrata-goswami-north-koreas-grand-strategy/, accessed on October 6, 2018.
35. James Wright, 'What we learned from the Korean War', *The Atlantic*, July 23, 2013 at https://www.theatlantic.com/international/archive/2013/07/what-we-learned-from-the-korean-war/278016/, accessed on December 5, 2017.

36. Leon Whyte, 'The Evolution of the US-South Korea Alliance', *The Diplomat*, June 13, 2015 at https://thediplomat.com/2015/06/the-evolution-of-the-u-s-south-korea-alliance/, accessed on December 5, 2017.
37. Kyle Mizokami, 'Here are the Five Weapons the US Army will need for the Next Korean War', *The National Interest*, November 5, 2017 at http://nationalinterest.org/blog/the-buzz/here-are-the-5-weapons-the-us-army-will-need-the-next-korean-23037, accessed on December 5, 2017.
38. Brian Padden, 'South Korea Wants Wartime Control of its Military', VoA, September 28, 2017 at https://www.voanews.com/a/south-korea-wants-out-of-us-military-control/4047790.html, accessed on December 5, 2017.
39. Ju Min-Park and James Pearson, 'South Korea says US Reaffirms it will pay THAAD Costs; Trump Calls Asia Allies', Reuters, April 29, 2017 at https://in.reuters.com/article/northkorea-usa-thaad/south-korea-says-u-s-reaffirms-it-will-pay-thaad-costs-trump-calls-asia-allies-idINKBN17W03H, accessed on December 5, 2017.
40. Stephen J. Adler, et al., 'Exclusive: Trump Says "Major, Major" Conflict with North Korea Possible but Seeks Diplomacy', Reuters, April 27, 2017 at https://www.reuters.com/article/us-usa-trump-exclusive/exclusive-trump-says-major-major-conflict-with-north-korea-possible-but-seeks-diplomacy-idUSKBN17U04E, accessed on December 6, 2017.
41. Mathew Carney, 'South Korean Village Become Centre of Protests Against THAAD Missile Defence System', ABC News, July 10, 2017 at http://www.abc.net.au/news/2017-07-11/south-korean-locals-protest-against-thaad-defence-system/8695448, accessed on December 6, 2017.
42. 'US, South Korea Begin Massive Military Exercises', NPR, December 4, 2017 at https://www.npr.org/sections/thetwo-way/2017/12/04/568263780/u-s-south-korea-begin-massive-military-exercises, accessed on December 6, 2017.
43. 'Foreign Ministry Spokesperson Geng Shuang's Regular Press Conference on July 4, 2017', Ministry of Foreign Affairs of the People's Republic of China at http://www.fmprc.gov.cn/mfa_eng/xwfw_665399/s2510_665401/t1475382.shtml, accessed on January 5, 2018.
44. 'Trump Says to Stop "Expensive", "Provocative" South Korea War Games', Reuters, June 12, 2018 at https://www.reuters.com/article/us-northkorea-usa-wargames/trump-says-to-stop-expensive-provocative-south-korea-war-games-idUSKBN1J80T5, accessed on June 15, 2018.
45. 'Joint Declaration of the Denuclearization of the Korean Peninsula' at https://peacemaker.un.org/sites/peacemaker.un.org/files/KR%20KP_920120_JointDeclarationDenuclearizationKoreanPeninsula.pdf, accessed on December 6, 2017.
46. For an excellent chronology, please see, 'Chronology of US-North Korean Nuclear and Missile Diplomacy', Arms Control Association, November

2017 at https://www.armscontrol.org/factsheets/dprkchron, accessed on December 6, 2017.

47. Ibid.
48. 'Joint Statement of the Fourth Round of the Six-Party Talks Beijing', US Department of State, September 19, 2005 at https://2001-2009.state.gov/r/pa/prs/ps/2005/53490.htm, accessed on November 15, 2018.
49. 'US, North Korea Resolve Macau Bank Dispute', NBC, March 19, 2007 at http://www.nbcnews.com/id/17658737/ns/world_news-asia_pacific/t/us-north-korea-resolve-macau-bank-dispute/#.Wk_Kt0qnGUk, accessed on January 5, 2018.
50. 'US Scientist Amazed by N. Korean Nuclear Facility', CNN, November 24, 2010 at http://www.cnn.com/2010/WORLD/asiapcf/11/23/north.korea.nuclear.facility/index.html, accessed on January 5, 2018.
51. Missy Ryan, 'China Assisting North Korean Missile Program: Panetta', Reuters, April 19, 2012 at https://www.reuters.com/article/us-usa-northkorea-china/china-assisting-north-korean-missile-program-panetta-idUSBRE83I1JQ20120420, accessed on January 5, 2018.
52. Paul Eckert and Arshad Muhammad, 'Satellite Image Suggests North Korea has Restarted Yongbyon Nuclear Reactor: US Group', Reuters, September 11, 2013 at https://www.reuters.com/article/us-korea-north-nuclear/satellite-image-suggests-north-korea-has-restarted-yongbyon-nuclear-reactor-u-s-group-idUSBRE98A1A720130912, accessed on January 5, 2018.
53. Stewart, Richard W., *The Korean War: The Chinese Intervention 1 November 1950-24 January 1951* at https://history.army.mil/brochures/kw-chinter/chinter.htm, accessed on December 7, 2017.
54. Eleanor Albert, 'The China-North-Korea Relationship', CFR Backgrounder, September 27, 2017 at https://www.cfr.org/backgrounder/china-north-korea-relationship, accessed on December 8, 2017.
55. 'China-Russia Share Opposition to US THAAD in South Korea: Xi', Reuters, July 3, 2017 at https://www.reuters.com/article/us-china-thaad-russia/china-russia-share-opposition-to-u-s-thaad-in-south-korea-xi-idUSKBN19O0N8, accessed on December 8, 2017.
56. Yue Yang, 'How China's South Korea Blockade Will Play Out, Politically and Economically', *Forbes*, March 20, 2017 at https://www.forbes.com/sites/ywang/2017/03/20/how-chinas-south-korea-boycott-will-play-out-politically-and-economically/#70ffcfc32c23, accessed on December 8, 2017.
57. Suli Ren, 'China's Sanctions over THAAD can sink Korea's Economy', *Barron's*, March 5, 2017 at https://www.barrons.com/articles/chinas-sanctions-over-thaad-can-sink-koreas-economy-1488773168, accessed on December 8, 2017.

58. Jonathan Cheng, 'South Korea Leader Warns Against Attack on North, Ahead of Trump's Asia Visit', *The Wall Street Journal*, November 1, 2017 at https://www.wsj.com/articles/south-korean-leader-warns-against-attack-on-north-ahead-of-trumps-asia-trip-1509530114, accessed on December 8, 2017. 'US Flies two Bombers over the Korean Peninsula in Show of Force', *Fortune*, October 11, 2017 at http://fortune.com/2017/10/10/us-south-korea-strategic-bombers-north-korea/, accessed on December 5, 2017.
59. Justin McCurry, 'China Accuses US of Putting Stability of Asia-Pacific at Risk', *The Guardian*, February 3, 2017 at https://www.theguardian.com/world/2017/feb/04/china-accuses-us-of-putting-stability-of-asia-pacific-at-risk, accessed on December 8, 2017.
60. 'China Washington Envoy Says US should Stop Threats over North Korea', Reuters, September 15, 2017 at https://www.reuters.com/article/us-northkorea-missiles-china-diplomacy/chinas-washington-envoy-says-u-s-should-stop-threats-over-north-korea-idUSKCN1BQ315, accessed on December 8, 2017.
61. Kallol Bhattacharjee, 'India, Japan, US, Australia Hold First 'Quad' Talks at Manila ahead of ASEAN Summit', *The Hindu*, November 12, 2017 http://www.thehindu.com/news/national/india-highlights-indo-pacific-cooperation-at-the-first-quad-talks/article20317526.ece, accessed on January 5, 2018.
62. Tara Coop, 'INDOPACOM, it is: US Pacific Command Gets Renamed', *Military Times*, May 30, 2018 at https://www.militarytimes.com/news/your-military/2018/05/30/indo-pacom-it-is-pacific-command-gets-renamed/, accessed on June 15, 2018.
63. Minnie Chan, 'China's Navy Put on Show of Strength for North Korea ... and the US East Asia Alliance', *South China Morning Post,* December 8, 2017 at http://www.scmp.com/news/china/diplomacy-defence/article/2123553/chinas-navy-puts-show-strength-north-korea-and-united, accessed on December 6, 2017.
64. Scott Neuman, 'US-South Korea Begin Massive Military Exercises', NPR, December 4, 2017 at https://www.npr.org/sections/thetwo-way/2017/12/04/568263780/u-s-south-korea-begin-massive-military-exercises, accessed on December 8, 2017.
65. Minnie Chan, 'Chinese Air Force Holds Drills in 'New Routes and Areas' near Korean Peninsula', *The South China Morning Post*, December 4, 2017 at http://www.scmp.com/news/china/diplomacy-defence/article/2122837/chinese-air-force-holds-drills-new-routes-and-areas, accessed on December 8, 2017.
66. Alex Lockie, 'China did something it's Never Done Before to Warn the US about Fighting North Korea', Business Insider, December 5, 2017 at http://www.businessinsider.com/china-north-korea-air-military-exercise-us-2017-12, accessed on December 12, 2017.

67. 'US Accuses China of "Lying for 25 Years" about North Korea', *South China Morning Post*, December 8, 2017 at http://www.scmp.com/news/world/united-states-canada/article/2123392/leading-us-senator-accuses-china-lying-25-years, accessed on December 12, 2017.
68. 'Remarks by President Trump before Cabinet Meeting', The White House, Office of the Press Secretary, November 20, 2017 at https://www.whitehouse.gov/the-press-office/2017/11/20/remarks-president-trump-cabinet-meeting, accessed on December 12, 2017.
69. 'Treasury Sanctions Trading, Labour, and Shipping Companies and Vessels to Further Isolate North Korea', US Department of Treasury, Press Centre, November 21, 2017 at https://www.treasury.gov/press-center/press-releases/Pages/sm0220.aspx, accessed on December 12, 2017.
70. Robert Delaney and Zhenhua Lu, 'US Imposes New Sanctions on Chinese and Russian Companies to Cut off North Korean Support', *South China Morning Post*, August 22, 2017 at http://www.scmp.com/news/china/policies-politics/article/2107874/us-imposes-new-sanctions-chinese-and-russian-companies, accessed on June 13, 2018.
71. Ibid.
72. Charlie Campbell, 'The US Imposes Secondary Sanctions on Chinese and Russian Firms over North Korea', *Time*, August 23, 2017 at http://time.com/4911882/north-korea-u-s-secondary-sanctions-china-russia-treasury/, accessed on June 13, 2018.
73. Krishnadev Calamur, 'How the US and China differ on North Korea', *The Atlantic*, November 28, 2017 at https://www.theatlantic.com/international/archive/2017/11/us-china-north-korea/546746/, accessed on December 12, 2017.
74. Bryan Schatz, 'A History of Missile Defense, from 'Star Wars' to 'Trump', *Mother Jones*, January 27, 2017 at athttp://www.motherjones.com/politics/2017/01/donald-trump-missile-defense-star-wars/, accessed on December 13, 2017.
75. David Axe, "Trump is Calling for a Missile Defense System That Already Exists", MotherBoard, January 27, 2017 at https://motherboard.vice.com/en_us/article/vvzdga/trump-missile-defense-system, accessed on November 1, 2018.
76. Euan McKirdy and Taehoon Lee, 'North Korea Accepts South's Offer to Meet for Talks', CNN, January 5, 2018 at https://www.cnn.com/2018/01/04/asia/north-korea-south-korea-talks-intl/index.html, accessed on June 13, 2018.
77. Patrick Frater, 'Trump-Kim: North Korean Leader Says Summit Like Being in a Sci-Fi Movie', MSN, June 12, 2018 at https://www.msn.com/en-us/movies/news/trump-kim-north-korean-leader-says-summit-like-being-in-a-sci-fi-movie/ar-AAyww1J, accessed on June 13, 2018.

8. Beijing and the House of Cards in the Korean Peninsula[1]

*Jagannath P. Panda**

While it was the Korean War in the 1950s that divided the future trajectory of the two Koreas, it was the 'momentous decision'[2] by the People's Republic of China (PRC) to intervene and support the Democratic People's Republic of Korea (DPRK or North Korea) as a war ally that became a defining element of that historic War. Therefore, no subject in the history of Northeast Asia can perhaps be complete without considering the Chinese perspective towards the Korean Peninsula.

As a resident power in Northeast Asia, China treated the Korean Peninsula as their backyard during the Korean War period. This was reflected in Mao Zedong's directives issued to the Chinese People's Volunteer's on January 19, 1951 stating, 'the Chinese comrades must consider Koreas cause as their own ... just the way we feel about our own country and treat our own people'.[3] Seven decades have passed since the War, but the same resolve is still reflected in China's approach towards the region: neither will it discard North Korea as an alliance partner; nor will it reduce its strategic grip over the region. President Xi Jinping's informal meeting with Kim Jong-un on March 28, 2018 confirmed this. The Chinese President was quoted as stating that it is important for China to carry 'forward the traditional friendship' between the two sides, and Beijing would aim to play a 'constructive role' in the peace and stability of the Korean Peninsula.[4] Even Xi Jinping's recent visit to North Korea, the first by a Chinese President after Hu Jintao's in 2005, reassured Pyongyang of the sustained Chinese support, and their "eternal friendship".[5]

On the other hand, Kim Jong-un's frequent visits to China in the recent past indicates how significant an actor China is, especially for North Korea, in influencing debates and decisions pertaining to the region.

This chapter examines China's current and future approach towards the Korean Peninsula, by mainly analysing critical issues that are central to peace and stability in the region. Notwithstanding the significance of the perspectives of other major powers, China's role and responsibility as a resident power will continue to heavily influence and determine the arc of debates in the Korean Peninsula. These debates vary between denuclearisation to complete denuclearisation, reunification, to peace and stability. If the three inter-Korean summits in 2018 have raised somewhat Korean expectations for peace, stability and eventually reunification, the historical US-North Korea summit was an 'epochal event', with Donald Trump and Kim Jong-un raising aspirations for 'opening up a new future', as the Joint Statement pledged.[6] No matter how significant these summits have been, the complexity of the issues surrounding the Korean Peninsula make those aspirations seem like a mere house of cards—whose fortune depends heavily on the direction of the Chinese breeze. Beijing's cautionary approach through its P-5 red-card of the United Nations Security Council (UNSC) legitimises its stance. To comprehend the velocity of this Chinese breeze, this chapter seeks to examine *four* critical questions.

Why and How Does Beijing Decide the Fortune of the House of Cards?

It is relatively easier to comprehend the 'why' aspect than the 'how' aspect in China's approach towards the Korean Peninsula. In fact, it is not difficult to underline why China will be the most decisive actor in shaping the fortune of the House of Cards since these are primarily constant in Chinese foreign policy. Being a resident power, a P-5 member of the UNSC and, most importantly, the alliance partner of North Korea, China holds *three* subtle but constant elements which help in outlining the 'why' aspect of its approach. The 'how' aspects are based on some more independent elements that are subject to change, and can be circumstantial. How China shapes the fortune of the region is, thus, a complicated and a continual subject that links up with a range of other issues, within and outside the Korean Peninsula—from denuclearisation and peace prospects to China's relations with other powers like the US. In order to have a realistic assessment of why and how China will profoundly leave an impact, it is necessary to establish the correlation between the two—why and how—by highlighting and understanding the Chinese strategic objectives, both in current and future contexts, in the Korean Peninsula.

Beijing possesses multiple strategic objectives in the Korean Peninsula,[7] though some of them are politically motivated. These include: (a) to maintain the status-quo of a divided Korean Peninsula that will serve China's political purpose; (b) to maintain Beijing's 'credibility as a patron and ally' of North Korea;[8] (c) to enhance economic contacts between China's northeast provinces and North Korea's northern regions;[9] (d) to maintain working yet stronger economic contacts with South Korea so that there is a more spread out network in the Korean Peninsula; (e) not to allow the US entirely to dictate the security conditions in the region; and, (f) to assure China's position as a determining factor in all important issues like denuclearisation and reunification. Some of these objectives are overlapping, and shed light on how complex China's overall policy approach is towards the region. Amidst these, two immediate objectives for China are: (a) to further enrich Beijing's influence in the post-Panmunjom period of the inter-Korean summit between Moon Jae-in and Kim Jong-un; and (b) to protect China's security interests in the region ahead of a nuclear North Korea and an unpredictable US foreign policy approach towards China.

At first glance, in order to increase its influence in the Korean Peninsula, Beijing would like to nurture and rebuild its relationship with a nuclear North Korea, its traditional ally.[10] Though the exact amount of leverage Beijing really enjoys with a nuclear North Korea remains a little unclear at present, it would be somewhat naive to infer that Beijing is not prepared to see and live with a nuclear North Korea. In fact, it is Beijing which has been instrumental, over the years, in helping North Korea to become a nuclear power.[11] It is, more than any other country, actually the most accustomed to seeing North Korea's continuous missile and nuclear tests over the last decade. If anything, Beijing seemed a little puzzled and undecided regarding its response to a now overt nuclear North Korea, especially with the international pressure building on China in using its proximity to Pyongyang to convince the latter to stop its nuclear programme. Rather, if anything, it has further made Beijing more uncertain—especially at times when Pyongyang overlooked or seconded the Chinese overtures in the course of its nuclearisation efforts. Hence, many deductions were drawn that a nuclear North Korea is more of a strategic liability than a strategic asset for Beijing.[12]

Following Pyongyang's emergence as a nuclear power, assumptions have fast emerged that China does not possess the same influence and command over North Korea that it enjoyed before the country became nuclear. In fact, many would argue that the nuclear card has offered Pyongyang enough international legitimacy to go in for independent diplomacy outside Chinese purview.[13] In addition, South Korea's proactive stance in promoting peace with North Korea and Donald Trump leading the American approach to initiate dialogue with Pyongyang directly have been some reference points which, perhaps, indicate that China is not the same central actor in the Korean Peninsula that it used to be. Strengthening this narrative further is the Panmunjom Declaration which mentions China's role only in passing in a quadrilateral format.[14] The Declaration offered special importance to the role of the US in a trilateral format with the two Koreas, apart from the Quadrilateral format involving China.

Do all of these really imply that China's role and influence in the Korean Peninsula has eroded? Inferences drawn from recent developments strongly suggest that today China's influence is clearly not the same on the Korean Peninsula as it used to be—at least not on its alliance partner, North Korea.[15] Moreover, Beijing has reasons to worry since the credit for the third inter-Korean summit has gone more in favour of Moon Jae-in's 'responsible' foreign policy and Donald Trump's smart outreach policy with the two Korea's. Some might argue that Pyongyang's consent to have an inter-Korean meet with Seoul is a result of American 'maximum pressure' strategy. The historic Singapore meet between Donald Trump and Kim Jong-un on June 12, 2018 and the Hanoi summit between the two in February 2019 further indicated that the American strategy has been working—at least in bringing the North Koreans provisionally to the negotiating table, albeit bilaterally. Beijing's primary worry concerns the capricious nature of American diplomacy, where President Trump might like to have a bilateral understanding with Kim Jong-un, taking South Korea into confidence. In conservative Chinese thinking, the greater concern is not to loosen its grip over the affairs of the Korean Peninsula, as a trilateral understanding involving North Korea-South Korea-US could possibly be the order of the future.[16] American troop presence in Northeast Asia, Moon Jae-in's position to allow American troops to stay back, and Seoul's refusal to remove the THAAD from South Korea are additional factors that have strengthened China's insecurity and vulnerability.

These developments are obviously critical, and very detrimental to Chinese interests. However, it would still be premature to state that the inter-Korean peace process is unfolding more with American assent or with the consent of the two Koreas. In other words, it would be reckless to draw the conclusion that the house of cards in the Korean Peninsula in upholding peace and stability is unfolding *without* Chinese consent and/or knowledge. If the earlier meetings that were held between Kim Jong-un and Xi Jinping in 2018 and 2019 have any clues to offer, China still maintains the edge as a resident power over other major powers or actors in the Korean Peninsula. The visits by Kim Jong-un to China were aimed not only at 'pay[ing] deference to Beijing' but also to reassure China over its apparent significance in the region.[17] Pyongyang's aim was also to seek more economic assistance from China to face or defy UNSC sanctions. Even though the sanctions over North Korea are yet to be removed, Xi Jinping's recent visit to Pyongyang makes a reassured and confident case about the continuous economic and security assistance from China.

Following the Trump-Kim meet in Singapore and Vietnam, China has taken the lead in shaping the global debate to ease international sanctions on North Korea. In fact, China continues to be North Korea's largest trading partner, and holds the potential to be the most pivotal economic partner post sanctions in times to come. What is more significant is that Chinese diplomacy had an effect on Donald Trump too, as was evident in the US deciding to cancel military exercises with South Korea temporarily. This was as per the 'suspension for suspension' approach which China demanded in lieu of North Korea stopping missile and nuclear tests.[18]

Therefore, no matter how much leverage Beijing enjoys currently with Pyongyang, a progressive approach will be noticed in China's policy towards nuclear North Korea. This is for a specific reason: enhancing the relationship with Pyongyang will allow Beijing to protect its security interests better than earlier. China's influence and interests in the region are complementary to each other. Therefore, it is difficult to single out any one factor that Beijing would like to focus on. Rather, Beijing would like to pursue a more multipronged foreign policy approach, strengthening its relationship with North Korea as much as consolidating its relations with South Korea.

In other words, the world will witness China preparing to pursue a more mature foreign policy, taking forward and making occasional and circumstantial changes to its traditionalist foreign policy towards the Korean Peninsula. China's strategic influence over North Korea has certainly weakened in recent years due to Pyongyang's defiant approach in choosing to go in for incessant missile and nuclear tests without taking China into much confidence. But the classical tone and tenor of the Sino-DPRK relations, and the depth in their political understanding is one vital factor that would continue to float Beijing's influence with Pyongyang, and the Korean Peninsula at large. Indeed, it is not the nuclear and missile programme that comes as the security guarantor for Pyongyang. Rather, it is China and its security alliance with Beijing that continues to stay as the biggest security guarantor for Pyongyang, one which Kim Jong-un will not like to lose. Nonetheless, a careful reading of the Panmunjom Declaration would suggest that Beijing is still very much the most influential actor in shaping the underlying spirit of the document, even though the Declaration just mentions China once under a quadrilateral dialogue format.

For instance, the prelude to the Panmunjom summit was the 'four cardinal principles' that China and South Korea restated during President Moon Jae-ins visit to China in December 2017. These 'four cardinal principles' were: deterring war in the Korean Peninsula; its denuclearisation; the promotion of peace and dialogue; and improvement of inter-Korean relations.[19] These principles figure highly in the Panmunjom Declaration (April 2018) and Pyongyang Declaration (September 2018), reflecting the Chinese balancing approach towards both the Koreas and the region itself. Therefore, neither the Panmunjom Declaration nor the Pyongyang Declaration really overlook China's prominence as it would perhaps appear from these two important document. This is primarily due to China's balancing approach towards the Korean Peninsula wherein its relationship with South Korea is a key factor. Sino-South Korean relations might have gone through a low phase after the deployment of THAAD; but neither China nor South Korea has abandoned their economic partnership. Rather, as a constant historical power in the Korean Peninsula, China is remodelling its policies and postures subtly, adding new content and conditions to its customary Korean Peninsula policy, with possible new revisionist elements as well.[20] These revisionist elements can be noticed primarily in *three* specific issues: (a) China's new approach towards a nuclear North Korea possibly by reviving and revisiting the scope of the 1961 treaty; (b) not allowing the denuclearisation debate going out of the Chinese grip; and (c) supporting the unification process in principle without disturbing the status-quo much.

How Committed is Beijing Towards a Nuclear North Korea?

In the post-Korean War period, one of the constant and critical axes in the Korean Peninsula was the Sino-DPRK security alliance formed in July 1961. With the signing of the Treaty of Friendship, Cooperation, and Mutual Assistance[21] in July 1961 between China and the North Korea, the world witnessed the arrival of the second security alliance in the Korean Peninsula after the historic US-RoK Mutual Defense Treaty signed in October 1953. Central to the US-RoK Mutual Defense Treaty was: to facilitate forward deployment of the American forces against the Chinese and the Russians while deterring a future North Korean attack on South Korea.[22] This 1953 treaty provided, on the one hand, front-line protection for Japan while convincing, on the other hand, the RoK to strengthen its economy rather than military, by extending a 'nuclear umbrella'.[23] A number of significant international developments between 1953 and 1961 shaped China's international behaviour and approach towards its neighbours, primarily North Korea, India, and the then Soviet Union. Yet, it was the US-RoK 1953 Treaty that actually encouraged China to nurture its relations with North Korea further, and eventually led to the signing of the July 1961 Treaty with Pyongyang. In fact, this 1961 treaty formalised the military alliance partnership between China and North Korea to define their relationship as the 'Lips and Teeth Alliance' in the years to come.[24]

Since the signing of this treaty, Beijing as a power has moved ahead, and global politics too has witnessed new changes on the Korean Peninsula. North Korea has gradually emerged as a nuclear power while China has established itself as a prominent global power. Beijing's commitment as an ally was never in question before North Korea started its missile and nuclear programme. Doubts over China's commitment towards North Korea started fast becoming an international debate following Pyongyang's missile and nuclear programme. What, therefore, needs to be examined is: how relevant is the 1961 Treaty of Friendship between the PRC and the DPRK? And, how committed is China towards North Korea as a nuclear power? Answering these questions would require a brief assessment of China's overall approach towards the two Koreas—North and South—both in historical and contemporary context.

If strategic, revolutionary, and ideological considerations were the primacies of China's approach towards the two Koreas traditionally, pragmatism and realism have become the prime features of Chinese policy at present.[25] China continues to bring its Communist legacy as a bonding factor between Beijing and Pyongyang. However, what is important to note is that a common revolutionary ideology and the 1961 Treaty between China and North Korea were the two central features of China's traditionalist policy approach towards the Korean Peninsula.[26] In other words, Beijing's traditionalist approach was heavily based on its North Korea policy.[27] A subtle change was noticed in the approach when China became a member of the United Nation (UN) and the UNSC in 1971. The 'open-door' foreign policy of Deng Xiaoping in 1978 equally internationalised China's outreach; an immediate effect of this was reflected in China's approach towards its immediate neighbourhood, Central Asia, South Asia, and also the Korean Peninsula.

Following the historic 1962 India-China war, relations between China and India started normalising from 1988 onwards. With the disintegration of the Soviet Union in 1991, China started viewing both Central Asia and Northeast Asia in a new way. What, however, significant was the establishment of Beijing's diplomatic relations with South Korea in August 1992 which increased the scope of Chinese policy towards the Korean Peninsula to become more non-North Korea centric. *The Times* published a piece in August 1992 stating the establishment of China-South Korea diplomatic relationship and indicating Beijing's increasing pragmatic foreign policy factored more on economics rather than on Communist ideologies.[28] In diplomatic ties between China and South Korea, a subtle change was noticed in Beijing's approach towards the region which was now based on directives favouring both the Koreas. Thus, any reflection on China's commitment towards the 1961 Treaty and its alliance with North Korea needs to be comprehended in terms of Beijing's overall approach towards the region—that is, factoring in a range of political and economic considerations.

This 57-year old Sino-DPRK treaty is still considered as the most important treaty of the region since it offers a guarantee to North Korea's security which is applicable even today. However, conventional debates suggest that a nuclear Pyongyang has become a 'strategic liability' more than a 'strategic asset' for Beijing.[29] This treaty has been extended from time to time, ratified every twenty years, and is now extending to 2021. It was originally based on 'Marxism-Leninism' and the 'principle of proletarian internationalism'.[30] In today's context, one could subject the relevance of these theories to substantial debates and discussions. But the Communist Party of China (CPC) still prefers to engage with the North Korean administration through these principles. For instance, CPCs International Department has been active recently in engaging with the North Korean side to promote exchange and revive the historical contacts between the two countries.[31] Besides, to accord a Communist legacy to their age-old bonding, Chinese media still makes a succinct case whenever possible by mentioning that the meetings between the Chinese President and North Korean leader is just not between the head of the states, but also between the ruling party chiefs. Therefore, the ideological pledge may seem to appear to be highly secondary in Sino-DPRK relations at present; but the ideological surface is still one strong medium of contact between the two sides. Chinese experts acknowledge the high importance that Beijing accords to 'its relations with the state and party of North Korea'.[32] Beijing's foreign policy is still very much guided by CPC's fundamentals of internationalism to which the 19th CPC report increasingly points or refers to.[33] Besides, what is significant to note in the Sino-DPRK context is the unchanged text of the 1961 Treaty which was renewed in 2001, implying that both sides still give importance to these principles, and like to carry forward this legacy before they bring any change to the text.

Nonetheless, an irrefutable relevance of the treaty is its Article II which outlines the military alliance between China and North Korea in a 'state of war' condition. Two points need explanation here: (a) how far North Korea would like to depend upon China's military after it has become a nuclear power; and (b) if the 1961 treaty will witness any change or modification in 2021 when the validity of the treaty will be reviewed. To answer these queries directly: North Korea would still like to indulge with China for a continued military understanding post-2021. This is specifically because it provides an assurance that China will act as a protector as and when North Korea needs protection. Pyongyang is not sure how the international situation will unfold in times to come even though inter-Korean relations are improving. Besides, for Pyongyang, there are doubts cast over the eventuality of its nuclear and missile capabilities, ahead of a 'complete denuclearisation' mandate. In order to not disturb the status quo of the military alliance partnership that it enjoys with Beijing, Pyongyang would, therefore, favour the renewal of the treaty post-2021.[34] From China's point of view, it would make sense to extend the validity of the treaty beyond 2021 as it would allow Beijing to maintain a closer security and military arrangement with North Korea. In fact, it will also allow Beijing to use Pyongyang as a 'buffer' between South Korea and the US in any negotiation or dialogue, since the 1961 treaty provides an umbrella that neither side will enter 'any action or measure' that is directed against any of them (Article III), and consult each other on 'important international issues' (Article IV). In other words, Beijing would like to renew the treaty beyond 2021 to ensure that Pyongyang will not move ahead to forge any meaningful or substantial understanding with either South Korea or with the US without consulting China.

Moreover, even though it appears from the Panmunjom and Pyongyang Declarations that China's role has been marginalised in the current context, the fundamentals of the Declarations endorse the Chinese historical essence in addition to the American essence in the Korean Peninsula. If the peace process after the Panmunjom summit continues, China *might* even like to modify the text of the 1961 treaty, given the unfolding environment between the two Koreas. In other words, the 1961 treaty would be extended further, with or without modification, since it is closely linked to China's national security objective. For China, while the immediate objective is not to reduce Beijing's grip over a nuclear North Korea, the long-term objective is to control the strategic environment of the Northeast Asia in favour of Beijing. This treaty allows China to be a constant factor both in the denuclearisation and reunification dialogue process where North Korea will be required to consult Beijing before taking any action or decision.

What would be China's Approach Towards Denuclearisation?

Both denuclearisation and reunification are debatable subjects where both the position and perspective of the critical actors, primarily China and the US, invariably differ from each other. The American pressure tactic of 'complete, verifiable, and irreversible' dismantling of North Korea's nuclear arsenals and facilities would be in juxtaposition with the Chinese standpoint which supports a gradual nuclear-free Korean Peninsula without really demanding a complete dismantling of North Korea's nuclear weapons. Further, China would like to provide an umbrella to Pyongyang in UNSC from the American pressure to conduct a "fully verified denuclearization" inspection by the IAEA that might utterly expose North Korea's internal security establishments to the outside world. Though Pyongyang has agreed "in principle" for verification by the IAEA, to follow concrete steps for nuclear disarmament leading to "complete denuclearization" remain the contested point on which China might raise objection, both within and outside the UNSC. Rather, Beijing would ensure that this IAEA verification process must commensurate with the removal of the UNSC sanctions. This shared perspective of China on denuclearisation with North Korea makes China the most important actor in the Korean Peninsula, which South Korea will find hard to openly object even though Seoul would expect Beijing to support a "fully verified" inspection eventually leading to "complete denuclearisation" process. For Seoul, restoring and maintaining peace is the utmost priority in the present scenario—

even more than 'complete denuclearisation'. Such a scenario only strengthens China's prospects in the region, making Beijing slowly emerge as the most significant player in the denuclearisation process, both within and outside the UN mandate.

What is important to note is that the crux behind the denuclearisation debate in the Korean Peninsula is not the issue of 'complete de-nuclearisation' but how to achieve it and then proceed with it. In fact, for Washington, 'complete, verifiable, and irreversible dismantlement' (CVID) is the principled position that the US would like to proceed with even though Washington realises that it is virtually impossible to achieve such a target in the near-term future. On the other hand, for Pyongyang, it is the bargaining chip in lieu of CVID, the removal of UNSC sanctions, and serves new opportunities to stimulate economic development.[35] For South Korea, it is the dialogue process on denuclearisation that matters, and which must ensue within a peaceful and stable environment.

Where does China stand in the entire scenario? Officially, China has commented on the issue of denuclearisation from time to time, signifying its importance as a P-5 country of the UNSC. Being 'committed' officially to a nuclear-free Korean Peninsula has helped Beijing maintain an international position, especially at the UNSC. An articulated Chinese position is aptly reflected in Chinese Foreign Ministry Spokesperson Geng Shuang's press conference held on June 12, 2018—coincidently on the same day as the Trump-Kim meeting in Singapore. The Chinese statement read,

> ... China is always committed to achieving the de-nuclearisation of the Korean Peninsula, upholding the peace and stability on the Peninsula and resolving the relevant issue through dialogue and consultation. To this end, China put forth the 'suspension for suspension' initiative and 'dual-track' approach. The facts have proven that the China-proposed 'suspension for suspension' initiative has been materialised and now the situation is also moving forward in the direction of the 'dual-track' approach.[36]

Underlying this statement is a much thought-out and long-drawn Chinese perspective on denuclearisation. These positions are certainly not permanent; rather, they are contingent upon the evolving politics in the region. Therefore, a careful analysis of this stated position unveils how critical China's position and perception is towards denuclearisation. In fact, Beijing's stance on denuclearisation is closely related to *three* aspects. First, Beijing wants the process of denuclearisation to proceed with concrete dialogue and consultation.[37] This allows Beijing to keep a close eye on the progress, and ensure that China is not left out of any negotiation or dialogue—or even consultation—concerning denuclearisation. Further, Beijing contends that the process of denuclearisation is a complicated chapter; hence it must proceed with peaceful dialogue.[38] This is so for historical reasons. China has been a signatory to the 1953 Armistice Agreement; therefore, any peace treaty in the Korean Peninsula, including denuclearisation, would have to involve China.[39]

Second, China's stance on denuclearisation is based on procedural peace mechanisms since this allows Beijing as a P-5 country to monitor and take control of the situation. A recent Chinese official statement points to this. The Chinese State Councillor and Foreign Minister, Wang Yi, stated that 'China believes that the most effective way is to promote denuclearisation in parallel with the building of a peace mechanism on the Peninsula, so that the two can be settled together'. He further stated that, 'The UN Security Council should also form consensus in a timely manner to facilitate and support this process'.[40] Beijing has always backed the Six-Party Talks even though they were not successful in stopping North Korea from going nuclear. Addressing denuclearisation through procedural mechanisms automatically allows China to become a central actor in building consensus in favour of North Korea by checking American pressure.

From the time of North Korea's withdrawal from the Nuclear Non-proliferation Treaty (that is, since 2003), China has followed the stance of uniting all relevant actors in the Korean Peninsula to seek consensus. Following the nuclear tests by North Korea, China's stated position to address the denuclearisation issue has seen a slight change: Beijing wants that denuclearisation should be addressed more through the UN mandate. China delicately pursues this position in the name of building trust. The Chinese media has often referred to the fact that 'trust building' is the key to the denuclearisation process.[41] In other words, Beijing's attempt has been to build a consensus on the denuclearisation debate in the UNSC where it could envision to play a constructive role.

Beijing wants that the denuclearisation process must be carried out within the purview of the UN where it will have a legitimate mandate to monitor, supervise, and control the process of negotiation as a P-5 country of the UNSC.

Third, to Beijing, the denuclearisation debate was more about the peace and stability in Korean Peninsula, which is China's immediate neighbourhood, rather than about technicalities. For a long time, Beijing had demanded the 'suspension for suspension' initiative to put a stop to North Korea's nuclear tests, and urged for a 'dual-track' approach to uphold peace and denuclearisation efforts in the region. Otherwise known as the 'dual suspension' initiative, Pyongyang agreeing to suspend its missile and nuclear programme in exchange for the suspension of the US-South Korea bilateral military exercise. President Trump's decision to suspend the US-South Korean joint exercises was in some way seen as a victory to the Chinese 'worldview' on the Korean Peninsula.[42]

Through a 'suspension for suspension' proposal, Beijing ensured that the US not only safeguards North Koreas 'security concerns' but also upholds its classical position that denuclearisation should be achieved systematically through a 'stage by stage' process and 'package solutions'.[43] The 'dual track' approach was to maintain peace and to address this, in which Beijing's call mostly prevailed. In other words, Beijing's 'dual-track' approach is based on a comprehensive approach, associated closely with the future of the Korean Peninsula, and based on dialogue and consultation. This stated Chinese position has been more beneficial for South Korea which was more in favour of North Korea stopping its nuclear and missile programme, and maintain stability.

The above stated Chinese position unveils a grander security calculus that is critical to Beijing's foreign policy approach in its neighbourhood. China's stance on denuclearisation is close to North Korea's stated position which is to achieve a 'complete' nuclear-free Korean Peninsula through a 'phased-by-phased' manner. In other words, China would not like to see North Korea or the Korean Peninsula becoming nuclear-free so soon. It serves the Chinese purpose, as Beijing does not want to allow the US to dictate terms over North Korea, and start having an edge in a trilateral format: US-North Korea-South Korea. Beijing realises that a nuclear North Korea is certainly not in its best interests; but it would like to carefully live with a nuclear North Korea and hold an edge, with Pyongyang pursuing a serious economic diplomacy that is key to North Korea's future. Pyongyang looks at Beijing for economic assistance, and will continue to do so. Being the largest trading partner of China, North Korea would like to take China into confidence in most denuclearisation debate.

Therefore, China's shared perspective with North Korea on denuclearisation is based on a strategy: not to allow a complete and abrupt denuclearisation, and try to make sure that North Korea continues to stay with China on a range of issues even though, at present, it is having frequent dialogues with the US and South Korea. Beijing's approach towards the Korean Peninsula—primarily towards North Korea's nuclear and missile programme—might seem to be contradictory all these years. However, what is important to note is that it was not without a purpose. Rather, it was based on a multi-faceted strategy to check and respond to US's growing influence over the region. Beijing would actually like to take advantage of the complex political environment relating to a nuclear-free debate which is more about the process of achieving it rather than about the definition of 'complete' or the technicalities of the issue. Beijing visualises a greater role in controlling the denuclearisation debate even though Pyongyang has agreed to a major disarmament by 2020.

Does China Support a Divided or Unified Korean Peninsula?

Officially, China continues to back a unified Korea to be brought about through a peaceful dialogue. It is imperative, however, to note that Beijing's stance on unification is a complicated chapter, relating to China's national security interests. In fact, it is equally important to note that, 'with or without unification', the Korean Peninsula is already witnessing continuous change.[44] Thus, any inferences regarding China's perspective on the issue needs to be analysed in evolving conditions, and Beijing's rapport with the state of affairs in the Korean Peninsula.

Besides, China's standpoint on a divided or unified Korea is a subject matter that is closely linked with China, both as an observer and participant.[45] A fine reflection of this dual role—of both observer and participant—is reflected aptly in the historic 1961 Treaty between China and North Korea. Article VI of this treaty outlines how the 'unification of Korea' is a process that should be realised through 'peaceful and democratic lines', keeping the 'national interests of the Korean people and the aim of preserving peace in the Far East'.[46] In other words, China holds a share for its role in the unification matter through this treaty. It has assured through all these decades that China will back more of a North Korea-led or North Korea-centred unification process, depending upon the situation in the 'Far East'—that is, the Korean Peninsula.

It remains unclear at present whether China would really like to see a North Korea-led or North Korean-centred unification process in region, especially with Pyongyang becoming a nuclear power. What evidently becoming clear is that China has maintained a delicate stance on the issue of unified Korea, since 'Pyongyang as a buffer against Western-style democracies' is useful for China.[47] Beijing strongly believes that any chance of unification would strengthen a 'Western-oriented peninsula' which will be detrimental to its own national security interests.[48]

Though the unification of the Korea is not a 'core interest' for China, any prospect of Korean unification will still invite China's attention in times to come.

This maybe because, for Beijing, a unified Korea would mean an increase in American influence on the Peninsula. This will not be conducive to China's strategic interests. Besides, a unified Korea would also mean the emergence of a stronger nation in the Northeast Asia which will change the balance of power equation in the region. In other words, it would mean the arrival of a politically strong country, increasing the odds of Korean interests being detrimental to Beijing's strategic interests. Therefore, China has always treaded carefully when expressing its views on Korean unification.

For instance, Beijing acted candid in approaching the inter-Korean leadership summit that was held in April 2018. Officially, it stated that the summit had a 'positive outcome' which would be beneficial for enhancing 'reconciliation' and 'cooperation' between the two Koreas. Stating that North Korea and South Korea 'belong to the same nation', China was vocal in supporting the dialogue between the two countries, and expressed hope in envisaging a peaceful political settlement of the Korean Peninsula.[49] These statements are, nevertheless, based on Beijing's own geopolitical interests in the region which are also closely linked to a number of other critical issues facing China currently.

First, Beijing would like to ensure that a unified Korea is pro-Chinese rather than pro-Western. Historically, China's position on Korean unification was noted in the secret cable communication drafted by the East German Embassy in Pyongyang on March 28, 1973 which stated: 'China will support Korean unification only when it is confident that a unified Korea will be pro-Chinese'.[50] The cable further states that: 'China was also concerned that a unified Korea, made up of over 50 million Koreans, will become more politically important and independent, and that a leader with political ambitions extending beyond the Korean peninsula will appear'.[51] This historical subtext on China is still relevant in the current context. Beijing would make sure that any prospects of Korean unification must be taking place with China's consent and coordination. In order to do that, China may install occasional changes or introduce new mediums of dialogue mechanisms on sensitive subjects like denuclearisation and unification. The attempt would be to promote the Chinese agenda, and not allow the two Koreas to undertake Western ways.

Second, China would like to support the current status-quo of the two Koreas while advocating principles for unification.[52] To attain this, Beijing may like to introduce new element of policies, a more revisionist oriented approach, by revisiting its traditional way of approaching the two Koreas. Rebuilding relationships with South Koreans may be given priority without compromising too much on its traditionalist alliance with North Korea. Sino-South Korean relations may witness steady progress where Beijing would aim to have a better consultative partaking in the prospects of the inter-Korean peace process without losing North Korea's confidence. South Korea might be an American ally, but South Korea's trading economy is closely linked, and somewhat regionally dependent on, trade and economic contacts with China.[53]

Even though the prospect of Korean unification is a distant dream and the meaning of unification is still an abstract concept, China's eventual aim would be to maintain a balance between the two Koreas while maximising its influence in the unification process. This is for a political purpose: under Xi Jinping's leadership, Beijing is aiming for the reunification of Taiwan with Mainland China under its 'new era' foreign policy—and sooner than many would like to anticipate. President Xi Jinping's speech at the 19th National Congress of the Communist Party of China (CPC) clearly indicates this.[54] Following this speech, many have even started foreseeing China occupying Taiwan forcefully by 2020,[55] though such a scenario will be an extreme one. Nevertheless, advocating and supporting Korean unification merely rhetorically serves the purpose of China, which would be aiming to encourage Taiwan to start preparing for a merger with Mainland China at some point.[56]

Importantly, neither does Beijing want to have a definite position on Korean unification, nor does it want to advocate its view hastily, since Taiwan's merger with it is one of its core interests. This has allowed Beijing to set an example to convince the relevant parties for a complete merger of Taiwan rather than adopting a compromising model, like the ones Hong Kong and Macau have set for themselves.[57] Taiwan's merger with China has been a debatable subject for a long time, along with the status of Hong Kong and Macau—even though both Hong Kong and Macau are, at present, seen as two important parts of China. These issues are sensitive for Beijing and relate to China's sovereignty issues. Therefore, China exercises caution in expressing specific views related to Korean unification as they might lead to spill-overs in Taiwan. Ideally, Beijing would aim to attain Taiwan's merger with Mainland China before any unification whatsoever in the Korean Peninsula. It would put China at a categorically better position to put forward its suggestions. Thus, depending on certain external circumstances like Taiwan's merger with Mainland China, Beijing might revise its position on Korean unification.

In conclusion, it is more in China's interests to have a divided Korea in its neighbourhood rather than a unified one. A unified Korea will not only alter the balance of power equation in Northeast Asia, but also alter China's political calculations in the broader Indo-Pacific region. Therefore, it goes without mentioning that China's role as a resident power in the region will definitely be pivotal in shaping the future of the Korean Peninsula. Since the inception of the Korean War on June 25, 1950, China's role has always been the most important factor not only in dividing North and South Korea but also in leading the non-Western bloc in global affairs.

China is, therefore, likely to pursue a more watchful approach towards the development in the Korean corridor for at least some time in the future. In other words, Beijing would like to play a cautious but constructive role in a region that had set the course for world politics in the 1950s with China's decision to support North Korea in the historic Korean War. If peace prospects continue to flourish in the post-Panmunjom period, China would like to play a balancing role between the two Koreas by maintaining equi-cordial relations with both. If the peace prospects fail to sustain, Beijing might like to persist with a traditionalist approach of maintaining 'exclusive' relations with North Korea. It would, thus, maintain economic-oriented relations with South Korea, anticipating a more robust US-China competition unfolding in the future. No matter what the prospects of peace are, China's role in the region will continue to remain defining, shaping the fortune of the precarious House of Cards in the Korean Peninsula.

Notes

* Dr. Jagannath P. Panda is a Research Fellow at the Institute for Defence Studies and Analyses (IDSA), New Delhi.

1. This essay builds on the author's earlier publication titled, 'Chinese revisionism in the Korean Corridor', *The Asian Age*, May 13, 2018 at http://www.asianage.com/360-degree/130518/chinese-revisionism-in-korean-corridor.html, accessed on October 31, 2018.
2. HaoYufan and ZhaiZhihai called China's decision to enter the Korean War a 'momentous decision'. They argue that this decision by China (to enter into the Korean War) was a legacy of the historical animosity between the Chinese Communist Party (CCP) and the US. The CCP viewed the United States as a foreign imperial power, threatening its existence. See, HaoYufan and ZhaiZhihai, 'China's Decision to Enter the Korean War: History Revisited', *The China Quarterly,* No. 121, March 1990, pp. 94–115.
3. Mao Tse-Tung, 'The Chinese Peoples Volunteers should cherish every hill, every river, every tree and every blade of grass in Korea', Directives to the Chinese Peoples Volunteers, January 19, 1951, *Selected Works of Mao Tse-Tung*, Vol. 5, 1977, p. 44.
4. 'Xi Jinping, Kim Jong-un hold talks in Beijing', *China Daily,* March 29, 2018 at http://www.chinadaily.com.cn/a/201803/29/WS5abae475a3105cdcf6514b55.html, accessed on October 26, 2018.
5. Andrei Lankov, 'Friends reunited: why the Kim-Xi summit was masterful political theatre', *NK News,* June 24, 2019 at https://www.nknews.org/2019/06/friends-reunited-why-the-kim-xi-summit-was-masterful-political-theater/, accessed on June 26, 2019.
6. 'Joint Statement of President Donald J. Trump of the United States of America and Chairman Kim Jong Un of the Democratic People's Republic of Korea at the Singapore Summit', The White House, June 12, 2018 at https://www.whitehouse.gov/briefings-statements/joint-statement-

president-donald-j-trump-united-states-america-chairman-kim-jong-un-democratic-peoples-republic-korea-singapore-summit/, accessed on October 30, 2018.

7. Dick K. Nanto and Mark E. Manyin, 'China-North Korea Relations', Congressional Research Service, CRS Report for Congress, December 28, 2010, pp. 1–22.
8. Ibid., p. 6.
9. Ibid.
10. Interview with Professor Haksoon Paik, President, Sejong Institute, South Korea.
11. See, Jagannath P. Panda, 'China's Approach to the North Korean Nuclear Crisis', IDSA Strategic Comment, October 31, 2016 at https://idsa.in/idsastrategiccomments/ChinaApproachtotheNorthKoreanNuclearCrisis_JPPanda_311006, accessed on November 1, 2018; Jagannath P. Panda, 'DPRKs Nuclear Provocations and the Indian Response', IDSA Strategic Comment, September 27, 2016 at https://idsa.in/idsacomments/dprk-nuclear-provocations-and-the-indian-response_jppanda_270916, accessed on November 1, 2018.
12. For example, Zhu Feng, 'Chinas North Korean Liability', *Foreign Affairs*, July 11, 2017, at https://www.foreignaffairs.com/articles/china/2017-07-11/chinas-north-korean-liability, accessed on October 31, 2018; see also, Leo Timm, 'A Fading Alliance Between China and North Korea', *The Epoch Times*, July 16, 2017 at https://www.theepochtimes.com/china-and-north-korea-a-fading-alliance_2267290.html, accessed on November 1, 2018); see also, Lee Seong-hyon, 'China-North Korea DefenseTreaty', *The Korea Times,* July 26, 2016 at http://www.koreatimes.co.kr/www/news/opinon/2016/07/197_210355.html, accessed on October 31, 2018.
13. Based on the author's interactions with many leading Chinese experts in South Korea during the author's stay in Seoul, June-July 2018.
14. 'Panmunjom Declaration', Inter-Korean Summit 2018: Panmunjom, *The Korea Times,* April 27, 2018, at https://www.koreatimes.co.kr/www/nation/2018/04/731_248077.html, accessed on October 31, 2018.
15. For instance, read, Eleanor Albert, 'The China-North Korea Relationship', Backgrounder, Council on Foreign Relations, March 28, 2018 at https://www.cfr.org/backgrounder/china-north-korea-relationship, accessed on November 2, 2018.
16. Jagannath P. Panda, 'Chinese revisionism in the Korean Corridor', *The Asian Age*, May 13, 2018 at http://www.asianage.com/360-degree/130518/chinese-revisionism-in-korean-corridor.html, accessed on October 31, 2018.
17. Lily Kuo, 'Kim Jong-un meets Xi Jinping for third time', *The Guardian,* June 19, 2018 at https://www.theguardian.com/world/2018/jun/19/

kim-jong-un-meets-xi-jinping-for-third-time, accessed on October 31, 2018.

18. Lily Kuo, 'China hails its indisputable role in outcome of Trump-Kim summit', *The Guardian,* June 13, 2018 at https://www.theguardian.com/world/2018/jun/13/china-hails-its-indisputable-role-in-outcome-of-trump-kim-summit, accessed on November 1, 2018.
19. '(3rd LD) Moon, Xi vow efforts to improve ties, peacefully denuclearize North Korea', Yonhap News Agency, December 14, 2017 at http://english.yonhapnews.co.kr/northkorea/2017/12/14/0401000000AEN20171214012052315.html, accessed on November 2, 2018.
20. Jagannath P. Panda, note 16.
21. Read the Full Text of the Treaty here. 'Treaty of Friendship, Co-Operation and Mutual Assistance Between the Peoples Republic of China and the Democratic People's Republic of Korea', July 11, 1961, *Peking Review*, 4(28), p. 5.
22. Kongdan Oh, 'U.S.-ROK: The Forgotten Alliance', Brookings East Asian Commentary, October 13, 2018 at https://www.brookings.edu/opinions/u-s-rok-the-forgotten-alliance/, accessed on October 30, 2018.
23. Ibid.
24. Chen Jian, 'Limits of the Lips and Teeth Alliance: An Historical Review of China-North Korean Relations', *Asia Programme Special Report,* No. 115, September 2003, pp. 4–10.
25. Kim Hakjoon, 'Chinas Korea Policy since the Tiananmen Square Incident', Proceedings of the Academy of Political Science, 38(2), *The China Challenge: American Policies in East Asia*, 1991, pp. 107–114.
26. Ibid.
27. Ibid., pp. 108–109.
28. Nicholas D. Kristof, 'Chinese and South Koreans Formally Establish Relations', *Times,* August 24, 1992, reprinted in *The New York Times* at https://www.nytimes.com/1992/08/24/world/chinese-and-south-koreans-formally-establish-relations.html, accessed on October 31, 2018.
29. Lee Seong-hyon, 'China-North Korea Defense Treaty', *The Korea Times,* July 26, 2016 at http://www.koreatimes.co.kr/www/news/opinon/2016/07/197_210355.html, accessed on October 31, 2018.
30. See, note 21.
31. Elizabeth Shim, 'Report: Chinese Communist Party official arrives in North Korea', *UPI,* April 13, 2018 at https://www.upi.com/Report-Chinese-Communist-Party-official-arrives-in-North-Korea/5821523624263/, accessed on November 7, 2018.
32. The Chinese expert on Korean Affairs, Lu Chao, from the Liaoning Academy of Social Sciences, holds this view. His views are quoted in the *South China Morning Post.* See, Teddy Ng, 'Xi Jinping to send right-hand

man Li Zhanshu to North Korea', *South China Morning Post,* September 4, 2018 at https://www.scmp.com/news/china/diplomacy/article/2162756/xi-jinping-send-right-hand-man-li-zhanshu-north-korea, accessed on November 7, 2018.

33. 'Secure a Decisive Victory in Building a Moderately Prosperous Society in All Respects and Strive for the Great Success of Socialism with Chinese Characteristics for a New Era', Full Text of Xi Jinpings report at 19th CPC National Congress, Delivered at the 19th National Congress of the Communist Party of China, October 18, 2017 at http://www.chinadaily.com.cn/m/shandong/yantai/2017-11/04/content_34175088.htm, accessed on November 7, 2018.
34. Dr. Wooyeal Paik of the Yonsei University argues that the 1961 Treaty 'still holds its legal ground even though many (in and out of China) argue that it's dead. This treaty can be revived and utilized when the two countries need to do something military against the US and its allies in Northeast Asia', author's interview with Wooyeal Paik.
35. Liu Zhen, 'China will have a role in North Koreas denuclearization, but not just yet, analysts say', *South China Morning Post,* June 15, 2018 at https://www.scmp.com/news/china/diplomacy-defence/article/2150864/china-will-have-role-north-koreas-denuclearisation-not, accessed on November 2, 2018.
36. Foreign Ministry Spokesperson, Geng Shuang's Regular Press Conference, June 12, 2018 at http://www.china-un.ch/eng/fyrth/t1568234.htm, accessed on November 2, 2018.
37. Li Zhao, 'China's role in denuclearization of Korean Peninsula', CGTN Live, June 10, 2018 at https://news.cgtn.com/news/3d3d414f3149444d78457a6333566d54/share_p.html, accessed on November 2, 2018.
38. Ibid.
39. Michael Walsh, 'Korea talks: What does China have to gain or lose from a potentially reunified Korean Peninsula?', ABC News, April 27, 2018 at https://www.abc.net.au/news/2018-04-25/north-korea-talks-will-they-help-or-hinder-china/9687834, accessed on November 2, 2018.
40. 'Chinese FM calls for joint efforts to solve Korean Peninsula issue', Xinhua, September 28, 2018 at http://www.xinhuanet.com/english/2018-09/28/c_137498994.htm, accessed on November 2, 2018.
41. 'Trust building is still needed for peninsula denuclearization', *China Daily,* July 8, 2018 at http://www.chinadaily.com.cn/a/201807/08/WS5b421457a3103349141e164e.html, accessed on November 2, 2018.
42. Wang Qingyun, 'Consider dual-track approach', *China Daily,* May 7, 2018 at http://www.chinadaily.com.cn/a/201805/07/WS5aef52d1a3105cdcf651c3c4.html, accessed on November 2, 2018.
43. Mu Xuequan, 'China advocates dual-track approach to solve Korean Peninsula nuclear issue: FM', Xinhua, May 4, 2018 at http://www.

xinhuanet.com/english/2018-04/05/c_137090767.htm, accessed on November 4, 2018.

44. Jonathan D. Pollack, 'Is Xi Jinping Rethinking Korean Unification?', Brookings, January 20, 2015 at https://www.brookings.edu/on-the-record/is-xi-jinping-rethinking-korean-unification/, accessed on November 7, 2018.
45. Ibid.
46. See, note 21.
47. Robert E. Kelly, 'Chinas Support for North Korea Kills Any Chance for Unification', *The National Interest*, April 17, 2017 at https://nationalinterest.org/feature/chinas-support-north-korea-kills-any-chance-unification-20227, accessed on November 5, 2018.
48. Todd Rosenblum, 'How to persuade China to abandon North Korea', *Politico,* July 18, 2017 at https://www.politico.com/agenda/story/2017/07/18/china-north-korea-american-troops-removal-000476, accessed on November 5, 2018.
49. 'China welcomes inter-Korean summit, extends congratulations', Xinhua, April 28, 2018 at http://m.china.org.cn/orgdoc/doc_1_29302 748824.html, accessed on November 5, 2018.
50. Cited in Kim Heung-Kyu, 'China's Position on Korean Unification and ROK-PRC Relations', The 2nd KRIS-Brookings Joint Conference, p. 232.
51. Ibid.
52. Dr. Wooyeal Paik of the Yonsei University argues that: 'China's basic position on the Korean peninsula is status quo. Unless China can obtain unexpectedly high compensation for supporting the unification (led by South Korea), it will support in talks, obstruct in behaviours'; author's interview with Dr. Wooyeal Paik.
53. Jagannath P. Panda, note 16.
54. Xi Jinping was explicit in his view when he said that, 'Resolving the Taiwan question to realize China's complete reunification is the shared aspiration of all Chinese people, and is in the fundamental interests of the Chinese nation. We must uphold the principles of 'peaceful reunification' and 'one country, two systems,' work for the peaceful development of cross-Straits relations, and advance the process toward the peaceful reunification of China'. See, 'Secure a Decisive Victory in Building a Moderately Prosperous Society in All Respects and Strive for the Great Success of Socialism with Chinese Characteristics for a New Era', Full Text of Xi Jinping's report at 19th CPC National Congress, Delivered at the 19th National Congress of the Communist Party of China, October 18, 2017 at http://www.chinadaily.com.cn/m/shandong/yantai/2017-11/04/content_34175088.htm, accessed on November 6, 2018.

55. For instance, see, Deng Yuwen, 'Is China planning to take Taiwan by force in 2020?', *South China Morning Post,* January 4, 2018 at https://www.scmp.com/comment/insight-opinion/article/2126541/china-planning-take-taiwan-force-2020, accessed on November 6, 2018.
56. Kim Heung-Kyu, 'Chinas Position on Korean Unification and ROK-PRC Relations', The 2nd KRIS-Brookings Joint Conference Paper, pp. 236–237; see also, Jagannath P. Panda, note 16.
57. For example, read, Ronald Tiersky, 'The China Model For Korean Unification', Real Clear World, February 26, 2018 at https://www.realclearworld.com/articles/2018/02/26/the_china_model_for_korean_unification_112724.html, accessed on November 6, 2018.

9. China-North Korea Military Relations

Mandip Singh

The Korean War saw the forging of a strong bond between the two armies. For three years, the Chinese People's Volunteers (CPV) fought alongside Kim Il-sung's North Korean troops against the US and, for five years after the war, Chinese troops remained stationed on the Korean Peninsula, many assisting in reconstruction projects. A large number of Chinese leaders of that campaign rose to be members of the Chinese elite. Korean War veterans like Lin Biao and Peng Duhai continued to maintain an emotional and sentimental connect with the KPA. Even elsewhere in the PLA, several Korean War veterans continued to patronise relations with the KPA. However, in 1958, threatened by the pro-China Yanan faction, Kim Il-sung purged the senior generals of the KPA, and cut off ties with the PLA to the detriment of the relationship.[1]

Kim Il-sung followed a deft policy of balancing relations with China and Russia. In 1961, China and North Korea signed a Treaty of Friendship, Co-operation, and Mutual Assistance—the only formal foreign military alliance signed by China—and committed one country to come to the aid of the other if attacked. Peng Duhai's ouster from power and Lin Biao's death in a suspicious air crash during the period of the Cultural Revolution in China led to a freeze in bilateral relations between the two neighbours. It was in 1970 that Premier Zhou Enlai became the first high level Chinese visitor in Pyongyang after seven years, and the two nations reiterated their 'blood-cemented militant friendship' that was as 'close as lips and teeth' once again.

Relations between the two continued to remain the purview of the political elite, and not much was exchanged between the two militaries through the 1970s. Differences continued to rock the fragile relations, with Mao refusing to support Kim Il-sung's succession plan to hand over power to his son Kim Jong-il, labelling it dynastic and anti-communist. In the meantime, Korea also failed to garner China's support to unify the Korean Peninsula at a time when China was seeking a rapprochement in its relations with the US.

It was the exchange of military visits in the early 1980s that renewed relations; there was also the transfer of 40 F-7 fighter planes (MiG 21) to North Korea. In addition, China provided North Korea with R-class submarines, AN-2 cargo carriers, silkworm ship missiles, and surface-to-surface ship missiles in an attempt to reassure North Korea of its commitment to the 1961 treaty. Deng Xiaoping mended fences with Kim when he gave his assent to the succession plan during the latter's visit to China with his son Kim Jong-il in 1982. However, China's reform under Deng was not to the dictator's liking as it undermined his absolute power, and the Hermit kingdom once again isolated itself from China.

The PLA began to push the military relationship in 1991 via the CPV-KPA Association and the General Staff Department. North Korea encouraged these exchanges as it provided them intelligence about the outside world. PLA's rationale's for pushing the enhancement of the military relationship was to help the KPA better understand the outside world, and make it more receptive to Chinese influence which was being orchestrated through a carefully managed engagement of the KPA leadership. By the mid-1990s, PLA-KPA relations spanned a wide range of military-to-military relations, which included high-level exchanges; visits by regional military commanders; dialogue between the foreign affairs bureaus, logistic, and equipment-related officials; military academy/CPV goodwill visits; and port visits by naval ships. However, since relations were largely politically driven, PLA-KPA meetings were merely symbolic, and skirted crucial military and security issues on the Korean Peninsula. Even within the Chinese establishment, the PLA had to grapple with the Chinese bureaucracy to make its influence felt on North Korean issues.

The Treaty of Friendship, Co-operation, and Mutual Assistance

It is essential to know the terms of the Treaty of Friendship, Co-operation, and Mutual assistance signed between China and North Korea in 1961 to understand relations today. Article II states,

> The Contracting Parties undertake jointly to adopt all measures to prevent aggression against either of the Contracting Parties by any state. In the event of one of the Contracting Parties being subjected to the armed attack by any state or several states jointly and thus being involved in a state of war, the other Contracting Party shall immediately render military and other assistance by all means at its disposal.

Further, Article V states,

> The Contracting Parties, on the principles of mutual respect for sovereignty, non-interference in each other's internal affairs, equality and mutual benefit and in the spirit of friendly co-operation, will continue to render each other every possible economic and technical aid in the cause of socialist construction of the two countries and will continue to consolidate and develop economic, cultural, and scientific and technical co-operation between the two countries.

The treaty renews every 20 years, and the right to cancel it can be invoked every five years, with advance notice of one year being provided.[2]

China's North Korea Policy

The prime concern of China is stability in the Korean Peninsula. North Korea is a buffer between China and the US supported South Korea which plays host to US personnel, missiles, and missile defence systems. '[For Beijing,] stability on the Korean Peninsula has always been prioritised over denuclearisation', says Ely Ratner of the Council on Foreign Relations. China fears a regime collapse in North Korea that would send a flood of North Korean refugees into China besides bringing the US on to its borders if South Korea succeeds in unifying the Korean Peninsula. In April 2017, the Chinese Foreign Minister Wang Yi said, 'if Pyongyang collapsed, refugees and armed North Korean soldiers, fissile material, or even nuclear fallout, could stream over the Yalu and Tumen rivers, which form the border with northeast China, presenting a major challenge to its own stability'.[3] Beijing has consistently urged the US and other world powers not to push Pyongyang for fear of precipitating the leadership's collapse, and triggering a possible nuclear war. 'Once a war really happens, the result will be nothing but multiple losses. No one can become a winner,' he argued.[4]

China is North Korea's immediate neighbour. It is axiomatic that stability in North Korea is critical to China's interests in the immediate neighbourhood. 'While China continues to want a denuclearised Peninsula, stability is its first priority. China prefers to live with a nuclear-powered but friendly neighbour to one with only conventional weapons, but that is unfriendly,' writes Paul Haenle, Director of the Carnegie-Tsinghua Center based in Tsinghua University in Beijing.[5] 'For China, North Korea is like a 'belligerent little brother', an upstart that needs to be mended time and again'. Mao Zedong described the relationship as the relation between 'lips and teeth' which, when translated, could be interpreted as 'If the lips are gone, the teeth will be cold'—a reference to the strategic importance of the North as a geographical security buffer.[6]

According to Jinhwan Oh and Jiyong Ryu, two Korean researchers, more Chinese citizens now 'view North Korea as a 'lipstick' (rather than 'lips'), which is increasingly expensive, despite its 'questionable quality, yet looks good to a cursory glance.'[7] Over the years, the relations have see-sawed swinging between brotherliness and bitterness, or as Oh and Ryu define them, as '...

[a pendulum swinging] between "lips and teeth" and "lipstick and teeth" on the basis of the characteristics of impending issues'.

China has been accommodative of North Korea for a number of other strategic reasons. China could use Pyongyang as a strategic lever to cause an overstretch to the US military in the event of a Taiwan contingency. US commitment to South Korea as well as Taiwan can be severely tested in the event of a coordinated action by North Korea to up the ante on the Korean Peninsula while China threatens or attacks Taiwan. According to *Stratfor*, a respected US military publication, in an assessment as far back as 1999,

> no amount of synchronised North Korean action can sufficiently make up for China's technical weaknesses to allow an invasion of Taiwan, a North Korean missile launch, along with a Chinese attack on small outer islands, could divide US resources. It would certainly divide US attention, and amplify the political effectiveness of both gambits.[8]

This was a possible reference to China finding ways to prevent US interference in an attack on the Taiwanese islands of Quemoy and Matsu.[9]

The other concern over the decades has been keeping the Korean Peninsula denuclearised, and ensuring that North Korean belligerence and its nuclear weapons programme does not have a cascading effect on the nuclearisation of South Korea and Japan. A nuclear standoff between the US and North Korea might disturb regional stability. Chinese leaders were alarmed at the mutual provocation in 2002–2003, and feared the danger that Pyongyang could be the next target of attack by the US after Iraq. Hochul Lee, in a *New York Times* report, alarmed China that the 'US was reviewing military options, including a surgical strike, bombing, and using tactical nuclear weapons over North Korean nuclear facilities.'[10] In China's calculus,

> A potential military conflict between the two countries would be the worst scenario for China, because Chinese leaders would

> have to decide whether to help North Korea in accordance with the China-North Korea alliance relationship, turning against the US, or to give up North Korea to maintain cooperative relations with the US. Either choice would be hardly acceptable for Chinese leaders.[11]

In an editorial in August 2017 in the *Global Times*, there was some clarity in China's stance on the worsening US-North Korea relations.

> China should also make clear that if North Korea launches missiles that threaten US soil first and the US retaliates, China will stay neutral. If the US and South Korea carry out strikes and try to overthrow the North Korean regime and change the political pattern of the Korean Peninsula, China will prevent them from doing so.[12]

In other words, China would support North Korea only if the US attacked first. But, if Kim Jong-un were to trigger a war, China would leave him to fend for himself. In an interesting conversation, some China experts have been of the opinion that the 'mutual assistance treaty of 1961 makes clear that they are meant to defend each other against aggression from external actor(s), rather than encourage one of them to attack external actor(s) in the first place.'[13] Thus, China has no obligation to defend North Korea if North Korea attacks another country. In fact, it is incumbent on China to support any UN initiative to intervene in such a crisis—'as a member of the UN, China shall support any UN effort to stop a North Korean attack, even by joining UN collective action against aggression by the North'.[14]

In sum, from the perspective of the Chinese leadership, the priorities for their country's policy toward North Korea are to:

- Ensure stability of the regime in North Korea, thereby ensuring it continues to be a buffer between the US and China.
- Ensure the denuclearisation of the Korean Peninsula.

- Avoid war from breaking out and, in doing so prevent a flood of refugees into its Northeastern provinces.
- Prevent US influence and domination of a unified Korea.
- Project itself as the final arbiter of any decision on the future of the Korean Peninsula.
- Retain leverages on North Korea.[15]

North Korea's China Policy

The bonhomie and close military relations between the two countries driven largely by the veterans of the two armies who had fought a bloody war together on the Korean Peninsula against the US and its allies. The relationship was cemented by the 'Treaty of Friendship, Cooperation, and Mutual Assistance', signed on July 11, 1961. Common Communist ideology and socialism kept the relationship cosy, even as North Korea played a fine balancing act between the Soviet Union and China. After all, Kim Il-sung had signed a similar Treaty of Friendship, Cooperation, and Mutual Assistance with Khrushchev barely six days earlier in Moscow, on July 6, 1961. The North Korean policy towards China was driven by three main interests: regime survival, regime legitimacy and economic assistance. China supported the regime, and gave it adequate legitimacy as it played off against the Soviet Union in ensuring a 'patron-client' relationship with North Korea. Besides trade, China provided for North Korea's energy needs in terms of coal and oil.

The end of the Cold War changed the equations considerably. The demise of the Soviet Union left Kim with few options. He enforced the twin policies of *Juche* (self-reliance) and *Songun* (military first) with a renewed vigour, having realised the changed international system and called for developing self-reliance and the stability of his regime through strengthening the military.[16] Meanwhile, China recalibrated its relations with South Korea, being impressed by the huge leap that South Korea had taken in its economic development. With improved diplomatic and trade relations, China moved away from North Korea, isolating the regime. The passing of Kim Il-sung cut off North Korea from the world in a kind of self-imposed isolation for almost three years. In the 1990s, famine killed an estimated two million people, with many resorting to 'eating a mixture of tree bark, roots and cabbage'.[17] Coupled with a failing economy and no industry, GDP growth is estimated to have fallen from 3.7 per cent in 2001 to 1.2 per cent in 2002, and then to –2.5 per cent in 2003.[18] Famine and negative growth forced China to come to North Korea's rescue—largely driven by China's self-interest of avoiding refugees from streaming across the Yalu river into China.

North Korea's relations with the Chinese leadership were defined by several developments. The period between 1994 and 2011 was laced with exasperation given the developments related to the ambitious nuclear and missile programme in violation of international agreements, sinking of the *Cheonan* (a South Korean warship), and shelling of South Korean territory in the Yeonpyeong Island in 2010, thus bringing the Koreas to the brink of war.[19] Convinced that regime survival was anchored in the development of asymmetric capabilities, he embarked on a dangerous path of developing nuclear weapons. Subsequently, North Korea unilaterally withdrew from the Treaty on the Non-Proliferation of Nuclear Weapons (NPT). Having conducted a series of six nuclear tests until 2017, North Korea has refused to be a party to the Comprehensive Nuclear-Test-Ban Treaty (CTBT), or the Chemical Weapons Convention (CWC). It has signed the Biological and Toxin Weapons Convention (BTWC) and the Geneva Protocol, but is believed to have a sizeable biological and chemical warfare programme.[20] Despite facing a crippling regime of international sanctions, and the failure of the China driven Six-Party Talks to denuclearise North Korea, Pyongyang continued to escalate tensions on the Korean Peninsula. As recently as November 2017, Kim Jong-un tested the Hwasong-15 ICBM which demonstrates major advancement in technology.

North Korea's Military Today

With the world's fourth largest army totalling 1.1 million men, North Korea has a defence budget of US$ 3.5 billion (2004–2014 figures), and equipped with vintage armaments. With a huge forward deployment of conventional artillery and missiles, it poses a persistent conventional threat to Seoul, the capital and largest city of South Korea, barely a few miles from the border. Kim Jong-un has only exacerbated the tension by upping the ante with his missile and nuclear weapons tests. 'The regime's nuclear arsenal could make it more aggressive in dealing with South Korea and the rest of the region,' says Siegfried Hecker, a Stanford University Professor. Punitive measures taken against Pyongyang seem to have emboldened Kim Jong-un's commitment to strengthening his military.[21]

North Korea had a vibrant small arms production line during the Cold War era, supplying USSR and Chinese designed weapons and replicas to a number of Latin American, African, and even non-state actors. After the collapse of the USSR, several Communist bloc countries turned arms producers, rivalling North Korea. As the arms industry dried up as a major source of income, North Korea turned to the production of missiles in the post-Soviet Union era. For a while, Iran and Pakistan benefitted from this technology; but, as missile control regimes became strict, and controls were imposed on nations proliferating ballistic missiles and nuclear weapons, the market for North Korean missiles—like the Nodong (a variant of the Scud)—turned cold. North Korea continues to have a fair sized defence industrial complex, with estimates varying from 50–100 sites. One input suggests that North Korea has fifty-four factories that produce conventional arms, of which eight make infantry weapons; eleven make ammunition and explosive munitions; and thirty-five produce larger weapons systems.[22]

North Korea's nuclear programme has been aided and assisted by a number of friendly countries over a period of time. During the early years, the programme was predominantly supported bt the USSR. The latter helped build a nuclear research reactor, provided missile designs, light-water reactors, and some nuclear fuel.[23] In the 1970s, China signed an agreement to produce missiles jointly, and Korean engineers participated in the production of the DF-61 programme.[24] The other partner was Pakistan: scientists from both nations met in Iran while working on ballistic missiles during the Iran-Iraq war. North Korea not only received designs for uranium warheads that Pakistan had obtained from China, but also gained access to centrifuge technology and designs from the Pakistani scientist Abdul Qadeer Khan. As quid-pro-quo, Pakistan received North Korean missile technology. Today, the North Korean missile inventory is impressive and threatens mainland US. Estimates of the nuclear stockpile vary reportedly from between 15–20 weapons to about 30–60 bombs.[25]

Figure 1: Map Showing North Korea-South Korea-US Missile bases and Facilities

Source: Prepared by GIS Lab, IDSA based on information gathered from Council of Foreign Relations and BBC.

China's Conundrum

The PLAs Shenyang Military Region bordering North Korea (now called Northern Theater Command) has been on the alert ever since Kim adopted a muscular and aggressive missile testing policy exacerbating tensions on the Korean Peninsula. The development of the railways into the Jilin province, and improved roads for move of mechanised formations have been evident since 2007.[26] In 2017, the Northern Theatre Command was deployed extensively along the Yalu River. Major General Wang Haiyun, a retired officer, reportedly said that the deployment was necessary as 'we can't let the flames of war burn into China.' He argued that,

> If it [US] attacked North Korea without Chinese approval, Beijing would have to intervene militarily, [and that] China must state that as a 'red line'. If war breaks out, China should without hesitation occupy northern parts of North Korea, take control of North Korean nuclear facilities, and demarcate safe areas to stop a wave of refugees and disbanded soldiers entering China's northeast.[27]

The level of readiness and the intent clearly demonstrates China's concern and commitment to control escalation while encouraging dialogue and a peaceful resolution to a potential flashpoint. Regular 'live-fire' drills and the movement of armoured fighting vehicles along the Yalu River are common. The PLA is prepared for an economic contingency, the influx of refugees, and even launching a swift offensive into North Korea, to capture maximum territory as a 'buffer' to US-South Korea presence along the Yalu River in the event of a war between the two Koreas.

China's relations with North Korea have seen a downslide ever since Pyongyang embarked on a policy of testing nuclear weapons to ensure regime survival. Much to the consternation of 'big brother' China, Pyongyang even refused to consult China on issues concerning the Korean Peninsula, often criticising Beijing for being soft on the US and its allies. Post the failure of the Six-Party talks, and Kim Jong-un's refusal to visit China until 2017, it became evident that China was losing leverage on North Korea and was even having to face criticism and ridicule from the world community for steadfastly supporting Kim's regime. Not that it was without its own national interests; but, as China grew in size and responsibility, it was impossible to be seen to be a party to Kim's shenanigans and yet be on the side of the world community. Beijing's attempts to resolve the issue through the Six-Party Talks failed ostensibly due to North Korea's stubborn refusal to halt or rollback its nuclear and missile programme. Not only did Kim Jong-il, but also his son Kim Jong-un later, continued to cock a snook at China till 2017, ignoring repeated calls to give up its nuclear programme. Over the years, China has been pacifying the North Korean regime by shielding Pyongyang from sanctions, punitive responses from US and its allies, particularly in UN.[28] The nuclear tests by Kim Jong-un were the proverbial 'last straw', and managing North Korea is proving to be a challenge for China.

In a slow but incremental manner, China began to apply the squeeze on North Korea. China has been recommending a 'double freeze'—a proposal for halting North Korea's nuclear and missile programme in exchange for the cessation of US-South Korea exercises in the Korean Peninsula and the seas around it. 'We think that the double freeze initiative is a viable approach in the current stage. Hope various parties can come to the path of dialogue and negotiations,' said the Chinese Foreign Ministry spokesperson, Geng Shuang.[29] But before the Singapore Summit, this has not found currency with the US, and China has agreed to join sanctions against Pyongyang, an indication of its inability to 'tame' Kim Jong-un. But the current negotiations in the Peninsula following the Singapore Summit appears to follow the 'suspension for suspension' approach. How long it will last following the developments in the Hanoi Summit remains to be seen.

In February 2017, it halted the import of coal from North Korea in accordance with the UN sanctions. Coal exports, which were permitted up to US$ 1 billion, were reduced to US$ 400 million, with China being the largest buyer. As early as March 2016, China had discreetly told Chinese companies to stop hiring North Korean workers, severely impacting as much as US$ 2.3 million which were coming into North Korea as remittances from abroad.[30] Although Pyongyang continued to be defiant, with the state run *Rodong Sinmun* quoted as saying, 'we will never put our nuclear weapons and ballistic rockets on the negotiation table',[31] it is apparent that the latest round of sanctions post the ballistic missile test on November 29, 2017 appears to have had an impact. The Chinese Commerce Ministry ordered a ban on the import of all types of North Korean food, machinery as also banned the sales of steel machinery and vehicles to North Korea. More importantly, all companies were banned from supplying any parts or weapons to the North Korean military.[32] This was in addition to the ban on textile exports and the import of North Korean coal, iron, and lead ore as well as seafood, imposed in September 2017.

All this has come with a cost to China. The border provinces of Jilin and Liaoning have seen a drop in economic statistics. For example, Liaoning province saw output shrink 2.5 per cent last year—the only province to register a downslide in growth. It reportedly dragged down China's growth rate to 6.7 per cent, the slowest in two decades. With North Korean labour gone, factories and businesses have been impacted. But, China believes that stability in its Northeast is more important to China than business. The media does not stop from eloquently suggesting that China too has made great sacrifices in ensuring peace in the Korean Peninsula.

There has been a flurry of diplomatic activity on the Korean Peninsula in the recent past. What is important to understand is whether these developments have fundamentally altered Chinese policy towards North Korea. Bill Gertz has quoted an authentic document of the Chinese government to argue that China continues to extend support to Kim Jong-un militarily, financially, and economically, in return for an assurance that he will stop testing nuclear weapons. The document, as recent as September 2017, directs concerned organs of government to,

> Give(s) Korea a stern warning, [and make further related] assurances to Korea at the same time, that is currently, Korea will not have to immediately give up its nuclear weapons, and that so long as Korea promises not to continue conducting new nuclear tests and immediately puts those promises into action, our country will immediately increase economic, trade, and military assistance to Korea.[33]

Clearly, China's military support to North Korea will not be compromised despite its international commitments and obligations.

Notes

1. 'Sino-North Korean Military Relations: Comrades-in-Arms Forever?' Royal United Services Institute for Defence and Security Studies (RUSI), June 17, 2004 at https://rusi.org/publication/sino-north-korean-military-relations-comrades-arms-forever, accessed on October 30, 2017.
2. Chris Bucher, 'China & North Korea Relations: 5 Fast Facts You Need to Know', Heavy, August 11, 217 at http://heavy.com/news/2017/08/china-north-korea-relationship-united-states-would-side-nuclear-attack-war/, accessed on December 8, 2017.
3. Adam Mount, 'How China Sees North Korea', *The Atlantic*, August 29, 2017 at https://www.theatlantic.com/international/archive/2017/08/china-military-strength-north-korea-crisis/538344/, accessed on October 31, 2017.
4. Eleanor Albert, 'The China-North Korea Relationship', Council on Foreign Relations, March 13, 2019 at https://www.cfr.org/backgrounder/china-north-korea-relationship, accessed on November 1, 2017.
5. Holly Eliyatt, 'Stability and strategy: Why is China so easy on North Korea?', *The Economic Times*, December 1, 2017.
6. Philip Wen and Christian Shepherd, 'China's relationship with North Korea is no longer as close as "lips and teeth"', Reuters, September 8, 2017.
7. Jinhwan Oh and Jiyong Ryu, 'The Effectiveness of Economic Sanctions on North Korea: China's Vital Role', *The Korean Journal of Defence Analysis*, 23(1), March 2011, pp. 117–131.
8. 'Rekindled Sino-DPRK Ties Offer Redefinition of Northeast Asian Security', Stratfor, August 17, 1999.
9. Ibid.
10. Hochul Lee, 'China in the North Korean Nuclear Crises: "interest" and "identity" in foreign behaviour', *Journal of Contemporary China,* 22(80), 2013, pp. 312–331.

11. Ibid.
12. 'Reckless game over the Korean Peninsula runs risk of real war', *Global Times*, August 10, 2017.
13. Shen Dingli, Bonnie S. Glaser, Michael Kovrig and Seong Hyon Lee, 'What Will China Do if the US attacks North Korea?' China-File conversation, September 21, 2017 at http://www.chinafile.com/conversation/what-will-china-do-if-us-attacks-north-korea, accessed on October 2, 2018.
14. Ibid.
15. See also William Boik, 'Understanding the North Korea Problem: Why It Has Become The "Land Of Lousy Options"', *The Letort Papers*, Strategic Studies Institute, US Army War College, Carlisle, PA, July 2011.
16. Also see, Sukhoon Hong, 'What Does North Korea Want from China? Understanding Pyongyang's Policy Priorities toward Beijing', *The Korean Journal of International Studies*, 12(1), June 2014, pp. 277–303.
17. Gloria Koo, 'China and North Korea: a Changing Relationship', *Stanford Journal of International Relations*, 2006 at https://web.stanford.edu/group/sjir/6.1.02 koo.html, accessed on October 5, 2018.
18. Ibid.
19. For more details on Kim Jong-Il's relations with China, see Hong Nack Kim, 'China-North Korea Relations after Kim Jong-Il', *International Journal of Korean Studies*, XVII(1) at http://icks.org/data/ijks/1482461222_add_file_2.pdf, accessed on March 26, 2018.
20. For details of the Six-Party Talks, see 'Factsheet of Arms Control Association', researched by Xiaodon Liang at https://www.armscontrol.org/factsheets/6partytalks, accessed on July 18, 2017.
21. Eleanor Albert, 'Backgrounder on North Korea's Military Capabilities', Council on Foreign Relations, June 6, 2018 at https://www.cfr.org/backgrounder/north-koreas-military-capabilities, accessed on November 7, 2017.
22. Andrea Berger II, 'North Korea's Contemporary Defence-Export Industry', Whitehall Papers, 84:1, 2015, pp. 35–62.
23. Eleanor Albert, 'North Korea's Military Capabilities', Council on Foreign Relations, January 3, 2018 at https://www.cfr.org/backgrounder/north-koreas-military-capabilities, accessed on April 15, 2018.
24. Ibid.
25. Ibid.
26. Bill Gertz, 'China Mobilizing Troops, Jets near Korea', *Washington Free Beacon*, April 1, 2013.
27. Jeremy Page, 'China Prepares for a Crisis along North Korea Border', *The Wall Street Journal*, July 24, 2017.
28. Edward Schwark, 'Old Ally, New Headaches: Will China Turn Cold on North Korea', Commentary RUSI, December 17, 2012.

29. Atul Aneja, 'Following North Korea's test, China reiterates call for "double freeze"', *The Hindu*, November 30, 2017.
30. Xander Snyder, 'Here's why China's Supposed Influence Over North Korea is a Bluff', *Mauldin Economics*, June 22, 2017.
31. Elise Hu, 'China's Leverage—And Its Limits—In North Korea', NPR, August 4, 2017 at https://www.npr.org/sections/parallels/2017/08/04/541104144/chinas-leverage-and-its-limits-in-north-korea, accessed on March 24, 2018.
32. 'China Tightens North Korea Trade Limits Under UN Sanctions', Associated Press, January 5, 2018.
33. Bill Gertz, 'China covertly offering North Korea missiles, aid to halt nuclear program', *The Washington Free Beacon*, January 2, 2018. The document is titled 'No. 000003 TOP SECRET Document of General Office of the Communist Party of China GOC Issuance (2017) No. 94 The Decision of General Office of the Communist Party of China on Conducting Communication and Coordination Work between Our Country and the Democratic People's Republic of Korea for Further In-depth Solution of Its Nuclear Issue' at https://freebeacon.com/wp-content/uploads/2018/01/PRC-Central-Committee-document-translation-revised.pdf, accessed on September 20, 2018.

10. South Korea's Approach to North Korea under President Moon Jae-in

Jojin V. John

The situation in the Korean Peninsula has witnessed a dramatic change since the beginning of 2018 with three inter-Korean Summits, North Korea-China Summits, and the two North Korea-US Summits. The change has been characterised by diplomacy and de-escalation taking centre stage as compared to the exchange of threats and heightened security tensions of 2017. Facilitated by summit diplomacy, it appears that the status quo in the Korean Peninsula is changing with the diplomatic opening of North Korea, improvement in inter-Korean relations, and a diplomatic breakthrough between Washington and Pyongyang. Following the South Korean President Moon Jae-in's visit to Pyongyang in September 2018, there are discussions on Chairman Kim's reciprocal visit to South Korea in 2019.

Among other factors, the proactive role of South Korea's President Moon Jae-in is a major factor in facilitating the diplomatic overturn that is currently underway in the Korean Peninsula. After assuming office in May 2017, President Moon insisted on a steadfast approach which played a central role in shaping developments in the Korean Peninsula. While adopting a strong deterrence approach in the context of the North Korean missile and nuclear provocation, President Moon committed to diplomacy and engagement. When the opportunity was presented in the context of the Pyeongchang Winter Olympics, Seoul not only worked to improve inter-Korean relations but also mediated between North Korea and the US.

Taking account of the developments in the Korean Peninsula, this chapter evaluates South Korea's policy towards North Korea under President Moon Jae-in, with special reference to the nuclear issue. In doing so, the chapter is organised thematically in five sections. After the introduction, the second section briefly evaluates the advancement of North Korea's nuclear and missile programme, and its implications for South Korean security. To locate President Moon's North Korea policy, the third section explains Seoul's North Korea conundrum from a domestic political perspective. The fourth section examines key aspects of South Korea's North Korea Policy of the Moon Jae-in administration. The sixth section provides some concluding thoughts highlighting the underlying imperatives and implications of Seoul's approach to North Korea.

North Korean Nuclear Threat: South Korean Perspective

On November 29, 2017, after successfully testing the Inter-Continental Ballistic Missile (ICBM) Hwasong-15, North Korean leader Kim Jong-un declared the completion of the 'state nuclear force'.[1] North Korea claimed that the missile reached an altitude of 4,475 km, and travelled some 950 km, with a flight time of 53 minutes.[2] The Union of Concerned Scientists assessed that if the missile was fired on a normal trajectory, its range would be more than 13,000 km (8,100 miles)—that is, capable of reaching Washington DC.[3] With that achievement, North Korea attained a milestone in its nuclear programme as was set forth by Kim Jong-un. During his New Year speech on January 1, 2017, Kim Jong-un declared that North Korea 'entered the final stage of preparation for the test launch of [an] intercontinental ballistic missile.'[4]

Since Kim Jong-un assumed power in 2011, the nuclear and missile programme has attained a new urgency. In February 2013, North Korea conducted its third nuclear test. Kim Jong-un's determination to advance the nuclear weapon programme was made clear with the announcement of the *byungjin* policy in March 2013. The *byungjin* doctrine commits the regime to the parallel development of nuclear weapons and economic progress. North Korea's Supreme People's Assembly amended its Constitution to declare North Korea as a 'nuclear weapon state'.[5] Since 2016, North

Korea has accelerated its WMD programme not only by increasing the frequency of missile and nuclear testing but also by making rapid advancements in its technical capability. In January 2016, North Korea conducted its fourth nuclear test, which it claimed was a hydrogen bomb. Although the yield of the test was higher compared to the previous test, many experts challenged North Korea's claim.[6] Another nuclear test, with a yield of 10–20 kt, was conducted in September 2016. Pyongyang claimed that the test 'confirmed the structure and specific features of movement of a nuclear warhead that has been standardised to be able to be mounted on strategic ballistic rocket.'[7] The sixth nuclear test in September 2017 was claimed to be a hydrogen bomb, capable of being used on the Hwasong-14 and Hwasong-12 ballistic missiles.[8] The test was estimated to produce a yield of 50–100 kt. There is no consensus among experts about the North Korean claim that the bomb was a thermonuclear warhead that could be mounted on an ICBM. However, in comparison to the previous tests, the yield indicates a substantial advancement in North Korea's nuclear programme.

Simultaneously North Korea also accelerated its ballistic missile testing since 2014. In 2016 alone, North Korea conducted more than two dozen missile tests. Among these tests, significant were the successful testing of Hwasong-10 (also known as the Musudan)—a mobile intermediate-range ballistic missile, and the first successful launch of the Pukkuksong-1 (KN-11)—a solid-fuelled, sea-based ballistic missile.[9] A significant advancement in missile capability was also observed in 2017. Among the 24 missile tests that North Korea conducted included the successful launching of the two ICBMs Hwasong-14 and Hwasong-15, and an intermediate-range ballistic missile (IRBM) called the Hwasong-12.[10] The successful testing of Hwasong-15 on November 28, 2017, was a milestone and a strategic game changer, as it puts the whole of continental US within its range. North Korea also claimed Hwasong-15 is 'capable of carrying a super-heavy nuclear warhead.'[11]

From the South Korean perspective, the heightened security challenge caused by the rapid advancement in North Korean WMD is not only from the fact that Pyongyang now is in possession of dangerous weapons but increasingly from the possibility of a military conflict between Pyongyang and Washington. Developments in 2017 have also brought about a shift in Washington's perspective on the North Korean nuclear problem. Washington's concerns with the North Korean nuclear problem has shifted from its earlier problematisation of an issue of non-proliferation and stability in the region to a security problem that is directly threating the US mainland. The shift in US perception was something which made Seoul very anxious. This shift in perspective was evident from President Donald Trump's talk of a 'military measures'.[12] The fear of being forced into a war prompted the South Korean President to state that his 'government will prevent a war at all cost'.[13]

The situation has also led President Moon to harden his rhetoric to Washington by saying that military action against North Korea should be decided by 'ourselves and not by anyone else'.[14] He also said that he is 'confident [that] the United States too will react calmly and responsibly', and reminded that 'peace on the Korean Peninsula will not come by force'.[15] The explicit remark to Washington on what it can or cannot do underscores how critical the situation is from the South Korean perspective.[16] The situation has also led Seoul to imagine the possibility of South Korea being sidelined in the process of resolving the nuclear and missile issues. This concern was reflected in a statement made by Lee Soo-hyuck, former chief negotiator for the Six-Party Talks and an assemblyman belonging to President Moon's Democratic Party. He said, because 'North Korea is one of the few countries on earth that can attack the US with missile capacity ... [the] paradigm has changed dramatically.' He argued, 'Washington is a player directly involved in the crisis.'[17]

Seoul's North Korean Conundrum

North Korea's nuclear threat has remained the most critical challenge to the national security of South Korea for the last three decades. However, Seoul remains ambivalent in its approach. The conundrum that Seoul faces in its policy toward Pyongyang is associated with a lack of domestic consensus on how to approach North Korea, which is an impediment to long-term policy planning and implementation. At the policy level, this problem is manifested by a dramatic shift in policies with a change of government. The political divergence is informed by a divide in Korean politics along ideological lines—between the progressives and the conservatives.

Since the democratic transition in the late 1980s, South Korea has experienced decade-long cycles of power transition between the conservative and progressive governments. The conservative governments of Roh Tae-woo and Kim Young-sam (1986–97), followed by the first progressive transition under Kim Dae-jung (1998–2002), and Roh Moo-hyun (2003–2007), and witnessed the return of the conservative governments under the leadership of Lee Myung-bak (2008–2012) and Park Geun-hye (2013–17). Each transition has featured a radical change in South Korea's North Korea policy. The conservatives favour a hawkish approach while the progressives prefer more engagement and cooperation. Since the early 1990s, policy changes have happened despite Pyongyang's nuclear weapons programme.[18]

The diverging policy paradigm between the conservative and the progressive governments is informed by their differing perspectives on North Korea, and the perception of 'North Korea' as a security challenge. According to Han and Jang, identity plays a major role: 'what is North Korea to South Korea?' is at the core of the puzzle. The policy paradigm switches with shifting perceptions of North's dual identity as a 'brother' and as an 'enemy'. The identification as 'brother' is informed by a nationalistic viewpoint; and the 'enemy' image by a realist worldview. The ideological preference is not strict among most South Koreans; rather, it swings between the two. It is not appropriate to provide a strict categorisation of conservatives as anti-North Korea, and the progressives as pro-North Korea. However, surveys suggest that North Korea presents the image of an 'enemy' to the conservatives, while the progressives identify North Korea as a 'brother'.[19] This divide between the progressives and conservatives has been a major point of contention in South

Korean domestic politics, and both have constantly clashed over their different policies on North Korea. They have differed in their perspectives on whether and how to engage, the method and scale of economic aid, the implementation of the existing agreements, the role of external actors (including the US), and the means and ways to establish a national consensus on the question of North Korea.[20] Though recent years have witnessed less polarisation between the progressive, centrist, and conservative groups, the ideological disposition is very evident, and is a critical factor in shaping South Korea's approach to North Korea.[21]

The ideological divergence also gives rise to differing perspectives of the South Korean perception of the North Korean security challenge, including the nuclear programme. Consequently, there are distinct policy paradigms between the two political forces. While recognising the North Korean nuclear programme as a significant security challenge to South Korea, the progressives do not see it in isolation. Instead they identify it in the broader context of the existing security dilemma in the Korean Peninsula. Hence, they see denuclearisation as a part of multiple processes of establishing a peace regime in the Korean Peninsula. On the other hand, the conservatives recognise North Korea's nuclear programme as the fundamental challenge to peace and stability in the Korean Peninsula. Hence, they propose denuclearisation as the precondition for inter-Korean engagement.

President Moon Jae-in's North Korea Policy

Throughout his political career, the progressive politician Moon Jae-in,[22] has argued for an engagement approach to North Korea. In his capacity as the Chief of Staff to former President Roh Moo-hyun, Moon was instrumental in organising the second inter-Korean Summit in 2007. President Moon assumed office in May 2017 in the midst of a heightened security tension following North Korea's frequent missile tests. In response, he adopted a stern approach to North Korean belligerence by conducting military drills and leading a diplomatic and economic pressure campaign.[23] While responding sternly, Moon also kept engagement and a dialogue option open. Even while facing an adverse situation, Moon declared that he is open to meet the North Korean leader. However, North Korea did not respond to the dialogue proposal until the beginning of 2018.

A breakthrough in the situation was created in January 2018, when North Korea announced its willingness to improve relations with South Korea. Seoul capitalised on the opportunity in improving inter-Korea relations, leading to North Korea's participation in the Winter Olympics and high level diplomatic engagements. Seoul's shuttle diplomacy paved the way for the April 27 inter-Korean Summit, and the first US-North Korea Summit on June 12. The swift and bold diplomatic move by Seoul in the context of the Winter Olympics not only facilitated the improvement in inter-Koreans relations but also played the critical role of mediating between Pyongyang and Washington.

The Panmunjom Declaration, signed between President Moon and Chairman Kim Jong-un at the inter-Korean Summit on April 27, 2018, committed to working towards improving inter-Korean relations, the de-escalation of military tension, and the establishment of a permanent peace regime in the Korean Peninsula.[24] The declaration reaffirmed the shared goal of a 'nuclear free Korean Peninsula' achieved through 'complete denuclearisation', and agreed to carry out their respective roles and responsibilities in this regard. The Panmunjom Declaration substantially draws from previous inter-Korean agreements, reflecting a continuity of the Sunshine era at some level.[25] For instance, on matters of inter-Korean economic relations, it evokes the agreements reached at the second inter-Korea Summit of October 2007. On military tension reduction and prevention of the use of force against each other, Panmunjom Declaration reaffirmed the Non-Aggression Agreement of December 1991. The commitment for a nuclear free Korean Peninsula the January 1992 Joint Declaration on denuclearisation. However, some aspects are unprecedented and proposed a time frame for undertaking tangible actions. Such elements included family reunion of separated families during Korean War in August 2018, high-level military talks to start in May and the setting up of liaison office. Above all Moon-Kim Summit created the environment for first US-North Korea Summit on June 12 in Singapore, which instrumental in bringing a détente in the Korean Peninsula creating a political environment for dialogue to undertake.

The inter-Korea Summit was, without a doubt, the result of a comprehensive and a steadfast approach pursued by the Moon administration over the last one year. President Moon laid out his North Korea Policy, 'Korean Peninsula Peace Initiative (KPPI)', in a speech delivered in Berlin on July 7, 2017,[26] and later apprised in a National Assembly speech.[27] The KPPI provided the basic framework to Seoul's North Korea policy by focusing on five principles. They are:

- primacy on maintaining peace and stability in the Korean Peninsula,
- denuclearisation of the Korean Peninsula,
- Seoul's primary role in resolving the inter-Korean issue,
- a peaceful resolution of the North Korean nuclear issue,
- a stern response to any North Korean provocation.[28]

Before articulating his North Korea approach, Moon also stated that Seoul has,

- no intetent to use force,
- no wish for regime collapse or change,
- no unification through absorption,
- and no artificial unification.[29]

The first principle highlights the overall thrust on achieving peace and stability in the Korean Peninsula as the primary goal. In doing so, it prioratised coexistance and copropserity over unification. In the context of heightened security tenstions in the Korean Peninsula, urgency was attributed to de-escalation to avoid military conflict. The insistence on de-escalation and stability attained a greater momentum since August 2017, following President Trump's 'fire and fury' remark inferring the possibility of a military operation to solve the nuclear issue.[30] President Moon vehemently opposed the idea of the military as a means of solving problems in the Korean Peninsula. He declared that that 'any military action to be taken on the Korean Peninsula requires South Korea's consent'.[31] He also stated that his 'government will prevent war at all cost ... [and] must peacefully resolve the North Korean nuclear issue no matter how many ups and downs there are.'[32] He also sought the support of China to oppose Washington's military option. During President Moon's state visit to China, Seoul and Beijing agreed upon four principles on the North Korea: no war on the Korean Peninsula; the denuclearisation of the Korean Peninsula, the peaceful resolution of all issues, including North Korean nuclear problem; and the improvement of inter-Korean relations.[33] Thrust on peace and stability is well reflected in the Panmunjom declaration.

The second policy direction focuses on the denuclearisation of the Korean Peninsula. President Moon proposed a step-by-step yet comprehensive approach to finding a solution to the nuclear issue. Such an approach is based on the belief that the nuclear problem cannot be solved without addressing the issue of North Korean's 'security concerns' and its diplomatic isolation. The step-by-step approach starts with a freeze of nuclear and missile tests and ends with the dismantling of the North Korean nuclear programme. The comprehensive plan seeks to replace the Armistice Agreement with a peace treaty, which also envisages an end of the diplomatic isolation of Pyongyang by improving relations with Japan and the US. President Moon emphasised 'the Joint Declaration on the Denuclearisation of the Korean Peninsula, signed by both South and North Korea, makes it impossible to accept or acknowledge North Korea as a nuclear power.'[34] He also added that 'South Korea will not develop or possess nuclear arms, either.'[35] President Moon outrightly rejected the idea of Seoul going nuclear, either by redeploying US tactical nuclear weapons or by developing its nuclear arsenal as propounded by some conservative politicians. In doing so,

President Moon is firmly upholding the moral high ground for the complete denuclearisation of the Korean Peninsula.

Though denuclearisation remains high on the agenda of Seoul's North Korea policy, its definition denuclearisation remains ambiguous. Seoul's ambiguity on the definition of denuclearisation is both tactical and political. Seoul recognises the fact that while it has major stake in the issue, its ability to resolve it is limited, and sees it as an issue to be settled primarily between Pyongyang and Washington. Seoul identifies its role as that of a facilitator in the process of US-North Korea denuclearisation. Hence, the meaning of denuclearisation and its details are something to be negotiated between North Korea and the US. In this regard, Seoul's effort was to create a political environment for the dialogue to start. Seoul managed to achieve that goal through the Panmunjom Declaration in which North Korea committed itself to denuclearisation. Though the Panmunjom Declaration is vague on the definition and process of denuclearisation, it has become clear what it is not. The denuclearisation does not mean a unilateral denuclearisation of North Korea but involves quid-pro-quo.

In contrast to the previous conservative administration, which followed Washington's lead on North Korea, President Moon stated Seoul's centrality in finding a solution to the North Korean problem. By declaring 'my country must sit in the driver's seat', he emphasizes the KPPI as a Seoul-led process. On proposing the KPPI, President Moon claimed that 'President Trump supported Korea's leading role', and has also reached consensus with President Xi on Seoul's leading role in engaging North Korea.[36] Thus, he argued that the 'conditions are finally being fostered' for a South Korea-led engagement process, indicating the support of Washington and Beijing.[37] On emphasising the centrality of the Korean people in shaping the course of inter-Korean relations, President Moon has invoked nationalist worldview of the South Korean progressives. He has pitched on the nationalist cause by arguing that 'the destiny of the Korean nation must be determined by Koreans.'[38] Hence, he also added that, 'the unfortunate past in which our destiny was determined against our will, such as colonial rule and national division, must never be allowed to recur'.[39]

The centrality of Seoul in shaping events in the Korean Peninsula features two aspects. First, it is reflected in the promotion inter-Korean relations and the facilitation of the diplomatic opening of North Korea. The second feature of South Korea's diplomacy is its mediating role between North Korea and the US, which resulted in the first ever Summit between the two countries. Seoul was successful not only in mediating between the two countries but, more importantly, in bringing Washington's position more close to that of Seoul. It can be argued that the Singapore Joint Statement in its aspiration is comparable, and takes its cue from Panmunjom Declaration.[40]

The fourth principle of President Moon's North Korea policy articulates an emphasis on the peaceful resolution of the nuclear problem. Since he became President, he has repeatedly been emphasizing that the 'North Korean nuclear issue must be resolved peacefully through dialogue'.[41] The emphasis has increased since August 2017 following Washington's repeated reference to the 'military option'.[42] President Moon's agreement with Chinese President Xi Jinping on the 'four principles' on North Korea was a signal to Washington on their shared opposition to Trump administration's suggestion of military means to solve the nuclear issue.[43] Seoul has also actively campaigned for sanctions and pressure against North Korea through bilateral and multilateral means, including the UNSC Resolutions. However, President Moon said that the tool of sanctions and pressure are 'the means to guide the North towards making the right choice and coming to the negotiating table.'[44]

As the fifth principle of his North Korea policy, President Moon focuses on a stern response to any North Korean provocation. The goal of stern response was promised to be achieved through 'retain (ing) overwhelming military superiority'.[45] While proposing dialogue and the promotion of inter-Korea relations, the President made sure that North Korean provocations are matched with force projection.

For instance, following Pyongyang's first ICBM launch in early July 2017, Seoul and Washington conducted a decapitation missile-firing drill. By conducting the unscheduled missile drill, President Moon emphasised that he was 'to react[ing] with more than just a statement.'[46] President Moon also reversed his position on the THAAD missile system in the wake of North Korea's continued missile provocation by ordering a 'temporary' deployment of the four additional launchers of the missile defence system.[47]

Since assuming office, President Moon has prioritised the enhancement of Seoul's deterrence posture vis-à-vis North Korea, relying on the US-Korea alliance, but also increasingly by pursuing an independent national security policy. On the objective of attaining military superiority, Seoul has increased its defence budget by 6.9 per cent, the highest rise since 2009. In the pursuit of an independent security strategy, President Moon has sought an early takeover of wartime operational control (OPCON). In this regard, President Moon said, 'Seoul should have wartime operational control to instil fear in North Korea and win the trust of the citizens,' and that 'retrieving wartime operational control will boost military development and place South Korea at the center of East Asian security, based on independent defense capabilities'.[48]

During President Trump's visit to Seoul in November 2017, Seoul and Washington agreed to step up 'collaboration to enhance Korea's self-defence capability to unprecedented levels'.[49] The summit announced three initiatives. First, Seoul and Washington agreed to immediately start deliberations on South Korea's acquisition and development of state of the art US military equipment. Second, both leaders agreed to eliminate the limits on the weight of South Korean missile warheads. Third, they announced the rotational deployment of US strategic assets in and around the Korean Peninsula. Seoul and Washington adopted the 2017 revised missile guideline, which eliminated the restriction on the weight of South Korean missile warheads. Under the US-Korea bilateral missile treaty (signed in 1979 and revised latest in 2012) South Korea was restricted to developing ballistic missiles with a range of up to 800 km and a payload weight of up to 500 km.[50] Though the weight cap of payload was removed, the 2017 revision still limits the range of the South Korean ballistic missile to 800 km. The unlimited warhead weight allowance would enable South Korea to make missile warheads which are heavier than one ton, which is capable of destroying North Korean underground facilities. In enhancing South Korea's defensive posture, Seoul is pushing to finish its three pillared defensive system: the Kill Chain, the Korea Air and Missile Defence (KAMD), and the Korea Massive Punishment and Retaliation (KMPR) at a date earlier than planned at the inception of the programme. These efforts reflect President Moon's persistence on 'peace based on strength' approach, and the pursuit of an independent national security strategy.

Conclusion

In retrospect, it could be argued that President Moon Jae-in's policy towards North Korea has featured a 'cautious engagement' through a comprehensive approach. The engagement approach that Moon proposed is different, at some level, from that of his progressive predecessors which were unconditional. President Moon's approach involves quid-pro-quo. The comprehensive aspect of Seoul's North Korea policy can be identified at two levels: inter-Korean relations and the international approach to the North Korean nuclear problem.

At the inter-Korea level, Seoul is pushing for an overall engagement with Pyongyang, including humanitarian, sports, cultural, political, and military. However, at the moment, the economic engagement is limited to feasibility studies because of international sanctions. During the four months after the April 27 Summit, inter-Korean relations have improved substantially. Developments include the setting up of a Liaison Office in the border city of Kaesong; a family reunion event, and two General level meetings (among other working level meetings) to reduce military tension. In the international approach to North Korean nuclear issue, Seoul has been campaigning for a comprehensive approach that involves simultaneously the process of denuclearisation, a peace regime, and the normalisation of US and Japan's relations with North Korea.

Another feature of Seoul's North Korea policy is the proactive role that South Korea played in bringing about a transformation in the situation in the Korean Peninsula. This role has two aspects. First, its lead role in promoting inter-Korea relations, and second, Seoul's mediating role in promoting US-North Korea engagement. Significant also is how Seoul's North Korea policy prioritises de-escalation and stability in the Korean Peninsula as well as create a political environment for dialogue. In the short term, Seoul wants to achieve a political commitment from North Korea and the US, which would set in motion the parallel process of denuclearisation, the establishment of a peace regime, and the diplomatic normalisation of North Korea. It can be argued that, through the Panmunjom and the Pyongyang Declarations, Seoul managed to break the status quo in the situation in the Korean Peninsula. In the mid to long term, through inter-Korean and US-Korean engagement, Seoul's attempt would be to carry forward and achieve the goal of denuclearisation, ending the Korean War, and the diplomatic normalisation of North Korea. In the process, attempts would be made to bring about economic reform in North Korea through an Inter-Korea economic engagement, and ensure peace and stability in the Korean Peninsula through the coexistence of the two Koreas. In the long term, President Moon's North Korea policy envisages an economic integration of the Korean Peninsula that would create a condition for promoting political unification.

President Moon's proactive approach has been instrumental in maintaining the diplomatic process, but not without challenges. The three-way meeting of Trump, Kim and Moon and the Trump-Kim Summit at the DMZ in June 2019, helped to maintain the diplomatic momentum. However, the ongoing US-China conflict and the lack of progress in the denuclearisation talks between Washington and Pyongyang have come to become significant challenges to President Moon's diplomatic efforts. Recent provocations by North Korea that including the firing of short-range missiles in July 2019 is adding a new set of challenges to President Moon's engagement policy.

Notes

1. 'DPRK Gov't Statement on Successful Test-fire of New-Type ICBM', KCNA, November 29, 2017 at https://kcna.kp, accessed on July 30, 2019.
2. Ibid.
3. David Wright, 'North Korea's Longest Missile Test Yet', November 28, 2017 at www.allthingsnuclear.org/dwright/nk-longest-missile-test-yet, accessed on July 30, 2019.
4. 'Kim Jong Un's 2017 New Year's Address', The National Committee on North Korea, January 1, 2017 at https://www.ncnk.org/resources/publications/kju_2017_new_years_address.pdf/file_view, accessed on July 30, 2019.
5. 'N. Korea "can't have" status of nation with nuclear weapons: Seoul', Yonhap News Agency, May 31, 2012 at english.yonhapnews.co.kr/search1/2603000000.html?cid=AEN20120531004500315, accessed on July 30, 2019.
6. 'N. Korea announces successful test of hydrogen bomb', Yonhap News Agency, 6 January 2018 at english.yonhapnews.co.kr/search1/2603000000.html?cid=AEN20160106004354315, accessed on July 30, 2019.
7. 'N. Korea conducts 5th nuclear test', Yonhap News Agency, September 9, 2018 at english.yonhapnews.co.kr/northkorea/2016/09/09/0401000000AEN20160909002554315.html, accessed on July 30, 2019.
8. 'N. Korea apparently conducts nuke test: S. Korea', The Yonhap News Agency, September 3, 2017 at english.yonhapnews.co.kr/news/2017/09/03/0200000000AEN20170903001360315.html, accessed on July 30, 2019.
9. 'North Korean Missile Launches & Nuclear Tests: 1984-Present', CSIS at https://missilethreat.csis.org/north-korea-missile-launches-1984-present/, accessed on July 30, 2019.
10. Ibid.
11. 'Kim Jong Un Guides Test-fire of ICBM Hwasong-15', KCNA, November 29, 2017 at https://kcna.kp, accessed on July 30, 2019.
12. John Wagner, 'Trump's national security adviser says U.S. no closer to war with North Korea than a week ago', *The Washington Post*, August 13, 2017 at https://www.washingtonpost.com/news/post - politics/wp/2017/08/13/trumps - national - security - adviser - says - u - s - no - closer - to - war - with - north - korea - than - a - week - ago/?utm_term=.e692afb4c904, accessed on July 30, 2019.
13. 'Moon vows more diplomatic efforts to denuclearize N. Korea', Yonhap News Agency, August 15, 2017 at http://english.yonhapnews.co.kr/northkorea/2017/08/15/0401000000AEN20170815002651315.html, accessed on July 30, 2019.
14. Peter Pae, 'South Korea to Prevent War at All Costs, President Moon Says', Bloomberg, August 15, 2018 at https://www.bloomberg.com/news/articles/2017-08-15/south-korea-will-prevent-war-at-all-costs-president-moon-says, accessed on July 30, 2019.

15. 'S. Korean leader urges N. Korea, US to resolve ongoing stalemate peacefully', Yonhap News Agency, August 14, 2017 at http://english.yonhapnews.co.kr/northkorea/2017/08/14/0401000000AEN20170814007352315.html, accessed on July 30, 2019.
16. Katherine S. Moon, 'Caught in the middle: How the North Korean threat is ultimately Seoul's problem', Brookings, September 21, 2017 at https://www.brookings.edu/blog/order-from-chaos/2017/09/21/caught-in-the-middle-how-the-north-korean-threat-is-ultimately-seouls-problem/, accessed on July 30, 2019.
17. 'S. Korea likely to be sidelined on N. Korea issues', *The Korea Times*, August 4, 2017 at www.koreatimes.co.kr/www/nation/2017/12/103_234139.html, accessed on July 30, 2019.
18. Han Kwan-soo and Jang Yoon-soo, 'South Korean Conservative and Progressive Views on North Korea', *Journal of the Korean Political Science Association*, Spring 2012, 46(1).
19. Keunsik Jung, *et al.*, *Unification Perception Survey*, Institute of Peace and Unification Studies, 2016 at tongil.snu.ac.kr/xe/esub910/86694, accessed on July 30, 2019.
20. Han Kwan-soo and Jang Yoon-soo, note 18.
21. Keunsik Jung, *et al.*, note 19.
22. Moon Jae-in, has a humble background. He is the son of refugee parents who fled to South Korea from the North during the Korean War. Before entering mainstream politics, Moon had a long activist career. He was a student activist during the 1970s, protesting against the military dictatorship of Park Chung-hee. In the 1980s, Moon, along with his lifelong friend Roh Moo-hyun who became the South Korean President in 2003, defended student and labour activists persecuted under military rule as a human rights lawyer. Moon served as the Chief of Staff of the Roh administration. Until elected as President in May 2018, he served as the leader of opposition following his defeat in the 2012 Presidential election against Park Guen-hye. From an ideological perspective, Moon, to a large extent, inherits elements from the two previous liberal presidents (Kim Dae-jung (1998–2002) and Roh Moo-hyun (2003–2008)) who adopted the *sunshine policy*, as their approach to North Korea, which included diplomatic talks, family reunions, and joint economic projects.
23. 'Moon to adopt "conditional dovish" approach to North Korea', *Korea Times*, May 9, 2017 at www.koreatimes.co.kr/www/nation/2018/02/356_229058.html, accessed on July 30, 2019.
24. 'Full text of joint declaration issued at inter-Korean summit', Yonhap News Agency, April 27, 2018 at english.yonhapnews.co.kr/northkorea/2018/04/27/0401000000AEN20180427013900315.html, accessed on July 30, 2019.

25. Previous inter-Korean agreements are: (i) 'South-North Joint Communiqué', July 4, 1972 at https://peacemaker.un.org/sites/peacemaker.un.org/files/KR KP_720704_The July 4 South-North Joint Communiqué.pdf; (ii) 'Agreement on Reconciliation, Non-Aggression, and Exchanges and Cooperation between South and North Korea', December 13, 1991 at https://peacemaker.un.org/sites/peacemaker.un.org/files/KR KP_911213_Agreement on reconciliation non aggression and exchangespdf.pdf; (iii) 'Joint Declaration of the Denuclearization of the Korean Peninsula', January 20, 1992 at https://peacemaker.un.org/sites/peacemaker.un.org/files/KR KP_920120_JointDeclarationDenuclearizationKoreanPeninsula.pdf; (iv) 'South-North Joint Declaration', June 15, 2000 at https://www.usip.org/sites/default/files/file/resources/collections/peace_agreements/n_skorea06152000.pdf; (v) 'Declaration on the Advancement of South-North Korean Relations, Peace and Prosperity', October 4, 2007 at https://www.usip.org/sites/default/files/file/resources/collections/peace_agreements/n_skorea10042007.pdf, accessed on July 30, 2019.
26. Moon Jae-in, 'Körber Global Leaders Dialogue with President Moon Jae-In in Berlin', Korber Foundation, Berlin at https://www.koerber-stiftung.de/mediathek/koerber-global-leaders-dialogue-with-president-moon-jae-in-in-berlin-1416.html; 'Full text of Moon's speech at the Korber Foundation', *Korea Herald*, July 7, 2017 at http://www.koreaherald.com/view.php?ud=20170707000032, accessed on August 5, 2017.
27. 'Address by President Moon Jae-in at the National Assembly Proposing the Government's Budget Plan for FY 2018 and Plans for Fiscal Operations', KOREA.NET, November 1, 2018 at http://korea.net/Government/Briefing-Room/Presidential-Speeches/view?articleId=149879&pageIndex=3, accessed on July 30, 2019.
28. Ibid.
29. 'Full text of Moon's speech at the Korber Foundation', *Korea Herald*, July 7, 2017 at http://www.koreaherald.com/view.php?ud=20170707000032, accessed on August 5, 2017.
30. 'Trump warns N. Korea will be met with fire and fury: reports', Yonhap News Agency, August 9, 2017 at english.yonhapnews.co.kr/news/2017/08/09/0200000000AEN20170809000651315.html, accessed on July 30, 2019.
31. 'Moon: U.S. won't take military option against N. Korea without Seoul's consent', Yonhap News Agency, August 17, 2017 at http://english.yonhapnews.co.kr/northkorea/2017/08/17/93/0401000000AEN20170817006153315F.html, accessed on July 30, 2019.
32. 'Moon vows more diplomatic efforts to denuclearize N. Korea', Yonhap News Agency, August 15, 2017 at http://english.yonhapnews.co.kr/northkorea/2017/08/15/0401000000AEN20170815002651315.html, accessed on July 30, 2019.

33. 'Leaders of S. Korea, China pledge joint efforts to improve ties, denuclearize N. Korea', Yonhap News Agency, December 14, 2017 at http://english.yonhapnews.co.kr/national/2017/12/14/0301000000AEN20171214013100315.html, accessed on July 30, 2019.
34. Moon Jae-in, 'Address by President Moon Jae-in at the National Assembly Proposing the Government's Budget Plan for FY 2018 and Plans for Fiscal Operations', Korea.NET, November 1, 2017 at www.korea.net/Government/Briefing-Room/Presidential-Speeches/view?articleId=150872, accessed on July 30, 2019.
35. Ibid.
36. 'Full text of Moon's speech at the Korber Foundation', *Korea Herald*, July 7, 2017 at http://www.koreaherald.com/view.php?ud=20170707000032, accessed on July 30, 2019.
37. Ibid.
38. Moon Jae-in, 'Address by President Moon Jae-in at the National Assembly Proposing the Government's Budget Plan for FY 2018 and Plans for Fiscal Operations', Korea.NET, November 1, 2017 at www.korea.net/Government/Briefing-Room/Presidential-Speeches/view?articleId=150872.
39. Ibid.
40. John Jojin, 'US-North Korea Summit: An Assessment', ICWA, June 21, 2018 at https://icwa.in/pdfs/VP/2014/USNKoreaAsessmentVP26062018.pdf, accessed on July 30, 2019.
41. 'Moon stresses solidarity with China in speech', *Korean JoongAng Daily*, December 16, 2017 at koreajoongangdaily.joins.com/news/article/article.aspx?aid=3042162, accessed on July 30, 2019.
42. President Trump, Twitter, August 11, 2017 at https://twitter.com/realDonaldTrump/status/895970429734711298; see also, John Wagner, 'Trump's national security adviser says U.S. no closer to war with North Korea than a week ago', *The Washington Post*, August 13, 2017 at https://www.washingtonpost.com/news/post - politics/wp/2017/08/13/trumps - national - security - adviser - says - u - s - no - closer - to - war - with - north - korea - than - a - week - ago/?utm_term=.e692afb4c904, accessed on July 30, 2019; see also, 'U.S. preparing for 'preventive war' with N. Korea: McMaster', Yonhap News Agency, August 6, 2017 at http://english.yonhapnews.co.kr/northkorea/2017/08/06/26/0401000000AEN20170806000200315F.html, accessed on July 30, 2019.
43. 'Leaders of S. Korea, China pledge joint efforts to improve ties, denuclearize N. Korea', Yonhap News Agency, December 14, 2017 at http://english.yonhapnews.co.kr/national/2017/12/14/0301000000AEN20171214013100315.html, accessed on July 30, 2019.
44. Moon Jae-in, 'Address by President Moon Jae-in at the National Assembly Proposing the Government's Budget Plan for FY 2018 and Plans for

Fiscal Operations', Korea.NET, November 1, 2017 at www.korea.net/Government/Briefing-Room/Presidential-Speeches/view?articleId=150872, accessed on July 30, 2019.

45. Ibid.
46. 'S. Korean president arrives in Berlin', Yonhap News Agency, July 5, 2017 at english.yonhapnews.co.kr/news/2017/07/05/0200000000AEN20170705005752315.html, accessed on July 30, 2019.
47. 'Moon orders more THAAD launchers to be deployed', Yonhap News Agency, July 29, 2017 at http://english.yonhapnews.co.kr/news/2017/07/29/0200000000AEN20170729001251315.html, accessed on July 30, 2019.
48. Choi He-suk, 'Moon says wartime operational control key to stronger military', *Korea Herald*, September 28, 2017 at www.koreaherald.com/view.php?ud=20170928000727, accessed on July 30, 2019.
49. https://www.whitehouse.gov/the-press-office/2017/11/07/remarks-president-trump-and-president-moon-republic-korea-joint-press, accessed on July 30, 2019.
50. Daniel Pinkston, 'The New South Korean Missile Guidelines and Future Prospects for Regional Stability', The Crisis Group, October 25, 2012 at https://www.crisisgroup.org/asia/north-east-asia/korean-peninsula/new-south-korean-missile-guidelines-and-future-prospects-regional-stability, accessed on July 30, 2019.

11. Russia and the North Korean Challenge

Manabhanjan Meher

The emergence of a North Korea possessing nuclear weapons is a serious blow to international non-proliferation efforts which undermine regional peace and stability and is causing security concerns around the world. It also poses a serious national security challenge for the US and its regional allies in Northeast Asia. Russia, which borders North Korea, would be affected in case of a large-scale war in the region. North Korean leadership thinks that the possession of nuclear weapons is the sole means to guarantee its existence. They believe that the presence of US military bases in South Korea and Japan as well as the regular military exercises with South Korean military in the region are a threat to the existence of North Korea.[1] The advancement of North Korea's nuclear weapons and missile programme has intensified debate among the major powers of the region.

The Korean Peninsula is surrounded by major powers such as Russia, China, and the US. Due to historical reasons, the Korean Peninsula is still under the shadow of the Cold War mind-set. The stakeholders in the Korean Peninsula including Russia, China, and the US—have different views on North Korea's non-proliferation and achieving the goal of complete denuclearisation remains a major challenge. The Russian government does not accept North Korea's nuclear status. The Russian Ambassador to the United Nations, Vassily A. Nebenzia, has maintained that 'Russia does not accept the Democratic People's Republic of Korea's claim to become a nuclear State and has supported all Security Council Resolutions demanding an end to the nuclear and missile programmes of Pyongyang, with a view to the denuclearisation of the Korean Peninsula.'[2] However, unlike the US, Russian Federation favours a more balanced approach, which not only relies on restrictions and pressure against Pyongyang but urges that the North Korean nuclear issue must be settled exclusively through negotiations.

This chapter examines Russia's larger interests in Northeast Asia, which are shaped by economic developments in the Russian Far East and the Siberia region which are intertwined with the Korean nuclear crisis. It scrutinises recent developments in Russia-North Korea relations, focusing on Russia's perception and its efforts in resolving the Korean nuclear crisis. The chapter emphasizes that Russian strategy towards the denuclearisation of the Korean Peninsula is closely linked to the deployment of THAAD in South Korea. It also highlights the active role of Russia in the United Nations for the peaceful resolution of the Korea crisis and the implementation of sanctions against North Korea.

Russia's Policy Towards Northeast Asia

Russia's policy towards Korean Peninsula is intertwined with its economic, political, and strategic motives in the region. Russia's policy toward North Korea is an important component of its general strategy towards Northeast Asia, which is now regarded by Moscow as a crucially important area. The Fourth Eastern Economic Forum, held in Vladivostok on September 11–13, 2018, played a significant role in bringing peace and stability to the Korean Peninsula by integrating Northeast Asia and the Russian regions of the Far East and Siberia into regional economic projects with neighbours. Addressing the session, Russian President Vladimir Putin emphasized the importance of three-way cooperation between Russia, South Korea, and North Korea. He stated that,

> I cannot fail but to highlight once again trilateral projects in infrastructure, energy and other spheres involving Russia, the Republic of Korea and the Democratic People's Republic

> of Korea. Normalising the situation around the Korean Peninsula is a key prerequisite for achieving progress on these projects.[3]

Earlier, during his visit to North Korea, the Russian Foreign Minister also pointed to the economic initiatives concerning trilateral projects involving the two Koreas and Russia in unifying railways, building a gas pipeline, and also in the electric power industry. He stated that,

> We discussed certain steps that can be made towards this, including the old idea of launching trilateral projects between the two Korean states and Russia to link their railway networks and to build a gas pipeline as well as energy projects.[4]

In the last decade, Russia has laboured hard towards entering Northeast Asia which is becoming the new centre of world politics and economy. This region offers the greatest potential for Russian energy export from the Russian Far East and Siberia region. However, these energy resources largely remain unexploited because of the absence of pipeline infrastructure. After the accomplishment of a liquefied natural gas (LNG) plant in Sakhalin in 2009, Russia has entered the Northeast Asian gas markets. In order to export these resources, Russia needs a ice-free port in the Russian Far East. John Bauer has correctly argued that,

> Vladivostok's limitations have recently led Russia to show interest in the North Korean port of Najin, situated in the remote north eastern corner of the Korean Peninsula. Unlike Vladivostok, Najin is ice free. It lies inside a special administrative region called Rason, one of four special economic zones in North Korea.[5]

As part of this approach, Russia aims to significantly expand its political and economic ties with its eastern neighbours, such as China, Japan, and the two Korean states. However, the instability on the Korean Peninsula is an important obstacle to the realisation of Russia's strategic programme to develop its economic role in Northeast Asia.

The recent initiatives taken by policy makers in Russia with regard to the Russian Far East region and Northeast Asia appear to be motivated more by geo-economics than by the geopolitics in the region. Russian scholar Sergey Sevastianov has noted that this trilateral project was planned a long time ago in August 2011, when the then North Korean leader Kim Jong-Il visited Russia and met with the then President Dmitry Medvedev. The two leaders during their meeting agreed to develop a plan of transportation of Russian gas of about 10 billion cubic meters initially to South Korea passing through the territory of North Korean. It would become a trilateral project with the active participation from the Russian Federation, South Korea, and North Korea. The construction of a gas pipeline from Russia to South Korea (its overall length would be more than 1100 km, while 700 km would pass through the North Korean territory).[6] But the plan couldn't be realised because of rapid advancement of North Korean nuclear programme in the last few years.

Subsequently, the South Korean government also launched the 'Eurasian Initiative' in 2013, aimed to speed up cooperation with Eurasian countries, including Russia. Both South Korean and Russian economies are complementary in recent years. Therefore, there is an objective and common interest to cooperate with the other. The report prepared by Jae-Young Lee, Vice President, Korea Institute for International Economic Policy (KIEP), specifically mentioned the involvement of North Korea into a mutually beneficial continental collaboration with new railways, energy transfer corridors, and trade exchange, thus providing the basis for peace and prosperity in the entire region. It also stressed that,

> In the future, these could be trilateral projects, bringing together the two Koreas and Russia. By participating in the construction and use of infrastructure, economic benefits that North Korea will get from participating in infrastructure projects will make it realize

the need to use its geopolitical location and become a partner in regional economic interaction.[7]

The Russian scholar Andrey Gubin has argued that 'Russia is still interested in [the] implementation of Trans-Korean projects within the framework of its new oriental diplomacy, joined with Chinese 'One Belt–One Road' plan and probably Korean 'Eurasian Initiative'.[8] Another report presented in Russian International Affairs Council, Moscow, experts from both Russia and South Korea have pronounced that,

> Normalisation of the inter-Korean relations would undoubtedly be facilitated by putting the following large Russian—South Korean—North Korean partnership projects into practice: the international rail corridor from Europe to Korea, the construction of a Russia—North Korea—South Korea gas pipeline, and the creation of a unified energy system in Northeast Asia, which includes regions in East Siberia and the Russian Far East.[9]

However, academics in Russia have both complementary and contrasting perspectives on this issue. Most of the analysts prefer the need for greater cooperation among Russia and its neighbouring countries in the region. The Russian scholar, Maxim Suchkov, has put forward that 'increasing cooperation with all states in the region is in the framework of what is deemed as Russia's "strategic pivot to Asia" and constitutes one of the reasons for Moscow's interest in engaging North Korea.'[10] Artyom Lukin contends that Russia is unlikely to become a major political player on the Korean Peninsula without possessing the necessary economic influence. He mentions that Russia is the major participant in three major economic projects. The most important is the laying out gas pipeline from Russia to South Korea via the North Korea. The second group of projects involve the export of Russian electricity to the Korean Peninsula. The third group of projects is the connectivity, to connect the Trans-Korean Railway to the Russian Trans-Siberian Railway.[11]

Nonetheless, the perpetuation of North Korea's nuclear programme further complicated the situations in Northeast Asia. Andrey Gubin argues that 'feasible economic and investment activity is possible only after [the] normalisation of North Korea's political behaviour.'[12] Likewise, Fyodor Lukyanov has also stated that,

> Any peaceful settlement on the Korean Peninsula would benefit Russia, because peace will open up new opportunities for important economic projects vital for the region. These may include the construction of a gas pipeline from Siberia to South Korea and the extension of the Trans-Siberian Railway connecting Asia and Europe, all the way to the south of the Korean Peninsula.[13]

Besides pointing to security concerns, Richard Weitz is of the opinion that,

> Russian officials are keen to reduce tensions on the Korean Peninsula and promote stability in the North to integrate Russia better into the prosperous East Asian region. They hope that closer ties with the Koreas and other Asian countries would facilitate Asian investment and technology transfers to Russia that would help modernise their economy and benefit Russian consumers and exporters.[14]

Finally, Vladimir Nelidov has asserted that,

> The issues of strategic balance in the region in general and the balance of military capabilities between Russia and the US in particular are also of great importance from the point of view of the security situation in Northeast Asia.[15]

Therefore, only propelling the complete denuclearisation of the Korean Peninsula could promote greater economic advantages to the Russian Far East and Siberia. Russia is the only major effective player in Northeast Asia that has a stable and deepening relationship with both Pyongyang and Seoul.

Russian Perceptions on Denuclearisation of the Korean Peninsula

Historically, North Korea was one of the friendly states of the former Soviet Union, and had extensive economic, political, and military ties with it. The Soviet Union assisted North Korea in training specialists in the nuclear research field, and the two countries signed an agreement on cooperation in the peaceful use of nuclear energy in early 1950 and built nuclear reactor in North Korea. However, later on, relying exclusively on their own efforts, North Korea modernised this reactor without the participation of Soviet experts.[16]

As a result of growing ideological differences with both the Soviet Union and China in the 1960s, the North Korean leadership saw their traditional partners with growing suspicion and decided to pursue the development of a nuclear deterrent in order to secure the state and government from external interventions.[17] Subsequently, in the 1970s, North Korean leader started working on the development of a domestic nuclear weapons programme. In mid-2000s, North Korea announced that it had developed nuclear weapons for their self-defence and to strengthen its nuclear deterrent conducted six nuclear tests till 2017.

The conventional view in Russia is that the North Korean nuclear and missile programme does not pose a serious challenge for the security of the Russian Federation, particularly in the Far East region. Russia advocates for North Korea returning to NPT. The Ambassador to the United Nations, Vassily A. Nebenzia, stated that,

> We call on the North Korean authorities to wind down their banned programmes and return as a non-nuclear State to the non-proliferation regime of the Treaty on the Non-Proliferation of Nuclear Weapons and the control of the International Atomic Energy Agency.[18]

In Russia, government officials and academics hold contradictory assessments regarding North Korea's nuclear programme. There exist various schools of thought when defining Russian policy towards North Korea.[19] The first school consists of activists and academics, sympathisers of the left parties and ultra-nationalists, including the Liberal Democratic Party of Russia (LDPR), which support the North Korean government and its policies, and put the blame on the alliance of US and South Korea for instability in the region. Communist Party leader, Gennady Zyuganov, has condemned US President Donald Trump's statement at the UN General Assembly about totally destroying North Korea. Zyuganov has called to pursue a diplomatic policy to solve the North Korean crisis. He stressed that 'I fully support the efforts on searching for a peaceful solution taken by [Russian President Vladimir] Putin and [Chinese President] Xi Jinping and many responsible politicians.'[20] During a meeting with the Minister Plenipotentiary at the North Korean Embassy to Russia, the LDPR leader, Vladimir Zhirinovsky, expressed his solidarity with the people and the leadership of North Korea. Zhirinovsky has asserted that,

> We are glad that there is such a country as North Korea on the Asian continent, and it is your country that the US is afraid of. We request to convey our profound solidarity to the North Korean leadership; we are with you these days. If necessary, deputies of the LDPR factions will come to Pyongyang and will stay there with the people of North Korea.[21]

Likewise, Kazbek Kutsukovich Taisayev, First Deputy Chairman of the Union of Communist Parties–Communist Party of the Soviet Union (UPC-CPSU), has stated that,

> The Communist Party of the Russian Federation and the Workers' Party of Korea have, for a long time, been united by a signed bilateral agreement. And the most important task for

> our party is to assist the DPRK and the Republic of Korea. We purposefully went to the unification of nations, to peace and good neighbourliness.[22]

The second group comprising of Russian scholars as well as leading policy makers believe that nuclear weapons are a 'powerful deterrent' which guarantee North Korea's sovereignty; however, they also compel North Korea to follow the UNSC sanctions. The Russian Foreign Minister, Lavrov, has argued that 'they will not attack North Korea because they know without a doubt that the country has a nuclear bomb.'[23] Correspondingly, while answering the questions of Russian journalists following his visit to China to take part in the BRICS Summit, President Putin stressed that,

> ...we cannot forget about what I just said about Iraq, and what happened later in Libya. Certainly, the North Koreans will not forget it. What can ensure security? The restoration of international law. We need to advance towards dialogue between all parties concerned.[24]

Addressing the general debate within the 72nd session of the UN General Assembly, Mikhail Ulyanov, Director of the Russian Foreign Ministry, stated that,

> Just like other countries, we strongly condemn Pyongyang's nuclear tests and ballistic missile launches in violation of the UN Security Council resolution. We supported the latest sanctions imposed by the UN Security Council. However, the sanctions are not a cure-all.[25]

A major section of Russian scholars agree with these perspectives. Russian scholar Artyom Lukin, Assistant Professor at the School of Regional and International Studies of the Far Eastern Federal University, is also of the opinion that,

> North Korea is driven by the basic instinct of survival in the face of actual and imaginary threats on the part of the US and South Korea. The only way for Pyongyang to safeguard itself against its external enemies and preserve sovereignty is to have nuclear weapons.[26]

Additionally, Georgy Toloraya believes that,

> DPRK's nuclear weapons are a deterrent. After Yugoslavia, Iraq, and Libya, one can hardly expect the leaders of the Pyongyang regime to sit on their hands and wait to be 'democratized.' The North Koreans make this very clear, saying that 'when a pack of wolves attacks you, only a fool lowers his gun.'[27]

This trend is the most dominant and influential in the Russian political sphere.

The third group blamed the North Korean leaderships for the critical situations in the region. For instance, Andrew Korybko argues that,

> In the Northeast Asian context, North Korea's missile and nuclear tests are creating the pretext to 'justify' the US's THAAD deployment to the peninsula, which both Russia and China consider as a latent threat to their nuclear second-strike capabilities with time, so from their perspective, it makes sense why they'd want to put multilateral pressure on North Korea to end these destabilising activities.[28]

Equally, Alexander Gabuev highlights that,

> These developments have negative consequences for Russian security interests, because they give the United States a legitimate pretext to develop its military infrastructure in and around the Korean Peninsula, including the recent deployment of THAAD. This is the major reason why Moscow continues its efforts with

> other members of the international community to limit DPRK missile and nuclear capabilities.[29]

On the other hand, there are a few politicians and scholars who believe that the deployment of THAAD in Korean Peninsula has led to the further acceleration of the arms race in Northeast Asia.

The Russian Attitude Towards the US Deployment of THAAD

South Korea and the US agreed on the deployment of the Terminal High-Altitude Area Defense (THAAD) systems in South Korea in 2016, after North Korea conducted its fourth nuclear weapon test and a satellite launch. Russia alleged that the North Korean missile threat was used as a pretext by the US for deploying THAAD systems adjacent to the borders of Russia and China.

Russian policy makers perceive the THAAD deployment in South Korea as a part of the larger vision of US's 'pivot' to the Asia-Pacific. It expands the already substantial network of missile defence systems encircling China and Russia. Leonid Slutsky, the Head of the State Duma's International Affairs Committee, warned that the deployment of THAAD in South Korea to counter North Korea may endanger Russia's security. According to him, 'Washington is creating a new regional segment of the US global missile defence system in North-Eastern Asia, close to the Russian border. This may put the security of our country at risk.'[30] In the same way, Vassily A. Nebenzia considers this deployment as

> An additional destabilising factor in the region has been the ramping up in the Republic of Korea of elements of the American Terminal High Altitude Area Defence anti-missile system. We have repeatedly stated that such moves are not only an irritant but undermine the military balance in the region generally, and jeopardise the security of neighbouring states.[31]

According to Professor Tolstokulakov, it is the arms race in Northeast Asia fuelled by the US following the deploying THAAD missile defence which is the main challenge in the region rather the North Korean nuclear programme.[32] Correspondingly, Anastasia Barannikova has blamed the US for making the Korean Peninsula a nuclear zone. She has asserted that,

> US tactical nuclear weapons in South Korea [withdrawn in 1991], the inclusion of nuclear weapons in joint exercises, and the nuclear umbrella guarantee extended to South Korea [are responsible for this].... As no country [has] ever offered the same guarantees to North Korea, it [has] decided to develop its own weapons.[33]

In this situation, Russia has taken the positions similar to China against THAAD's deployment in the Korean Peninsula saying that this could further worsen the situation around in the Peninsula. Russian Foreign Minister, Sergey Lavrov, also raised concerns, stating,

> The potential of the US anti-missile complex, which includes the THAAD systems, is definitely of concern to our strategic forces and is having a negative effect on the security of not just Russia but also China and other countries. This is why we have been acting against the Pentagon's dangerous plans jointly with our Chinese partners.[34]

The Press Statement released by Deputy Foreign Minister of Russia, Igor Morgulov and Assistant Foreign Minister of China, Kong Xuanyou, after the Russia-China Dialogue on Security in Northeast Asia in May 2017 highlighted,

> the developments on the Korean Peninsula and in Northeast Asia, and expressed mutual concern at the serious deterioration of the situation in the region following Pyongyang's continued pursuit of its missile and nuclear programmes, and also the disproportionate military action of the United States and its allies, including the deployment of THAAD missile defence systems on South Korean territory.[35]

The deployment of THAAD system does seem to pose some threat to Russia which compelled both Russia and China to move closer on the issue in the region.

Russian Position on the UNSC Sanctions on North Korea

The UNSC has passed several resolutions condemning North Korea's nuclear activities. The UNSC has passed a number of resolutions since North Korea's first nuclear test. The Resolution 1718 passed in 2006 demanded that North Korea to stop further nuclear testing, and prohibited some military supplies and luxury goods export to North Korea. It highlighted that,

> All Member States shall prevent the direct or indirect supply, sale or transfer to the DPRK, through their territories or by their nationals, or using their flag vessels or aircraft, and whether or not originating in their territories, of any battle tanks, armoured combat vehicles, large calibre artillery systems, combat aircraft, attack helicopters, warships, missiles or missile systems as defined for the purpose of the United Nations Register on Conventional Arms.[36]

However, the UN sanctions authority didn't prohibit humanitarian assistance to flow into North Korea.

In violation of the UNSC's resolutions, North Korea carried out several ballistic missile tests, and conducted a sixth nuclear test in 2017. As a result, the 15-member UNSC passed Resolution 2375 against North Korea, slapping harsh sanctions against it by branding its nuclear build-up as a 'threat' to international peace and security. Subsequently, the UNSC adopted Resolution 2397, imposing the strongest sanctions on North Korea till date. The Security Council tightened sanctions on the country, severely restricting fuel imports and other trade as well as the ability of its citizens to work abroad. It stated that,

> Unanimously adopting resolution 2397 (2017), the Council limited the country's imports of refined petroleum to 500,000 barrels for

> 12 months starting on 1 January 2018, with crude oil capped at the current levels for that period. It also called for the repatriation of all its nationals earning income abroad, with some humanitarian exceptions, to the Democratic People's Republic of Korea within 24 months.[37]

Sanctions against North Korea have also been imposed by a number of other countries. The US, along with Japan, have also sanctioned North Korea beyond the measures imposed by the Security Council. The US has imposed unilateral sanctions on North Korea. For instance, Donald Trump administration has imposed more sanctions on the business establishments those who engaged with North Korea. In September 2017, US President Trump approved the Treasury Department blocking from the US financial system any foreign businesses or individuals that facilitate trade with North Korea. The North Korea Sanctions Advisory (of the Department of Treasury), on February 23, 2018, has further prohibited the following things: (i) any transactions or dealings with the Government of North Korea or the Workers' Party of Korea; and (ii) direct or indirect exports and imports to or from North Korea of nearly all goods, services, and technology.[38] These restrict more economic activities, and target a larger list of individuals and businesses than the UN sanctions. The US has led the passage of UNSC sanctions resolutions and along with its allies, has dedicated to continue strengthening unilateral sanctions to complement them until North Korea reverses course.

It is not only the US and its allies but also Russian and Chinese leaders have reservations over North Korea's nuclear test. Even they decided to vote in favour of the UNSC resolution against North Korea. In order to comply with a UNSC resolution, Russian President Vladimir Putin issued a decree imposing sanctions on North Korea. The decree came into force on October 14, 2017. The decree presumes additional restrictions in compliance with the resolution, including on trade, economic, financial, scientific, and technical cooperation with North Korea. The decree also presumes sanctions against 11 North Korean individuals and 10 entities related to Pyongyang's nuclear programme. There is also a list of materials, technologies, and products that are banned from being exported to North Korea.[39]

Many observers have been doubtful as to what extent these sanctions would even be enforced. It has been alleged that North Korea, with help and aid from countries like China, Russia, and Iran, continues to disregard UN and US sanctions to pursue its nuclear programme.

Russia continues to develop close economic interests associated with North Korea; though, the official trade volume remains low, and continues to decrease. On the September 17, 2012, the leaderships of Russia and North Korea signed an agreement on the settlement of the North Korea's debt to the Russian Federation on loans which was previously granted by the former Soviet Union. In 2014, North Korean authorities have showed an extraordinary level of openness and willingness to cooperate in negotiations with the Russians and at the same time asserted to create favourable business conditions for Russian companies to invest.[40] Subsequently, the bilateral turnover stood at US$ 76.8 million in 2016 as reported by the Federal Customs Service of Russia. At the one hand, North Korean exports to Russia (US$ 8.8 million) included frozen fish (24.6 per cent), parts and accessories for tractors (22.3 per cent), articles of apparel and clothing accessories (16 per cent), and wind musical instruments (12.4 per cent). On the other hand, Russian exports to North Korea (US$ 68 million) consisted mainly of bituminous coal (75 per cent), lignite (5 per cent), petroleum oils and gas (4 per cent), as well as wheat (5 per cent), and frozen fish and crustaceans (3 per cent).[41]

The transportation of petroleum products from Russia to North Korea, which includes gasoline and diesel fuel, is projected to be within the range of 200,000–300,000 tons per year. The process of fuel shipments from Russia to North Korea are carried by North Korean coastal tankers that load at Russian Far Eastern ports, such as Vladivostok, Nakhodka, and Slavyanka. All Russian oil supplies to North Korea are carried out by private companies, and executed on the basis of world market prices.[42] It has also been alleged that they possibly include some premium mark-up for the risks involved in dealing with a heavily sanctioned country.[43]

It is reported that Russian tankers have frequently supplied fuel to North Korea in violation of UNSC sanctions. For instance, a report prepared by the Asan Institute for Policy Studies (July 2018) titled 'The Rise of Phantom Traders: Russian Oil Exports to North Korea', provide figures regarding North Korea's oil imports from Russia. The report states that,

> A former high level official working for North Korea's Office 39 claimed in 2017 that North Korea had been importing between 200,000–300,000 tons of fuel from Russia every year using oil brokers based in Singapore. More recently, oil tankers under a number of different national flags were spotted engaging in ship-to-ship transfer of oil, in a clear bid to avoid sanctions enforcement. In several of these instances, Russian tankers were involved.[44]

The US, on the other hand, has claimed that the sales of oil or oil products from Russia evidently violated the UN sanctions imposed on North Korea. The UNSC Sanctions Committee 1718 with reference to oil sales to North Korea from December 2017, cited that 'All Member States are prohibited from supplying, selling, or transferring crude oil that exceeds the aggregate amounts of 4 million barrels or 525,000 tons per 12-month periods from December 22, 2017.'[45] During her remarks at a UNSC Briefing on Non-proliferation and the Implementation on September 17, 2018, Ambassador Nikki Haley argued that,

> North Korea continues to illegally procure refined petroleum products with the help of Russia. Not only that, when we pursued UN designation of the Patriot and other North Korean, Russian, and other country-flagged ships that have been found to be illegally transferring oil, Russia consistently blocked these designations in the sanctions committee.[46]

In contrast, Russia refutes the claims made by the US on violations on UNSC Resolutions. The Russian Ambassador to the United Nations, Vassily Nebenzia, said,

> With regard to the oil tanker *Patriot*, the Panel of Experts itself stated that it was not in violation of the sanctions regime. That statement is in the original draft of the report. It is untrue that we allegedly removed the section about violations made by a Russian company. That is a lie.[47]

Meanwhile, in August 2018, the Treasury Department of the US imposed sanctions on one of the Russian bank accusing it of processing transactions for North Korea in violation of United Nations sanctions. The US has alleged that a Russian bank had assisted a transaction with a person prohibited by US for his alleged involvement with North Korea's nuclear weapons programme.[48] The US further alleged that Russia has allowed thousands of new North Korean labourers into the country with new work permits which according to US is violation UN sanctions. It is said more than 10,000 new North Korean workers have been registered in Russia, since the sanction has imposed.[49]

The United Nations Security Council in August 2018 has adopted guidelines designed to facilitate humanitarian assistance to North Korea. Entitled 'Guidelines for Obtaining Exemptions to Deliver Humanitarian Assistance to the Democratic People's Republic of Korea'. The Committee stated that international and non-governmental organizations can request exemptions from sanctions on North Korea in order to provide their humanitarian assistance. This Security Council guidelines which comes in the middle of the US continued effort for strict enforcement of sanctions on North Korea.

In the meanwhile, Russia has blocked the US request to the UNSC Sanctions Committee on North Korea (1718) regarding introducing international sanctions against individuals and several legal entities, which includes the Russian commercial bank Agrosoyuz that allegedly involved in illegal activities which are violating the sanctions imposed against country. The statement released by the Foreign Ministry suspected that,

> The US-presented evidence in support of this proposal is totally unconvincing. We cannot accept the pressure exerted by the US delegation in the UN Security Council and its subsidiary bodies, which has already become a norm. By means of an artificially tightened deadline, it is trying to push through its own decisions without taking into account the opinion of the other members. Clearly, Washington is trying to keep Pyongyang under maximum pressure as long as possible, in effect, up to the completion of the denuclearisation process. This policy is destructive for settling the issues of the Korean Peninsula and evokes extreme resentment.[50]

The US and Russia faced off over North Korean sanctions at the UNSC on September 17, 2018 in a tense exchange over what Washington is calling 'systematic' Russian violations of the sanctions, and an attempt to cover it up. Ambassador Nikki Haley said that,

> Russia is actively working to undermine the enforcement of the Security Council's sanctions on North Korea. They are systematic. Russia has engaged in a concerted campaign in the Security Council to cover up the violations of sanctions, whether they're committed by Russia or citizens of other states.[51]

In contrast, Russia's Representative to the UNSC, Vasily Nebenzya, alleged that US authorities have artificially created tension around the report by the UNSC's sanctions committee on North Korea. He rejected claims that Russia exerted pressure on the UN sanctions committee's experts. He argued that,

> The US is striving in a forceful and aggressive manner to suppress the UN Security Council in this area, and one gets an impression at times the US Administration has developed a habit for mixing up

> the UN Security Council and Washington's own National Security Council. They say that Russians are allegedly seeking to exert pressure on the expert team. We would like to put an end to such allegations once and for all.[52]

Defending Russia with regards to the violation of UNSC sanctions, Vasily Nebenzya specified that,

> The sanctions committee on the Democratic People's Republic of Korea is a clear example of what the destructive behaviour of some of its members leads to. It seems that the Committee is seen by the United States as a kind of club meant to punish the Democratic People's Republic of Korea for its intransigence in the negotiations.[53]

However, not only Russia and China but a tally of 52 states—as revealed by the Institute for Science and International Security in their report—were found to be violating the UNSC sanctions from the period January to September 2017. Nine governments were found to be involved in military-related cases of North Korean sanctions violations, including: Angola, Egypt, Eritrea, Mozambique, Myanmar, Sudan, Syria, Tanzania, and Uganda. It also discovered that twenty countries were involved in the import of goods and minerals from North Korea, including coal, copper ore, iron/steel, nickel, silver, and zinc which are sanctioned by UN. The countries importing these goods as reported to the Panel were: Barbados, Bolivia, Chile, China, Colombia, Costa Rica, El Salvador, Ghana, India, Ireland, Malaysia, Mexico, Mozambique, Nicaragua, Pakistan, Philippines, Russia, South Korea, Thailand, and Vietnam.[54] Most of the observers have expressed serious apprehensions about these violations, and also questioned the effectiveness of the sanctions if such conditions persist for a long time.

The United States has disagreed with Russia and China several times during the debate at the United Nations over their demand for the easing of sanctions against North Korea. The Russian Ambassador to UN, Vassily Nebenzia, pointed that,

> It will be impossible to settle the nuclear issue on the Korean peninsula through sanctions and pressure on Pyongyang alone. Sanctions should not be used to strangle the Democratic People's Republic of Korea economically or worsen its humanitarian situation. That applies especially to unilateral restrictions, which affect civilian sectors that have nothing to do with the country's nuclear-missile programmes and are one reason for the serious deterioration in the population's living conditions.[55]

Despite their support for the resolution via an affirmative vote, Russia and China have openly questioned the effectiveness of these economic sanctions on North Korea. Furthermore, Russia has stressed need for concrete initiative to resolve the crisis several times in UN rather tightening sanctions on North Korea. The solution to the Korean Peninsula's nuclear issue cannot be complete unless sanctions against Pyongyang are lifted. Addressing the 72nd session of the UN General Assembly within the General Debate, Mikhail Ulyanov, Director of the Russian Foreign Ministry Department, stated that,

> We supported the latest sanctions imposed by the UN Security Council. However, the sanctions are not a cure-all. The problem can be resolved only politically and diplomatically. The pressure can only be successful if it is backed by active diplomacy and a creative search for effective solutions.[56]

Likewise, Russian Foreign Minister, Sergey Lavrov, echoed the same idea after talks with his North Korean counterpart Ri Yong-ho. Answering a question raised by a journalist, he noted that,

> We assume that a complete resolution cannot be achieved until all the sanctions are lifted. It is up to the negotiators to make this happen, but in any case it would be impossible to achieve this in a single round. The same applies to denuclearisation. For this reason, this should be a step-by-step process with reciprocal moves at each of the stages.[57]

In the same way, the Russian scholar, Alexander Gabuev, has argued that,

> The sanctions do not provide an ultimate solution to the DPRK missile and nuclear problems. Pyongyang will try to secure the possession of nuclear-capable ICBMs, and the international community has no real tools to prevent it since military tools are not applicable, and since China and Russia will not support crippling sanctions on the DPRK that would enable internal regime change.[58]

As a replacement which moved beyond sanctions, Russian Ambassador to the UN, Vassily Nebenzia, placed an alternative solution. He said that,

> We proposed a reasonable and realistic alternative to the ultimatum logic of the sanctions, which has proved unworkable time and again. The alternative consisted of the following: beginning implementation of not just the sanctions-related parts of the aforementioned resolutions of the Security Council, but also those of the provisions calling for a peaceful political and diplomatic settlement of the nuclear issue on the Korean Peninsula through dialogue and negotiation.[59]

Hence, there exists a level of consensus among Russia and China within the UNSC to find a diplomatic solution to the Korean crisis.

Russia in Six-Party Talks and New Russia-China Initiatives

Russia professed that peace and stability on the Korean Peninsula is possible only through cooperation and coordination with both Korean governments. Russia proposes the diplomacy and consultations the best way to resolve the North Korean nuclear issue. As the Russian expert on the Asia-Pacific, Alexander Lukin, has said,

> Russia is interested in the security of its borders, consequently in the political stability of both Korean states. Any war or loss of control on developments in the peninsula, in consideration of the presence in North Korea of nuclear weapons, could easily directly affect the adjoining Russian territory, capable of causing casualties, an ecological catastrophe, a flood of refugees, and other dangerous consequences.[60]

The main purpose of the Six-Party Talks were based on dismantling North Korea's nuclear programme launched in 2003. The Six-Party Talks were a sequence of multilateral meetings involving all major regional actors including China, Japan, North Korea, the US, South Korea, and Russia. However, the process has been stalled over the years by North Korea's repeated missile and nuclear weapons tests. While answering Sergei Brilyov's question in the meeting of Eastern Economic Forum in September 2018, President Putin argued that,

> North Korea was promised security guarantees in exchange for its denuclearisation efforts, as you have just pointed out. North Korea has taken certain steps to denuclearise—it blew up its nuclear test site, destroyed it, but it apparently expects something in return. We have the format of six-party talks. And the international community can give such guarantees, including those secured by the presence of nuclear powers in these agreements. China and Russia are parties to these talks.[61]

Georgy Toloraya has noted that 'Russia would like to see multiparty security and cooperation systems emerge in Northeast Asia. The Six-Party Talks had provided a unique opportunity to try a multilateral approach to solving the thorny issues that plague the region.'[62] Professor Igor Tolstokulakov of the Far Eastern Federal University of Russia has argued that sanctions would not work with North Korea and suggested closer cooperation between regional powers including China, Russia, the US, Japan, and South

Korea in order to find peaceful and acceptable solution to Korean crisis which also require the active participation of from the side of Pyongyang.[63]

However, it is only Russian Federation which consistently promoted the Six-Party Talks at every forum and, to a certain extent, so did China; but other parties, such as the US, Japan, South Korea and, most importantly, North Korea, do not seem to be interested in reviving the process at this moment. This has also been acknowledged by the Russian Ambassador to North Korea, Alexander Matsegora. During an interview to the Russian News Channel in February 2018, he stated that the resumption of the Six-Party negotiations on the denuclearisation of the Korean Peninsula is unlikely at the moment. But it is possible in the future.[64]

Besides the Six-Party Talks, the Russian Federation has also put forward the idea of a phased approach to the settlement of the basic issues of the Korean Peninsula. Russia and China signed a joint statement in July 2017 in Moscow on the Korean Peninsula to coordinate efforts in finding a solution to the crisis, and achieving lasting peace and stability in Northeast Asia. The joint call came as a result of the meeting between the Chinese President Xi Jinping and the Russian President Vladimir Putin in Moscow. The Joint Declarations, signed on July 4, 2017 with reference to Korean Peninsula, reads as follows:

> Our common foreign policy priorities include a comprehensive resolution of the Korean Peninsula issue with a view to ensuring peace and stability in Northeast Asia. We have agreed to actively promote our common initiative based on Russia's stage-by-stage plan for a Korean settlement and China's initiatives for a parallel freeze of nuclear missile activities in the DPRK and the large-scale military exercises by the United States and the Republic of Korea.[65]

The Chinese Ambassador to the UN, Wu Haitao, welcomed this proposal and stated that,

> The joint proposal of China and Russia is practical and feasible and is aimed at promoting the peaceful settlement of the nuclear issue of the Korean peninsula and the maintenance of peace and stability on the peninsula. As such, we hope that the proposal will elicit responses and support from the parties concerned.[66]

Regarding this joint initiative, Russian scholars Mikheev and Fedorovsky argue that,

> It is also significant that the Russian-Chinese initiative was developed outside of the framework of preliminary consultations with Pyongyang, for which it was also a surprise. Such a situation undoubtedly reduces the productivity of joint Russian-Chinese efforts to normalise the situation on the Korean Peninsula.[67]

Moreover, peace and stability in Northeast Asia is possible only when appropriate measures are taken on denuclearisation of North Korea and, at the same time, restraining large-scale joint exercises by the US and the South Korea. Whatever may be the outline prepared by Russia and China, the main actors—such as the US and North Korea—were not involved. Hence, its implementations does not seem feasible in the near future. Russia continues discussions with North Korea in both bilateral and tripartite (including China) formats. Recently, the Deputy Foreign Ministers of Russia Igor Morgulov, along with his Chinese and North Korean counterparts held talks in Moscow in October 2018 in which they insisted that the UNSC reverse its policy of anti-Pyongyang sanctions. This is the first time they have officially raised this issue in the format of a trilateral meeting. A joint communiqué released after the consultations in Moscow stated that,

> Taking into account the important steps towards denuclearisation made by the Democratic People's Republic of Korea, the sides believe the UN Security Council should start in due time revising the sanctions against the DPRK. There is general understanding

> that this process, the priority goal of which is to establish mutual trust, should be of a step-by-step and synchronised character and accompanied by reciprocal steps of the involved states.[68]

Russia recognises the situation in the Korean Peninsula as one of the major global seats of tension, and has always campaigned a non-nuclear status for the Korean Peninsula, and pledged its support for denuclearisation in every possible way.

The Russian Attitude to Summit Diplomacy and the Way Forward

The situation in the Korean Peninsula has changed since the inter-Korea Summits and the historic meeting between President Trump and Chairman Kim Jong-un. The Russian Foreign Ministry issued a press released stating that,

> We welcome the successful holding of the meeting between the leaders of the two Korean states in Panmunjom on April 27. We regard it as a significant step by Seoul and Pyongyang to national reconciliation and the establishment of strong relationships of independent value. We have a positive view of the agreements enshrined in the Panmunjom Declaration on the results of the inter-Korean summit. We are ready to facilitate the establishment of practical cooperation between the DPRK and the Republic of Korea, including through the development of tripartite cooperation in the railway, electricity, gas and other industries.[69]

In an answer to a question from TASS news agency regarding the non-mention of Russia in the declaration, the Russian Deputy Foreign Minister, Igor Morgulov, replied that,

> Russia will not drop out of the process; on the contrary, it is determined to continue searching for solutions to all the problems of the Korean Peninsula in the most proactive manner.

> By the way, the Russian-Chinese roadmap for the Korean peace settlement, drafted in 2017, clearly sets out Russia's position on this matter. This position implies that the process of signing a peace treaty that would replace the Armistice Agreement is solely the subject of bilateral relations between North and South Korea, and should be conducted by Pyongyang and Seoul. In fact, the Panmunjom Declaration reflects this approach. Russia has no legal grounds or motives to become a party to this treaty.[70]

Similarly, Moscow has always welcomed any steps aimed at the denuclearisation of the Korean Peninsula. In a press release, the Foreign Ministry noted,

> We welcome the talks of the Chairman of the DPRK State Council Kim Jong-un and US President Donald Trump on July 12 in Singapore. We proceed from the belief that the normalisation of US-North Korean relations, a commitment to which is stated in the final joint statement, is an inalienable part of the comprehensive settlement of the Korean Peninsula issues, including the nuclear issue.[71]

The Vladivostok summit held on April 25, 2019 turn out to be the first face-to-face meeting between Russian President Vladimir Putin and North Korean leader Kim Jong-un. Both the leaders thoroughly discussed bilateral relations and their prospects and dwelled on issues linked to the situation on the Korean Peninsula, in particular the denuclearisation problem but there was no joint declaration. The meeting came two months after the unproductive summit in Hanoi in February 2019 between North Korean leader Kim Jong-un and US President Trump. Addressing at the official reception on behalf of the President of Russia, President Vladimir Putin retaliated that there is no alternative to resolving the Korean Peninsula issue through diplomatic means. He noted 'We welcome DPRK's steps to establish direct dialogue with the United States and normalise relations between North and South Korea. We proceed from the premise that there is no alternative to a peaceful resolution of the nuclear and other problems in the region.'[72]

Russia has been one of the main actor on the Korean Peninsula. It continues to be a major partner in wide range of political, economic, and social links with North Korea. While criticising North Korea for testing nuclear weapons, Russian government representatives have also questioned Western countries for their failure to address with reference to their previous promises to North Korea. Russia is the only major player in Northeast Asia that has a stable relationship with both the Koreas. It has constantly and consistently appealed to the global community collectively to resolve the issue through dialogue and consultations. Russia anticipates that the positive tendencies, which have appeared recently in the ongoing negotiating process on regulating the situation on the Korean Peninsula, might gather momentum in the near future.

Notes

1. Eleanor Albert, 'What to Know About the Sanctions on North Korea', The Council on Foreign Relations, 2018 at https://www.cfr.org/backgrounder/what-know-about-sanctions-north-korea, accessed on October 23, 2018.
2. Vassily A. Nebenzia, 'Non-proliferation/Democratic People's Republic of Korea', Security Council Seventy-Second Year, 8042th Meeting, UN Security Council Meeting Open Debate on DPRK, September 11, 2017 at http://www.un.org/en/ga/search/view_doc.asp?symbol=S/PV.8042, accessed on October 20, 2018.
3. Vladimir Putin, 'Eastern Economic Forum: Plenary Session', Russian President's Website Resources, September 12, 2018 at http://en.kremlin.ru/events/president/news/58537, accessed on October 20, 2018.
4. Sergey Lavrov, 'Foreign Minister's remarks and answers to media questions following talks with Foreign Minister of North Korea, Ri Yong-ho Pyongyang', The Ministry of Foreign Affairs of the Russian Federation, May 31, 2018 at http://www.mid.ru/en/maps/kp/-/asset_publisher/VJy7Ig5QaAII/content/id/3240604, accessed on October 20, 2018.
5. John W. Bauer, 'Unlocking Russian interests on the Korean Peninsula', U.S. Army Website, September 28, 2009 at https://www.army.mil/article/27946/unlocking_russian_interests_on_the_korean_peninsula, accessed on October 20, 2018.

6. Sergey Sevastianov, 'Russia and Northeast Asia Energy Security', The Daniel K. Inouye Asia-Pacific Center for Security Studies (DKI APCSS), 2012 at https://apcss.org/wp-content/uploads/2012/09/Chapter3.pdf, accessed on October 20, 2018.
7. Lee Jae-Young, 'The New Northern Policy and Korean-Russian Cooperation', No. 76 Valdai Papers, October 2017 at http://valdaiclub.com/files/16143/, accessed on October 20, 2018.
8. Andrey Gubin, 'Shall we secure DPRK to be secured?', Russia and the Asia-Pacific Region Community, Russian International Affairs Council (RIAC), Moscow, February 28, 2016 at http://russiancouncil.ru/en/blogs/dvfu-en/2339/, accessed on October 22, 2018.
9. I.S. Ivanov (ed.), 'Security and Cooperation in Northeast Asia: the Russian-South Korean Experts Joint Paper', Working Paper No. 25, Russian International Affairs Council, Moscow, 2015, p. 12 at http://russiancouncil.ru/en/activity/workingpapers/bezopasnost-i-sotrudnichestvo-v-severo-vostochnoy-azii-sovme/, accessed on October 25, 2018.
10. Maxim Suchkov, 'North Korea's Nuclear, A View from Moscow', Analytics and Comments, Russian International Affairs Council (RIAC), Moscow, June 14, 2018 at http://russiancouncil.ru/en/analytics-and-comments/columns/asian-kaleidoscope/north-korea-s-nuclear-a-view-from-moscow/?sphrase_id=18856023, accessed on October 29, 2018.
11. Artyom Lukin, 'Why Russia Is Still Playing Second Fiddle in Korean Geopolitics', Expert Opinion, Valdai Discussion Club, Moscow, August 21, 2018 at http://valdaiclub.com/a/highlights/russia-second-fiddle-in-korea/?sphrase_id=433795, accessed on October 20, 2018.
12. Andrey Gubin, note 8.
13. Fyodor Lukyanov, 'Russia can be the honest broker in Korean diplomacy', Russia in Global Affairs (Moscow), June 18, 2018 at https://eng.globalaffairs.ru/redcol/Russia-can-be-the-honest-broker-in-Korean-diplomacy-19620, accessed on October 20, 2018.
14. Richard Weitz, 'Russian Policy toward North Korea: Steadfast and Changing', *International Journal of Korean Unification Studies*, 24(3), 2015, p. 15.
15. Vladimir Nelidov, 'Regional Security in Northeast Asia and the Russia-Japan-US Triangle', Policy Brief, No. 16, May 2018, The Russian International Affairs Council (RIAC), Moscow, p. 4.
16. Alexander Zhebin, 'A Political History of Soviet-North Korean Nuclear Cooperation', in James Clay Moltz and Alexander Y. Mansourov (eds), *The North Korean Nuclear Program: Security, Strategy and New Perspectives from Russia*, Routledge, London and New York, 2000, pp. 27–31.
17. Valery I. Denisov, 'Nuclear Institution and Organization in North Korea', in James Clay Moltz and Alexander Y. Mansourov (eds), *The North*

Korean Nuclear Program: Security, Strategy and New Perspectives from Russia, Routledge, London and New York, 2000, pp. 21–23.

18. Statement by Ambassador Vassily A. Nebenzia, Permanent Representative of the Russian Federation to the United Nations, at the Security Council meeting on Non-proliferation/Democratic People's Republic of Korea, Permanent Mission of the Russian Federation to the United Nations, New York December 15, 2017 at http://russiaun.ru/en/news/dprk1512, accessed on October 20, 2018.
19. Alexander Lukin, 'Russian Strategic Thinking Regarding North Korea', The Asan Forum, The Asan Institute for Policy Studies, Seoul (South Korea), October 7, 2013 at http://www.theasanforum.org/russian-strategic-thinking-regarding-north-korea/, accessed on October 20, 2018.
20. 'Russia's communist party leader slams Trump's statement on North Korea as provocation', ITAR-TASS News Agency (Moscow) September 20, 2017 at http://tass.com/politics/966596, accessed on October 29, 2018.
21. 'Zhirinovsky expresses profound solidarity with N. Korea', Interfax News Agency, Moscow, April 18, 2017 at http://www.interfax.com/newsinf.asp?y=2012&m=7&d=21&id=748930, accessed on October 20, 2018.
22. Kazbek Taysaev, 'We welcome the formation of peace on the Korean Peninsula. South Korea is an equal player for everyone in the international arena', Press Service of the CA SKP-KPSS, International Department, Communist Party of the Russian Federation , Moscow, September 20, 2018 at https://kprf.ru/international/new-world/179058.html, accessed on October 20, 2018.
23. Sergey Lavrov, 'Foreign Minister Sergey Lavrov's interview with Itogi Nedeli for the NTV network', The Ministry of Foreign Affairs of the Russian Federation, Moscow, September 24, 2017 at http://www.mid.ru/en/web/guest/foreign_policy/news/-/asset_publisher/cKNonkJE02Bw/content/id/2873322, accessed on October 20, 2018.
24. Vladimir Putin, 'Vladimir Putin's news conference following BRICS Summit', Russian President's Website Resources, September 5, 2017 at http://en.kremlin.ru/events/president/news/55535, accessed on October 2, 2018.
25. Mikhail Ulyanov, 'Remarks by Mikhail Ulyanov, Director of the Foreign Ministry Department for Non-Proliferation and Arms Control and Representative of the Russian Federation at the First Committee of the 72nd session of the UN General Assembly, within the General Debate', The Ministry of Foreign Affairs of the Russian Federation, Moscow, October 4, 2017 at http://www.mid.ru/en/web/guest/general_assembly/-/asset_publisher/lrzZMhfoyRUj/content/id/2887054, accessed on October 30, 2018.
26. Artyom Lukin, 'The Korean Nuclear Missile Crisis: It Takes Three to Tango', Analytics and Comments, Russian International Affairs Council

(RIAC), Moscow, August 23, 2017 at http://russiancouncil.ru/en/analytics-and-comments/analytics/the-korean-nuclear-missile-crisis-it-takes-three-to-tango/, accessed on October 20, 2018.

27. Georgy Toloraya, 'The Korean Peninsula: Is There a Nuclear War Coming?', Analytics and Comments, Russian International Affairs Council (RIAC), Moscow, January 20, 2016 at http://russiancouncil.ru/en/analytics-and-comments/analytics/teatr-koreyskogo-poluostrova-zhdat-li-yadernoy-voyny/?sphrase_id=18856023, accessed on October 20, 2018.
28. Andrew Korybko, 'Multipolar Sanctions on North Korea: Sell-Out or Strategic?', ORIENTAL REVIEW: International Open Dialogue Research e-journal, August 14, 2017 at https://orientalreview.org/2017/08/14/multipolar-sanctions-north-korea/, accessed on October 20, 2018.
29. Alexander Gabuev, 'A Russian Perspective on the Impact of Sanctions', The Carnegie Endowment for International Peace, Moscow Centre, August 3, 2017 at http://carnegie.ru/2017/08/03/russian-perspective-on-impact-of-sanctions-pub-72723, accessed on October 20, 2018.
30. 'MP warns US deployment of THAAD system in South Korea jeopardizes Russia's security', ITAR-TASS News Agency (Moscow), March 7, 2017 at http://tass.com/politics/934381, accessed on October 20, 2018.
31. Vassily A. Nebenzia, 'Non-proliferation/Democratic People's Republic of Korea', Security Council Seventy Second Year, 8118th Meeting, UN Security Council Meeting Open Debate, November 29, 2017 at https://www.un.org/en/ga/search/view_doc.asp?symbol=S/PV.8118, accessed on October 20, 2018.
32. Igor Tolstokulakov, 'North Korea should be treated as an equal partner', Hanns Seidel Foundation Korea, Seoul, January 30, 2018, in 'Search of Trilateral Cooperation in North East Asia', Conference on the Future Development of South Korea-Russia Relations at https://korea.hss.de/en/news/detail/in-search-of-trilateral-cooperation-in-northeast-asia-news2494/, accessed on October 20, 2018.
33. Charles Knight, 'A Russian Perspective on Korean Denuclearization', interview with Anastasia Barannikova, Lobelog: Institute for Policy Studies, Washington DC, February 18, 2018 at https://lobelog.com/a-russian-perspective-on-korean-denuclearization/, accessed on October 2, 2018.
34. Sergey Lavrov, 'Russia's Foreign Minister Sergey Lavrov answers questions from readers of the newspaper *Argumenty i Fakty*', The Ministry of Foreign Affairs of the Russian Federation, Moscow, March 29, 2017 at http://www.mid.ru/en/web/guest/foreign_policy/news/-/asset_publisher/cKNonkJE02Bw/content/id/2709721, accessed on October 20, 2018.
35. 'Press release on the meeting of the Co-chairmen of the Russian-Chinese Dialogue on Security in Northeast Asia', The Ministry of Foreign Affairs of the Russian Federation, Moscow, May 22, 2017 at http://www.mid.

ru/en/web/guest/maps/cn/-/asset_publisher/WhKWb5DVBqKA/content/id/2763229, accessed on October 20, 2018.

36. 'Resolution 1718 Adopted by the Security Council at its 5551st meeting', on UN Security Council Meeting Open Debate on DPRK, October 14, 2006 at http://www.un.org/ga/search/view_doc.asp?symbol=S/RES/1718(2006), accessed on October 20, 2018.
37. 'Security Council Tightens Sanctions on Democratic People's Republic of Korea', Unanimously Adopting Resolution 2397, 2017, Security Council, 8151ST Meeting (PM), SC/13141, UN Security Council Resolutions on DPRK, December 22, 2017 at https://www.un.org/press/en/2017/sc13141.doc.htm, accessed on October 20, 2018.
38. 'Sanctions Risks Related to North Korea's Shipping Practices', North Korea Sanctions Advisory, Department of Treasury, The U.S. Department of the Treasury, Washington, D.C., February 23, 2018 at https://www.treasury.gov/resource-center/sanctions/OFAC-Enforcement/Documents/dprk_vessel_advisory_02232018.pdf, accessed on October 20, 2018.
39. 'Putin Signs Decree Imposing Restrictions on North Korea', Sputnik News Agency, Moscow, October 16, 2017 at https://sputniknews.com/world/201710161058276769-putin-decree-north-korea-sanctions/0, accessed on October 20, 2018.
40. Liudmila Zakharova, 'Economic cooperation between Russia and North Korea: New goals and new approaches', *Journal of Eurasian Studies* 7, 2016, p. 154.
41. Artyom Lukin, 'Nuclear Weapons And Russian-North Korean Relations', Foreign Policy Research Institute, November 27, 2017 at https://www.fpri.org/article/2017/11/nuclear-weapons-russian-north-korean-relations/, accessed on October 20, 2018.
42. Artyom Lukin and Lyudmila Zakharova, 'Russia-North Korea Economic Ties: Is There More Than Meets the Eye?', report by the Foreign Policy Research Institute, Philadelphia, October 6, 2017 at https://www.fpri.org/wp-content/uploads/2017/10/Russia-DPRK-Economic-Ties.pdf, accessed on October 20, 2018.
43. Artyom Lukin, note 41.
44. 'The Rise of Phantom Traders: Russian Oil Exports to North Korea', Asan Report, The Asan Institute for Policy Studies, July 2018 at file://C:/Users/idsa/Downloads/Asan-Report-The-Rise-of-Phantom-Traders3.pdf, accessed on October 20, 2018.
45. '1718 Sanctions Committee (DPRK), Supply, sale or transfer of all refined petroleum products to the DPRK', Reporting on the supply, sale or transfer of all refined petroleum products to the DPRK by Member States, Security Council Committee resolution on DPRK at https://www.un.org/sc/suborg/en/sanctions/1718/supply-sale-or-transfer-of-all-refined-petroleum, accessed on October 20, 2018.

46. Nikki Haley, 'Remarks at a UN Security Council Briefing on Non-proliferation and the Implementation and Enforcement of UN Sanctions on North Korea', The U.S. Mission to the United Nations (USUN), September 17, 2018 at https://usun.state.gov/remarks/8613, accessed on October 20, 2018.
47. Vassily Nebenzia, 'Non-proliferation/Democratic People's Republic of Korea', United Nations Security Council, Seventy-third Year, 8353rd Meeting, UN Security Council Meeting Open Debate on DPRK, September 17, 2018 at https://www.un.org/en/ga/search/view_doc.asp?symbol=S/PV.8353, accessed on October 20, 2018.
48. Sasha Ingber, 'Russian Bank Hit with Sanctions for Helping North Korea', National Public Radio (NPR), Washington, DC, August 3, 2018 at https://www.npr.org/2018/08/03/635465039/russian-bank-hit-with-sanctions-for-helping-north-korea, accessed on October 20, 2018.
49. Bob Fredericks, 'Russia may have violated UN sanctions by giving work permits to North Korean laborers', *New York Post*, August 2, 2018 at https://nypost.com/2018/08/02/russia-may-have-violated-un-sanctions-by-giving-work-permits-to-north-korean-laborers/, accessed on October 20, 2018.
50. 'Comment by the Information and Press Department on the US application tó the UN Security Council Sanctions Committee on North Korea (1718) on expanding sanctions', Press Release, Ministry of Foreign Affairs of the Russian Federation, The Ministry of Foreign Affairs of the Russian Federation, Moscow, August 10, 2018 at http://www.mid.ru/en/maps/kp/-/asset_publisher/VJy7Ig5QaAII/content/id/3316726, accessed on October 20, 2018.
51. Nikki Haley, 'Remarks at a UN Security Council Briefing on Non-proliferation and the Implementation and Enforcement of UN Sanctions on North Korea', The U.S. Mission to the United Nations (USUN), September 17, 2018 at https://usun.state.gov/remarks/8613, accessed on October 20, 2018.
52. 'Russian envoy slams US policy towards North Korea', ITAR-TASS News Agency (Moscow), September 17, 21018 at http://tass.com/politics/1021986, accessed on October 20, 2018.
53. Vasily Nebenzia, note 47.
54. David Albright, Sarah Burkhard, Allison Lach and Andrea Stricker, '52 Countries Involved in Violating UNSC Resolutions on North Korea throughout most of 2017', Institute for Science and International Security, Washington, DC, March 9, 2018 at http://isis-online.org/isis-reports/detail/52-countries-involved-in-violating-unsc-resolutions-on-north-korea-througho, accessed on October 20, 2018.
55. Vassily A. Nebenzia, note 18.

56. Mikhail Ulyanov, 'Remarks by Mikhail Ulyanov, Director of the Foreign Ministry Department for Non-Proliferation and Arms Control, and Representative of the Russian Federation at the First Committee of the 72nd session of the UN General Assembly, within the General Debate', The Ministry of Foreign Affairs of the Russian Federation, Moscow, October 4, 2017 at http://www.mid.ru/en/web/guest/general_assembly/-/asset_publisher/lrzZMhfoyRUj/content/id/2887054, accessed on October 20, 2018.
57. Sergey Lavrov, 'Foreign Minister Sergey Lavrov's remarks and answers to media questions following talks with the Foreign Minister of North Korea, Ri Yong-ho Pyongyang', The Ministry of Foreign Affairs of the Russian Federation, Moscow, May 31, 2018 at http://www.mid.ru/en/maps/kp/-/asset_publisher/VJy7Ig5QaAII/content/id/3240604, accessed on October 20, 2018.
58. Alexander Gabuev, note 29.
59. Vassily A. Nebenzia, 'Non-proliferation/Democratic People's Republic of Korea', Security Council, Seventy Second Year, 8042th Meeting, UN Security Council Meeting Open Debate on DPRK, September 11, 2017 at http://www.un.org/en/ga/search/view_doc.asp?symbol=S/PV.8042, accessed on October 20, 2018.
60. Valery Denisov and Alexander Lukin, 'Russia, China, and the Korean Peninsula', in Gilbert Rozman (ed.), *Joint US-Korea Academic Studies*, Volume 25, 2014, Princeton University at http://www.keia.org/sites/default/files/publications/alexander_lukin.pdf, accessed on October 20, 2018.
61. Vladimir Putin, 'Eastern Economic Forum Plenary Session', Russian President's Website Resources, September 12, 2018 at http://en.kremlin.ru/events/president/news/58537, accessed on October 20, 2018.
62. Georgy Toloraya, 'The Six Party Talks: A Russian Perspective', *Asian Perspective*, 32(4), p. 62.
63. Igor Tolstokulakov, note 32.
64. 'Revival of six-party talks on North Korea unlikely now: Russian Ambassador', ITAR-TASS News Agency (Moscow), February 8, 2018 at http://tass.com/politics/989032, accessed on October 20, 2018.
65. 'Press statements following Russian-Chinese talks, Vladimir Putin and President of the People's Republic of China Xi Jinping made statements for the press following Russian-Chinese talks', Russian President's Website Resources, July 4, 2017 at http://en.kremlin.ru/events/president/news/54979a, accessed on October 20, 2018.
66. Wu Haitao, 'Non-proliferation/Democratic People's Republic of Korea', Security Council Seventy second year, 8237th meeting, UN Security Council Meeting Open Debate on DPRK, December 15, 2017 at https://

www.un.org/en/ga/search/view_doc.asp?symbol=S/PV.8137, accessed on October 20, 2018.

67. V. Mikheev and A. Fedorovsky (eds), 'Crisis and New Political Agenda for the Korean Peninsula and the Regional Powers', Moscow, IMEMO, Institute of World Economy and International Relations of the Russian Academy of Sciences (IMEMO) Publication 2018 at https://www.imemo.ru/files/File/en/publ/2018/2018_001.pdf, accessed on October 20, 2018.
68. 'Russia, China, North Korea call for review of sanctions against Pyongyang', ITAR-TASS News Agency (Moscow), October 10, 2018 at http://tass.com/world/1025315, accessed on October 20, 2018.
69. Comment by the Information and Press Department on the inter-Korean summit, The Ministry of Foreign Affairs of the Russian Federation, Moscow, April 27, 2017 at http://www.mid.ru/en/maps/kp/-/asset_publisher/VJy7Ig5QaAII/content/id/3194904, accessed on October 20, 2018.
70. Igor Morgulov, 'Deputy Foreign Minister Igor Morgulov's answer to a question from TASS news agency about Russia's role in the settlement process on the Korean Peninsula', The Ministry of Foreign Affairs of the Russian Federation, Moscow, April 28, 2018 at http://www.mid.ru/en/maps/kp/-/asset_publisher/VJy7Ig5QaAII/content/id/3204522, accessed on October 20, 2018.
71. Comment by the Information and Press Department on the US-North Korea Summit in Singapore, The Ministry of Foreign Affairs of the Russian Federation, Moscow, June 12, 2018 at http://www.mid.ru/en/maps/kp/-/asset_publisher/VJy7Ig5QaAII/content/id/3256544, accessed on October 20, 2018.
72. Vladimir Putin, 'Speeches at the official reception on behalf of the President of Russia', Russian President's Website Resources, April 25, 2019 at http://en.kremlin.ru/catalog/persons/599/events/60369, accessed on July 31, 2019.

12. Rethinking Japan's North Korea Strategy: In Cross-Currents between Kim Jong-un and Donald Trump

Titli Basu

As Chairman Kim Jong-un attempts to redefine strategic stability in the Korean Peninsula, Japan's North Korea policy is caught between a rock and a hard place. While the Korean Peninsula is often considered as a 'dagger pointed at the heart of Japan', North Korea has lately emerged as a key variable shaping Tokyo's official narrative, articulating the case of the most severe security environment in its post-war history.[1] Considerable advancement in North Korea's nuclear and ballistic missile programme has raised fierce policy debates in Japan on key strategic and security concerns, including how to realise a complete, verifiable, and irreversible dismantlement of all North Korea's Weapons of Mass Destruction (WMD), including biological and chemical weapons as well as its ballistic missiles of all flight ranges. Also debated is how to evolve a better alliance management mechanism, and balance US's extended deterrence commitment versus the intensification of alliance decoupling concerns.

As North Korea tests the resilience of Japan's post-war security orientation, will Tokyo pursue the option of going nuclear, given the stockpile of 47 metric tons of plutonium? Or will it further advance the political debate on acquiring strike capabilities (*teki kichi kōgeki*)? Other questions also arise. Is Prime Minister Shinzo Abe's domestic political priority concerning the abduction issue isolating Japan in the fast altering regional strategic environment? And most importantly, how can Japan pursue its interests in the face of difficult challenges looming in the region with regard to realising denuclearisation while dealing with a 'rational'[2] Kim Jong-un on the one hand, and an unconventional US President Trump on the other?

This article first sieves Japan's North Korea conundrum from its security and foreign policy discourse as well as its domestic political agenda. Subsequently, the article critically analyses the North Korean factor in the US-Japan alliance, and weighs Japan's policy options, including economic sanctions, political and diplomatic alternatives; evaluates Japanese evolving defence posture; and finally, unpacks the regional response as Japan adapts incrementally to reinforce alliance deterrence capabilities, and assumes greater responsibility for its own security.

Japanese Policy Discourse on North Korea

Under Chairman Kim Jong-un, North Korea has undeniably advanced its nuclear and ballistic missile programme at an unanticipated pace. Since he assumed responsibility, North Korea has conducted four nuclear weapons tests and over 80 ballistic missile tests[3] on a variety of platforms, including ballistic missiles launched over the Oshima Peninsula and the Cape Erimo of Hokkaido Prefecture in violation of United Nations Security Council (UNSC) Resolution 2375, and the Hwasong-15 ICBM falling within Japan's Exclusive Economic Zone (EEZ) in the latter half of 2017. Confrontational rhetoric from the North Korean regime underscoring Tokyo's 'war hysteria' amounting to possible 'nuclear clouds' in Japan have raised concerns for Prime Minister Shinzo Abe who, in turn, has argued in his policy speeches at the National Diet that 'it is no exaggeration to say that the security environment surrounding Japan is the most severe in post-war history'.[4]

As China advocates a 'dual track' approach vis-à-vis the Korean Peninsula, Japan has shaped its 'maximum pressure' campaign, and argued that 'sanctions are the tool to make North Korea understand that there is no other way but to change its policy'[5] and urged for effective implementation of UN sanctions, in addition to secondary sanctions. At the 2017 United Nations General Assembly, Japan cautioned that dialogue is employed as a tool by Pyongyang for 'deceiving us and buying time', and that 'not dialogue, but pressure' is the way forward in making Pyongyang relinquish its nuclear and ballistic missile programmes in a complete, verifiable, and irreversible manner.[6] In December 2017, Ambassador Koro Bessho, Permanent Representative of Japan to the United Nations and also the Security Council President for December, argued that the furtherance of nuclear and missile development 'could never be tolerated and maximum pressure would be applied to end it'.[7]

Japan's mistrust of North Korea is shaped by its experience with the regime, drawing from the outcome of the Agreed Framework, Six-Party Talks, and the Japan-DPRK Pyongyang Declaration. For instance, in the case of Korean Peninsula Energy Development Organisation (KEDO), instituted following the Agreed Framework, Japan disbursed approximately 40 per cent of its one billion dollar pledge till 2002 in the hope of making Pyongyang abandon its nuclear programme only to realise that North Korea was vigorously pursuing its uranium enrichment programme simultaneously. Under Japan's presidency at the UNSC, Resolution 2397 was adopted in December 2017 wherein Japan urged 'not [to] yield to any provocative actions', and 'enhance pressure' on Pyongyang to the 'maximum degree in order to urge it to change its policies'.[8]

However, with the historic Trump-Kim Summit in June 2018 in Singapore, Japan's maximum pressure policy campaign got diluted. While international enforcement of the sanctions did play an important role in making North Korea revisit its strategy, major powers responded to Chairman Kim's charm offensive and pursued diplomatic channels to engage with the regime. Even though Japan expressed support for the unfolding diplomatic initiatives, it has urged the international community to be united in the implementation of the unanimously adopted UNSC Resolutions given that the 2018 annual cap on petroleum products is violated by exploiting the well-established mechanisms to evade sanctions by way of ship-to-ship transfers and the selling of fishing rights.[9] The latest Japanese Defense White Paper released in August 2018 evaluates the 'unprecedentedly serious and imminent threat' emanating from North Korea because for Japan, which is well within the range of Nodong missiles, there is 'no change to the underlying status of the North Korean nuclear and missile threat'.[10] Meanwhile, the Foreign Ministry Diplomatic Blue Book 2018 has emphasised the challenges associated with the North Korean proliferation of WMDs comprising the probability of acquisition by terrorist organisations, thus constituting 'a major threat to the entire international community, including Japan'. As the diplomatic whirlpool has unfolded in the Korean Peninsula since the beginning of 2018, Japan has suggested offering US$ 2.8 million[11] with the objective of supporting the International Atomic Energy Agency (IAEA) inspections as the denuclearisation programme moves ahead.

Japan's North Korea policy has approached Pyongyang's nuclear and missile programme, together with the abduction issue. Tokyo seeks a 'comprehensive resolution of outstanding issues' comprising nuclear and missile issues in addition to the abductions issue, 'which continues to be the most important'[12] within its framework of 'dialogue and pressure' and 'action for action' approach. Moreover, Japan has made the normalisation of relations conditional on the resolution of the abduction issue.[13] Normalisation talks between Japan and North Korea since the early 1990s have stumbled over several issues, including North Korea's assertion that normalisation can be realised only after settling the past by way of a Japanese apology; compensation; returning the Korean cultural assets taken away during Japanese occupation; as well as extending legal status to ethnic Koreans residing in Japan.[14] Differences over Tokyo's insistence on the use of the term economic assistance vis-à-vis Pyongyang's demand for war reparation and compensation and the legality of the 1910 Treaty of Annexation between the Empire of Japan and the Empire of Korea has further complicated the process. However, with the 1998 Taepodong missile launch over Japan, and the following developments related to Pyongyang's nuclear weapons programme, compelled Japan to cultivate a more pragmatic approach, including initiatives like the first Japan-North

Korea Summit in 2002. However, normalising relations with North Korea has proved to be a daunting task. On one hand, the nuclear issue encompasses variables beyond Japan's control and requires a multilateral approach while the abduction issue, on the other hand, is of a bilateral nature and domestic sentiments on this subject are sometimes exploited by Japanese right-wing elements which have influenced the normalisation process.[15]

Prime Minister Abe has been personally invested in the abduction issue with the institution of Headquarters for the Abduction Issue in the Cabinet Secretariat in 2006. While Japan broadly aligns its North Korea policy with the US, but there are instances when national sentiments and Prime Minister Abe's commitment towards the abduction issue has reflected some flexibility in Tokyo's approach. For instance, Tokyo's minor easing of sanctions in 2014 (following the Stockholm meeting) including elevating the limits on the reporting of cash remittances and permitting port-calls by North Korean vessels as Chairman Kim pledged to renew investigations into, and institute a special investigation committee on, the abduction issue. While this has reflected minor differences between the Japanese and the US and South Korean approach at that point in time, nevertheless the concessions made by Japan were nominal, and did not influence Japan's compliance with UN sanctions on North Korea's proliferation.[16] However, the North Koreans failed to deliver on their commitments.

Debating the North Korea Variable in US-Japan Alliance

For Japan, the stakes are very high in the Korean Peninsula. North Korea has emerged as one of Japan's top priorities as policymakers deliberate how to weave Japan's North Korea strategy. As Japan's strategic community debates the North Korea puzzle, there is a school of thought which perceives four scenarios regarding how the North Korean situation will unfold.[17] In the first case, a possible improvement of US-North Korea relations is perceived where Chairman Kim undertakes incremental steps towards denuclearisation, but does not give up all his country's nuclear weapons and initiate economic reforms and undo barriers to access financial and technical assistance. Thus, President Trump can project the success of his North Korea policy in contrast to President Obama's strategic patience in the run-up to the 2020 elections. The second case underscores an expectation gap scenario. The US has outlined the target dates of 2020–2021 to realise denuclearisation. However, Pyongyang's delaying tactics may eventually lead the hardliners in the US administration to adopt a more confrontational approach, including military options. The third case is a bad peace scenario in which the US may well decide to diminish its security obligation towards South Korea in response to Pyongyang's bargain not to target continental US which ultimately will erode the decades-old US alliance network in East Asia. The fourth—and most unlikely—scenario is if Kim is sincere about unfolding socio-economic reforms in the hermit kingdom, although this may very well end up destabilising the regime.

While President Trump and Prime Minister Abe broadly share concerns on the consequences of a nuclear North Korea, Japan has several concerns regarding US's approach to the North Korea conundrum.[18] Since the alliance with the US lies at the core of post-war Japanese foreign and security policy, and functions as a 'public good' maintaining regional stability, Prime Minister Abe has invested heavily on building trust with President Trump. But, with the unfolding contours of President Trump's North Korea policy in the run up to the Singapore Summit and the subsequent developments thereafter, the key concern is whether Washington's discussions with Pyongyang are actually serving Tokyo's national security interests. Keeping Tokyo out of the loop;[19] decoupling ICBMs and short and medium range ballistic missiles; ignoring human rights issues in the Singapore Summit; the fault lines in trade matters (including the initiation of investigation by the Department of Commerce under Section 232 of the Trade Expansion Act of 1962 with the objective of determining if auto imports 'threaten to impair the national security') is testing the metal of the US-Japan alliance.[20] President Trump has not given Tokyo much latitude with his transactional approach, whether it is tariffs on steel and aluminium or demanding

Japan to purchase more American weapon systems for its defence or sharing more responsibility concerning the forward deployment of US forces even though Japan reportedly paid ¥191 billion or 86.4 per cent of the total cost in 2015 and pays the largest share compared to other allies.[21]

Even though the US-Japan alliance survived several geopolitical tensions during the Cold-War and post-Cold War era, how to reinforce the robustness of the alliance framework under President Trump's 'America First' policy on the one hand, and manage an 'unprecedentedly serious and imminent threat' posed by Pyongyang on the other, presents several policy challenges for Prime Minster Abe. Concerns over the reliability of US extended deterrence on the one hand, and the decoupling of the Japan-US alliance on the other, are intensifying. The fate of US allies in Northeast Asia depend on the extended deterrence and the American nuclear umbrella for their security at a time when Pyongyang is investing in dividing the security guarantor from its allies with a threat to attack continental US. North Korea has considerably raised the stakes vis-à-vis the US commitment towards its allies, and compelled Washington to consider if it would trade its homeland for its allies. While North Korea's objective is to drive a wedge between the US and its allies, and is attempting to use the threat of ICBMs to decouple the US-Japan alliance, there is a school of thought which argues that while American bases in Japan could be the initial target of North Korean attack but as the sophistication of its nuclear and missile programme encompasses continental US, the Trump administration may not defend Tokyo or Seoul in order to avoid nuclear attack on Los Angeles, San Francisco or, possibly, even Washington, thus decoupling the traditional alliances.[22]

Meanwhile, a February 2018 Department of Defense report to the US Congress has argued that 'North Korea ultimately seeks the capability to strike the continental United States with a nuclear-armed ICBM. This pursuit supports North Korea's strategy of deterring the United States as well as weakening US alliances in the region by casting doubt on the US commitment to extended deterrence. In the long term, North Korea may see nuclear weapons as permitting more frequent coercive behaviour and may further increase Kim Jong-un's tolerance for risk'.[23]

One of biggest preoccupations amongst the Japanese strategic community today is to analyse how events will unfold in the Korean Peninsula and, more importantly, how they will influence US's responsibility as a security provider and an alliance partner. Japan is weighing the implications of a possible decoupling on the one hand and the fear of entrapment/abandonment on the other. With the Trump administration's 'America First' approach, Prime Minister Abe has genuine concerns that the US is rather focussed on ICBMs instead of medium-range missiles and short-range missiles which constitute a severe threat to Japan and in case North Korea succeeds in negotiating an agreement with the US to leave out the medium-range ballistic missiles, it will drive a wedge in the decades-old US-Japan alliance. Thus, one school of thought argues that, as President Trump negotiates denuclearisation with Chairman Kim, it should not be at the cost of sacrificing US security arrangements with Japan. While US negotiations with North Korea should not make Japan and South Korea vulnerable to danger, the use of force should avoid entrapping Japan in a military conflict.[24] As the Trump administration advocates that 'all options are on the table' including military pressure and limited use of force, it will lead to retaliation from the North, thereby entrapping the US allies who would suffer enormous devastation and subsequent abandonment. The policy objective should be to counter Pyongyang's decoupling attempt by investing in reinforcing the alliance. Previous US negotiations with North Korea adeptly balanced both security assurances on the one hand, and alliance commitment on the other. Japan's concern over decoupling is not new. Earlier, when North Korea proposed a non-aggression pact with the objective of guaranteeing regime stability with the US, there were concerns regarding withdrawal of American forces from South Korea and Japan, and even rationalising the development of 'retaliatory nuclear weapons'.[25]

Even with de-escalation of tensions in the Peninsula since early 2018 and the subsequent charm offensive by Chairman Kim, the possibility of Pyongyang parting ways with its nuclear weapons is unlikely, and hence deterrence will continue as the salient regional security management feature. As the discourse on alliance decoupling has gained momentum with North Korean advancement of the ICBM, it underscores the criticality of US extended deterrence for allies. The 2018 US Nuclear Posture Review has been reassuring to Japan as it has urged for developing new nuclear submarine-launched cruise missiles, in addition to low-yield nuclear options. It is important to note that Japanese policy makers do not favour reintroducing tactical nuclear weapons in South Korea as they will be high-priority targets for Pyongyang, in addition to redirecting resources away from conventional capabilities. Japan's most important goal is to keep the US invested in the Northeast Asian security architecture, and sustain the reliability of extended nuclear deterrence. Contingencies in the Korean Peninsula will have severe security implications for Japan, and hence Tokyo actively participates in strengthening deterrence by hosting American bases and by enabling Self-Defense Forces (SDFs) to support American forces during a Korean contingency. Adapting to the changes in the Korean Peninsula, the US-Japan alliance has updated operational coordination by way of the revision of the 1978 US-Japan Defense Cooperation Guidelines in 1997 and in 2015. The focus of the Security Treaty has moved from Article V concerning an armed attack on Japanese territory to Article VI securing international peace and security in the Far East.

Just as during the Korean War, Japan hosted key operating bases for the US military fighting for the United Nations Command and South Korea, in any future contingency, US forces are likely to use the air bases in Misawa, Yokota, and Kadena; naval bases in Yokosuka and Sasebo; naval and marine air bases in Atsugi and Iwakuni; and the marine air station in Futenma. Meanwhile, Japan has invested around US$ 18 billion on missile defence systems, agreed to initially provide non-combat support to US forces in 1997 in 'situations in areas surrounding Japan' with reference to Korean contingencies, and provide intelligence, transport, maintenance, and other support to the US military operating in defence of South Korea. Subsequently, in 2015, Japan agreed to provide combat support to US forces and shoot down North Korean ballistic missiles targeting Guam or Hawaii, conduct anti-submarine warfare operations to protect the American Navy, and sweep mines in the waters near North Korea, thus aiding US amphibious landing operations.

One key issue pertaining to Korean contingency is the debate concerning Japanese consent vis-à-vis the use of the bases. This has deepened the fault lines between Japan and South Korea. Even though in 1969, Prime Minister Eisaku Sato argued that securing South Korea was critical for maintaining Japan's national security, and thus permitted the US to utilise facilities within Japan in case of a contingency, Prime Minister Abe categorically articulated that, in the case of contingencies in the Peninsula, Japan would require the US to engage in prior consultation before using the bases for aiding South Korea.[26] Meanwhile, Seoul argues that American forces stationed in Japan are expected to offer rear-area logistical and strategic support and, thus, automatically employed to South Korean defence during any contingency. Meanwhile, in the case of any contingency, North Korea will exert pressure on Japan not to permit the use of bases for the defence of South Korea which will, in turn, create stress in the US-Japan alliance.

Reinforcing deterrence within the US-Japan alliance framework is imperative for Japan. Several policy recommendations have been proposed, including developing a robust deterrence posture in cooperation with South Korea; developing concerted planning between the US and its allies with the aim of responding to North Korea's nuclear threat by developing standard operating procedures for information sharing as regards American nuclear use, and design a well-coordinated decision-making and responsibility-sharing system; synergising allies' Extended Deterrence Dialogue (EDD) and Defense Programme Guidelines implementation; retaining the thrust of the US-Japan-South Korea trilateral cooperation, especially with regard to exchanging information on missile launches, anti-mine warfare, non-combatant evacuations during conflict, furthering intelligence, surveillance, and reconnaissance (ISR) cooperation with the objective of maximising defence; and developing Japanese strike capability in order to avert alliance decoupling; and to improve deterrence by supplementing US strike capability during war.[27]

Another top priority for North Korea is to replace the Armistice Agreement with a peace declaration, and subsequently a peace treaty establishing a peace regime. Once the peace regime is established, the relevance of the Cold War structures existing in the Korean Peninsula will need to be revisited, including the future of the United Nations Command (UNC) in Seoul and the UN Rear Headquarters in Japan. The UNC was initially headquartered in Japan till 1957, and subsequently moved to Korea. The Rear Headquarters in Japan was initially in Camp Zama and then in the Yokota Air Base, and is allowed to use the seven American military bases in Japan.[28] Once the Korean War ends officially, it would imply the end to the UNC. Any negotiation to establish a peace regime should not affect US alliances in the region.

Managing the North Korean Conundrum

It has been argued that both economic sanctions and military pressure would be necessary to manage the North Korean threat. However, these are only 'necessary conditions for a diplomatic solution and are not ends in and of themselves'.[29]

*Economic Pressure:*Prime Minister Abe has invested heavily in arguing the merits of employing economic pressure on the regime in order to address the North Korean nuclear threat. The Japanese Maritime Self-Defense Force and the Japan Coast Guard plays an active role when it comes to monitoring the implementation of UNSC Resolution 2375 and 2397 which forbids member states from engaging in ship-to-ship transfers of goods to or from North Korean-flagged vessels. In addition to implementing UNSC sanctions, Japan has employed secondary sanctions, and has reportedly frozen the assets of more than one hundred entities and individuals. With the aim of realising the common goal of complete, verifiable, and irreversible denuclearisation of the Korean Peninsula, Japan is working with China and Russia, in addition to the US and South Korea, for effective implementation of the relevant UNSC Resolutions. In the initial years, the UNSC Resolution failed to produce the intended impact as the scope was restricted to barring the exports of luxury items, and materials required for WMD and military development. China played a critical role in obstructing the US from deepening the sanctions on the civilian sector, given its concerns for the regime stability. Subsequently, President Obama's strategic patience created more space for China to play a bigger role in shaping the debate on North Korea. Critics have often interpreted this strategic patience as strategic outsourcing to China.[30] However, a policy shift unfolded in 2016 as President Trump discarded the strategic patience approach, adopted a hard line stance on North Korea, and stepped up the rhetoric.

Diplomatic Tools: Besides economic pressure, Japan has engaged in managing North Korea by stepping up trilateral diplomatic and military cooperation with South Korea, which in turn strengthens the US alliance network in Northeast Asia. Sustaining constructive trilateral cooperation is of key importance to Japan in achieving the complete, verifiable, and irreversible dismantlement of all weapons of mass destruction and ballistic missiles of all ranges. Japan has coordinated its policies within the Japan-US-South Korea trilateral framework at the Foreign Ministers and Defense Minister's level while pursuing the effective implementation of the pertinent UNSC Resolutions. The three navies are stepping up interoperability with anti-submarine drills and missile defence drills. Japan prefers a trilateral coordinated approach to pursue the objective of augmenting the effectiveness of missile defence systems, train and exercise together while preparing for a crisis, and coordinate in case of non-combatant evacuation operations during a contingency. Japan is acutely aware that it is the sole regional power who is struggling to find space in the diplomatic whirlpool unfolding in the Korean Peninsula since the PyeongChang Winter Olympics in February 2018. Japan has worked tirelessly to establish direct consultation with Pyongyang with the aim of representing its interests. However, the secret consultation with North Korean officials—first in Ulan Bator and subsequently in Vietnam—did not translate into a much anticipated Abe-Kim meeting on the side-lines of the Eastern Economic Forum in Vladivostok. Thus, political, diplomatic, and military coordination with the US and South Korea bilaterally and in a trilateral framework remains a key policy choice. In this regard, Japan and South Korea needs to invest more diplomatic capital in managing their bilateral relations given the escalating tensions over history and trade issues.

Meanwhile, Japan has stepped up diplomatic pressure on North Korea at regional forums, including at the Association of Southeast Asian Nations (ASEAN) related frameworks like the ASEAN Regional Forum (ARF), the ASEAN Defence Ministers' Meeting (ADMM)-Plus and East Asia Summit (EAS), and at the UNGA. It has strongly articulated the significance of achieving the complete denuclearisation of North Korea, the implementation of the pertinent UNSC Resolutions by the international community, and the resolution of the abduction issue. Japan was a key player in the now defunct Six-Party Talks, the regional multilateral framework designed to manage the North Korean crisis. In addition to pursuing verifiable denuclearisation, Japan has underscored the need for the normalisation of relations, in keeping with the Pyongyang Declaration—that is, 'on the basis of the settlement of [the] unfortunate past and the outstanding issues of concern' at the Six-Party Talks.[31] However, critics have argued that Japan has pursued its individual national interests within the Six-Party Talks which sometimes did not align with the views of other members. Arguably, Japan's narrow focus on the abductions issue had isolated it from China and South Korea, both of whom felt that, as Japan articulates human rights violations, it refrains from owning up responsibility for its own historical baggage in the World War II era.[32]

Defending Japan: As the North Korean nuclear and missile threat augmented under Chairman Kim, the Japanese defence administration took a policy decision to 'drastically'[33] develop ballistic missile defence capabilities. Tokyo has a multi-tier defence system, with upper and lower tier interception by the Aegis-equipped destroyers and the Patriot PAC-3 respectively. In December 2017, the National Security Council and the Cabinet decided to further introduce two Aegis Ashore batteries with the goal of reinforcing upper tier interception by the Aegis-equipped destroyers. Japan will use two Lockheed Martin Aegis Ashore systems, with LMSSR radars, which will permit response against lofted trajectory projectiles. It is likely to be operational in 2023, and the batteries will be deployed in Akita and Yamaguchi prefectures. In order to improve response capability, SM-3 Block II advanced ballistic missile interceptor is developed by Japan in cooperation with the US. In addition, Japan has set up a civil-defence early-warning system with the Emergency Information Network (Em-Net) system and the J-Alert system.

Even though Japan has an exclusively defence-oriented policy, Tokyo has long weighed the prospects of acquiring strike capabilities, with the objective of doing counterforce operations against North Korean missiles. Japan is also introducing the Joint Strike Missile (JSM) for its F-35A stealth fighters and adjusting existing Japanese F-15 fighters to be equipped with Long-Range Anti-Ship Missiles (LRASM) and extended-range Joint Air-to-Surface Standoff Missiles (JASSM-ER). Japan is advancing its air defence capabilities with emphasis on the Pacific Coast, remodel Izumo destroyers to facilitate the use of STOVL aircraft in emergency situation. The Council on Security and Defense Capabilities in the New Era was instituted in 2004 which argued that, in order to cope with missile threats, 'deterrence with strike capability as well as defensive measures is deemed important'.[34] Despite the exclusively defence-oriented posture of the Japanese security policy, acquiring strike capability is not debarred altogether, given the proliferation of ballistic missiles.[35] Japan's voluntary restrictions on acquiring offensive weapons are aimed at underscoring its proclamation not to invade another country. Nevertheless, given the historical trajectory of Japan, the acquisition of strike capability will raise concerns in the region.

Discussions in the political circuit on debating Japan's nuclear options are unfolding including several political figures, such as Taro Aso, Yokobatake, Tomomi Inada, Fumio Kishida, and Nakagawa arguing for a thorough debate on the nuclear option. In 2002, when Abe was serving as Deputy Chief Cabinet Secretary, he suggested that the possession of nuclear weapons is constitutional within the limits of what is minimally necessary for self-defence. While Japan has maintained its three non-nuclear principles—upholding not possessing, not producing, and not permitting the import of nuclear weapons—the academic debate on Japan developing its own nuclear deterrent has gained traction. It is important to note that Japan's 'nuclear allergy' coexists conveniently with the 'nuclear umbrella'. Moreover, the three non-nuclear principles of the 1960s coexisted with the Cold-War era's secret agreements with the US. Japan's capability in terms of technology, and having a stockpile of 47 metric tons of plutonium, do present the option of it acquiring nuclear weapons. However, Japan has opted instead for nuclear restraint, owing to its identity as a non-nuclear weapon state, its devotion to nuclear non-proliferation and disarmament, and realistic security considerations.[36]

In the late 1960s, at the same time as Japan articulated the three non-nuclear principles, the government commissioned an internal report exploring a cost and benefit analysis of Japan's nuclearisation in a comprehensive way, which resulted in two secret reports in 1968 and in 1970.[37] These studies recommended that Japan should adapt a multi-dimensional attitude, comprising political and economic initiatives to ensure its national security, and that its non-nuclear weapon state identity acts as a positive element for its national security. Furthermore, the report argued that Japan's nuclear arsenal may caution the US and lead to Tokyo's diplomatic isolation. Later in the 1990s, Japan's then Defense Agency instituted a few internal study groups to analyse the nuclear deterrent option in the post-Cold War setting. A 1995 'Report on the Problems of the Proliferation of Weapons of Mass Destruction' also reflected that acquiring nuclear weapons is not desirable as it may wane the US nuclear umbrella and endorse nuclear proliferation. Furthermore, this may destabilise Japan's prospects as a trading nation, and thus suggested focussing on conventional defence rather than the nuclear option. The nuclear debate in Japan picked up further following Pyongyang's missile and nuclear tests in the subsequent years. Even though the taboo on discussing the nuclear weapons option is loosening, Japan will have a difficult journey in terms of gaining public support for acquiring its own nuclear deterrent.

The Way Ahead

With the fast altering geopolitical landscape in Northeast Asia, what Japan's North Korea policy needs is political and strategic creativity to secure Japan's national interests. As President Trump expects Japan to assume larger responsibilities for its own security within the alliance framework, the fundamental challenge before Prime Minister Abe is to strike a balance between sharing the greater burden in ensuring regional security as part of the long-standing alliance with the US on one hand, and factoring in regional sensitivities on the other. Since Prime Minister Abe came to power in December 2012, Japan has unmistakably marked a departure in its post-War security orientation. His resolve to buttress Japan's deterrent capabilities has raised concerns in the region that still suffers from the complex historical baggage of Imperial Japan. As Japan adapts to the fast altering geostrategic environment, and incrementally expands the scope of Article 9, creates more latitude for SDF operations, bolsters the missile defence systems, and reinforces deterrence capabilities, it has prompted a regional response which argues that, in order to defend Japan's normalisation agenda, conservatives often employ an 'external threat' or the 'enemy state' notion. In particular, North Korea has developed a discourse that sternly critiques Prime Minister Abe for using North Korea for rationalising the reorientation of Japan's security policy, and argued that 'in the past Hitler called for a fight against communism to justify the war, but at present Abe is trumpeting the theory of confrontation with the DPRK to rationalise the militarisation of Japan for reinvasion. There is no difference between them'.[38] The North Korean state news agency, KCNA has underscored that Tokyo is investing in military capabilities under the pretext of North Korea, wanting 'reinvasion' and 'militarism' at a time when a favourable environment of a detente is being attempted on the Korean Peninsula.[39]

With regard to denuclearisation, Japan has aligned and pursued its national interests in cooperation with the US and South Korea. At present, Japan lacks direct leverage with North Korea, and this has constrained Prime Minister Abe's ability to influence and shape critical negotiations. Its economic leverage in terms of offering economic aid—in case Chairman Kim delivers on denuclearisation—will in all likelihood be conditioned on the progress in the bilateral abduction issue despite Prime Minister Abe's offer to meet Chairman Kim without preconditions in May 2019. Given this, the US-Japan alliance will continue to remain at the core of Japan's North Korea policy more than ever to safeguard Japan's national security interests amidst the altering regional balance of power.

Notes

1. 'Policy Speech by Prime Minister Shinzo Abe to the 195th Session of the Diet', Prime Minister of Japan and His Cabinet, November 17, 2017 at https://japan.kantei.go.jp/98_abe/statement/201711/_00006.html, accessed on October 15, 2018.
2. Shane Harris, 'Gaps remain in CIA's understanding of North Korean nukes, spy chief says', *The Washington Post*, January 23, 2018 at https://www.washingtonpost.com/world/national-security/gaps-remain-in-cias-understanding-of-north-korean-nukes-spy-chief-says/2018/01/23/9eb4cd62-006f-11e8-93f5-53a3a47824e8_story.html?noredirect=on&utm_term=.67f4182dd1f7, accessed on October 15, 2018.
3. 'North Korea's Nuclear and Ballistic Missile Programs', Congressional Research Service, August 2, 2018 at https://fas.org/sgp/crs/nuke/IF10472.pdf, accessed on October 15, 2018.
4. 'Policy Speech by Prime Minister Shinzo Abe to the 196th Session of the Diet', Prime Minister of Japan and His Cabinet, January 22, 2018 at https://japan.kantei.go.jp/98_abe/statement/201801/_00002.html, accessed on October 15, 2018.
5. 'Threats and challenges posed by North Korea to international peace and security', Ministry of Foreign Affairs, December 15, 2017 at https://www.mofa.go.jp/fp/unp/page4e_000729.html, accessed on October 15, 2018.

6. 'Address by Prime Minister Shinzo Abe at the Seventy-Second Session of the United Nations General', UN New York, September 20, 2017 at https://gadebate.un.org/sites/default/files/gastatements/72/jp_en.pdf, accessed on October 15, 2018.
7. 'Security Council Tightens Sanctions on Democratic People's Republic of Korea, Unanimously Adopting Resolution 2397 (2017)', Security Council, 8151ST Meeting (PM), SC/13141, December 22, 2017 at https://www.un.org/press/en/2017/sc13141.doc.htm, accessed on October 15, 2018.
8. 'Comment by Prime Minister Shinzo Abe on the Adoption of a Resolution by the United Nations Security Council concerning North Korea's Ballistic Missile Launch and Other Activities', Ministry of Foreign Affairs Japan, December 23, 2017 at https://www.mofa.go.jp/fp/unp/page11e_000016.html, accessed 15 October 2018, accessed on October 15, 2018.
9. 'Bright Future Awaits If Democratic People's Republic of Korea Fulfils Promises of Complete Denuclearisation, United States Tells Security Council', Security Council, 8363rd Meeting, SC/13525, September 27, 2018.
10. 'Press Conference by the Defense Minister', Ministry of Defense Japan, August 28, 2018 at http://www.mod.go.jp/e/press/conference/2018/08/28a.html, accessed on September 15, 2018.
11. 'Over ¥300 million offered for IAEA inspections as Japan bids to remain player in global response to North', Kyodo, March 11, 2018 at https://www.japantimes.co.jp/news/2018/03/11/asia-pacific/japan-offer-300-million-north-korea-nuclear-inspections-tokyo-looks-remain-player-global-response/#.W7xUHugzbIU, accessed on October 15, 2018.
12. 'Comment by Prime Minister Shinzo Abe, on the Adoption of a Resolution by the United Nations Security Council concerning a series of ballistic missiles launches and other activities conducted by North Korea', Ministry of Foreign Affairs, Japan, June 3, 2017 at https://www.mofa.go.jp/fp/unp/page4e_000618.html, accessed on October 15, 2018.
13. 'Policies and Concrete Measures for Resolving the Abduction Issue', Secretariat of the Headquarters for the Abduction Issue, Government of Japan, January 25, 2013 at https://www.rachi.go.jp/en/shisei/taisaku/images/20130125honbukettei.en.pdf, accessed on October 15, 2018.
14. Mark E. Manyin, 'North Korea-Japan Relations: The Normalization Talks and the Compensation/Reparations Issue', CRS Report for Congress, The Library of Congress, June 13, 2001 at https://www.globalsecurity.org/military/library/report/crs/RS20526.pdf, accessed on October 15, 2018.
15. Tsuneo Akaha, 'Japan and the recurrent nuclear crisis', in Linus Hagstrom and Marie Soderberg (eds), *North Korea Policy: Japan and the Great Powers*, Routledge, London and New York, 2006.
16. Sheila A. Smith, 'Pyongyang's New Overtures and Abe's Diplomacy', 38 North, May 31, 2014 at https://www.38north.org/2014/05/ssmith053114/ accessed on October 15, 2018.

17. Narushige Michishita, 'Four scenarios for the Korean Peninsula's future', Prime Minister's Office of Japan, Japan House, Consulate General of Japan in Los Angeles, October 16, 2018.
18. Abraham M. Denmark, 'Old Territory and New Horizons in the US-Japan Alliance', in Shihoko Goto (ed.), *US National Security Strategy: Implications for the US-Japan Alliance*, Wilson Centre at https://www.wilsoncenter.org/sites/default/files/asia_180315_us_national_security_strategy_web.pdf.
19. Sheila A. Smith, 'Can Tokyo survive Trump?' *East Asia Forum Quarterly*, 10(3), July–September 2018.
20. 'US Department of Commerce Initiates Section 232 Investigation into Auto Imports', US Office of Public Affairs, May 23, 2018, at https://www.commerce.gov/news/press-releases/2018/05/us-department-commerce-initiates-section-232-investigation-auto-imports, accessed on October 15, 2018.
21. Ayako Mie, 'How much does Japan pay to host U.S. forces? Depends on who you ask', *The Japan Times*, January 31, 2017, at https://www.japantimes.co.jp/news/2017/01/31/national/much-japan-pay-host-u-s-forces-depends-ask/#.W59AxegzbIU; see also, 'How much does Japan pay to host U.S. military forces?' *The Mainichi*, May 30, 2016, at https://mainichi.jp/english/articles/20160530/p2a/00m/0na/017000c, accessed on October 15, 2018.
22. Kazuto Suzuki, 'Japan's View of the North Korean Threat', Istituto AffariInternazionali (IAI) Commentary, March 2018, at http://www.iai.it/en/pubblicazioni/japans-view-north-korean-threat, accessed on October 15, 2018.
23. 'Military and Security Developments Involving the Democratic People's Republic of Korea 2017', Office of the Secretary of Defense, February 13, 2018, at https://fas.org/irp/world/dprk/dod-2017.pdf, accessed on October 15, 2018.
24. Hideya Kurata, 'From Non-proliferation to Regional Talks, then to Collective Security and Deterrence the Third North Korean Nuclear Crisis from a Historical Perspective', *Japan Review*, 1(3), Spring 2018.
25. Masashi Nishihara, 'North Korea's Trojan Horse', The *Washington Post*, August 14, 2003, at https://www.washingtonpost.com/archive/opinions/2003/08/14/north-koreas-trojan-horse/f9a9152c-797d-44c8-876e-de1bcee14ec1/?noredirect=on&utm_term=.e3feaf38791e, accessed on October 15, 2018.
26. Toby Dalton, Narushige Michishita and Tong Zhao, 'Security Spillover: Regional Implications of Evolving Deterrence on the Korean Peninsula', Carnegie Endowment for International Peace, June 2018, at https://carnegieendowment.org/files/CP_336_DaltonMichishitaZhao_Korea_final1.pdf, accessed on October 15, 2018.

27. James L. Schoff and Sugio Takahashi, 'Strengthening U.S.-Japan Alliance Deterrence', Asia Strategy Initiative, Policy Memorandum 1, Sasakawa Peace Foundation, at https://www.spf.org/jpus/investigation/pdf/doc_spf_asi_memorandam001.pdf, accessed on October 15, 2018.
28. 'Push for Korean peace throws fate of UN forces into doubt', Nikkei, June 18, 2018, at https://asia.nikkei.com/Politics/Trump-Kim-Summit/Push-for-Korean-peace-throws-fate-of-UN-forces-into-doubt, accessed on October 15, 2018.
29. Hideya Kurata, 'From Non-proliferation to Regional Talks, then to Collective Security and Deterrence: The Third North Korean Nuclear Crisis from a Historical Perspective', *Japan Review*, 1(3), Spring, 2018.
30. Ibid.
31. 'Joint Statement of the Fourth Round of the Six-Party Talks', US Department of State, Beijing, September 19, 2005 https://www.state.gov/p/eap/regional/c15455.htm, accessed on October 15, 2018.
32. Emma Chanlett-Avery, 'North Korea's Abduction of Japanese Citizens and the Six-Party Talks', CRS Report for Congress, March 19, 2008, at https://fas.org/sgp/crs/row/RS22845.pdf; see also, Michael R. Auslin, 'Japanese Perspectives on the Six-Party Talks and the North Korean Nuclear Crisis', in *Tomorrow's Northeast Asia*, Joint US-Korea Academic Studies, Volume 21, 2011, at http://keia.org/sites/default/files/publications/jukas_2011-11_auslin.pdf, accessed on October 15, 2018.
33. 'Defense of Japan 2018 (Digest)', Ministry of Defense, August 2018, at http://www.mod.go.jp/e/publ/w_paper/pdf/2018/DOJ2018_Digest_0827.pdf, accessed on September 20, 2018.
34. 'Japan's Visions for Future Security and Defense Capabilities in the New Era: Toward a Peace Creating Nation', The Council on Security and Defense Capabilities in the New Era, Prime Minister of Japan and His Cabinet, August 2010, at https://www.kantei.go.jp/jp/singi/shin-ampobouei2010/houkokusyo_e.pdf, accessed on October 15, 2018.
35. Sugio Takahashi, 'Dealing with the Ballistic Missile Threat: Whether. Japan Should Have a Strike Capability under its Exclusively Defense-Oriented Policy', NIDS Security Report No 7, December 2006, at file:///H:/EAR%20TB/MY%20DRAFT%20MATERIAL/strike%20capability.pdf.
36. Mike M. Mochizuki, 'Japan Tests: The Nuclear Taboo', *Non-proliferation Review*, 14(2), July 2007.
37. Yuri Kase, 'The Costs and Benefits of Japan's Nuclearisation: An Insight into the 1968/70 Internal Report', *The Non-proliferation Review*, Summer 2001.
38. 'KCNA on Abe's reckless remarks', Korean Central News Agency, DPRK, February 4, 2014, retrieved July 12, 2014 at http://www.kcna.co.jp/index-e.htm, accessed on October 15, 2018.

39. 'KCNA Denounces Japan for Harassing Peace', Korean Central News Agency, DPRK, August 27, 2018 at https://kcnawatch.co/newstream/1535421663-26759344/kcna-denounces-japan-for-harassing-peace/, accessed on September 27, 2018.

PART III
India and the Korean Peninsula

13. Korea in India's Look and Act East Policy

Prashant Kumar Singh[1]

This essay attempts to analyse how India's Look and Act East Policy (LAEP) has unfolded in the Korean Peninsula.[2] It underscores the convergences and divergences between India-ROK (South Korea) and India-DPRK (North Korea), and discusses the prospects of a Peninsula-level implementation of the LAEP. The essay argues that an imaginative implementation of this policy in the Peninsula can, indeed, enrich the discourse on the LAEP, and can project India as a committed and responsible stakeholder in the peace, stability and prosperity of the Asia-Pacific.

Even though Southeast Asia was considered to be the focus of Prime Minister P.V. Narasimha Rao's Look East Policy (LEP), introduced in the early 1990s, the ambition to extend it further, to include the entire Asia-Pacific, was noticeable even in its early phase.[3] Two decades later, in November 2014,[4] Prime Minister Narendra Modi renamed LEP as the Act East Policy (AEP). However, the term Look and Act East Policy (LAEP) would be preferable for two reasons: firstly, it captures the evolution of the policy, and brings to the fore the nuances of its implementation; secondly, its results are yet not uniform. While it has yielded results in India's relations with the ROK, that qualify it as being in the Act East phase, it is uncertain whether India's relationship with the DPRK can even be properly described as being in the Look East phase.

The Look and Act East Policy (LAEP)

The LAEP seeks to introduce India as a regional player in East Asia, or the Asia-Pacific, by providing a geo-civilisational view of India's engagement with the region, on the basis of geographical contiguity and the historical connections of civilisation and culture.[5] It is, in a way, about bringing East Asia back into India's cultural imagination, after the long colonial rupture in Asian history.[6] Economic, political, and security convergence underpins this geo-civilisational view.

The visits of Rabindranath Tagore and Jawaharlal Nehru—the two pioneers of *Asianism* or Asian solidarity—to various parts of East Asia marked a fresh start in the relationship in the first half of the 20th century. Under Prime Minister Nehru, India's engagement with regional struggles, decolonisation, anti-imperial struggles, in the late 1940s and 1950s, defined India's *Asianism*. However, the Cold War was to soon catch up with India's *Asianism*. While India championed the cause of the Non-Aligned Movement (NAM), some countries in the region chose the US-led South East Asia Treaty Organisation (SEATO), which was created in 1955, or were US allies outside it. Besides, the socio-cultural orientation of the Indian elite towards the West for historical reasons, India's uninspiring economic and military conditions and, especially, its defeat in the War with China in 1962, gave a serious jolt to its *Asianism*, and to its standing as a regional leader.[7]

The transition from Nehru and Tagore's *Asianism* to the geo-civilisational view had to wait till the post-Cold War period. The end of the Cold War helped Prime Minister Narasimha Rao redefine India's national interest in terms of pragmatism and economic development. His search for capital, after the balance of payment crisis hit the country in 1991, took him to the East Asian countries,[8] such as Singapore, ROK, and Japan, and also to Hong Kong and Taiwan. This coincided with the opening up of economic opportunities in the region. Around the same time, China's economic rise had begun to take off, which the regional countries saw as an opportunity.[9] On its part, India recognised the region as a natural destination, beyond South Asia, for fulfilling its larger aspirations. Incidentally, India and the region have geographical contiguity and historical connections, and there is no security-strategic friction between them. Thus, the region also seemed to visualise India as a strategic hedge vis-à-vis China.[10] This then was the backdrop in which India re-approached the region under the LEP.

Since the early 1990s, the LEP has had a broad mandate to strengthen relations with the region. New objectives have been added as engagement with the region has matured. It has evolved by strengthening bilateral relationships through bilateral economic, political, and security ties (early 1990s–2003), by promoting India's multilateral integration with the region and by extending the geographical scope of the policy (2003–08), and promoting strategic ties (2008–14).[11] By the time the policy was renamed in 2014, the demand for an enhanced delivery-efficient LEP, with intensified strategic cooperation, had gained traction. The name change was in keeping with this demand.[12]

Besides, at present, the LAEP is, to a large extent, contributing to India's conception of 'a free, open, natural and inclusive' Indo-Pacific region. The Indo-Pacific as a concept, strives to remove the artificial divide between the regions by highlighting the metaphor of oceanic contiguity between the Indian Ocean and the Pacific Ocean,[13] of which Southeast Asia remains the fulcrum.[14]

Korea in the LAEP: Civilisational and Historical Dimensions

India-Korea ties (that included both ROK and DPRK) have their share of historical affinity. Although two-way Buddhist missionary contacts were the norm in India-East Asia cultural ties in ancient times, India as the country where Buddhism originated, remains the point of reference, in any study of these pilgrimage and religious learning-related missionary contacts. However, what is distinctly and uniquely Korean is Korea's cultural consciousness relating to the legend of the marriage of the Korean King Suro with Suriratna, an Indian princess from Ayodhya, the sacred city of Lord Rama's birth. Substantial sections of Korean society consider the prince and princess to be their ancestors.[15] This is unlike the Hindu legacy in Southeast Asia, which according to scholars has an India connection.

However, ancient Buddhist missionary contacts slipped through the cracks of history. Contacts re-emerged in the early 20th century in the form of anti-imperialism, which was however too sporadic and inconsequential, unlike, for example, the contacts between Indian freedom fighters and the Chinese leaders fighting against the Japanese aggressors. The legacy of India-Korea contacts, lives on, in Rabindranath Tagore's lyrical appreciation of Korean culture, which he shared with Korean student revolutionaries in the 1910s and 1920s, during his Japan visits. Thus, the celebration of the shared Buddhist and Hindu heritage and Tagore's legacy does help in constructing a cultural framework for a relationship under the LAEP. However, it has to be noted that bilateral ties only began to become more meaningful post World War II, especially during the Korean War (1950–53). Therefore, the relationship is a theme of contemporary history.[16] In this period, India-Korea relations have been through a convoluted journey of discovery, estrangement, and rediscovery.

India and the Korean War (1950–53)

India and Korea came closer in the wake of the division of Korea. Cold War politics set the process of division in motion in 1945, soon after World War II. India was in the United Nations Temporary Commission on Korea (UNTCOK), set up in 1947, for overseeing elections in North and South Korea. Later, it joined the United Nations Commission on Korea (UNCOK) as a member, which was created at the UNTCOK's recommendation in 1948. India's contribution to peace efforts during the Korean War (1950–53) is an important chapter in the history of its interaction with the Korean Peninsula. India chaired the Neutral Nations' Repatriation Commission (NNRC) (1953–54). The NNRC was created to resolve the issue of the repatriation of prisoners of war (POWs). The humanitarian service rendered by India's 60th Field Ambulance in South Korea has been duly recorded.[17] Prime Minister Jawaharlal Nehru's efforts for brokering peace in the Korean Peninsula by providing a channel of communication between the People's Republic of China (PRC), the USSR, and the US are well known. He had a role in bringing the warring sides in the Korean War (PRC, North Korea and US, and South Korea) to the negotiating table.[18] Nehru saw the Korean problem as part of the larger problems plaguing Far East Asia that included the Korean problem, the Formosa issue (Cross-Strait issue), and the conflict in Indo-China.[19] He perceived the link between these problems and the international isolation of the PRC. India's unbiased involvement in Korean affairs received international appreciation. It underlined how Nehru's foreign policy made India influential in international politics, in spite of it being a newly independent country. India's action during the Korean crisis pointed to the non-aligned course its foreign policy would take in the coming years.

India Withdraws and Maintains Equidistance

India's strictly neutral stance in UNTCOK and NNRC left both South and North Korea somewhat dissatisfied. India withdrew from Korean affairs once the Armistice was signed in 1953. By the end of the 1950s—partly due to its frustration at the lack of progress in the inter-Korea dispute and partly due to the deepening Cold-War fault-lines—India lost interest in the Korean Peninsula. Besides, India became more and more absorbed in dealing with the challenges in its immediate neighbourhood. Moreover, India's move away from the Peninsula also reflected the general level of India's relations with East and Southeast Asia, or the Asia-Pacific region, after Nehru's short-lived *Asianism* in the 1940s and 1950s—a theme which has been previously discussed. Both India and East Asia, in general, had a different understanding of the geopolitical space vis-à-vis each other during this time. For the reasons previously discussed, India was not able to describe itself as an East Asian country. For the East Asian countries too, India was a socially and culturally unfamiliar South Asian country.[20]

Incidentally, in the 1960s, when South Korea was striving to industrialise itself and moving away from being a poor agricultural country, it displayed a keen interest in India's Five-Year Plan, and explored the possibility of seeking Indian assistance. However, India did not have the capacity to match the assistance offered by the US and others, to the ROK.[21] This explains India's estrangement from Korea after the Korean War. India maintained strict equidistance from both South and North Korea for around the next four decades. India set up consular contacts in 1962, and established ambassadorial relations in 1973 with *both* Koreas, simultaneously.[22] Indian dignitaries who visited the Peninsula during that period reportedly included both the ROK and the DPRK in their itineraries. India remained cautious about not making any political comment on the issues between the ROK and the DPRK. It did not accept South Korea's proposal to release a joint statement during President Chun Doo-hwan proposed visit in 1983, which eventually did not materialise. It also did not agree for a minister-level India-ROK joint commission at the time.[23]

India-ROK-DPRK: Rediscovery and Mutual Oblivion

India-ROK relations, which remained insignificant[24] during the Cold War, had to wait till the 1990s to be renewed. Business contacts which had begun showing promise in the early 1980s now finally took off. It should be noted that, despite the equidistance policy, India had empathy for the ROK. Since India tilted towards the USSR-led socialist camp during the Cold War, it supported the DPRK's entry into NAM in 1975, which the ROK was not eligible to join on account of the US bases in the country. However, on its part, India discouraged the DPRK from using NAM as a platform against the ROK. At the 1983 NAM Summit in New Delhi, India as the chair did not allow the Korean issue to overshadow the meet.[25] Thus, the positive history of the late 1940s and early 1950s ensured that the estrangement and neglect remained benign. Therefore, when economic imperatives acquired salience in their relations in the 1980s, there was no resistance from either side. South Korea's growing economic stature drew the attention of India because of its evolving pro-business policies. On the other hand, the DPRK's nuclear and missile cooperation with Pakistan became a security concern for India in the 1990s. Moreover, North Korea went into self-imposed isolation after the disintegration of the USSR.[26] Hence, India-DPRK relations gradually lapsed into mutual oblivion, which will be discussed separately.

The ROK in the LAEP

Prime Minister Rao abandoned the equidistance policy in 1993 when he visited South Korea without travelling to North Korea. This could be considered an early example of his LEP, though this policy was widely perceived to have been aimed towards Southeast Asia, in the beginning. Rao was the first Indian prime minister to visit the ROK.[27] In brief, India's dire need for capital forced it to ignore the equidistance policy, which South Korea, in its search for foreign markets, welcomed. South Korean companies responded positively to India's call for the enhancement of economic cooperation under the LEP in the early 1990s. During this time, South Korea was focusing on outbound investment. Geopolitically, India's pragmatism converged with South Korea's growing foreign policy pragmatism as it, on its part, had changed its attitude towards communist countries,[28] that included India, which although not a communist country, was considered to be close to the USSR.

The LAEP passes the test with considerable distinction in respect of India-ROK bilateral relations. These relations reiterate the fact that there can be no uniform implementation of the policy. A successful economic partnership between India and ROK has paved the way for a broader strategic partnership between them, unlike India's relations with Japan, wherein strategic considerations seemed to take a lead. In forging the partnership with the ROK, India has appeared mindful of the strategic context of Northeast Asia, which is beset with complications involving South Korea, US, China, North Korea, and Japan. India's LAEP engagement with the ROK is based on issues and themes—that are independent and without reference to any third country, as for instance China. On the other hand, India figures prominently in South Korean diplomatic projects such as the Global Korea and the New Asia Diplomatic Initiative,[29] which symbolise its aspirations for middle power status beyond Northeast Asia. Thus, the relationship has the potential for playing an important a role in the strategic networking, of middle and major powers such as South Korea, Australia, India, and Japan.

Premise and Canvas of the India-ROK Strategic Partnership

The period between 2008 and 2014 saw significant progress in India's strategic ties with the region. Major strategic agreements with countries such as Australia, Japan, ROK, and Vietnam were concluded around this time. India's strategic partnerships, with Australia, Japan, and the ROK are rooted in the principles of democracy and the rule of law, which imply cooperation, stability, dialogue, and people-to-people friendship. The positive premises of enlightened self-interest and mutual benefit form the basis of the LAEP that shapes India-ROK relations. The two countries had signed a Long Term Cooperative Partnership for Peace and Prosperity (LTCPPP) in 2004. However, there was "rapid expansion and diversification" of bilateral relations after they signed the Strategic Partnership Agreement in 2010. Since then, the relationship has carved out a well-defined comprehensive space for itself. A study of primary documents—such as the political and official-level joint communiqués and the actual instances of cooperation—highlights the shared norms and guiding principles of the relationship. These include the common quest for: international and regional peace; stability and security; democracy; the rule of law; rule-based order; and the promotion of free market. These norms and objectives strengthen the complete spectrum of the relationship comprising "stronger high level political cooperation, open economic and trade environment, and deeper cultural understanding".[30] In order to realise this vision, the two countries have strengthened: "bilateral strategic communication channels in the political and security field"; "the institutional framework for economic cooperation" to "create more favourable conditions for further expansion of trade and investment"; deepened "mutual understanding by expanding cultural exchanges and people-to-people interactions" by cooperating "with each other as partners on the regional and international stages".[31] Thus, the two countries have identified an expansive deliberative space to: "enhance mutual familiarity"; "promote reciprocal benefits"; and build an understanding with regard to the complex international and regional strategic scenario.

Strategic Convergence between India and the ROK

The India-ROK relationship gained traction after 2010, which was a landmark year as it saw the operationalisation of the Comprehensive Economic Partnership Agreement (CEPA) signed in 2009, as well as the relationship being declared a 'Strategic Partnership.' Prime Minister Modi's visit to South Korea in 2015 witnessed the upgrading of this 'Strategic Partnership' to a 'Special Strategic Partnership.'[32] The frequency of high-level bilateral visits has notably gone up after 2010.

The progress in strategic arenas has, thus, followed the progress in the economic sphere. The 2010 and 2015 versions of the Strategic Partnership marked the transformation of bilateral relations into a relationship that is different from ordinary bilateral relations. It highlights the willingness of both countries to delineate the prospects for convergence in their strategic interests, and harness them. Although much remains to be achieved, the discussion in the previous section has thrown light on the normative framework and common objectives the two countries have articulated for their strategic cooperation. Policy coordination between India's LAEP and the Connect Central Asia policies with the ROK's Eurasia Initiative and the North East Asia Peace and Cooperation Initiative (NAPCI) is sought to create an integrated and shared Asian geopolitical space.[33] The ROK describes India as 'a central pillar of ROK's New Southern Policy',[34] propagated by President Moon Jae-in, in his election manifesto of 2017. It forms part of his larger North East Asia Plus Community for Responsibility-sharing (NEAPC) vision, which consists of the NEA Community Platform, the New Northern Policy and the New Southern Policy. While the first platform is about regional security, the other two policies seek to promote prosperity. India and ASEAN were both mentioned in the 'New Southern Policy' in his 2017 manifesto.[35]

Multilateral interactions: Around the beginning of the second phase of the policy in 2003, India began pushing for multilateral integration with the Asia-Pacific region. It joined various mini-lateral and multilateral processes, such as the Mekong-Ganga Cooperation (MGC) in 2000; the Bay of Bengal Initiative for Multi-Sectoral Technical and Economic Cooperation (BIMSTEC) in 2004; and the East Asia Summit (EAS) in 2005 for this. In keeping with their endorsement of a liberal democratic world order, India and the ROK engage with each other in the EAS, the ASEAN Regional Forum (ARF), the ASEAN Defence Ministers' Meeting-Plus (ADMM+), the Asia Cooperation Dialogue (ACD), the G-20, and the Nuclear Security Summit (NSS). In these forums, they have voiced their support for issues such as UNSC reforms, the North Korean nuclear issue, and non-proliferation.[36] Importantly, the ROK has all along pledged its support for India's claims for membership of the four main multilateral export control regimes—the Nuclear Suppliers Group (NSG), the Missile Technology Control Regime (MTCR), the Australia Group, and the Wassenaar Arrangement.[37] Likewise, India supports the recommencement of the Six-Party talks on the North Korean nuclear issue. Incidentally, the Six-Party talks include ROK, DPRK, China, the US, Japan, and Russia. The talks began in 2003 and continued intermittently till 2009, when the DPRK pulled out from the talks.

Bilateral political, security and defence cooperation: India's strong bilateral political, security, and defence relations with Japan, Vietnam, and Singapore are prominent examples of the LAEP's success. To a great extent, relations with them derive their strength from congruity in their strategic perceptions. In case of Singapore especially, relations are supported by strong people-to-people ties that have historically existed between them. However, as for cooperation with the ROK in these domains, political and security cooperation is thus far under-utilised. Besides, there is a lack of strong people-to-people bonding and ties despite various government-sponsored cultural commemorations and celebrations. Therefore, the focus of their strategic partnership is on strengthening consultative mechanisms relating to political and security issues. Their focus is also on strengthening bilateral high-level exchanges by way of regular summit level meetings, the meetings of foreign and defence Ministers, the vice minister-level foreign and security 2+2 Dialogue, and the interaction between their National Security Council structures.[38]

Functional level security cooperation: In addition to the need for strategic consultations, a functional security and defence cooperation between the two countries has also been outlined. Staff-level talks, joint defence research and development, UN peacekeeping cooperation, think-tank level track 1.5 dialogues, military exchanges, joint naval exercises, anti-piracy cooperation in the Gulf of Aden, defence logistics and industry development, as well as shipyard level collaboration are all part of the functional cooperation visualised in their Strategic Partnership documents.[39] This is consistent with India's defence and security cooperation with other major countries in the region. However, in terms of institutionalisation, regularity, frequency, and the substance of cooperation, the India-ROK strategic partnership lags behind India's strategic partnerships with Japan, Vietnam, and Singapore.

Non-Traditional Security (NTS) cooperation: The two countries identify cooperation in non-traditional security as an important subject for deepening their strategic engagement. NTS cooperation within the maritime domain, which finds an important place in India's LAEP engagement, is also a focus in the India-ROK strategic partnership. International anti-terror cooperation has emerged as an important feature in India's broader international engagement and in its LAEP. The ROK has commercial interests in West Asia. South Korean citizens have been the targets of terrorists in West Asia and East Africa.[40] South Korea has also been a victim of terrorist activities, allegedly carried out on behalf of North Korea.[41] Incidentally, South Korean forces have fought terrorism and jihadi forces in

Afghanistan with the US-led coalition forces.[42] In this backdrop, the two countries seek 'an early conclusion of negotiations on the Comprehensive Convention on International Terrorism' and the prioritising of a broader anti-terror cooperation which includes the dismantling of 'terrorist safe havens and infrastructure, disrupt(ing) terrorist networks and their financing, and stop(ping) cross-border movement of terrorists.'[43]

High-end technology cooperation: The two countries have several more actionable interests and capabilities in high-end technology cooperation. Cyber security is one such domain. An important MoU with regard to a Future Strategy Group "for cooperation in cutting edge technologies for the 4th Industrial revolution" was signed during President Moon Jae-in's India visit in July 2018. This MoU covers the "Internet of Things (IOT), Artificial Intelligence (AI), Big Data, Smart Factory, 3D Printing, Electric Vehicle, Advance Materials and affordable healthcare for the elderly and disabled." Separate MoUs were signed for cooperation in biotechnology and bio-economics, and for ICT and telecommunications cooperation. MoUs between India's Council for Scientific and Industrial Research (CSIR) and ROK's National Research Council of Science and Technology (NST), and Research Design and Standards Organisation (RDSO) and the Korea Railroad Research Institute (KRRI) for science and technological cooperation were also signed during the visit.[44] Earlier, the two sides established the India-ROK ICT Policy Forum in 2014. They have also initiated policy consultations on cyberspace. The first of these was held in 2014. India was a major participant in the 2013 Seoul Conference on Cyberspace. India's Computer Emergency Response Team (Cert-In) and the Korea Internet & Security Agency (KISA) signed an MOU on cyber security in 2014.[45] In addition, they are cooperating in nuclear technology for peaceful purposes. They regularly hold exchanges relating to civil nuclear energy under the Agreement for Cooperation in the Peaceful Uses of Nuclear Energy.[46] Cooperation between the Indian Space Research Organisation (ISRO) and the Korea Aerospace Research Institute

(KARI) has research as well as commercial aspects. ISRO and KARI have promoted regular working-level talks for cooperation in deep space tracking and communication support, data sharing—particularly data received from India's Chandrayan-1. India has also offered its services for launching South Korean satellites.[47]

The LAEP and India-ROK Economic Relations

As economic imperatives shaped the adoption of the LEP in the early 1990s, economic relations have been the mainstay of India-ROK relations since that period. Their economic ties figure very prominently in India's economic integration with the Asia-Pacific. India has signed Free Trade Agreements (FTAs) with ASEAN, and also separately with Singapore, Thailand and Malaysia. It has signed the Comprehensive Economic Partnership Agreement (CEPA) with Japan and the ROK.

India and ROK signed the CEPA in 2009. Economic relations stand out in the entire matrix of India-ROK relations. Given the minuscule economic engagement of the early 1990s, the relationship has registered remarkable growth. In 1990, the two countries only had $ 488 million worth of trade, which rose to US$ 1.4 billion in 2000. The latest data for Financial Year (FY) 2016–17 is US$ 16.80 billion. Bilateral trade achieved a record high of US$ 18.1 billion in FY 2014–15. In 2000–01, the ROK was India's 19th ranking trade partner. As per the data for FY 2016–17, it is now India's 9th largest trading partner. India's trade with ROK constitutes around 2.55 per cent of India's total trade.[48] CEPA has, thus, had a positive impact on bilateral trade.

The ROK's cumulative investment from April 2000 to September 2015 stood at $ 1.67 billion. It was the 14th largest investor in India, accounting for 0.63 per cent of the total FDI in India. According to the data provided by India's DIPP, metallurgical industries lead the pack in receiving FDI from the ROK, followed by the auto sector, prime movers, machine tools, and hospital and diagnostics—in that order.[49] Companies such as POSCO, Hyundai Mobis, and Doosan Heavy Industries & Construction have been leading investors in India since 2000.[50] Fast moving consumer goods (FMCG) companies—for example LG and Samsung, and the automobile company Hyundai—are very popular in Indian households. In all, around 300 South Korean companies are doing business in India, employing approximately 40,000 Indians, as per 2014 data.[51] On the other hand, Indian giants such as Tatas and Mahindra & Mahindra have also made some acquisitions in South Korea. Indian companies in the ROK are mainly operating in the automobile, IT, and pharmaceutical sectors.[52]

However, while India's investment in the ROK is yet to take off, ROK's investment in India is also stagnant. Besides, India has a trade deficit of approximately US$ 8 billion in bilateral trade. Moreover, India-ROK trade figures are way short of the ROK's with China, Japan, the US, and Vietnam. Thus, there are many business prospects still for the two countries. Under its Make in India programme, India is inviting South Korean investment and technical expertise for its Smart City Project, the steel sector, the Swacch Bharat Abhiyan (Clean India Campaign) which can draw lessons from Saemaul Undong (SMU), a South Korean rural development programme of the 1970s. Similarly, there are prospects for cooperation between the Korean Green Economy initiative and India's search for green technology. Further, the two countries are desirous of entering into frontier areas of business cooperation that include cooperation in shipbuilding, maritime infrastructure, and space commerce. As previously mentioned, India has expressed its willingness to launch satellites for South Korea.

India is also seeking South Korean assistance for modernising the Indian shipbuilding industry, and for joint projects in shipping and maritime logistics.[53] Cooperation in the shipbuilding industry deserves some more attention. India's military and commercial naval capacity requires augmentation, and its capabilities need modernisation on a priority basis as ships and vessels are becoming obsolete. In India, the acquisition of such platforms, particularly in the defence sector, is a tardy process. Besides, in view of the growing energy demand, India requires a large number of Liquid Natural

Gas (LNG) tankers, which are technologically advanced ships. The ROK's shipbuilding expertise can help India augment capacities and update its capabilities through joint production ventures in this strategically important sector.[54]

During President Moon Jae-in's India visit in July 2018, the two countries issued a statement regarding an Early Harvest Package, for revising and upgrading their Comprehensive Economic Partnership Agreement (CEPA) to further liberalise bilateral trade. They have a US$ 50 billion target for bilateral trade by 2030. The Package includes goods, services, and investments. Early harvest offers have been made, "for 35 items each, while including yoga instructors and taekwondo instructors in the list of professionals under Sporting and other Recreational Services category." Korea offered zero duty for 15,000 tonne of shrimps from India, while India would implement duty reduction "for three broad categories of Korean imports" over the next 10–15 years. The ROK will reciprocate by reducing duties, "in equal 8–10 annual instalments." Under Early Harvest, the two countries decided to liberalise visas for "intra-corporate transferee". Thus, efforts have been made to expand bilateral trade and make it more balanced.[55]

India-ROK Relations in a Cultural Perspective

Apart from a liberal normative framework, the two countries have laid emphasis on the cultural side of their relationship, which strives to connect the countries with each other on the basis of a shared ancient Hindu and Buddhist cultural heritage. This places the relationship within the ambit of reviving Asian cultural connectivity, an idea that India and many regional countries have vigorously pushed in recent years. This contributes to the efforts towards creating a shared identity within a common geo-civilisational space which, in the Indian view, may be termed as the Indo-Pacific. In keeping with this, promoting the legend of King Suro and Suriratna,[56] and fostering Buddhist linkages have become important themes in the cultural interactions between the two countries. An MoU to upgrade and renovate the monument commemorating Princess Suriratna in Ayodhya was signed during

Moon Jae-in's visit.[57] Given its considerable Buddhist population, South Korea is a participant in the Nalanda University project—an East Asian Summit (EAS) project in the Indian state of Bihar.[58] The project aims at reviving the ancient Nalanda University, which was a famous Buddhist centre of learning. During their visits to South Korea, Prime Minister Modi in 2015, and earlier Prime Minister Manmohan Singh in 2014, gifted a sapling from the holy Bodhi tree to President Park.[59] In 2015, India participated in the Masterpieces of Early Buddhist Sculpture exhibition in South Korea.[60] This promotion of a shared cultural heritage along with other activities, like student exchanges, scholarships and fellowships, as well as cultural festivals is part of their vision for promoting cultural connectivity.

In keeping with this, the two countries have also undertaken several other initiatives, such as amending "the bilateral Air Services Agreement with a view to enhancing flight connectivity and to covering more cities",[61] as well as a Visa Simplification Agreement in 2012.[62] India approved "tourist visa-on-arrival facilities to ROK nationals" in 2014.[63] These sustained activities might help to develop better people-to-people bonds beyond the ambit of the state over the long term.

The LAEP and China as a Factor in the India-ROK Relationship

As has been indicated in the beginning of this essay, the LAEP is widely perceived to have intensified India's strategic engagement with the region, especially keeping China in view. Notably, its strategic partnerships with Japan and Vietnam are more clearly viewed as attempts to hedge against the Chinese strategic challenge. However, as far as the India-ROK strategic partnership is concerned, there are few grounds for inferring that India and the ROK have shared strategic assessments, or that China determines their strategic convergence. The mere articulation of shared liberal democratic norms and principles does not make their partnership China-centric. India's capabilities for strategic manoeuvring in the Korean Peninsula remain limited for the following reasons:

- **China's Pre-eminence in Peninsular Affairs:** The Peninsula lives in China's economic, political, and military shadow. Ever since the Korean War, it has been a stakeholder in Peninsular affairs.[64] China is treaty-bound to defend DPRK.[65] It is opposed to the US military presence in the ROK. As has been already mentioned, China is one of the Six-Party countries.
- **India's Distance from Korean Affairs:** Although in think-tank interactions, South Korean interlocutors may wish to understand India's perspective on the inter-Korea issue with regard to India's experiences of partition in 1947, or they may recall India's positive role in Korean affairs in the late 1940s and early 1950s, any mediation by India in Peninsular disputes has always remained far-fetched. India has hardly ever shown any such interest or inclination.[66] Nor is such an interest shown by either ROK, or DPRK, or any of other countries from the Six-Parties. In fact, India does not appear to have any viable *locus standi* in the security and political issues between North and South Korea.
- **Different Strategic Concerns and Responses:** There are considerable differences in the two countries' strategic concerns and their response to the Chinese strategic challenge. The ROK's security concerns originate from North Korean aggression and its missile and nuclear programme; whereas India has multiple strategic concerns such as the border dispute with China, Pakistan-sponsored cross-border terrorism, and jihadi terrorism. Even though the two countries may view China's rise with concern, it is difficult for India and ROK to adopt a common attitude towards China.[67] India's strategic divergence vis-à-vis China is far more complex. South Korea mainly diverges from China on the issues of North Korea and the US military presence in the region. However, it also acknowledges China's capacity to contribute to resolving issues with DPRK.
- **Differing Perceptions of Japan's Place in Regional Affairs:** India and South Korea also differ in their perceptions regarding Japan's role in regional strategic affairs. While India and Japan

appear to have emerged as natural strategic partners, with far greater convergence in their strategic perception of China, South Korea has historical grievances against Japan, and is suspicious of its potential re-emergence as a military power. It is, thus, on the same page as China with regard to concerns about Japan's possible militarisation and the historical issue of Japanese war crimes in China and Korea, in the first half of the 20th century.[68] Also, while the potential of India-ROK relations contributing to operationalise the vision of an Indo-Pacific region from India's vantage point is all too evident, it must be remembered that Japan has co-authored this idea with India and US. For this reason, South Korea's response to this idea may not be very enthusiastic.[69]

- **Weak Strategic Infrastructure:** The 'software' of India-ROK strategic partnership is still developing. Their partnership shows more promise in high-end technological-commercial cooperation and the defence industrial sector. However, in terms of a meaningful political and diplomatic coordination over regional issues, it has to go a long way.

In view of these considerations, a balance-of-power proposition in the India-ROK relationship vis-à-vis China is, thus, unworkable.

The LAEP and DPRK: Don't Shut all the Doors[70]

The Indian Minister of State (MOS) for External Affairs, General V.K. Singh, paid a visit to the DPRK in May 2018.[71] The visit immediately hit the headlines as this was the first minister-level visit from India's side since 1998.[72] The Minister for External Affairs, Sushma Swaraj, stated that "due to our bilateral relations, General V.K. Singh visited DPRK,"[73] at Foreign Minister Ri Yong-ho's invitation.[74] Notwithstanding Swaraj's clarification that the visit had nothing to with the upcoming Trump-Kim Singapore summit in June 2018, or her denial that the minister travelled to mediate in order to salvage the summit (which seemed to be in jeopardy at that moment), the timing of the visit is difficult to overlook.[75] Immediately before the visit, India had sent an Indian Foreign Service (IFS) officer as its Ambassador to Pyongyang after a considerably long break. The two previous Ambassadors were not from the IFS.[76] Any possible Indian mediation in Peninsular affairs has all along been explored by academicians and experts in think-tanks, on the basis of India's role in the late 1940s and early 1950s, in Korean affairs. India's rare contacts with the DPRK supported this exploration.[77] One will have to wait to learn whether the visit had any close or remote connection with the summit. For now, the North Korean invitation highlighted the rare distinction that India enjoys, of holding consultations with an isolated DPRK, from time to time.

Decline in Relations

India-DPRK relations began to decline from the late 1990s onwards. DPRK's self-imposed international isolation that began in the early 1990s, the clandestine North Korea-Pakistan missile and nuclear nexus, and the emergence of US-DPRK strains in the late 1990s over the latter's non-committal approach to the Non-Proliferation Treaty (NPT), explain the decline. Incidentally, during this time, India was busy mending its fences with the US, post-Pokhran sanctions in 1998.[78] The stopping of minister-level visits from India, after the last one in 1998, is a prominent example of the decline in the relationship. However, Indian parliamentarians, officials and North Korean ministers and other high officials, continued to travel to each other's countries. Moreover, the channels of communications have remained open all along. Even though bilateral relations are negligible, New Delhi is one of the few capitals, where the guests from Pyongyang receive a warm welcome. In fact, India's diplomatic contacts with the DPRK are a curiosity in concerned circles.

Humanitarian Framework for Relations: Aid and Consultation

India is not in favour of shunning or isolating the DPRK. It maintains its traditional contacts with the poverty and hunger stricken North Koreans within a humanitarian framework. Thus, it approves the DPRK's participation in the Ministry of External Affairs (MEA)-

initiated Indian Technical and Economic Cooperation (ITEC) Programme. North Korean diplomats participate in the Professional Course for Foreign Diplomats (PCFD). The PCFD is run by the MEA's Foreign Service Institute (FSI). India has periodically provided humanitarian assistance to North Korea, directly or through the UN World Food Programme (WFP in 2011). Incidentally, DPRK also donated US$ 30,000 to the Prime Minister's National Relief Fund after the Tsunami hit India's southern coast in 2004. The two countries have held the Foreign Office Consultations (FOC) since 2000. The last FOC was held in Pyongyang in 2011. They also set up Joint Secretary-Director General level talks in 2013.[79] The then Indian external affairs minister, Salman Khurshid, and the then DPRK Foreign Minister Pak Ui-chuan met on the side-lines of the East Asia Summit held in Brunei in 2013.[80] Notably, the *MEA Annual Report 2014–2015* made a mention of the DPRK's support for the following: India's candidature to the United Nations Human Rights Council (2015–17); the Intergovernmental Committee for the Safeguarding of Intangible Cultural Heritage for 2014–18; and the post of Secretary General of the Asia-Pacific Telecommunity for the term 2015–18. Earlier, the DPRK did not receive specific mention in the reports, in such contexts.[81] The 12th Cultural Exchange Programme for 2017-20 between the two countries "is in the final draft stage."[82]

The latest available information according to media sources suggests that India is, perhaps, DPRK's second largest trading partner after China. In 2013, Sojin Shin, a Singapore-based scholar, recorded India as North Korea's third largest trading partner.[83] The latest Indian figure for bilateral trade for 2017–18, is US$ 82.63 million, while it was US$ 208.45 million in 2014–15.[84] The figure seems to have gone down on account of stricter UN sanctions against DPRK. These figures are not great, and no match for the India-ROK economic relationship, yet they do have symbolic value.

Perceiving New Momentum in the Relationship

Since Foreign Minister Ri Su-yong's visit to India in April 2015, relations have gained new momentum. While General V.K. Singh's recent visit was the first minister-level visit from India in 20 years, Foreign Minister Ri's visit also took place after a long break. Foreign Minister Ri urged India to include his country in its LAEP. Later, in August 2015, the Indian minister of state for home, Kiren Rijiju, remarked that India "should have good bilateral ties" with North Korea, which is "an independent country and a member of the United Nations." He underlined "greater trade and commerce" as the basis for enhancing relations.[85]

In September 2017, the media reported that the US expected India to curb its diplomatic contacts with the DPRK. Foreign Minister Swaraj, however, in October 2017, advised the US Secretary of State, Rex Tillerson, that it was important that, 'Some of their [US] friendly countries should maintain embassies there so that some channels of communication are kept open.'[86] Finally, sending an Indian Foreign Service officer to Pyongyang as Ambassador, followed by the visit of a minister to the country, was a subtle upgrading of the ties in 2018.

General V.K. Singh's Visit and the LAEP

The fact that the DPRK interlocutors briefed the visiting minister about "some of the recent developments in the Korean Peninsula" (the obvious reference was to the Singapore Summit), and the minister reiterated "India's support to the joint peace initiative of DPRK and Republic of Korea (ROK) ... encouraging both sides for their efforts towards [the] establishment of peace and prosperity on the Korean Peninsula" indicated the strategic nature of the dialogue and consultation. During the dialogue, General Singh was assured that, "as a friendly country, DPRK will never allow any action that would create concerns for India's security." This was with reference to the history of proliferation between North Korea-Pakistan. Besides, the visit witnessed the two countries' decision to explore cooperation in various aspects of people-to-people relations "to mark 45 years of establishment of diplomatic relations between the two countries".[87] Thus, the visit extended India's LAEP to the DPRK.

Understanding the Motivations behind the Relationship

India seems to have been motivated by a variety of considerations in insisting on continuing its relations with the DPRK. Foreign Minister Swaraj's refusal to curtail India's diplomatic presence in Pyongyang should be seen as India's unwillingness to give up its historical presence in the region, and in the country. Any yielding on this count will negate India's self-image of being an independent player in the region, its idea of strategic autonomy and its LAEP mandate to increase the country's footprint in the Asia-Pacific. Besides, it would be only wise to keep the DPRK engaged, particularly when isolating Pakistan on terror, and since security-related issues remain a top priority for India. North Korea's assurance to General Singh is instructive in this regard. Moreover, the DPRK is very much a member of the UN General Assembly. India needs its vote and cooperation on several issues in the UN. Furthermore, the DPRK has a prospective economic value in view of its unexplored minerals market, particularly the strategically important rare earth elements (REE).[88] Likewise, the DPRK's renewed interest in India may be seen in the context of President Kim Jong-un's perceived willingness to reduce dependence on China, and a willingness to engage with the international community. Since 2011, the DPRK under Kim Jong-un has appeared to be sending signals to Russia, Japan, and some Western countries.[89] The Trump-Kim Singapore summit was the culmination of this change.

Unification and Nuclear Issues in the Peninsula and India

India supports peaceful unification of the two Koreas. One may argue that a peaceful, stable, and unified Korea in the Asia-Pacific would be in India's strategic interest. India reaffirms its commitment to "peace and stability in the Korean Peninsula" but wants the unification issue to be left to "the Korean people to decide and to do by themselves."[90] Thus, it opposes any regime change approach. However, India also supports the de-nuclearisation of the Korean Peninsula. It opposes Pyongyang's nuclear programme and other proliferation activities and thus complies with the UN sanctions on DPRK.[91] India welcomed the Singapore Summit, describing it as "a positive development". The MEA press release issued then succinctly captures India's position:

> India has always supported all efforts to bring about peace and stability in the Korean Peninsula through dialogue and diplomacy. We hope that the outcomes of the US-DPRK Summit will be implemented, thus paving the way for lasting peace and stability in the Korean Peninsula. We also hope that the resolution of the Korean Peninsula issue will take into account and address our concerns about proliferation linkages extending to India's neighbourhood.[92]

India must be one of the few, if not the only country, outside the Six-Party countries that receives the briefings from the DPRK on nuclear and other issues. Foreign Minister Salman Khurshid in 2013,[93] Foreign Minister Swaraj in April 2015, and now Minister of State V. K. Singh have all discussed these crucial issues with their North Korean counterparts.[94] It can be inferred that they discuss these issues in their dialogue mechanisms as well. The ROK was reported to have explored the possibility of Indian mediation in inter-Korean affairs in the 1980s. At present, the left political constituencies there, have occasionally shown an interest in mediation by India.[95] However, as India has barely shown any interest in strategic issues in the Korean Peninsula after the Armistice in 1953, Indian mediation has remained a subject of academic discussions only. Yet, if the original stakeholders were to decide to involve other major countries to ensure trust in the dialogue process, India may be a good choice for them.

Conclusion

Thus, the LAEP engages with the Peninsula in the independent bilateral contexts of India's relations with the ROK and the DPRK. India-ROK relations, manifestly, dominate the LAEP for their economic salience. On the other hand, any suggestions regarding India-DPRK relations are still exploratory.

India-ROK economic relations, which have progressed from very weak to strong, symbolise the success of LAEP, though much potential remains untapped. On the other hand, the security and diplomatic dimensions of strategic partnership are largely aspirational, as the strategic framework needs more fleshing out in terms of institutionalisation, regularity and frequency. Also, trade in the high technological sectors of strategic importance is yet to take off. Besides, more investment in cultivating strong people-to-people bonding is needed to make the relationship move beyond being government-led. On the whole, the India-ROK strategic partnership will blossom within the framework of economics and culture, in the short to the medium-term. The larger political and diplomatic aspects are unlikely to become as pronounced as they are in the India-Japan or, to an extent, in the India-Vietnam strategic partnership. Finally, the overall report card of the LAEP in the ROK is satisfactory. 'New substance, more speed and greater content'[96] in bilateral relations is however still required.

As for India-DPRK relations, structural factors will restrict any effective LAEP explorations in the DPRK in the short term, though the situation may change in the medium-term, depending on strategic developments in the Peninsula. India should maintain its humanitarian ties as well as consultation and dialogue with the DPRK. It should also continue with its present small-scale capacity building programmes. The LAEP demonstrates India's strategic autonomy through these ties. When the situation in the Peninsula with regard to North Korea seems to be optimistic, there will be all the more reason to stay the course. India should promote people-to-people exchanges. It should explore ways to deepen trade and development-oriented investment, without violating the UN sanctions. The LAEP objective now should be to do the ground-work for the time when North Korea, re-engages the international community. However, all this should be done while being mindful of the ROK's sensibilities, which are far too important for India.

As for an integrated view of the Korean Peninsula in LAEP, the top priority should be accorded to enhancing the mutual awareness between India and the two countries. India should speak through the scholarly community and civil-society on unification, denuclearisation, as well as developmental issues relating to these countries. Efforts can be made to jointly engage the two Koreas in semi-official and unofficial dialogue. This integrated view is desirable, as a stable Korean Peninsula is in India's larger interests. The LAEP should project India as a committed and responsible stakeholder in the region.

Notes

1. The author, an Associate Fellow at the East Asia Centre, IDSA, can be reached at prashant.idsa@gmail.com
2. This essay has evolved from the paper 'India-South Korea Relations in a China Context: Convergence, Divergence and the Future', which the author presented at the World Congress for Korean Politics and Society 2017 (Rebuilding Trust in Peace and Democracy), the Korean Political Science Association (KPSA), Yonsei University, Seoul, Republic of Korea, on June 23, 2017. The essay also draws on the author's previous paper on 'North Korea: An Advance Frontier of India's "Act East"?' *Special Feature*, IDSA, December 1, 2015 at https://idsa.in/specialfeature/north-korea-indias-act-east_psingh_011215.
3. Prime Minister P.V. Narasimha Rao's speech at the ISIS in Singapore in 1994 is considered as being the earliest and most definitive articulation of the Look East Policy (LEP). See also, Pinak Ranjan Chakravarty, 'Bridging the Hiatus of History: India's Look East Policy', in Amar Nath Ram, *India's Asia-Pacific Engagement: Impulses and Imperatives,* Manohar, New Delhi, 2015, p. 58.
4. '"Look East" Policy Now Turned into "Act East" Policy: Modi', *The Hindu*, November 13, 2014 at http://www.thehindu.com/news/national/look-east-policy-now-turned-into-act-east-policy-modi/article6595186.ece, accessed on March 21, 2018.
5. Ancient India had notable Hindu and Buddhist cultural and trade contacts with the region, particularly during the Chola period. Coastal India and regional countries such as Thailand and Cambodia reflect this legacy in their religion, temples, customs and traditions, religious texts, and languages. During the Turko-Afghan Delhi Sultanate and the Mughal Empire, India developed an Islamic connect with the region. During this period, Muslim traders played an important role in spreading Islam in South East Asia, especially from India's south west coast (modern Kerala). These contacts,

however, were lost during colonial rule from the late 18th century onwards, though this era saw exploitation-based contacts facilitated by the needs of the colonial masters, such as the sending of the sugarcane planters to Fiji and other countries. However, the Indian diaspora spread across the region during this period. See, Pinak Ranjan Chakravarty, note 3, in Amar Nath Ram, note 3, pp. 59–60.

6. Christophe Jaffrelot, 'India's Look East Policy: An Asianist Strategy in Perspective', *India Review*, 2:2, 2003, pp. 35–68.
7. D.R. Sardesai, 'India and Southeast Asia', in B.R. Nanda (ed.), *Indian Foreign Policy: The Nehru Years,* Nehru Memorial Museum & Library and Sangam Books, New Delhi, 1990, pp. 98–101. See also, Rajiv Sikri, *Challenge and Strategy: Rethinking India's Foreign Policy,* Sage India, New Delhi, 2009, pp. 112–115.
8. Christophe Jaffrelot, note 6, pp. 35–68.
9. Rajiv Sikri, note 7, pp. 112–115.
10. Rajiv Sikri, note 7; Also see, S.D. Muni, 'India's 'Look East' Policy: The Strategic Dimension', in Rajshree Jetly and Shanthie Mariet D'Souza (eds), *Perspectives on South Asian Security*, World Scientific, Singapore, 2013, pp. 67–99; Harsh V. Pant, 'India in the Asia-Pacific: Rising ambitions with An Eye on China', *Asia-Pacific Review*, 14(1), 2007, pp. 54–71.
11. Amar Nath Ram, 'Introduction' in Amar Nath Ram, note 3, pp. 15–19; C. Raja Mohan and Darshana M. Baruah, 'India's "Look East" Policy: The Maritime Dimension', in Amar Nath Ram, note 3, pp. 192–194; Ramadhani, Eryan, 'Lost in Southeast Asia: India's "Look East" Policy Revisited', *Yonsei Journal of International Studies*, 6(2), 2014, pp. 316–333. There is always some variation in the classification of phases by various scholars.
12. Parbati Sen Vyas, 'India's "Look East" and "Enhanced Look East" Policies', in Amar Nath Ram, note 3, pp. 133–134.
13. Baladas Ghoshal, 'Geo-civilisational Links and Role of Soft Power: Towards Deepening ASEAN-India Cultural Relations', Centre for Indian Studies, January 9, 2018 at http://cis.org.vn/article/2504/geo-civilizational-links-and-role-of-soft-power-towards-deepening-asean-india-cultural-relations-part-2.html, accessed on March 21, 2018.
14. C. Raja Mohan and Darshana M. Baruah, 'India's Look East Policy: The Maritime Dimension', in Amar Nath Ram, note 3, pp. 194–198; Kapil Kak, 'Indo-Pacific Security and Defence: India's Challenges and Policy Options' in Amar Nath Ram, note 3, pp. 182–185; 'The Indo-Pacific Defining A Region', Stratfor at https://worldview.stratfor.com/article/indo-pacific-defining-region, accessed on March 21, 2018.
15. Skand Tayal, *India-Republic of Korea Relations: Engaged Democracies,* Routledge, New Delhi, 2014, pp. 1–9.

16. Ibid., pp. 1–21.
17. Skand Tayal, note 15, pp. 24–43; Skand Tayal, 'Looking Back at 40 Years of India-Korea Relations and Future Perspectives', in Rajat Kathuria and Samjana Joshi (eds), *Forty Years of India-Korea Relations and Looking Ahead,* ICRIER, New Delhi, 2014, pp. 47–62.
18. John Garver, *China's Quest: The History of the Foreign Relations of the People's Republic of China,* Oxford University Press, New York, 2016, p. 83.
19. Skand Tayal, note 15, pp. 28–29.
20. David Brewster, *India as an Asia Pacific Power,* Routledge, New York, 2012, p. 65.
21. Sheela Kaul, 'India and the Two Koreas', Working Paper 2, Seminar on India and East Asia, June 26–28, 1967, Nainital, Indian School of International Studies (ISIS), New Delhi, p. 6.
22. 'India-Korea (ROK) Relations', MEA at https://www.mea.gov.in/Portal/ForeignRelation/Korea__ROK__June_2014_.pdf, accessed on March 23, 2018.
23. Skand Tayal, note 15, p. 75.
24. Sheela Kaul, note 21, pp. 6–7.
25. Skand Tayal, note 15, p. 70.
26. Prashant Kumar Singh, 'North Korea: An Advance Frontier of India's "Act East"?', *Special Feature,* IDSA, December 1, 2015 at http://www.idsa.in/specialfeature/north-korea-indias-act-east_psingh_011215, accessed on March 25, 2018.
27. Skand Tayal, note 15, pp. 82–83.
28. Prashant Kumar Singh, note 26.
29. Scott Bruce, John Hemmings, Balbina Y. Hwang, Terence Roehrig and Scott A. Snyder, 'Global Korea: South Korea's Contributions to International Security', Report, Council on Foreign Relations (CFR), at https://www.cfr.org/report/global-korea, accessed on March 25, 2018; see also, Na Jeong-ju, 'Summit and S. Korea's "New Asia Initiative"', *The Korea Herald,* March 30, 2010 at http://www.koreaherald.com/view.php?ud=20090601000110, accessed on March 25, 2018.
30. 'India-Republic of Korea Joint Statement for Expansion of the Strategic Partnership', MEA, January 16, 2014 at http://www.mea.gov.in/bilateral-documents.htm?dtl/22752/India+Republic+of+Korea+Joint+Statement+for+Expansion+of+the+Strategic+Partnership, accessed on March 29, 2018.
31. Ibid.
32. 'India-Korea (ROK) Relations', note 22; 'India—Republic of Korea Joint Statement For Special Strategic Partnership', May 18, 2015, Press

Information Bureau (PIB), Government of India at http://pib.nic.in/newsite/PrintRelease.aspx?relid=121821, accessed on March 29, 2018.

33. 'Joint Statement', note 32, PIB, May 18, 2015; 'Keynote Address by President Park Geun-hye of the Republic of Korea at the Eastern Economic Forum in Russia', September 3, 2009 at http://mofa.go.kr/webmodule/htsboard/template/read/engreadboard.jsp?typeID=12&boardid=14195&seqno=317327&c=&t=&pagenum=1&tableName=TYPE_ENGLISH&pc=&dc=&wc=&lu=&vu=&iu=&du=, accessed on May 3, 2018; 'NAPCI, North East Asia Peace and Cooperation Initiative 2016', Korean Ministry of Foreign Affairs (MOFA), at http://napci.net/eng/images/sub/eng_book.pdf, accessed on May 5, 2018.
34. 'India and Republic of Korea: A Vision for People, Prosperity, Peace and our Future', MEA, July 10, 2018 at https://www.mea.gov.in/bilateral-documents.htm?dtl/30041/India_and_Republic_of_Korea_A_Vision_for_People_Prosperity_Peace_and_our_Future, accessed on September 27, 2018.
35. Jaehyon Lee, 'Korea's New Southern Policy towards ASEAN: Context and Direction', Asian Institute for Policy Studies at http://jpi.or.kr/skyboard/download.sky?fid=4975&gid=7073&code=jpiworld, accessed on September 27, 2018.
36. 'Joint Statement', note 32, PIB, May 18, 2015; 'Joint Statement', note 30, MEA, January 16, 2014; 'Transcript of Foreign Secretary's Briefing on Prime Minister's visit to Seoul', MEA, March 21, 2012 at http://www.mea.gov.in/bilateral-documents.htm?dtl/19093/Transcript+of+Foreign+Secretarys+briefing+on+Prime+Ministers+visit+to+Seoul, accessed May 3, 2018; 'Transcript of Media Briefing by Official Spoke sperson and Joint Secretary (East Asia)', MEA, January 13, 2014 at http://www.mea.gov.in/in-focus-article.htm?22738/Transcript+of+media+briefing+by+Official+Spokesperson+and+Joint+SecretaryEast+Asia+January+13+2014, accessed on May 3, 2018.
37. 'Joint Statement', note 32, PIB, May 18, 2015.
38. Ibid.
39. 'India, Korean Naval Ships to Conduct Joint Military Exercises', *India Today*, November 15, 2014 at http://indiatoday.intoday.in/story/india-korea-joint-military-exercises-korean-navy-indian-navy-roks-choi-young-roks-cheoji-ins-rajput-ins-sumitra/1/400985.html, accessed on May 7, 2018; 'India-South Korea Coast Guards to Jointly Hold Naval Exercises', *The Times of India*, June 6, 2017 at https://www.google.co.in/#q=india+south+korean+naval+exercise&spf=1497459309115, accessed on May 7, 2018; 'Transcript of Media Briefing' note 36, MEA, January 13, 2014.
40. Choe Sang-Hun, 'Afghan Hostage Crisis Transfixes South Korea', *New York Times*, July 26, 2007 at http://www.nytimes.com/2007/07/26/world/asia/26iht-korea.4.6849627.html?pagewanted=all, accessed on June 7,

2018; John Power, 'On Heels of North Korean Threat, South Korea Now Fears Islamic Terror', *Asia Times*, January 21, 2016 at http://www.atimes.com/article/on-heels-of-north-korean-threat-south-korea-now-fears-islamic-terror/, accessed on June 7, 2018.

41. Robert Park, 'North Korea's Legacy of Terrorism', *World Affairs* (Online) at http://www.worldaffairsjournal.org/article/north-korea%E2%80%99s-legacy-terrorism, accessed on June 7, 2018.
42. Lee, Jong-Heon, 'Seoul to Resend Troops to Afghanistan', *UPI,* October 3, 2009 at http://www.upi.com/Top_News/Special/2009/10/30/Seoul-to-resend-troops-to-Afghanistan/UPI-33291256914946/, accessed on June 7, 2018.
43. 'Joint Statement', note 32, PIB, May 18, 2015.
44. 'List of MoUs/Documents signed between India and the Republic of Korea during the State Visit of President of Korea to India', MEA, July 10, 2018 at https://www.mea.gov.in/bilateral-documents.htm?dtl/30040/List_of_MoUsDocuments_signed_between_India_and_the_Republic_of_Korea_during_the_State_Visit_of_President_of_Korea_to_India, accessed on September 27, 2018.
45. 'Joint Statement', note 30, MEA, January 16, 2014.
46. Ibid.
47. 'Joint Statement', note 32, PIB, May 18, 2015.
48. The trade data is from the website of Department of Commerce, EXIM Bank, India, which can be accessed at http://commerce.nic.in/eidb/default.asp, accessed on June 10, 2018.
49. 'FDI Synopsis on Country South Korea', Department of Indian Policy and Promotion (DIPP), Government of India at http://www.dipp.gov.in/sites/default/files/fdi_synopsis_korea.pdf, accessed on June 10, 2018.
50. Ibid.
51. 'Transcript of Media Briefing' note 36, MEA, January 13, 2014.
52. 'FDI Synopsis on Country South Korea', note 49.
53. 'Joint Statement', note 32, PIB, May 18, 2015; 'Joint Statement', note 30, MEA, January 16, 2014.
54. Sudhakar Vaddi, 'India Finds a New Friend', *Millennium Post,* July 10, 2018 at http://www.millenniumpost.in/opinion/india-finds-a-new-friend-308710, accessed on September 27, 2018.
55. 'List of MoUs/Documents' note 44, MEA, July 10, 2018; 'A Vision for People, Prosperity, Peace and our Future', note 34, MEA, July 10, 2018; Jyoti Mukul, 'India-Korea CEPA: Harvest Deal by 2019 Even as Two Nations Stick to Guns', *Business Standard,* July 10, 2018 at https://www.business-standard.com/article/economy-policy/india-korea-cepa-harvest-deal-by-2019-even-as-two-nations-stick-to-guns-118071001401_1.html, accessed on September 27, 2018; T.C.A. Sharad Raghavan, 'India,

South Korea Agree on Framework to Improve Trade', *The Hindu*, July 10, 2018 at https://www.thehindu.com/news/national/india-south-korea-agree-on-framework-to-improve-trade/article24382342.ece#, accessed on September 27, 2018.

56. Skand Tayal, note 15, pp. 1–9.
57. 'List of MoUs/Documents', note 44, MEA, July 10, 2018; see also, Geeta Mohan, 'India, S Korea and the Ayodhya Connect', *India Today*, July 11, 2018 at https://www.indiatoday.in/mail-today/story/india-s-korea-and-the-ayodhya-connect-1282323-2018-07-11, accessed on September 27, 2018.
58. 'India-Republic of Korea Joint Statement: Deepening the Strategic Partnership', MEA, March 25, 2012 at http://mea.gov.in/bilateral-documents.htm?dtl/19070/India++Republic+of+Korea+Joint+Statement++Deepening+the+Strategic+Partnership, accessed on June 10, 2018.
59. 'Joint Statement', note 32, PIB, May 18, 2015; 'Joint Statement', note 30, MEA, January 16, 2014.
60. 'Joint Statement', note 32, PIB, May 18, 2015.
61. Ibid.
62. 'Joint Statement', note 30, MEA, January 16, 2014.
63. Ibid., 'Tourist Visa-on-Arrival Extended to Republic of Korea', MEA, April 16, 2014 at http://mea.gov.in/press-releases.htm?dtl/23205/Tourist+VisaonArrival+Extended+to+Republic+of+Korea, accessed on June 12, 2018.
64. Bonnie S. Glaser and Yun Sun, 'Chinese Attitude towards Korean Unification', *International Journal of Korean Unification Studies*, 24(2), 2015, pp. 71–98.
65. 'Treaty of Friendship, Co-operation and Mutual Assistance Between the People's Republic of China and the Democratic People's Republic of Korea', Chinese Communism Subject Archive, at https://www.marxists.org/subject/china/documents/china_dprk.htm, accessed on September 27, 2018; see also, Ankit Panda, 'China and North Korea Have a Mutual Defense Treaty, But When Would It Apply?', *The Diplomat*, August 14, 2017 at https://thediplomat.com/2017/08/china-and-north-korea-have-a-mutual-defense-treaty-but-when-would-it-apply/, accessed on September 27, 2018; 'China, Russia Share Opposition to U.S. THAAD in South Korea: Xi', Reuters, https://www.reuters.com/article/us-china-thaad-russia-idUSKBN19O0N8, accessed on September 27, 2018.
66. David Brewster, note 20, p. 74.
67. Changhee Parksee, 'India and Korea in a Changing Asia: From Distant Neighbours to Strategic Partners', in Rajat Kathuria and Samjana Joshi (eds), note 17, pp. 70–73.

68. Jonathan Eyal, 'South Korea Needs New Thinking on Foreign Policy', *The Strait Times*, May 15, 2017 at http://www.straitstimes.com/opinion/south-korea-needs-new-thinking-on-foreign-policy, accessed on June 16, 2018; see also, Ben Forney, 'South Korea's 3 Foreign Policy Blind Spots', *The Diplomat*, February 25, 2017 at http://thediplomat.com/2017/02/south-koreas-3-foreign-policy-blind-spots/, accessed on June 16, 2018.
69. Hiroshi Minegishi, 'South Korea Balks at Joining US-Japanese 'Indo-Pacific' Push', *Nikkei Asian Review*, November 11, 2017, at https://asia.nikkei.com/Politics/South-Korea-balks-at-joining-US-Japanese-Indo-Pacific-push, accessed on September 27, 2018.
70. This section on Unification and Nuclear Issues in the Peninsula and India, and some bits of Conclusion draws on this author's 'North Korea: An Advance Frontier of India's "Act East"?', Special Feature, IDSA, December 1, 2015 (online) at https://idsa.in/specialfeature/north-korea-indias-act-east_psingh_011215. Some bits of information and analysis are reproduced from Special Feature with the editor's consent.
71. For an exclusive discussion on this visit, see Prashant Kumar Singh, 'V.K. Singh's 'Surprise' Visit to Pyongyang: Reading the Tea Leaves', Strategic Vision, MCSSTW, IIR, NCCU, Taipei (Accepted & under process of publication).
72. 'Visit of Minister of State for External Affairs General Dr. V.K. Singh (Retd.) to the Democratic People's Republic of Korea', MEA, May 16, 2018 at http://www.mea.gov.in/press-releases.htm?dtl/29899/Visit_of_Minister_of_State_for_External_Affairs_General_Dr_VK_Singh_Retd_to_the_Democratic_Peoples_Republic_of_Korea, accessed on June 20, 2018.
73. 'Annual Press Conference by EAM on Completion of 4 Years of Government', MEA, May 28, 2018 at http://www.mea.gov.in/media-briefings.htm?dtl/29927/Annual_Press_Conference_by_EAM_on_completion_of_4_Years_of_Government_Translation_, accessed on June 20, 2018.
74. Ibid.
75. 'Trump Says US-North Korea Summit may be "in Three-Four Weeks"', BBC, April 29, 2018 at http://www.bbc.com/news/world-us-canada-43938535 accessed on June 21, 2018; Barbara Starr and Zachary Cohen, 'US B-52 Bombers Changed Flight Plan after North Korea Threatened Trump Summit', CNN, May 19, 2018 at https://edition.cnn.com/2018/05/18/politics/us-b-52-route-change-north-korea/index.html, accessed on June 21, 2018.
76. K.P. Nayar, 'Atul Malhari Gotsurve: Delhi's Man in Pyongyang is an IFS Officer', *The Indian Express*, May 23, 2018 at http://indianexpress.com/article/india/finally-delhis-man-atul-malhari-gotsurve-in-north-korea-ambassador-ifs-officer-5187383/, accessed on June 23, 2018.

77. 'Why is US Pleased with India's Outreach to North Korea?', Scroll. In, April 16, 2015, accessed on June 29, 2018; Skand Tayal, note 15, pp. 230–231; 'Breaking the Cycle of North Korean Provocations', Hearing before the Senate Committee on Foreign Relations, United Senate, Statement by Assistant Secretary of State Kurt Campbell, Washington, March 2011, p. 12 at https://www.ncnk.org/resources/publications/Breaking_the_Cycle_Hearing_Transcript.pdf, accessed on June 29, 2018.
78. Prashant Kumar Singh, note 26, pp. 6–8.
79. Ibid., p. 5.
80. Ibid.
81. Ibid., p. 8. *Annual Report, 2014–15*, Policy, Planning and Research Division, Indian Ministry of External Affairs, New Delhi, p. viii at http://www.mea.gov.in/Uploads/PublicationDocs/25009_External_Affairs_2014-2015__English_.pdf, accessed on June 29, 2018.
82. 'India DPRK Relations', Country Brief, August 2018, Ministry of External Affairs at http://www.mea.gov.in/Portal/ForeignRelation/india__dprk_bilateral_brief_for_mea_website.pdf, accessed on September 15, 2018.
83. Sojin Shin, 'Political Risks in India-North Korea Ties: Analysis', ISAS Brief, Singapore, No. 382, July 2015, p. 4.
84. See 'Export-Import Data Bank', Department of Commerce, Ministry of Commerce & Industry, Government of India at http://commerce-app.gov.in/eidb/iecnt.asp, accessed on July 1, 2018.
85. Kallol Bhattacherjee, 'India Reaches Out, Wants to Upgrade Ties with North Korea', *The Hindu*, September 16, 2015, accessed on July 5, 2018.
86. Jayanth Jacob, 'India will Retain North Korea Diplomatic Mission, Sushma Tells Tillerson', *Hindustan Times*, October 25, 2017 at https://www.hindustantimes.com/india-news/india-will-retain-north-korea-diplomatic-mission-sushma-tells-tillerson/story-gtAFzLKYzUqjdl3jj3jkQI.html, accessed on July 5, 2018.
87. 'Visit of Minister of State', note 72, MEA, May 16, 2018.
88. Kallol Bhattacherjee, note 85.
89. Prashant Kumar Singh, note 26, pp. 10–11.
90. 'Transcript of Media Briefing', note 36, MEA, January 13, 2014.
91. 'India Imposes New Restrictions on Trade with North Korea, Say Govt Sources', *Business Standard*, March 7, 2018 at https://www.business-standard.com/article/economy-policy/india-imposes-new-restrictions-on-trade-with-north-korea-say-govt-sources-118030700899_1.html, accessed on July 7, 2018.
92. 'India Welcomes the US-DPRK Summit', MEA at http://www.mea.gov.in/press-releases.htm?dtl/29973/India_Welcomes_the_US_DPRK_Summit, accessed on July 7, 2018.

93. Elizabeth Roche, 'India Raises Nuclear Proliferation Issue with North Korea', *Live Mint*, July 1, 2013.
94. 'North Korea Foreign Minister in India, Meets Sushma Swaraj', First Post, April 14, 2015 at http://www.firstpost.com/world/north-korea-foreign-minister-india-meets-..., accessed on July 12, 2018.
95. Tayal shared information with the author.
96. 'Joint Statement', note 32, PIB, May 18, 2015.

14. India's North Korea Relationship: A Case of Limited Aims and Strategic Calculations

M.S. Prathibha

India's desire to maintain sustained and friendly contact with North Korea has been the subject of speculation and intense international scrutiny. Though India had to comply with the United Nations Security Council sanctions, it maintained medical and food assistance to North Korea amidst mounting international sanctions against North Korea's nuclear and missile tests. Even the intense pressure from the United States under the administration of President Donald Trump to get India to close diplomatic relations with North Korea failed to fructify. Thus, India's commitment to defend its diplomatic presence shows that it has specific strategic objectives to achieve in its relationship with North Korea.

In fact, India articulates its relationship with North Korea through seeking long-term benefits in its policy planning but pursuing limited aims in its approach. In other words, India does not endeavour any grand objective, especially given its limited influence in the Korean Peninsula. Nevertheless, India wants to convey specific security concerns to North Korea and sensitise it to the Indian security interests. Further, India's policy predicts that it would not have any immediate gains but long-term benefits from its strategic partnership with North Korea. Moreover, this long-term benefit would depend on India having strategic patience to maintain sustained contact with North Korea to build mutual trust in the relationship.

Thus, India's relationship with North Korea is predicated on future gains depending on India's ability to extract limited benefits by negotiating on mutual concerns in the Indian subcontinent and the Korean Peninsula. In other words, India's security concerns would have to be reflected in any peace process in the Korean Peninsula, making it the most challenging of Indian foreign policy objectives due to its limited influence and presence in the region. In fact, India would have to convince many stakeholders in the Korean Peninsula, including the elusive North Korean leadership to that a peace process that includes resolving proliferation challenges would have a positive impact not only on India's security environment but also on the stability of the Korean Peninsula. Intense engagement and the upgradation of ties is, thus, the optimal solution in this scenario. A review of India's interaction in the recent years, especially the elevation of diplomatic ties with North Korea are indicative of this type of strategic thinking. It however raises questions regarding the extent of India's leverage to influence North Korea's cooperation in exposing proliferation linkages in its nuclear programme. A historic account also shows that why the nature of Indian engagement has changed over the years and became more pragmatic in its engagement in the Korean Peninsula.

India's Historic Involvement and Its Legacy

India's engagement in the Korean affairs began at the outbreak of hostilities in the Korean Peninsula. Contrary to popular opinion in India that it had played a welcome role in the Korean peace process, Indian Prime Minister Jawaharlal Nehru found himself at odds with great power politics. The needs of the US, the Soviet Union, and China were contrary, and the responsibility of maintaining amiability rested in Jawaharlal Nehru's hands. India was the Chair in the United Nations Commission that oversaw the Korean elections in 1947 as well as UN activities regarding the Korean War, leading it to play an important role in the Neutral Nations Repatriation Commission. Besides contributing to the armistice negotiations, India also sent the 60th Para Field Ambulance Platoon during the

Korean War, which provided medical and surgical assistance to the wounded allied soldiers in the war. This medical unit moved along with the allied troops into the battle zone during the Korean War and established a field hospital. They were the only qualified medical unit that assisted the US 187th Regimental Combat Team at Munsan in their parachute jump.[1]

India's diplomatic role in the negotiations to end the Korean War remains its most intense phase of engagement; indeed it was also the most challenging one. The American and British pressure on Nehru to support their initiatives, and his fear that the conflict would be dragged to a wider war was a constant source to apprehension to him.[2] Nehru's efforts were focused on attempting to find a common ground between the US, the UK and China, and preventing the UN from passing any resolution that could be used to engage in a wider war in the Korean Peninsula. This was evident in India's efforts in warning the US to not cross the 38th parallel because of the threat of Chinese intervention, which was not taken seriously. Moreover, India was also involved in the armistice agreement through drafting proposals that could be acceptable to both sides, in particular with regard to the exchange of prisoners of war.

Thus, India's involvement was neutral in North Korea, which has been significantly different from that of US and South Korea. For instance, India did not support the draft that led North Korea to be called an 'aggressor' in the Korean conflict; indeed, it was responsible for diluting those terms by ending it as 'breach of the peace'.[3] India has never been hostile to the North Korean sentiments as much as the Western powers. This has influenced Indian policy in its engagements with North Korea due to the lack of moral high-ground in its actions. Despite not supporting the antagonist view of North Korea by the West, India nevertheless attempted to address the concerns of the Western powers by condemning the pre-emptive attack by North Korea in the Korean War. Further, in the case of the Korean Peninsula, India's objections remained only with reference to the disposition of the Americans to view the Korean question as a wider war against the Communists in defence of Western interests.

Moreover, South Korea's then President, Syngman Rhee, viewed India's neutral role as being that of a Communist sympathiser, and was vehemently opposed to the Indian participation in the negotiations. South Korean sentiments were so hostile that President Rhee subsequently refused to let the Custodian Force—India (CFI)—to land on the South Korean territory, which later led the United Nations Command to airlift the Indian troops to Inchon. More troops were airlifted later by the American troops into the demilitarized zone.

As the lead in the Repatriation Commission, India also saw the Commander of the Commission, General S.M. Thimayya, overseeing the toughest prisoners of war exchange. By the end of the ordeal, whether it was General Thimayya or Jawaharlal Nehru, they did end the engagement with general dissatisfaction over the conduct of the stakeholders in the Korean Peninsula as they were censured from all sides for their presumed cordiality with other.[4]

Limited Indian Aims in North Korea

While Indian foreign policy after the 1962 war with China underwent major revisions focusing on *realpolitik* and emphasising a foreign policy based on national interests, India maintained diplomatic contact with North Korea officially 1973 onwards. Obvious reasons include membership in the Non-Aligned Movement, and a shared consensus on the need for cooperation among developing countries, popularly known as the South-South cooperation. However, China's nuclear test in October 1964 and the subsequent cooperation between Pakistan and China on nuclear matters raised issues of proliferation in India's security calculations. The exposed nuclear and missile proliferation links between North Korea and Pakistan in the 1990s did not disrupt India's relationship with North Korea, and the period remains decade of renewed cooperation with North Korea. For instance, India signed the agreement on scientific cooperation in 1994, and signed 'Protocol on Cooperation' between the foreign affairs departments of both the countries.[5]

Nonetheless, India's relationship with North Korea became limited in its aims. The extent of the Pakistani connection with the North Korean nuclear programme soon became clear to Indian policy-makers.[6] In the 1990s and early 2000s, Indian intelligence sources became more aware of the extent of nuclear and missile deals between the two countries. The opening of a dialogue with North Korea was intended to expose the proliferations links of Pakistan. For instance, in a question in the Lok Sabha to the Minister of State, Ministry of External Affairs (MEA), V.K. Singh, on the role of India in the Korean question, Singh answered that North Korea's 'proliferation links directly impacts India's national security', and 'any solution to the Korean Peninsula must take into account and address the concerns about the proliferation linkages of DPRK's nuclear and missile programmes'.[7] Thus, India believes that since North Korea was a signatory to the Non-Proliferation Treaty (NPT), it should be held responsible, and has condemned the nuclear tests of North Korea due to its concerns on its proliferation activities.[8]

The security challenge seems to be significant because Pakistan's proliferation linkages with North Korea started in the 1980s, and continued with high level cooperation from the Pakistani establishment, and with tacit approval from China.[9] For instance, the range of Pakistani assistance is varied. Pakistan's relationship with North Korea was laid by Zulfikar Ali Bhutto's visit in 1976. He convinced the US to engage North Korean officials as part of the Korean peace process. This echoed the Chinese position on the matter, and Pakistan convinced the US by including more stakeholders such as Japan, and thereby in exchange, elevated Pakistan's relationship with North Korea.[10] Obviously, the actual nuclear and missile part of the relationship started in the early 1990s, when the A.Q. Khan Research Laboratories (KRL) began its Ghauri missile programme with North Korean assistance. There might have also been some cooperation between the two countries on uranium melting information in the late 1980s.

A.Q. Khan also travelled to North Korea in the 1990s, where he was attempting to convert the No Dong missile into Ghauri missile.

Later, Pakistan's economic woes led it to expand its cooperation with North Korea and, around 1997, might have started nuclear transfers—such as centrifuge and enrichment designs—to North Korea. In the early 2000s, American satellites captured missile components were being loaded in Pyongyang into a Pakistani cargo plane. In addition, after China joined the NPT in 1992, it has been reticent to engage in direct nuclear transfers to Pakistan in its nuclear programme. Thus, in Indian view, China tacitly approves the Pakistani-North Korea relationship.

The complexity of decades-long Pakistan-North Korea nuclear and missile connection has made India more than determined to maintain its diplomatic contact with the North Korean leadership. Thus, the aims of India towards North Korea are limited to its proliferation activities, and India hopes to bring North Korea into a more international set-up in its strategic calculations. In this scenario, India hopes that North Korea's international socialisation might end its preference for underground dealings in sensitive technologies. As has been the case with other countries, socialisation also includes more regulations and control systems being in operation, and the export of nuclear and missile technologies being verified by international agencies. Thus, India's long-term policy planning wants to leverage North Korea's desire for more international cooperation to wean it away from the Pakistan-China axis. North Korea's thorny partnership with China[11] fuels its policy to engage with the outside world, which facilitates India's assumptions.

Trump, India and North Korea: Strategic Calculations

The policies of US President Donald Trump towards North Korea have had a transformational effect on the Peninsula. The effect these have had on India shows how far North Korea has been on India's strategic calculations. When President Donald Trump announced his policy to engage North Korea, and the subsequent summit held between him and Kim Jong-Un in Singapore, India stated that it

> welcomes the United States-DPRK Summit held in Singapore. This is a positive development. India has always supported all efforts to bring about peace and stability in the Korean Peninsula through dialogue and diplomacy. We hope that the outcomes of the U.S.-DPRK Summit will be implemented, thus paving the way for lasting peace and stability in the Korean Peninsula.[12]

When the two Koreas signed a joint statement on ending hostilities and engage in denuclearisation in the Peninsula, India also welcomed this development. The Ministry of External Affairs (MEA) said in a statement,

> India welcomes the just concluded inter-Korean Summit meeting held in Pyongyang on September 18–20, 2018. India has been constantly supportive of all such efforts to bring about peace and stability in the Korean Peninsula through dialogue and diplomacy.[13]

Immediately after the summit, India sent the Minister of State of External Affairs, V.K. Singh to North Korea to capitalise on the relationship. The meeting was kept secret until the North Korean agencies released the news of the visit, including pictures. The visit was preceded by India selecting a new Ambassador, Atul Gotsurve, one of first Indian Foreign Service (IFS) officers to be appointed to Pyongyang. Where diplomatic access to the top leadership is extremely limited, both Gotsurve and V.K. Singh met many of the top leadership officials in North Korea. These hard fought gains are the only leverage that India has with Pyongyang to convince the leadership not to follow any policies in the future that could be detrimental to India's interests.

India's hope is that through the denuclearisation process and other measures, such as security guarantees from the US, North Korea would be brought into the larger export control mechanism, and probably, in the vetting process, the proliferation links could be investigated to the satisfaction of India. Probably, India believes that these could discredit Pakistan's proliferation record in a more substantial manner, and further impinge on its membership to nuclear regimes. China is very much in favour of bringing Pakistan into the nuclear regimes (such as Nuclear Suppliers Group (NSG)) and, in Indian view, its past record and lack of domestic mechanism regarding the control of illegal activities of high-level officials in the Pakistan government—and sometimes the complicity of the Pakistani government itself—makes one suspect that it would not engage in such activities in a more brazen manner. The Indian lack of trust in Pakistani commitments to non-proliferation norms has made it very wary of Pakistan's entry being touted as a purely energy-based need to acquire nuclear power capability.

Thus, even in the trilateral meeting between the US, India, and Japan, the Indian foreign minister Sushma Swaraj made an appeal that the proliferation linkages 'must be exposed and those accountable must be held responsible'.[14] When V.K. Singh visited North Korea, he also expressed concerns about proliferation in particular in India's neighbourhood, indirectly pointing fingers at Pakistan. On the other hand, North Korea emphasised that it would not allow any actions that would be of concern to Indian security.[15] This means that India would have to negotiate to convince North Korea to reconsider any dealings in the future that would have an adverse impact on India. These security concerns aside, and true to his historic involvement with the region, India has supported the peace process in the Peninsula as have many other countries.

Despite grave concerns regarding the future of the changing nuclear environment in the Indian neighbourhood, and despite also the emboldened Pakistani establishment's propensity to pursue a more vigorous nuclear weapons development programme (aided no doubt by the lack of civilian control on its nuclear weapons policy), India has nevertheless remained steadfast in maintaining its diplomatic contact with North Korea. When the Trump administration was attempting to cut off all contact with North Korea—especially pressurising India to cut off diplomatic ties—India had to refuse based on these calculations. In her talks with the then US Secretary of State Rex Tillerson, India's Foreign Minister, Sushma Swaraj, categorically dismissed any move on India's part to close down its embassy in North Korea. She maintained that 'embassies of some of ... friendly countries should remain there so that some channels of communications remain open.'[16] India had already complied with UN sanctions against Pyongyang under US pressure in 2017 on all exports except humanitarian and medical supplies, and issued an affidavit regarding this matter. Even with the international sanctions, in 2017–2018, around US$ 16 million worth of refined petroleum products was exported to North Korea.

In short, India's strategic calculations seem to be that if President Trump's negotiations with North Korea become successful and an agreement is achieved, then both aid and international investment could transform its economy. The reliance of North Korea on China's refined goods would reduce as the world markets would be open to them. The illegal and underground dealings would not be needed as much in order to procure hard cash, and the economy would stabilise slowly. In this regard, India's continuous trade with North Korea means that it has an available source of traders who understand the market needs of North Korea, and enable it to achieve economic and trade relations with India. Since India has shown its credentials in resisting US pressure on North Korea on closing diplomatic contact, and as a part of its diplomacy in general, India has to showcase that North Korea has a reliable partner in times of crises.

India hopes to capitalise on this goodwill that has been created in its relationship with North Korea in the belief that a more engaged North Korea does not have to be in a dependent relationship with China. It is generally known that North Korea has never been comfortable with its dependence on China and, at times, even resents its relationship. One of the reasons for its drive to negotiate with the US bilaterally is also to underscore its independence from other stakeholders in the region, including China and Japan.

India in a Quagmire?

Thus, the pressing issue has been to implement both India's limited aims in North Korea as well as its strategic calculations in the uncertain political environment present in the peace process. Not only would the interactions of the two Koreas be paramount but also the interests of other stakeholders—such as China, the US, Russia, and Japan—would play a far greater role than India. Improving relations with both the Koreas as well as pursuing strategic objectives without upsetting the delicate balance seems to be India's policy. The political will to play a disruptive role in the peace process seems to be very low. In the 1950s, even though India operated from the perspective of a non-aligned state, its involvement though worthy was considered disruptive. But that is not the case now.

Nevertheless, Prime Minister Modi has made statements that indicate India's priorities in the peace process. For instance, he stated that India is a 'stakeholder' in the peace process when South Korean President Moon Jae-in visited India in July 2018. This is a term which has been reserved mostly for the four players that are considered crucial for reaching a settlement: the US, China, Russia, and Japan. Prime Minister Modi reiterated that 'proliferation linkages between North-East Asia and South Asia are a matter of concern to India. Therefore, India is also a stakeholder in the peace process. We will do our bit to ensure peace'.[17] As mentioned above, India has been pressing for a probe into North Korea's nuclear proliferation linkages with Pakistan, and demanded that those responsible for them should be held accountable.

However, being a stakeholder means that the particular country's interests are taken into consideration or seen as an influence on the process. While it is acknowledged that India has limited influence in the Korean Peninsula, it has been the second or third largest trading partner of North Korea for decades, and has opened up opportunities in the region. The high-level visits suggest that at least there have been some conclusions reached by the North Korean leadership that a relationship with India would serve its national interests. Or alternatively, in the absence of other major countries that are democratic and friendly to the regime, India would give some legitimacy to the North Korean leadership.

However, in India's concerns, the biggest impediment seems to be the ever-present Pakistan's relationship with North Korea. It cannot be forgotten that even though it was not acceptable by international norms, Pakistan did assist North Korea in its nuclear endeavours. From North Korean records, it is clear that its desire for a nuclear weapons programme has been a long term dream, and assistance from Pakistan has been as crucial as has been assistance from China. Such historic ties cannot be changed even though the fortunes of North Korea are being transformed. In fact, the easing of tensions would enable North Korea to deepen its interactions with Pakistan even though the latter would like to prevent any investigations in the nuclear network. If North Korea agrees to expose some of Pakistan's nuclear proliferation activities, it would severely impact its credentials on being a responsible nuclear power. What India hopes is that its centrality to the many of the regimes—such as Indo-Pacific strategy or an inclusive Asian architecture—has meant that it has some limited sway over the future of Asia. Due to the desire of both South Korea and Japan to expand its market access to India to reduce their dependence on China, India's deepening strategic partnerships with these countries might subsequently increase the role that India can play in the security of East Asia.

With the Pakistan's NSG membership looming, India would not like to see its inclusion without any investigation into the A.Q. Khan network, especially after he was given some protection against international investigation. For instance, a new report of a letter written by a North Korean official, Jeon ByungHo, provided by Dr. Khan to a scholar named Simon Henderson, was made public in a news article. According to news reports, the letter exposes Pakistan's dealings in which North Korea offered a bribe of three million dollars in exchange for documents and nuclear components.[18] This news report offered India the necessary ammunition to reiterate its long-held conclusion that Pakistan's nuclear activities with North Korea has been carried out with the knowledge of Pakistani government.[19] It is clear that India hopes to use its growing relationship with North Korea to curtail and checkmate Pakistan's credentials as a responsible nuclear power.

Nevertheless, Pakistan's ambition to enter the NSG to counter perceived Indian aggression as well as support from China ensures that India will have to confront Pakistan's involvement in various nuclear regimes. India's policy of bringing up proliferation risks whenever the North Korean denuclearisation talks are being discussed are some of the ways in which the concerns are highlighted regularly. Since the security relationship between North Korea and Pakistan has never been diluted, this becomes the most significant foreign policy objective of India in the Korean Peninsula.

Thus, the Korean peace process offers a unique opportunity for India to push for an international investigation into the proliferation links in Pakistan, and expose A.Q. Khan network in a concrete way. However, how exactly India will influence or push countries in this direction remains to be seen, and depends on the tolerance of other stakeholders to involve India in the peace process. Obviously, India would also have to maintain neutrality in the actual settlement so as to not upset the two Koreas, especially since India's engagement with South Korea seems to be growing steadily. Nor can it afford to create an impression that its close partnership with the US will prevent it from pursuing a neutral approach to the peace process.

Prospects for India-North Korea Strategic Partnership

India's North Korea relationship in the immediate future seems to be working on efforts to veer it away from the Pakistan-China orbit. Thus, India has been patient in accepting that the relative gains would be lesser even if the risks it takes to maintain its diplomatic contact with North Korea would be more. The risks would imply any negative impact of resisting US pressure on North Korea on the US-India bilateral relationship. Relative gains would mean that India might not be successful in convincing the North Korean regime to expose, or agree to an investigation on proliferation links, or could only convince North Korea to refrain from any more proliferation activities in the future.

These risks might be high and the gains limited, but the continued high-level contact between India and North Korea shows that India has agreed to this. In Indian strategy, even the relative gains, however small, are worth the high risks to its diplomacy. This shows the importance of the partnership with North Korea. Given this importance, it is highly likely that India might pursue a strategic partnership with North Korea if the conflict in the Korean Peninsula continues to reduce. If strategic partnership with South Korea continues to deepen because of the recent thaw in South Korea-China relations because of THAAD deployment and the dependence of Chinese trade on the South Korean economy, then India might request that its interests in the Peninsula could be addressed as well.

Whether the denuclearisation process in the Korean Peninsula should essentially contain the investigation and dismantling of proliferation networks and links or whether it could be a choice between the two remains of utmost importance. Also, how far North Korea would be willing to show its commitment to denuclearisation would also become a variable in deciding this process. Thus, India's support in encouraging North Korea to denuclearise would serve the India-South Korea strategic partnership and, at the same time, India's acknowledgement that there are legitimate North Korean interests in seeking security guarantees with the US would also enable it to present its views to the North Korean regime.

Thus, strategic partnership with North Korea would essentially contain two choices for Indian foreign policy makers. One approach, which might be of greater difficulty, would be to convince North Korea for a UN investigation into proliferation links. India would then have to highlight this proliferation investigation as part of the condition for denuclearisation and NPT norms. This would not be easy to achieve due to resistance not only from the North Korean regime but also from China, which is crucial to any settlement on the Korean Peninsula. Secondly, the less troublesome approach is to dismantle proliferation and implement an export control mechanism on North Korea that might prevent any future dealing, in particular with Pakistan. This might not help India in its opposition to Pakistan's NSG membership or in exposing its proliferation networks, but it might prevent future such associations.

Both these choices might provide a guarantee that there are repercussions to the touting of proliferation norms and principles. However, the extent to which India can influence these choices remains to be seen. Already such efforts are seen as part of India's strategy to dismantle Pakistan's nuclear weapons programme. In fact, the US-India partnership is particularly seen as antithetical to Pakistan's strategic weapons capabilities.[20] Thus, any efforts of reining in Pakistan's proliferation activities could be seen as an effort to weaken its security, and supporting India.[21]

Therefore, India's North Korean relationship faces complex challenges, given the objectives India wants to achieve in the Peninsula. While historically India's concerns were limited to reining in the local conflict to its logical conclusion and restricting the spill-over effects of superpower politics, the current scenario seems to have altered in one significant aspect. Unlike China, India has no interest in deciding the terms of the peace settlement or reunification between the two Koreas. It does, however, want to influence the denuclearisation process. Even within the denuclearisation process, India only wants the proliferation links to be acknowledged or investigated, depending on its capability to convince the stakeholders. Such limited aims also mean that, on the one hand, it does not create intense impact on North Korean interests; on the other hand, it is also convenient to dilute such demands as they are not considered tantamount to the settlement process.

Notes

1. Paul M. Edwards, *United Nations Participants in the Korean War: The Contributions of 45 Member Countries,* McFarland and Company Inc Publishers, North Carolina, 2013, pp. 136–138.
2. Robert Barnes, 'Between the Blocs: India, the United Nations, and Ending the Korean War', *The Journal of Korean Studies*, 18 (2): 263–286, 2013. See also, Sandeep Bhardwaj, 'India and the Korean War: Damned are the

Peacemakers', *Revisiting India*, February 3, 2014 at https://revisitingindia.com/2014/02/03/india-and-the-korean-war-damned-are-the-peacemakers/, accessed on July 12, 2016.

3. 'Resolution 84, Complaint of Aggression upon the Republic of Korea', UNSCR at http://unscr.com/en/resolutions/84, accessed on February 2, 2019.
4. 'Foreign Relations of the United States, 1952–1954, Korea, Volume XV, Part 2', Memorandum by the Secretary of State to the President, October 21, 1953 at https://history.state.gov/historicaldocuments/frus1952-54v15p2/d774, accessed on December 23, 2018. Also See 'The Deputy Representative for the Korean Political Conference (Young) to the Department of State', Foreign Relations of the US, 1952–1954, Korea, Volume XV, Part 2, January 15, 1954 at https://history.state.gov/historicaldocuments/frus1952-54v15p2/d853, accessed on December 23, 2018, Swapna Kona Nayudu, 'The Peacekeepers', *Motherland*, December 8, 2014 at http://www.motherlandmagazine.com/the-peacekeepers/, accessed on November 12, 2018.
5. 'India-DPR Korea Relations, Ministry of External Affairs, Foreign Relations', October 2017 at https://www.mea.gov.in/Portal/ForeignRelation/2_DPR_Korea_October_2017.pdf, accessed on February 25, 2018.
6. Suzanne Goldenberg, 'Pakistan Helped North Korea Make Bomb', *The Guardian*, October 19, 2002 at https://www.theguardian.com/world/2002/oct/19/pakistan.northkorea, accessed on December 12, 2018.
7. 'Question No. 889 Ties With North Korea', February 7, 2018, Lok Sabha at https://www.mea.gov.in/lok-sabha.htm?dtl/29427/QUESTION+NO889+TIES+WITH+NORTH+KOREA, accessed on December 12, 2018.
8. 'Press Statement on Nuclear Test Conducted by DPRK', September 3, 2017 at https://mea.gov.in/press-releases.htm?dtl/28911/Press_Statement_on_Nuclear_Test_conducted_by_DPRK, accessed on January 12, 2019.
9. Adrian Levy and Catherine Scott-Clark, *Deception: Pakistan, the United States and the Secret Trade in Nuclear Weapons*, Walker and Company, New York, 2007.
10. Samuel Ramani, 'The Pakistan-North Korea Consensus', *The Japan Times*, September 5, 2016 at https://www.japantimes.co.jp/opinion/2016/09/05/commentary/world-commentary/pakistan-n-korea-nexus/, accessed on October 25, 2018.
11. For the extent of differences between the two countries, see Andrew Scobell, *China and North Korea: From Comrades-in-Arms To Allies at Arm's Length*, Strategic Studies Institute, 2014 at http://ssi.armywarcollege.edu/pdffiles/pub373.pdf, accessed on December 18, 2018.
12. 'India Welcomes the US- DPRK Summit', MEA at https://www.mea.gov.in/press-releases.htm?dtl/29973/India_Welcomes_the_US_DPRK_Summit, accessed on January 12, 2019.

13. 'India Welcomes the Inter-Korean Summit Meeting Pyongyang', MEA, September 20, 2018 at https://www.mea.gov.in/press-releases.htm?dtl/30417/Indias_response_to_InterKorean_Summit_meeting_in_Pyongyang, accessed on February 13, 2019.
14. 'India Seeks Probe into Nuclear Proliferation Links Between Pakistan, North Korea', *The Economic Times*, July 12, 2018 at https://economictimes.indiatimes.com/news/defence/india-seeks-probe-into-nuclear-proliferation-links-between-pakistan-north-korea/articleshow/60741819.cms, accessed on November 17, 2018.
15. 'North Korea Pledges Not To Create Security Concerns for India', *The Economic Times*, May 17, 2018 at https://economictimes.indiatimes.com/news/defence/north-korea-pledges-not-to-create-security-concerns-for-india/articleshow/64200202.cms, accessed on December 23, 2018.
16. 'Transcript of Question and Answer Session During Media Interaction by External Affairs Minister and US Secretary of State', MEA, October 25, 2017 at https://mea.gov.in/media-briefings.htm?dtl/29051/Transcript_of_Question_amp_Answer_Session_during_Media_Interation by External_Affairs_Minister_and_US_Secretary_of_State_October_25_2017, accessed on October 17, 2018.
17. Suhasini Haider, 'India a Stakeholder in Korean Peace', *The Hindu*, July 11, 2018 at https://www.thehindu.com/todays-paper/tp-national/india-a-stakeholder-in-korean-peace/article24384085.ece, accessed on November 12, 2018.
18. David E. Sanger, 'Pakistani Army Linked in Letter to Nuclear Sale', *The New York Times*, July 7, 2011 at https://www.nytimes.com/2011/07/08/world/asia/08khan.html, accessed on November 13, 2018.
19. Dipanjan Roy Chaudhury, 'In NSG Fight, India to Raise Pakistan Links with North Korea', *The Economic Times*, July 11, 2018 at https://economictimes.indiatimes.com/news/defence/in-nsg-fight-india-to-raise-pakistan-links-with-north-korea/articleshow/54301690.cms, accessed on November 18, 2018.
20. Munir Akram, 'A Strategic Challenge', *Dawn*, April 29, 2018 at https://www.dawn.com/news/1404556, accessed on November 1, 2018.
21. Drazen Jorgic, 'U.S. Sanctions Pakistani Companies Over Nuclear Trade', Reuters, March 26, 2018 at https://www.reuters.com/article/us-pakistan-usa-sanctions/u-s-sanctions-pakistani-companies-over-nuclear-trade-idUSKBN1H20IO, accessed on December 2, 2018.

PART IV
Beyond the Singapore Summit

15. Singapore to Hanoi: Southeast Asia and the Korean Peninsula

Anushree Chakraborty

Southeast Asia's determination to be a norm entrepreneur not only within its region but also in relation to its external partners is conspicuous.[1] It is no surprise that both the historic meetings in 2018 and 2019 between Chairman Kim Jong-un and President Donald Trump's took place in Singapore and Hanoi. *Singapore served as the ASEAN* Chair in 2018, *and its diplomatic balancing act among the major powers* is *well acknowledged. Moreover, Singapore* has *maintain*ed *diplomatic relations with North Korea since 1975.* As Former US Ambassador to Singapore, David Adelman *noted,* Singapore was ideal because it has been 'an honest broker between East and West.'[2] Earlier, in 2015, Singapore hosted another unprecedented summit between two rival countries, Chinese President Xi Jinping and Taiwan's then-President Ma Ying-jeou—the first such meeting since the founding of the People's Republic of China in 1949. For the second summit, Hanoi was preferred which represents one of the fastest growing economies in Asia following their emergence from the ravages of the War with the US.

Southeast Asia has sought relations with North and South Korea, despite the complexity of their relationship among themselves and with the major powers. Can Southeast Asia play a role in defusing tension in Korean Peninsula? The fact that Singapore spent US$ 20 million[3] for hosting the Trump-Kim summit in June 2018 suggests how important Singapore considered its role as a venue. Although Singapore is not the mediator, it nevertheless realises the reputational cost attached to it, both for itself as well as for the region. Both

President Trump and Chairman Kim chose Singapore as a neutral venue. Moreover, Singapore did have a healthy trade relations with North Korea before the United Nations Secuirty Council (UNSC) sanctions came into effect. The city state has also nurtured diplomatic ties with the hermit kingdom.

Southeast Asia and the Two Koreas

Geographically, the Korean Peninsula is in the Southeast Asian backyard. Their common regional heritage in the past continued the flow of interaction and exchanges between Southeast Asian countries on the one hand, and Japan, the Koreas and China on the other. Thus, the ongoing interaction between Southeast Asian countries and the two Koreas are nothing new. The Cold War divided the Koreas in the Peninsula and they became two nations competing with each other. During this period, Southeast Asia's engagement with the Korean Peninsula suffered. Association of Southeast Asian Nations (ASEAN) as a regional organisation is changing East Asian dynamics and building a new foundation for engagement, including bringing the Koreas into their congregation. This chapter examines the nature and profile of Southeast Asia's engagement with the North Korea and South Korea. It analyses the nuclear crisis arising from North Korea, and evaluates what role Southeast Asia has played hitherto, and the potential thereafter.

Southeast Asian countries and the two Koreas have had diplomatic relations since their independence in the 1940s and 1950s. Beyond Singapore, North Korea has economic engagements in Southeast Asia. Geographical proximity plays an important role in carrying out commercial interests with most Southeast Asian countries. The UNSC Sanctions Committee Report suggests that North Korea had shipped coal to several ports, including in Russia, China, South Korea, Malaysia, and Vietnam. North Korea has strong arms export linkages with some Southeast Asian states as well as the rest of the world. Its arms export is an important source of income, including small arms, training and consulting, and praetorian guard services. In 1998, the North Koreans admitted that it exported missiles to Iran, Syria, Iraq, Libya, Nigeria, Pakistan, and Egypt. Malaysia plays a crucial part of arms trading with North Korea.[4] In Southeast Asia, Pyongyang has been involved in assisting Myanmar on missile technology. Myanmar reportedly received ballistic missile systems from North Korea along with conventional weapons, including multiple rocket launchers and surface-to-air missiles.

North Koreans are often found to be involved in illicit activities, such as smuggling, drug trafficking, and counterfeiting, thereby another possibility for financing the trade gap. Drug trade, North Korean counterfeit currency, and several such unlawful activities are operational in Southeast Asian countries.[5] For example, Singapore has reportedly played a key role in allowing North Koreans access to illicit financial service offerings; Singapore-based Chinpo Shipping was fined in 2016 for facilitating weapons shipments in violation of UN sanctions.[6] In 2015, North Korea's then-Foreign Minister, Ri Su-yong, visited Bangkok and asked Thailand to invest in his country.[7] Pyongyang operates restaurants in Thailand, Malaysia, Laos, Cambodia, Nepal, and across China as well as in the Middle East and Africa. Thailand exports commodities to Pyongyang via China, therefore escaping detection. Malaysia has an air route and, until recently, had visa-free travel with Pyongyang to attract more tourists from the country. However, Malaysia and North Korea were embroiled in a diplomatic crisis over the investigation of Kim Jong-nam, the half brother of North Korean leader Kim Jong-un, who was killed at Kuala Lumpur International Airport in February 2017. Another country which has strong connections with North Korea is Cambodia—North Koreans funded the museum and helped restoring near Angkor Wat in Cambodia.

Southeast Asian countries often articulates their approach towards the Korean Peninsula related developments through ASEAN. At present, the ASEAN regional organisation offers itself as a platform for dialogue for the individual Southeast Asian and Northeast Asian countries, wherein the relation with South Korea is deeper and more structured, while North Korea remains relatively reclusive. Pyongyang carries out its exchanges with individual ASEAN members within the ambit of informal and unofficial interactions. In fact, ASEAN members are among the restricted few countries with which North Korea maintains diplomatic relations. Among the ASEAN members, Indonesia, Vietnam, Laos, Cambodia, and Malaysia have embassies in Pyongyang.

Southeast Asia's vision of the Korean Peninsula was blurred with the image of it being a conflict zone, overshadowed by nuclear proliferation and the strategic rivalry of Cold War era. As a result, for Southeast Asian regional organisation like ASEAN, built with the aim of forging a community of ten nation states with greater linkages and prosperity, the Korean Peninsula provided limited attraction. The conflict in the Korean Peninsula reflects of the relics of Cold War, which ASEAN members have deliberately tried to leave behind. With the ASEAN plus three framework, and the ASEAN Regional Forum (ARF) formed during the 1990s for greater economic and security integration, ASEAN as a central regional grouping was merely interested in bringing the two Koreas into its circle for broader regional influence. Moreover, South Korea, one of the four Asian tigers, developed into advanced and high-income industrialised economy, specialising in manufacturing consumer electronics and information technology. Southeast Asia clearly wanted to take advantage of South Korea's success through greater linkages. As the ASEAN plus three (involving ten ASEAN members plus Japan, China, and South Korea) format embarked on playing a leading role in Southeast Asia's prosperity, a common destiny with the Northeast Asia, both economically or strategically, became a *sine qua non.*

The Northeast Asian strategic landmass is witnessing dramatic changes with the rise of China and its challenges to US global hegemony is shaping the broader East Asia. On the other hand, the durability of President Trump's commitment towards stability in Asia is under serious doubt. The two pillars of Asian security are the US and China. The increasing aggressive posturing among these two super powers are shrinking the strategic space for the small and medium sized countries in Southeast Asia, thereby calling for a greater need for ASEAN to remain engaged in regional issues including the Korean Peninsula.

ASEAN's Political Engagement with the Two Koreas

The theory of international relations is predominantly focused on the power play among major powers and their balancing act. It is oblivious to the attempt of small countries to acquire and exploit power.[8] ASEAN is a prime example in the post-Cold War era of an organisation trying to build normative values and an institutional architecture for regional cooperation. ASEAN has played a significant role in norm diffusion while intervening among the great powers in Asia.[9] It's norms of non-interference, respect for sovereignty, consensus-building, and non-confrontation provides assurance for the smaller as well as major powers in maintaining the status quo. At the political level, ASEAN has refrained from attributing any status of Dialogue Partner, Sectoral Dialogue Partner, and Development Partner to North Korea. Nonetheless, they hold summit and ministerial conferences on the occasion of bilateral visits and multilateral meetings. North Korea has persistently sent high level delegations to attend ASEAN meetings. It maintains embassies in all ASEAN countries except for the Philippines and Brunei. Pyongyang maintains visa-free travel and several financial linkages with Southeast Asian countries. The so-called hermit kingdom is, in fact, not so isolated in Southeast Asia since it carries out both illicit and legitimate trade in addition to maintaining closer people to people contact. For example, King Sihanouk of the Royal Government of Cambodia has had a close relationship with North Korea over the decades, to the extent that his personal body guards have been North Koreans.[10] This is the reason why former Secretary of State, Rex Tillerson, prioritised North Korea in his first meeting with the ten ASEAN foreign ministers in Washington in 2017.[11] The US realises the depth of Southeast Asia-North Korea relations, and the fact that UN sanctions or diplomatic pressure would not be effective until North Korea continues to have close ties with China and Southeast Asian countries.

As far as South Korea is concerned, ASEAN has established deeper institutional linkages. ASEAN first established the Sectoral Dialogue Partnership with South Korea in November 1989. Thereafter, there was no looking behind since, after according full Dialogue Partner status at the 24th ASEAN Ministerial Meeting in 1991 in Kuala Lumpur, within thirteen years ASEAN and South Korea concluded a Joint Declaration at the ASEAN-South Korea Summit in 2004 in Vientiane, which became the basis of their future collaboration. ASEAN subsequently accelerated its ties, realising Seoul's economic potential by establishing the Korea Centre in 2009, and cemented them further by elevating the comprehensive cooperation to a strategic partnership in the very next year. South Korea received a status similar to that of China and Japan in accordance with the regularisation of the ASEAN plus three (China, Japan, Korea) Summit following the 2nd ASEAN plus three Summit in 1998. The convergence between South Korea and ASEAN became explicit given their dialogue covering all-encompassing issues related to politics, security, economy, society, and culture, in addition to the latest developments in in the Korean Peninsula.[12]

Moreover, South Korea meets regularly with ASEAN at the ASEAN Regional Forum and East Asia Summit which provides adequate space for security and geopolitical interaction. South Korea was, in fact, among the early signatories outside ASEAN to accede to ASEAN's Treaty of Amity and Cooperation (TAC) in November 2004 in Vietnam. After Seoul, eighteen countries, including the European Union, joined TAC. In 2009, South Korea came up with the proposal named the 'New Asia Initiative' in Jakarta. This was the former President Lee Myung-bak's pet project wherein he wanted to align with countries of Australia, Indonesia, Japan, China, and India to represent the interest of Asian nations in the international arena. Although the initiative failed to gather momentum, it nevertheless implied a shift of South Korea's focus from Northeast Asia to the entire Asian region.

There are several landmark agreements under ASEAN tutelage which helped in strengthening ASEAN and South Korea relations.

The ASEAN Integrated Initiative (2000), the Joint Declaration on Comprehensive Cooperation Partnership (2004), and the Korea-ASEAN Action Plan (2005) are some of these platforms built to further the cause. As compared to this, ASEAN's engagement with North Korea is dismal. In fact, the ASEAN website does not display any engagement between ASEAN and North Korea in any sector, except for Joint Statements issued by member states condemning the nuclear tests carried out by Pyongyang. Considering that Southeast Asia is a nuclear weapons free zone, ASEAN's hard-line response to North Korea's nuclear pursuit seems pertinent. Therefore, the only official lens through which ASEAN looks at North Korea is through nuclear proliferation.

ASEAN and South Korea are fully aware of the vacuum existing in East Asia due to the lack of regional institutional mechanisms. They are, therefore, addressing this inadequacy by forming interactive formats such as the East Asia Study Group (EASG), the East Asia Vision Group (EAVG), and the Korea-ASEAN Centre with the aim of building an East Asian Community. Notably, people-to-people interaction between ASEAN and the Korean Peninsula—and particularly with South Korea—is profound; in fact, it is deeper than political links. For example, the 'Korean Wave' travelling from South Korea to Southeast Asia in the name of Hallyu, is one talking point. K-pop, movies, and cuisine depicts South Korea's visible presence in Southeast Asia.

Regional Security Challenges and Cooperation

In a letter to the ASEAN Secretary General on March 23, 2017, North Korean Foreign Minister Ri Yong-ho expressed his 'expectations that ASEAN which attaches great importance to the regional peace and stability will make an issue of the US-South Korean joint military exercises at ASEAN conferences'. He added that ASEAN should take a 'fair position and play an active role in safeguarding the peace and safety of Korean Peninsula'.[13] This letter highlights the fact that ASEAN has earned the reputation of an impartial regional player, keen to work towards the peace and prosperity of the region. North Korea's dependence on China is compulsion, while ties with the ASEAN are spontaneous. Surin Pitsuwan, the former Secretary General of ASEAN, expressed how he managed to bring North Korea into the ASEAN Regional Forum (ARF) membership, while applauding ASEAN as the only multilateral institution having North Korea as a member.[14]

In the Korean Peninsula, the Koreas' divergent alignment complicates their relationship. South Korea's alliance with the US comes into conflict with its relations with North Korea, since Pyongyang is a communist country, having close ties with its communist neighbour China. North Korea is ruled with an iron fist under the hereditary succession of a single family of the Kim clan. On the other hand, South Korea transformed itself into one of the fastest growing economies in Asia, known for its shipbuilding and high-tech products around the world. As Andreas Meyndt noted, 'the differences between the two countries in almost all respects could hardly be any greater.'[15] In this conflicting environment, Southeast Asia's strategic importance to South Korea is not trivial. A point of reference is Seoul's controversial deployment of an American missile shield system which led to China's boycott of South Korean companies and pop stars, and banning their tour packages to South Korea in protest. In turn, South Korea had to seek closer integration with Southeast Asia in the neighbourhood, benefitting the latter. South Korean President, Moon Jae-in, once commented that ASEAN is 'as important' as the United States and other neighbours.[16]

At the institutional level, both North and the South Korea are members of the ASEAN Regional Forum (ARF). Although ARF produced limited success, nevertheless it is presently the sole platform available primarily for the Asian countries (since there are non-Asian members as well) to talk on security, and cooperate on non-traditional security challenges. The post-Cold War period witnessed the rise of transnational challenges and the subsequent realization of the need for a multilateral set up to address them. Thus, under the ambit of ARF, ASEAN acted remarkably by bringing in both the Koreas (although ideologically divergent) to the same podium, and encourage a dialogue on broader security issues. ASEAN's norm entrepreneurship is striking since, for the first time, ARF gave space for frank dialogue and consensus-based decision making to incompatible countries (North and South Korea; the US and Russia) on the same table, and helped build norm-diffusion of security under a common destiny. Although once operative, the Six-Party Talks never mentioned ARF notwithstanding the fact that all members of the Talk were members of ARF. Nonetheless, ARF played a significant role in confidence building measures, and made modest gains in building the sense of a strategic community.

The East Asia Summit, another initiative of ASEAN, is based on the premise of the centrality of ASEAN.[17] The inclusion of South Korea in this exclusive group highlights Southeast Asia's eagerness to strategically integrate with the Korean Peninsula. Therefore, there is noticeable asymmetry in ASEAN's engagement with the two Koreas. South Korea is closely tied with the ASEAN because of its economic might, while North Korea is still isolated and largely informal in its dealings.

Southeast Asia's Economic Engagement

In the 1970s, the former CIA Director, Robert Gates, described North Korea as a 'black hole' and the 'toughest intelligence target in the world'.[18] Economic data is often cited as a state secret, making it impossible to get a real picture of North Korea.[19] The overwhelming part of North Korea trade is dominated by China; but the non-China part of its trade has Southeast Asian footprint. Notably, North Korea's policy of *Juche* turned them into a hermit country, maintaining complete isolation from the rest of the world. China is, by far, North Korea's main trade partner. Barter transactions and aid to North Korea fuels the existing Chinese economic preponderance. Moreover, China finances more than half of the North Korean deficit. Following China, North Korea's trade partners are South Korea, Russia, Germany, and Southeast Asian countries.[20]

Table 1: North Korea's Trade with ASEAN Countries (unit: US$ million)

ASEAN Partners	North Korea's Average Export to ASEAN		North Korea's Average Import from ASEAN	
	2009-12	2013-16	2009-12	2013-16
Brunei Darussalam	4.15	0.55	0.00	0.06
Cambodia	0.82	0.39	1.34	1.08
Indonesia	27.21	4.80	6.82	2.72
Lao People's Democratic Republic	0.74	0.06	0.00	0.12
Malaysia	0.05	0.88	4.84	2.64
Myanmar	0.01	0.92	0.09	1.71
Philippines	0.00	15.67	7.07	39.02
Singapore	5.01	0.77	37.60	37.23
Thailand	17.43	10.73	31.13	81.90
Vietnam	0.00	0.00	0.00	0.00

Source: Constructed from Trade Map data (https://www.trademap.org/Index.aspx)

The aforementioned data highlights North Korea's trade figures with individual Southeast Asian countries. The Southeast Asian countries' large volume of trade with the pariah state is primarily unreported, thereby making it difficult to estimate the amount of North Korea's ties with its south-eastern neighbours.[21] The data suggests that the trade between North Korea and the Southeast Asian countries is negligible. In fact, the figures suggest that, after 2012, both export and import to and from Southeast Asia has reduced. There was no trade figure with Vietnam, in spite of the fact that both are communist countries. However, North Korea imports a substantial amount from Thailand, indicating a jump in the period 2013–16. Among the Southeast Asian countries, Philippines and Indonesia are two countries, in addition to Thailand, having trade with North Korea.

The 1997 Asian financial crisis paved the way for furthering integration between China, Japan, South Korea and ASEAN, which eventually resulted in the institutionalisation of ASEAN+3.

Table 2: South Korea's Trade with ASEAN Countries (unit: US$ billions)

ASEAN Partners	South Korea's Average Export to ASEAN		South Korea's Average Import from ASEAN	
	2009-12	2013-16	2009-12	2013-16
Brunei Darussalam	0.21	0.18	1.62	1.23
Cambodia	0.41	0.62	0.07	0.20
Indonesia	10.60	9.37	14.04	10.65
Lao People's Democratic Republic	0.12	0.16	0.01	0.02
Malaysia	6.11	7.86	9.34	9.58
Myanmar	0.72	0.73	0.22	0.51
Philippines	6.49	8.61	3.25	3.38
Singapore	18.15	18.42	8.59	9.11
Thailand	6.91	7.13	4.54	5.00
Vietnam	11.55	25.96	4.13	9.37

Source: Constructed from Trade Map data

Although China and Japan are bigger trading partners than South Korea, nonetheless, South Korea remains the fifth largest trading partner of ASEAN. South Korea is the fifth largest investment partner of ASEAN as well. In the aftermath of Agreements on Goods and Services, the ASEAN-ROK Free Trade Area (AKFTA) was signed, which came into effect on January 1, 2010. At the Commemorative Summit, both ASEAN and South Korea agreed to target US$ 200 billion of a two-way trade volume by 2020. Both sides have formed institutional mechanisms which will facilitate deeper integration and liberalisation. For example, the ASEAN-Korea Working Group on Economic Cooperation, the ASEAN-Korea Business Council, the ASEAN Connectivity Coordinating Committee, etc. Tourism is another thrust area. The number of Korean tourists arriving in ASEAN countries reached 5.83 million in 2015. The number of Southeast Asian tourist arrivals in South Korea reached 1.6 million in 2015 which is the third largest number of foreign visitors to Korea after China and Japan.[22]

South Korea has been supporting ASEAN to narrow the development gap through the Initiative for ASEAN Integration

(IAI). It has contributed US$ 5 million to support five IAI projects, followed by a further US$ 5 million each for the IAI for the period of 2008–2012 and 2013–2017. In addition to that, South Korea is one of ASEAN's aid donors, with aid amounting to US$ 2.56 billion.[23] This is modest in comparison to its other East Asian partners; nevertheless, South Korea's development story from being an ODA beneficiary to aid donor is an important learning lesson for Southeast Asian countries, especially for those facing the middle income trap problem like Indonesia, and/or struggling with their economic development.[24]

The Role of Southeast Asia Towards Korean Geopolitics: The Nuclear and Reunification Quagmire

Instability and nuclear proliferation in the Korean Peninsula is one of the most serious security concerns for the world. Jacques L. Fuqua notes the 'it was the result of decisions made during the last years of World War II in planning for the defeat of Japan, its ultimate surrender, and the disposition of the fruits gained through its territorial aggrandizement, that Korea became as we know it today—a nation divided'.[25] Today, Korean geopolitics is largely the result of policies of the great powers and the inter-relationships among them. North Korea's nuclear enterprise is, therefore, its bargaining chip, considering the fact that no peace treaty has been signed. This means that the Korean War has not officially ended. Pyongyang is well aware that nukes are its security guarantee and, therefore, North Korean leaders have always set the precondition that Pyongyang would eventually abandon nuclear weapons if the US pledged not to invade their country.

Southeast Asia has played barely any role in the Korean peace talk. Nonetheless, Singapore and Hanoi acting as a venue for the Trump-Kim summit showcases Southeast Asia's potential as a sincere broker of peace in the Peninsula.[26] Southeast Asia is geographically close to the Korean Peninsula and, therefore, a stakeholder. Moreover, the fact remains that any fallout from nuclear proliferation would have serious repercussions for them. In the past, Korean peace talks have been driven by the major powers: primarily the US, China, Japan, and Russia. In 2017, North Korea tested its most advanced hydrogen bomb that could be loaded onto an intercontinental ballistic missile (ICBM). Thereafter, in April 2017, during the 30th ASEAN Summit in the Philippines, ASEAN expressed 'grave concern', and urged North Korea to comply with the UN Security Council Resolutions on its nuclear programme. ASEAN has taken this stand since the 1990s, when each time North Korea achieved a nuclear milestone, triggering geopolitical complications in the region. ASEAN's response over the decades has always implied their grave concern towards the Korean nuclear situation. It is fully conscious of its constraints to achieve any solution on this issue. This does not, however, undermine their effort towards putting up a firm but measured approach in its interaction with North Korea and encourage any dialogue that has been taking place between the two Koreas.

Southeast Asia's calculated approach on North Korea is a defence mechanism to avoid taking sides either with the US or China. Probably, this is the reason why ASEAN has not gone beyond issuing statements of concern. ARF has been the only platform wherein North Korea has been engaged through back door diplomacy and encouraged talk. ASEAN member countries have always responded against North Korea's misadventure, and are aware of playing at the right side of the fence. Malaysia took steps by terminating its visa-free travel arrangement for North Korean citizens in early 2017 and, in late September, banned travel by its own citizens to North Korea—a significant step for the only country whose nationals were allowed visa-free travel to North Korea.[27] Similarly, the rest of the ASEAN countries have drastically reduced their commercial ties, thereby abiding the UN sanctions.

ASEAN's role as a facilitator of dialogue is well established, given its inclusion of North Korea in 2000 in the ARF—the bloc's flagship regional security meeting which involves 27 countries across the Asia Pacific. ASEAN's sensitivity towards sovereignty and its insistence on non-interference in the internal matters of other countries is well acknowledged by the two Koreas. This normative cushion brings diplomatic ease for any kind of dialogue to start off. ASEAN also represents an alternative front for both North and South Korea to escape from over-dependence on major powers like China and the US, respectively. The involvement of the major powers will invariably put the Korean Peninsula's interest behind their broader strategic calculations. For example, China insists on the withdrawal of American troops from South Korean soil as a precondition for Korean peace talks. This is primarily because China does not seek a united Korea fearing the attrition of its influence vis-à-vis the US. On the other hand, President Trump's aggressive pursuit of North Korea through twitter and other diplomatic channels is simply not a benevolent act regarding denuclearisation; rather, it is a broader strategy of curtailing China's sphere of influence. In this sense, ASEAN has an advantage considering its lack of vested interest in engaging with both the Koreas.

Conclusion

The historic Trump-Kim meeting held at Singapore and Hanoi brought attention to Southeast Asian region. The global media attention on Singapore and Hanoi during the meetings and the presence of the US leader in Singapore and Hanoi brought the spotlight on US's relations with Southeast Asia. For example, the US Secretary of State, Mike Pompeo's meeting with Singapore's Minister for Foreign Affairs, Vivian Balakrishnan, during the latter's presence in the city state, centred their discussion on US cooperation with Southeast Asia, in view of the upcoming ASEAN summit in November 2018. This is noteworthy because the Trump administration has created a perception that they are loosening their ties with Southeast Asia. President Trump's withdrawal from the Trans-Pacific Partnership (TPP) and his absence in the East Asia Summit are some of the highlighters.

Meanwhile, the historic inter-Korean meeting led to the outlining of the objective of 'a nuclear-free Korean Peninsula' and 'complete denuclearisation' as a common goal of the two Koreas.[28] Although these meetings are the beginning, and any real effort towards denuclearising North Korea will be a long process that requires multiple rounds of negotiations and steps to build trust. Herein, in this long journey of negotiations, Southeast Asia could step in and significantly contribute to a congenial environment for dialogue.

The fact that Southeast Asia and the Korean Peninsula share a common destiny is frequently acknowledged at the Summit meetings. The psychological distance between ASEAN and South Korea has erased over the decades, thanks to the ASEAN+3 framework. Similarly, North Korea shares historic and commercial links with the Southeast Asian countries. It could be advocated that Southeast Asia should play more meaningful role in the Korean peace talks. ASEAN can succinctly fill in the trust deficit that North Korea suffers from under the major power entanglement. Therefore, the letter dated March 23, 2017 written by North Korean Foreign Minister Ri Yong-ho, is most suggestive: in it North Korea has desperately appealed for fair play since it criticises the annual US-South Korean military exercises as pushing the state of affairs on the Peninsula to the 'brink of war'.

In recent years, ASEAN came under criticism over the issues such as South China Sea dispute and the Rohingya crisis in Myanmar. The human rights violations and democratic deficit in many of these countries draws much flak as well. At this junction, in the absence of institutionalised diplomatic multilateral mechanisms like the Six-Party Talks, ASEAN and its forums are keen to cleanse their image by providing the requisite dialogue platforms to the conflicting parties. Singapore's hosting of the first historic summit between the Presidents of the US and North Korea and the subsequent Hanoi summit proves Southeast Asia's relevance in global affairs. Undeniably, ASEAN's contribution in bringing stability in East Asia would enhance its salience while encouraging its big neighbour China to appreciate its sensitivity on the South China Sea dispute. Thus, any leeway in the Korean nuclear conundrum would enable a larger strategic space for ASEAN, and warrant its centrality.

Notes

1. Laura Allison-Reumann, 'The Norm-Diffusion Capacity of ASEAN: Evidence and Challenges,' *Pacific Focus*, 32(1), April 2017, p. 6.
2. Annabelle Liang, 'Here's why Singapore was chosen to host the summit between Trump and Kim Jong Un', Associated Press, May 10, 2018 at https://globalnews.ca/news/4201913/singapore-donald-trump-kim-jong-un/, accessed on September 22, 2018.
3. Royston Sim, 'Trump-Kim summit will cost about $20 m to host—a cost Singapore willing to pay for regional stability: PM Lee', *The Straits Times*, June 10, 2018 at https://www.straitstimes.com/singapore/trump-kim-summit-will-cost-about-20-million-to-host-says-pm-lee, accessed on September 22, 2018.
4. Ibid.
5. North Koreans have shifted toward the production of methamphetamine in recent years. North Korean pharmaceutical labs reportedly have the capacity to process 100 tons of opium a year.
6. John Park, 'Restricting North Korea's Access to Finance,' Statement before the House Committee on Financial Services Subcommittee on Monetary Policy and Trade, July 19, 2017; see also, Fathin Ungku, 'Singapore slaps US$ 180,000 fine on North Korea-linked shipper,' Reuters, January 29, 2016 at https://www.reuters.com/article/us-chinpo-shipping-singapore-northkorea/singapore-slaps-s180000-fine-on-north-korea-linked-shipper-idUSKCN0V70JV, accessed on September 22, 2018.
7. Richard S Ehrlich, 'Thailand-North Korea ties in the spotlight', *Asia Times*, June 22, 2017 at http://www.atimes.com/article/thailand-north-korea-ties-spotlight/, accessed on September 22, 2018.
8. Zhai Kun, 'The ASEAN Power', in Ron Huisken (ed.) *The Architecture of Security in the Asia-Pacific,* ANU Press, Canberra, 2009.
9. Jiajie He, 'Normative Power in the EU and ASEAN: Why They Diverge', *International Studies Review*, 18(1), March 1, 2016, pp. 92–105. This is an interesting article highlighting how ASEAN is building norms and maintaining relevance in the developing world which is facing great powers or a regional hegemon.
10. Surin Pitsuwan, 'Korea's Changing Roles in Southeast Asia: Expanding Influence and Relations', Key note Address at The Asia Foundation International Conference in Seoul, March 19–21, 2008 at https://asiafoundation.org/resources/pdfs/SurinPitsuwantranscript.pdf., accessed on September 22, 2018.
11. Jake Maxwell Watts and Ben Otto, 'Tillerson Presses Asian Nations to Clamp Down on North Korea,' *The Wall Street Journal*, August 8, 2017.
12. ASEAN-Korea Centre at http://www.aseankorea.org/eng/ASEAN/ak_overview.asp, accessed on September 22, 2018.

13. David Han, 'North Korea Threat: How Should ASEAN Respond?' RSIS Commentary, No. 094, May 15, 2017, p. 1.
14. Surin Pitsuwan, note 10.
15. Andreas Meyndt, 'Nuclear Proliferation and Multilateralism on the Korean Peninsula', Master's Thesis, Tallinn University of Technology, 2017 at file:///C:/Users/Debasish/Downloads/Tuumarelvustamine+ja+multilateraalsed+suhted+Korea+poolsaarel.pdf, accessed on September 22, 2018.
16. 'China's Rebuff of South Korea Is ASEAN's Gain', *The Straits Times*, Singapore, September 16, 2017 at https://www.rsis.edu.sg/media-highlight/idss/chinas-rebuff-of-south-korea-is-aseans-gain/#.WuAr5C5ubIU, accessed on September 22, 2018.
17. Established in 2005, the East Asia Summit is a unique Leaders-led forum of 18 countries of the Asia-Pacific region, formed to further the objectives of regional peace, security and prosperity. It has evolved as a forum for strategic dialogue and cooperation on political, security, and economic issues of common regional concern, and plays an important role in the regional architecture. There are six priority areas of regional cooperation within the framework of the EAS. These are: Environment and Energy, Education, Finance, Global Health Issues and Pandemic Diseases, Natural Disaster Management, and ASEAN Connectivity. Indian Prime Ministers have participated in all the Summits since its inception, thereby suggesting its importance to India. For more details, see, http://mea.gov.in/aseanindia/about-eas.htm.
18. Paul French, *North Korea: The Paranoid Peninsula: A Modern History*, Zed Books, London and New York, p. xiii.
19. There are a number of reasons why North Korean statistics are problematic. These include the fact that statistical methodology in the DPRK is rarely explained and is thought to be relatively basic; that centrally planned economies notoriously have dubious statistics; that the North Korea has its own internal security reasons for not making all figures known internationally; and that there may be some official under-reporting in order to attract aid. Additionally, politics remains paramount in North Korea, including in terms of the gathering of statistics. Where possible, the problems with verifying statistical data are explained, and the possible differences in calculation commented upon in the text.
20. Marcus Noland, 'North Korea's External Economic Relations', Peterson Institute for International Economics, at https://piie.com/commentary/speeches-papers/north-koreas-external-economic-relations#5, accessed on September 22, 2018.
21. North Korea has several commercial and arms cooperation links with individual Singaporean firms and Myanmarese government. Most of these dealings are clandestine in nature. The UN report mentioned below provides substantial evidences regarding these connections. For more, see 'Report

of the Panel of Experts established pursuant to resolution 1874 (2009)', United Nations Security Council, March 5, 2018 at http://www.un.org/ga/search/view_doc.asp?symbol=S/2018/171, accessed on September 22, 2018.

22. 'Overview of ASEAN-Republic of Korea Dialogue Relations', ASEAN at http://asean.org/storage/2012/05/Overview-ASEAN-ROK-Dialogue-Relations-As-of-15-June-2017.pdf, accessed September 22, 2018.
23. 'ASEAN—South Korea Economic Relations: The Way Forward', ASEAN Studies Programme at http://thcasean.org/read/articles/338/ASEAN-South-Korea-Economic-Relations-The-Way-Forward#_edn9, accessed on September 22, 2018.
24. Ibid.
25. Jacques L. Fuqua, Jr., *Nuclear Endgame,* Praeger Security International, Westport, Connecticut, 2007, p. 45.
26. Although Singapore acted in its individual capacity as a venue for the US and North Korea, nonetheless it has the support and encouragement of ASEAN. In the past, several countries within ASEAN—namely, Indonesia, the Philippines, Thailand—have acted as an honest peace broker if not serving as a venue for conflicting parties.
27. Sheena Chestnut Greitens, 'North Korea's activities in Southeast Asia and the implications for the region', November 29, 2017, Brookings, at https://www.brookings.edu/articles/north-koreas-activities-in-southeast-asia-and-the-implications-for-the-region/#footref-17, accessed on September 22, 2018.
28. Choe Sang-Hun, 'Kim Says He'd End North Korea Nuclear Pursuit for U.S. Truce', *The New York Times*, April 29, 2018 at https://www.nytimes.com/2018/04/29/world/asia/north-korea-trump-nuclear.html, accessed on September 22, 2018.

16. The Denuclearisation of the Korean Peninsula: Possible Outcomes of the US-North Korea Dialogue

Balachandran Gopalan and *Jyotishman Bhagawati*

The idea of denuclearisation of the Korean Peninsula was introduced in the 'Joint Declaration of the Denuclearisation of the Korean Peninsula' signed between the two Koreas on January 20, 1992, which entered into force on February 19, 1992. The Declaration committed both sides to refrain from building or receiving nuclear weapons, possessing nuclear reprocessing and uranium enrichment facilities and to establish a Joint Nuclear Control Commission to mutually inspect agreed-upon locations on both sides for verification.[1] Even though the declaration never materialised, its stated goals continue to be the ultimate objective- which all countries, directly or indirectly affected by North Korea's nuclear programme, have agreed to in-principle. However, the denuclearisation of the Korean Peninsula continues to remain a distant dream, with Pyongyang refusing to fully cooperate with any initiative taken by concerned countries or the international community.

There is a broad agreement that North Korea is a de-facto nuclear weapons state.[2] Although estimates of the country's nuclear stockpile vary among experts, according to US intelligence, Pyongyang holds around 30 to 60 nuclear bombs.[3] The question of whether North Korea possesses thermonuclear bombs is a matter of debate; but there is little doubt about its ability to build a powerful nuclear bomb, especially after it conducted its sixth and the most powerful nuclear test in September 2017. The test was five to ten times as powerful as its preceding test, leading many to suggest that the device was probably a hydrogen bomb, with an estimated yield between 100 to 200 kilotons.[4]

North Korea has also tested a range of missiles, including short range, intermediate range, as well as submarine launched ballistic missiles (SLBMs). In November 2017, Pyongyang announced that it had successfully tested the new Hwasong-15 Intercontinental Ballistic Missiles (ICBMs), which analysts estimate, could reach anywhere in the US mainland.[5]

In response to the latest nuclear and missile activity by North Korea, the United Nations Security Council (UNSC) imposed hard-hitting sanctions, designed to target the North's economic lifeline, which includes, among others, capping the import of petroleum products at 500,000 barrels a year, and crude oil at 4 million barrels a year.[6] These sanctions have severely hit North Korea, to the extent that the country's armed forces had to scale back their annual winter military drills in order to conserve oil.[7]

However, subsequently the sanctions are not hurting the Kim Jong-un regime as much as they did earlier—because of some alleged relaxations on the part of China and Russia in enforcing the sanctions, especially with ship-to-ship transfers and the monitoring of border trade.[8] Probably, as a consequence, the North Korean attitude towards denuclearisation has also not been very convincing as it has not taken any credible steps in furtherance of denuclearisation since the Trump-Kim Summit, except shutting down the Punggye-ri nuclear test site—which had, in fact, already lost its utility after the sixth test. Therefore, it would be fair to say that the status-quo, as of today, continues to exist.[9] Even though the Pyongyang Declaration of September 2018 talks about North Korea offering to 'permanently dismantling its Dongchang-ri missile engine test site and launch platform under the observation of experts from relevant countries', but permanent dismantling of the Yongbyon nuclear facilities is contingent on the US reciprocity in accordance with the spirit of the Singapore Summit.

But having said this, the possibility of North Korea entering into an agreement on denuclearisation cannot be ignored, as much as the possibility of both the sides failing to come to an agreement as witnessed in Hanoi. Thus, this chapter, attempts to analyse the possible scenarios and the implications of each of them for the region.

What would 'Denuclearisation' Entail?

The prevailing situation in the Korean Peninsula has been complicated further by the differing versions of 'denuclearisation' among the stakeholders in the region. China and North Korea share a similar definition in that they want a nuclear-free Korean Peninsula; but they also want the US to withdraw its troops from the region and end its nuclear umbrella in South Korea and Japan. On the other hand, draw-down of troops is not an option for the US, which is insisting on a complete, verifiable, and irreversible dismantling of North Korea's nuclear weapons and the associated infrastructure and facilities as soon as possible.[10] At the very least, denuclearisation, for the US would mean the absence of nuclear weapons and related materials or efforts, no stock of unsafeguarded nuclear weapons grade fissile material production (plutonium or highly enriched uranium), and no production of nuclear weapons capable fissile material. This divergence in the understanding of denuclearisation is acting as a stumbling block for meaningful dialogue and cooperation between the US and North Korea.

Nevertheless, for negotiations to succeed, some compromises will have to be worked out. For the US, which now faces a direct threat from North Korea, any denuclearisation deal must include, as a minimum, the following foundational steps.

- North Korea will have to stop all fissile material production for explosive purposes. That means the North cannot produce highly enriched uranium or plutonium.
- An accounting of all past fissile material production has to be made which would also include the materials used for testing nuclear weapons and the dismantling of the nuclear weapons stock.

- Additionally, access must be given to all the North Korean personnel, previously or presently employed in its nuclear activities.
- It would also require that North Korea sign the Nuclear Nonproliferation Treaty (NPT) as well as the 'Additional Protocols' of the International Atomic Energy Agency (IAEA), to make sure that they are not working on nuclear weapons related non-nuclear activities.

If the US cannot get North Korea to agree to even one of these components, there cannot be any assurance of denuclearisation. It must, however, be noted that North Korea did agree to certain verifications during the discussions held from October 1-3, 2008, between North Korean negotiators and the US negotiating team that visited Pyongyang on behalf of the Six Parties.[11] The US-North Korea understanding on verifications comprised several agreements which included, among others, allowing experts from the six countries as well as non-nuclear states to participate in the verification activities, agreement on the use of scientific procedures (like sampling) as well as the agreement that the verification protocol will apply to both uranium-based and plutonium-based programmes.[12] However, the understanding was reached with Kim Jong-il, Kim Jong-un's father. Whether the current North Korea leader abides by the commitments made by his father remains to be seen.

The denuclearisation of the Southern Peninsula had already taken place in 1991, following a unilateral decision by the Bush administration in the US to withdraw all tactical nuclear weapons from South Korea after being continuously deployed there for 33 years with an all-time high of 950 approximate warheads in 1967.[13]

However, it is unlikely that North Korea will subject itself to all the components mentioned above without getting some concessions in return. Therefore, it is likely that the final endpoint might be similar to the Iran Nuclear Deal—that is, a step by step sanctions removal in return for the above steps by North Korea.

The following are the stages that might be convenient to all the parties in the region:

- Foundational Steps from North Korea (as mentioned above).
- After following up with these foundational steps, North Korea might expect some initial sanctions relief which might include relaxation on petroleum imports as an initial step. However, in order to be able to trade freely, North Korea will have to declare their past production of fissile materials as well as the scientists involved in the nuclear programme. Like in the case of the Iran deal, the IAEA will also have to submit periodic reports to ensure that North Korea is complying with the deal, and the IAEA is given complete access to their nuclear programme.

New Leaders, New Complexities in the Korean Peninsula

According to some reports, during President Trump's June 12 summit with Kim Jong-un, he reportedly made a vow to the North Korean leader that he would soon sign a peace 'declaration' to end the Korean War.[14] President Trump allegedly also made the same promise to Kim Yong Chol, a top North Korean official at the White House on June 1, just 11 days before the much famed summit with Kim Jong-un.[15] While a peace declaration is not the same as a peace treaty—it would, however, be a formal endorsement of peace in the Korean Peninsula, which would increase North Korea's leverage to eventually get the US into signing a peace treaty and withdraw its roughly 28,500 troops stationed in the southern Peninsula. President Trump has already questioned the logic behind stationing such a large force abroad, and spending billions of dollars on it.

South and North Korea, on the other hand, are on the same page in prioritising an end-of-war declaration or a peace treaty.[16] This is a major divergence with the US, which has been demanding that the North give up its nuclear programme before it can be granted any concessions. This divergence is also due to the domestic political pressures in the respective states. South Korea wants the US to give 'something significant' to Kim Jong-un to build the domestic political will for denuclearisation, while the US is wary of repeating past mistakes again.[17] However, according to Harry Kazianis, a North Korean expert at the Centre for National Interest think-tank in Washington, the idea of a peace declaration might be a good thing for President Trump since he could then be seen as a legacy builder that would reflect well for his administration, if successful.[18] It is also something that Pyongyang desperately wants, and Seoul is also supportive of. Besides, a peace declaration will not have any strong legal basis for the US to withdraw its troops from the region—though, it would certainly start the process for the signing of a peace treaty and would reflect a significant concession on the part of the US before getting anything substantial in return from North Korea.

Despite President Trump's apparent willingness to sign a peace declaration, senior officials like National Security Advisor, John Bolton, and then Secretary of Defence, James Mattis, have voiced their opposition to the signing of any such agreements unless North Korea gives up much of its nuclear arsenal upfront.[19] It seems likely, that due to the stiff resistance from within the administration, since the Trump-Kim summit, the US has been demanding progress on denuclearisation before embracing any formal peace declaration. However, there seems to be a lot of confusion between President Trump and his administration. While the President is vocal about Kim being a very good person, his administration has continuously been putting a lot of North Korean entities in the sanctions list. Since January 24, 2018, the US Treasury department has added at least 41 entities, 22 individuals, and 34 shipping vessels to its list of sanctioned entities.[20] These include not just North Korean businesses and people but also a few Chinese entities, one Russian bank and a Turkish company for breaking the North Korean sanctions. As opposed to the urgency reflected on the part of the Trump administration for denuclearisation, experts say that denuclearisation will take years to materialise.

However, the US position on this issue is somewhat weakened by the order of points made in the joint statement after the Singapore Summit, where the first and second points called on the US and North Korea to build 'a lasting and stable peace on the Korean

Peninsula', commitment to denuclearisation was placed third.[21] Going by the joint statement, analysts believe that for North Korea, it would mean prioritising a declaration and a peace treaty, rather than denuclearisation.[22] At the same time, it would be difficult for the US to budge under pressure at this moment. However, if the US does not follow up on this, will North Korea agree for denuclearisation? If one looks at its past record as well as the amount of progress made between the Singapore and Hanoi summits towards denuclearisation, North Korea's behaviour does not inspire much confidence.

How Can Such an Agreement be Worked Out?

This brings us to the next bone of contention. In the case of the Joint Comprehensive Plan of Action or the JCPOA, the agreement was reached by Iran and the P5+1 States (China, France, Russia, the US, UK and Germany). But, how can an agreement for thc denuclearisation of the Korean Peninsula take shape, and who can be a party to it? The following are some of the possibilities, if an agreement happens at all,

- It could be a bilateral agreement between the US and North Korea. However, like in the case of the JCPOA, other countries like China, Russia, South Korea, and Japan could also be interested parties. The Korean Armistice Agreement, which brought about a ceasefire between North and South Korea was a multilateral agreement between the UN Command, China, and North Korea. Thus, it is most likely that it will not be a bilateral treaty but one formalised by the UN, and ratified by the US, North Korea, South Korea, and China.[23]
- The IAEA must be involved in it as it is the only body whose 'Safeguards' and 'Additional Protocols' have international legitimacy.
- The North Korean requirements would be the lifting of the sanctions as soon as the agreement is signed. However, the US and the West would know that once the conditions are removed, it would be very difficult to reimpose them, given the current international scenario in which, US relations with China and

Russia are difficult. In the case of the JCPOA, it was far easier for the six parties (P5+1) since there were no nuclear weapons, and Iran had to sign the Additional Protocols before the sanctions were lifted. Also, given the past experiences with North Korea, the US would be averse to any sanctions relief for North Korea until it fully complies with the agreement.

- Since the Libyan example is often cited by North Korea to justify its nuclear programme, the US, in order to dispel such doubts, can guarantee that it will not be involved in any regime change activity. However, this will not be enough since the North Koreans are well aware that revolutions can be sparked off and supported from within as well, as the Arab Spring has demonstrated. This is where the US will have to work out something different, since it cannot guarantee regime continuity.

One could say the sanctions can be lifted once all steps related to denuclearisation are taken up by the Kim Jong-un regime. As mentioned above, that would include, among others, the proper accounting of all nuclear materials and nuclear weapons by international agencies, the signing of the NPT and the Additional Protocols by North Korea, and access to all personnel and facilities involved in the nuclear programme. If such a deal happens, denuclearisation might become the foundation for the development of US-North Korean ties in the future.

However, it is extremely unlikely that the North Koreans would agree to have the sanctions remain in place until the whole process of denuclearisation is completed. They would be looking for reciprocal concessions from the other side. On the other hand, the West would not be comfortable with this method, knowing North Korea's past records. Therefore, if such a stalemate persists, there might not be any agreement at all and the status-quo will continue.

Since the re-imposition of the UN sanctions will be difficult given the current international political climate, the US will have a tough call to take if the Russians and Chinese start engaging in trading with North Korea. This was evident when US Secretary of State, Mike Pompeo, and US Ambassador to the UN, Nikki Haley, held a press stakeout at the UN on July 20 and informed member states that North Korea has already exceeded the import limit of petroleum products established by the sanctions regime. Pompeo noted that the US had recorded at least 89 illegal ship-to-ship transfers of petroleum products during the first five months of 2018. When the US requested the sanctions committee to issue a statement that would inform the member states about the North Korean breach and call upon members to enforce sanctions measures, China and Russia blocked the committee from issuing any statement, arguing the need for more time to examine the US claims.[24] This shows that it is very unlikely that the UNSC will re-impose sanctions against North Korea in case the current sanctions are lifted. Consequently, the US will be left with the only choice of imposing secondary sanctions on any entity dealing with North Korea. This might also be used by the US as a pressure tactic against countries like China and Russia to curb their activities with North Korea. Since the existential threat of North Korean nuclear weapons will still be present, this is likely to be the only viable option for the US.

Incidentally, the December 2017 sanctions also state that if North Korea conducts further nuclear or ICBM tests, it will be subjected to additional sanctions.[25] However, whether that will be an automatic one or whether it has to be re-voted by the UNSC members is open to discussion. However, if it is an automatic provision, the US can also block any attempt by China and Russia to withdraw or limit the automatic sanctions on North Korea—just like China and Russia blocked the sanctions committee from issuing a statement in July.[26]

However, what this scenario does not include is the US bombing of North Korea, since the situation that will arise out of any negotiation failure will be the same situation that prevailed before. While for North Korea, the best scenario would be not to conduct any tests, not to sign the agreement and allow leakages to take place.

Conclusion

The recent summit meeting between Kim Jong-un and Donald Trump in Singapore have created certain degree of hope of realising a denuclearised Korean Peninsula. However, while China and North Korea seems to be on the same page regarding denuclearisation, the US and South Korean positions reflect a divide.

South Korea is concerned more with the (phased) removal of sanctions on North Korea, irrespective of denuclearisation, in order to engage in greater economic, political and cultural ties with its northern sibling. But the US is unwilling to compromise on its stand for complete denuclearisation of North Korea. This is primarily because of the fact that North Korean nuclear weapons do not lead to any additional existential threat for South Korea. The North's conventional superiority is enough to create havoc in Seoul. On the other hand, Pyongyang cannot pose any existential threat to continental US without its nuclear bombs and its associated delivery systems. As a consequence, the US finds itself in a peculiar position in the region as it unequivocally rejected any selective waiver of sanctions, unless the DPRK agrees to a complete and verifiable withdrawal of its nuclear weapons. Adding to the complexities for the US is President Trump's lack of diplomatic acumen, which is being leveraged by North Korea to extract concessions from the US.

Meanwhile, North Korea is also reeling under a lot of stress due to the hard-hitting UN sanctions which has crumbled its economy. Although oil smuggling to the country continues to take place, trade in other commodities has witnessed a sharp decline. This has made the North Koreans desperate for sanctions relief—but they are still unwilling to part with their nuclear weapons, which is currently their sole guarantor of security from the US.

Besides, other major players in the region—like China, Russia and Japan have considerable stakes in the Korean Peninsula too, which further increases the complexity of the denuclearisation process, since any agreement will most likely be a multinational one, which has to take into account the interests of all the relevant parties.

Due to the vested interests of all parties in the region, coming to a consensus on such a critical issue as denuclearisation continues to be a lengthy affair. Analysing past records as well as the recent developments in the region, and taking into account the divergent interests of the various stakeholders in the Korean Peninsula, a few scenarios have been envisaged in this chapter which might emerge following the Trump-Kim Summit. While there exists a lot of potential outcomes, the most probable assessment of the region suggests that the denuclearisation of the Korean Peninsula is not going to happen soon, especially since North Korea has not shown any real resolve to demonstrate such intentions, other than offering some symbolic gestures. On the other hand, the US administration has hardened its position on denuclearisation by continuously adding more and more entities to the sanctions list. By putting North Korea under continuous economic strain, the US is currently in a more advantageous position, although Kim Jong-un has been able to garner support from South Korea and its traditional allies for its position on denuclearisation. However, it remains to be seen how long the virtual stalemate between the two countries' position continues.

Notes

1. Joshua Pollack, 'Denuclearization of the Korean Peninsula: Reviewing the Precedents', Arms Control Wonk, June 10, 2018 at https://www.armscontrolwonk.com/archive/1205354/denuclearization-of-the-korean-peninsula-reviewing-the-precedents/, accessed on August 7, 2018.
2. Van Jackson, 'Is North Korea a Nuclear State?' *The Diplomat,* March 26, 2015 at https://thediplomat.com/2015/03/is-north-korea-a-nuclear-state/, accessed on October 22, 2018.
3. Eleanor Albert, 'North Korea's Military Capabilities', Council on Foreign Relations, June 6, 2018 at https://www.cfr.org/backgrounder/north-koreas-military-capabilities, accessed on August 7, 2018.
4. Julie Vitkovskaya and Joby Warrick, 'North Korea's nuclear weapons: What you need to know', *The Washington Post,* March 9, 2018 at https://www.washingtonpost.com/news/worldviews/wp/2018/03/06/5-things-to-know-about-north-koreas-nuclear-weapons/?noredirect=on&utm_term=.f20648450a41, accessed on August 7, 2018.

5. Eleanor Albert, note 3.
6. UNSC-2017. Resolution 2397 (2017), Resolution, 'United Nations: Meetings Coverage and Press Releases'. United Nations, December 22, 2017 at https://www.un.org/press/en/2017/sc13141.doc.htm, accessed on August 8, 2018.
7. Michael R. Gordon and Jonathan Cheng, 'North Korea, Under Sanctions Strain, Dials Back Military Exercises'. *The Wall Street Journal,* January 29, 2018 at https://www.wsj.com/articles/north-korea-under-sanctions-strain-dials-back-military-exercises-1517227829, accessed on August 8, 2018.
8. 'August 2018 Monthly Forecast', Security Council Report-2018 at https://www.securitycouncilreport.org/monthly-forecast/2018-08/, accessed on August 8, 2018
9. The DPRK has also offered to shut down the Yongbyon nuclear facility as also allow 'international' (not IAEA) observers to visit its facilities- but such steps have been taken in the past as well after the Six-Party Talks in 2007, only for Pyongyang to walk out of negotiations in 2009.
10. Josh Smith, 'Differing views of 'denuclearization' complicate North Korea talks', Reuters, March 28, 2018 at https://www.reuters.com/article/us-northkorea-missiles-denuclearisation/differing-views-of-denuclearization-complicate-north-korea-talks-idUSKBN1H40YI, accessed on August 8, 2018.
11. 'U.S.-North Korea Understandings on Verification', US Department of State, October 11, 2008 at https://2001-2009.state.gov/r/pa/prs/ps/2008/oct/110924.htm, accessed on September 26, 2018.
12. Ibid.
13. Hans M. Kristensen and Robert S. Norris, 'A history of US nuclear weapos in South Korea', *Bulletin of the Atomic Scientists*, 73(6): 2017, pp. 349–357.
14. Alex Ward, 'Exclusive: Trump promised Kim Jong Un he'd sign an agreement to end the Korean War', Vox, August 29, 2018 at https://www.vox.com/2018/8/29/17795452/trump-north-korea-war-summit-singapore-promise, accessed on September 27, 2018.
15. Ibid.
16. Kang Jin-kyu, 'Moon still working on declaration to end war', *Korea Joongang Daily*, July 12, 2018 at http://koreajoongangdaily.joins.com/news/article/article.aspx?aid=3050495, accessed on October 22, 2018.
17. Edward Wong, 'Why Is the U.S. Wary of a Declaration to End the Korean War?', *The New York Times*, August 13, 2018 at https://www.nytimes.com/2018/08/13/world/asia/korea-peace-treaty-trump-us.html, accessed on September 27, 2018.
18. Alex Ward, note 14.
19. Ibid.

20. '2018 OFAC Recent Actions, October 2018', US Department of The Treasury at https://www.treasury.gov/resource-center/sanctions/OFAC-Enforcement/Pages/OFAC-Recent-Actions.aspx, accessed on October 20, 2018.
21. 'Joint Statement of President Donald J. Trump of the United States of America and Chairman Kim Jong-un of the Democratic People's Republic of Korea at the Singapore Summit'- Press Release, The White House 2018, Washington, D.C. at https://www.whitehouse.gov/briefings-statements/joint-statement-president-donald-j-trump-united-states-america-chairman-kim-jong-un-democratic-peoples-republic-korea-singapore-summit/, accessed on September 28, 2018.
22. Edward Wong, note 17.
23. Uri Friedman, 'The Deceptively Simple Promise of Korean Peace', *The Atlantic,* April 27, 2018 at https://www.theatlantic.com/international/archive/2018/04/north-south-korea-peace-treaty/558932/, accessed on October 22, 2018.
24. 'August 2018 Monthly Forecast', Security Council Report-2018 at https://www.securitycouncilreport.org/monthly-forecast/2018-08/ accessed on October 22, 2018.
25. UNSC-2017. Resolution 2397, note 6.
26. Rodrigo Campos and Hyonhee Shin, 'U.N. Security Council imposes new sanctions on North Korea over missile test', Reuters, December 22, 2017 at https://in.reuters.com/article/northkorea-missiles/un-security-council-imposes-new-sanctions-on-north-korea-over-missile-test-idINKBN1EG0HS, accessed on August 23, 2018.

Index